BLOOD
AND
MONEY

BLOOD AND MONEY

War, Slavery, Finance, and Empire

David McNally

Haymarket Books
Chicago, Illinois

WITHDRAWN

© 2020 David McNally

Published in 2020 by
Haymarket Books
P.O. Box 180165
Chicago, IL 60618
773-583-7884
www.haymarketbooks.org
info@haymarketbooks.org

ISBN: 978-1-64259-133-0

Distributed to the trade in the US through Consortium Book Sales and Distribution
(www.cbsd.com) and internationally through Ingram Publisher Services International
(www.ingramcontent.com).

This book was published with the generous support of Lannan Foundation and
Wallace Action Fund.

Special discounts are available for bulk purchases by organizations and institutions.
Please call 773-583-7884 or email info@haymarketbooks.org for more information.

Cover design by Rachel Cohen.

Printed in Canada by union labor.

Library of Congress Cataloging-in-Publication data is available.

10 9 8 7 6 5 4 3 2 1

For Helen, John, and Marilyn

And in memory of Colin Barker, Joyce and Ken Ferguson,
and Ellen Meiksins Wood

CONTENTS

Foreword and Acknowledgments

This book has been many years in the making. It originated in efforts to make sense of world money as a critical concept for the understanding of modern capitalism. As so often happens, this interest coincided with others—including the questions of slavery and the rise of capitalism—in ways that took me down unanticipated paths. Eventually, I found myself toiling at the crossroads of money and slavery in the ancient Greco-Roman world. And from there, I kept crossing history's bridges to later historical complexes of war, slavery, finance, and empire—from early modern Britain to the US empire today. The result, I hope, is a unique historical interpretation of money and power in the making of our world.

The first presentation of some of these arguments came in my Deutscher Memorial Prize Lecture at the 2013 Historical Materialism Conference at the University of London. A revised version of that lecture appeared the next year as "The Blood of the Commonwealth: War, the State and the Making of World-Money," in *Historical Materialism* (vol. 22, no. 2). I thank the journal's editors and the conference organizers for their support.

As work on the book proceeded, I benefited from insightful feedback on several chapters from Colin Barker, Sue Ferguson, Holly Lewis, Geoff McCormack, and Colin Mooers. I extend my warmest thanks and appreciation to all of them. I especially remember, with sadness and great affection, the encouragement I received from Colin Barker, who expressed great excitement about this project and insisted on reading some of its chapters while battling the cancer that took him from us. Colin was a true friend, a wonderful, generous socialist, and an incisive radical thinker.

Work on this book was regularly halted as we lost others along the way. My loving partner, Sue Ferguson, lost both of her parents, Joyce and Ken, in 2016 and 2017, respectively. They are remembered with love and affection.

My dear friend and former teacher Ellen Meiksins Wood passed in 2016. Outside of asking Ellen one small question concerning my research on ancient Greece, I did not have the benefit of her sharp and discerning opinions on the arguments I have made here. Ellen might have differed with me on many points in the analysis that follows. But she would have been pleased, I think, that I have honored her injunction to always do the necessary historical investigation before pronouncing oneself on matters like these.

While I was working on this book, I moved from Toronto's York University to the University of Houston. Big thanks are due to my colleagues and students at York, where I first launched this project. My warm reception in the Department of History in Houston has been a true joy, for which I am grateful to all my colleagues there. For their kindness, generosity, and support, special thanks are due to Donna Butler, Philip Howard, Tom O'Brien, Raul Ramos, Linda Reed, Paul Scott, Abdel Razzaq Takriti, and Cihan Yüksel Muslu. Their support has meant the world to me as I make a new home in Houston. I am truly thrilled that *Blood and Money* will roll off the presses as my first book as a member of the UH Department of History.

I also want to recognize the inspiring activists of the Convict Leasing and Labor Project (CLLP) in Sugar Land, Texas, with whom I have been privileged to work since my arrival in Houston. I will say something more about them in my next book, which will be devoted to the relationship between slavery and capitalism. That question forms much of the backdrop to their efforts to preserve and memorialize the remains of ninety-five African American convict laborers found in 2018 at the site of the former Imperial Prison Farm in Sugar Land. I particularly want to acknowledge the decades of work in this area by CLLP founder Reginald Moore, the keeper of the flame, and to recognize the dedication to this cause of Sam Collins, Barbara Jones, Naomi Carrier Mitchell, and Liz Austin Peterson.

At the heart of my life is the love and support of Sue Ferguson and of our amazing children, Adam, Sam, and Liam. Once again, Sue has been with me on this journey every step of the way, while toiling away at a book of her own. As pleased as I am to be sending *Blood and Money* to Haymarket Books, I truly cannot wait for Sue's book launch. As for our boys, they continue to be endless sources of joy, love, laughter, and celebration. I thank them and hug them all.

In this day and age especially, authors ought to be immensely appreciative to editors and publishers dedicated to the process of writing and producing high-quality books. I cannot say enough about the wonderful folks at Haymarket Books. I particularly want to thank John McDonald and Anthony Arnove for their support and encouragement, my manuscript editor, Ashley Smith, for his valuable and insightful comments, and copy editor, Sam Smith, for their meticulous attention to the manuscript.

I am extremely fortunate to have my parents with me at this stage of my life. All of them have dealt with health challenges in recent years, yet each has managed to keep moving forward with good humor and love for the people in their lives. My mother, Helen, continues to amaze with the support she gives to beleaguered souls, and with her love for all of us. My father, John, endlessly warms my heart with the abiding interest he takes in my writing and my social justice commitments, and in the accomplishments of his grandchildren. Marilyn McNally came into my life, and those of my sisters, when I was a teenager. Her love and support for me, and for my siblings, Terri, Sandra, and Steven, has meant the world to all of us.

I dedicate this book to these three elders—Helen, John, and Marilyn. I further dedicate it to the memories of Joyce and Ken Ferguson, Colin Barker, and Ellen Meiksins Wood. They have passed on, but in our hearts they remain.

Introduction

I t is remarkable how deferential people can be, even progressive people, when it comes to the subject of money. In a recent critical work debunking mainstream economics, for instance, the author instructs us that "monetary and financial systems are among human society's greatest cultural and economic achievements." Turning to the Bank of England, the same author confidently proclaims it to have been "a great civilizational advance."[1] I beg to differ. Rather than a benign medium for promoting the exchange of goods, money has been a technology of power. This is not to deny that it has facilitated trade (though it *is* to deny the absurd myth that money emerged out of barter).[2] It is merely to insist that money and finance are enmeshed within matrices of social power and tend to reproduce them.[3]

Critical theory insists that objects are not separable from their histories. Every object is defined by the process of its emergence and development. Rather than mere externalities, these processes are intrinsic to objects themselves.[4] Where money is concerned, I submit that every layer of its sedimentation is mingled with the blood of slaves, of soldiers, of the colonized, of the exploited and oppressed. Notwithstanding the considerable differences between monetary regimes throughout history, these features have been at the core of each. And they are histories that must be ruptured if violence and domination are to be overcome.

In what follows, I contend that financial history is soaked in blood—blood that has flowed in the tracks of slavery, war, and empire. Thus, the arguments that follow are decidedly unconventional. Even among historians contributing to the major (and important) resurgence in the study of capitalism in the United States, the predominant picture on offer is too often that of "a capitalism born without blood," as one commentator put it.[5] This bloodless image of capitalism owes something to the way the global economic crisis of 2009 focused attention on esoteric financial instruments, such as collateralized debt obligations and credit default swaps. So abstracted are these instruments from the everyday production of goods and services that it is all too easy for analysts to plunge into descriptions of mortgage-based derivatives and computerized trading as if there were no larger system in which people toil in sweatshops, warehouses, stores, and fields—and as if financial profits did not ultimately derive from these labors.[6] To lose sight of such spaces, however, and of the bodies that toil there, is to succumb to a profound fetishism. It is to fail the critical test of tracking abstract financial technologies to the human labors that underpin them. In this respect, the chapters that follow might be considered an exercise in *de-fetishizing* criticism—one that connects the study of monetary and financial history to a phenomenology of the laboring body.

The theoretical work of tethering money to the body and its labors draws from insights that originate with Marx. In his 1844 "Notes on James Mill," for instance, the young Marx turned his sights to the role of credit in the modern monetary system. "The substance, the body clothing the *spirit of money* is not money, paper, but instead it is my personal existence, my flesh and blood," he wrote. "Credit no longer actualizes money-values in actual money but in human flesh and human hearts."[7] In this profound observation, Marx urged that the monetary values changing hands in the credit system are rooted—*actualized*, as he put it—in human flesh, in the body and its pains. Monetary power is thus vampiric, a ghostly presence haunting human flesh and blood.[8] Because of this, credit and money also colonize our hearts—by means of perverse love of lucre, and by means of our mortal fear of the servitude that can accompany debt.

To start from the body is thus an essential protocol. However, human bodies are always enmeshed in history. Human life is the domain of *historical bodies* that carry traces of collective legacies of labor, desire, technology, domination, suffering, and resistance.[9] An assessment of the record of money must therefore situate bodies in networks of power and oppression—among them class, patriarchy, and slavery. More than this, since class societies are always at war (or preparing for war), our protocol requires us to locate the immersion of historical bodies in relations of organized violence. In what follows, I extend this insight to monetary history from the ancient Mediterranean and Middle East to contemporary globalized capitalism. Exploring a range of monetary technologies that have taken shape in societies organized around war, slavery, and colonial plunder, I show that these are *intrinsic* elements of the history of money, not background stage effects.

When it comes to modern capitalist society, I consider Marx's analysis of money—as an expression of the logic of generalized commodity exchange—to be indispensable.[10] But money existed prior to capitalism and obeyed social logics distinct from it, even if these were grounded in domination. Indeed, Marx was well aware that the investigation he conducted in *Capital*, volume 1, operates at a preliminary level of theoretical abstraction. Concerned to delineate money's basic logic in capitalist society, Marx initially bracketed consideration of credit markets, the banking system, the nation-state, public debt, and international finance. But all of the latter—and their entanglements with war and war finance—are essential to any actual *history* of money.[11] To trace this history requires an analysis of the commodity logic of money that incorporates the operations of the state. Marx recognized as much. He understood that states determine the unit of measure (e.g., dollars, yen, euros, yuan) within their sovereign territory. "Coining, like the establishment of a standard of prices, is the business of the State," he remarked. And he further observed that the "different national uniforms worn at home by gold and silver as coins," or by paper currencies, are all governed by the nation-state.[12] It is these different modalities of money—coin, paper currencies tied to precious metal, inconvertible paper money—that shape the history of *monetary regimes*.

To be sure, money's most developed operations occur in an international space that exceeds the sovereignty of national states, which is why *world money* occupies the highest level in Marx's theory. Yet, the global level is not an empty space. It is constituted in and through world competition among capitals and international rivalry between dominant nation-states. Integral to a theory of world money, therefore, is the analysis of international conflict and war—which is perhaps why Marx's plan for his critique of capitalism was meant to culminate in books on the state, foreign trade, and the world market.[13] This is fitting, since national currencies that have attained status as world money have done so on the basis of colonialism, empire, and war. As soon as we approach monetary regimes and institutions in these terms, we can readily appreciate the problems with describing, say, the formation of the Bank of England as "a great civilizational advance." It was instead, as we will see, an advance in the technology of war finance. For its first century, the bank arranged payment for the ships, guns, and soldiers with which the British Empire fought France. And there is nothing particularly unique about the Bank of England in this regard: as one economist observed, all the "central banks in existence before 1850 were chartered in the context of war."[14]

But war finance did not originate with modern society any more than money did. For this reason, this volume begins long before the rise of capitalism: with the emergence of full-fledged money in the ancient West Asia, and its crystallization in Greece. In so doing, it foregrounds the crucial role of the slave trade in the development of markets in the Mediterranean region. By beginning here, I also highlight payment for mercenary soldiers as an integral element in the origin of state-produced ancient coinage, which comprised the first *modular form* of money. I further show that ancient elites considered the hiring of mercenaries, and of wage laborers generally, as a variation on the purchase of slaves. All of this reinforces Marx's account of the "primitive accumulation of capital" as a multifaceted process of bloody dispossession. Money appears in Marx's story as a decisive instrument by which capital emerges into the world "dripping from head to toe, from every pore, with blood and dirt."[15]

But money does not play the same role in all systems of social life and production. For this reason, these chapters make no claim to offer a general *theory* of money across the ages. Theory must be specific to its historical objects of study. Instead, these chapters proffer a unique *historical account* of money: one that demonstrates that in all class societies money is enmeshed in practices of domination and expropriation.[16] I further suggest that three *modular forms* of general-purpose money can be identified in the broad sweep of socioeconomic history, all of them issued by states: metallic coinage, paper banknotes legally backed by precious metal, and paper fiat money untethered to any commodity. The classic instances of each emerged, respectively, in the silver coins of ancient Athens, the notes issued by the Bank of England (founded in 1694), and the US dollar following its detachment from gold in 1971. Each of these modular forms characterizes a historical epoch.[17] Equally significant, I show that each developed as a solution to specific challenges associated with war finance. That war was endemic in ancient Greek society is obvious from even a passing acquaintance with Homer's epics. That it was also deeply imbricated in the emergence of money is a central argument of the first two chapters, which also point to imperial Rome as the heir to Greece's monetary innovations.

Long after the demise of the Roman Empire, coinage continued to operate as the modular form of money in Europe, the Middle East, and Asia. Notwithstanding a decline in the degree of monetization in Europe after Rome's collapse, metallic coinage remained the prevailing means of payment and exchange. As Eurasian commercial life accelerated in the later medieval period, so did military conflict.[18] By 1270 CE, silver coins and bullion comprised a form of world money that lubricated trade from Western Europe to China.[19] And just as war became increasingly commercialized in this period, so commerce became increasingly militarized. One scholar observes that for six centuries in Europe, from the Middle Ages into the early modern period, "people bought and sold military manpower like a commodity on the global market."[20] This refers, of course, to the purchase of mercenary soldiers. So historically significant were mercenaries that, in the thirteenth century CE, Egypt came under the rule of descendants of enslaved mercenary soldiers, known as the Mamluks.

As we move into the era of the rise of capitalism in Europe, war and the hiring of mercenaries moved into higher gears. With states seeking new means of conducting and funding military conflict, the Bank of England perfected its machinery of war finance. In so doing, it established the *second* modular form of money. But it could do so only on the basis of new social relations of production and a new form of political power, one that internalized market imperatives within the very heart of the modern state. The power of capital, and its necessary manifestation in war, became constitutive of the bourgeois order.[21] Just as modern banking was a regime of war finance from its inception, so was capitalism a system of *war capitalism*—and it remains so today.[22] This is the story at the heart of chapters 3 and 4.

By the twentieth century's Thirty Years' War (1914–45), the United States had attained dominance within global capitalism. Essential to its rise was a long internal struggle to adopt the second modular form of money, paper notes tied to gold and secured by a central bank. But, as much as it ascended to imperial hegemony through this form of money, the United States was also to destroy it. At the height of the Vietnam War, in 1971, the monetary arrangements integral to war capitalism underwent a seismic shock when the US government disconnected its currency from gold, thereby reconstituting the dollar as an imperial fiat money. Since then, state fiat monies have become the general form of late capitalist money—its *third* modular form—and have brought with them new modalities of financial turbulence and turmoil of the sort witnessed in the 2009 global financial crisis. I explore this epochal departure, and its lasting reverberations, in chapter 5.

In writing a counter-history of money organized around ancient Greece and Rome, Britain, and the United States, there is a risk that the reader will imagine these to be the world's great innovators. Yet, even in the domain of empire, these states were often mere imitators. One can make the case that the empires of Persia, Babylon, and early Islam, and those of the Mongols, Ottomans, Mughals, and Khazars, exceeded what the Greeks achieved in many domains. The Mongols under Genghis Khan (Temüjin) and his successors, for instance, established "the largest land empire in history."[23] And China undertook the world's first sustained experiment with paper money, albeit one that collapsed and thus failed to establish a new modal form (outlined in chapter 2). My focus is on Greece, Britain, and the United States only because their exercises in destruction and domination, war and empire, were underpinned by monetary innovations that became generalized. This is also why they figure prominently in the global history of colonialism, which is a central part of the story told here. All of this further serves to remind us why anti-colonialism is essential to the prospect of a world beyond empire and war.

The chapters that follow also deploy an interdisciplinary approach to the study of money and its history. Epic poets—like Homer and Hesiod—enter our analysis, as do novelists such as Daniel Defoe and Herman Melville. This has to do with the capacity of literature to break through the obfuscation that so frequently surrounds economic questions, particularly monetary ones. As the gadfly economist John Kenneth Galbraith observed, "The study of money, above all other fields in economics, is the one in which complexity is used to disguise truth or to evade truth, not to reveal it."[24] And these evasions at the heart of mainstream economics serve to protect power and privilege. To the degree to which they pierce such mystifications, poets and philosophers often have more to teach us about the study of money than economists do.

This volume is thus intended as a work of demystification. It is also "an experiment in history, solidarity, and hope," to borrow a formulation from radical scholar Vincent Harding.[25] The *history* it traces is one of money, slavery, empire, and war. The *solidarity* it embraces is with the oppressed across the ages. And the *hope* it nurtures is in a future free of violence and oppression. I will have succeeded if this work makes some small contribution to that cause.

CHAPTER 1

"Droves I Took Alive and Auctioned Off as Slaves"

War, Slavery, and Ancient Markets

Half a century before the dawn of the Christian era, a Roman provincial governor gazed with delight at the loot from a recent military campaign. Exulting in his gains, the governor, known to posterity as Cicero, dashed off a letter to a friend. "As I write," he enthused, "there is about 120,000 sesterces on the platform."[1] In fact, there were no sesterces, the predominant Roman coin of the time, atop the platform he regarded. No, rather than coins, it was human beings he observed—enslaved humans, taken as plunder by the army. Yet, Cicero was in one sense speaking truthfully. What he perceived was indeed a heap of coins. After all, the people before him were commodified humans, readily translatable into a monetary equivalent. Our Roman politician might not have known their names, but he knew their approximate market value. So developed was exchange in enslaved humans, so routine was the economic transformation of persons into money, that Cicero simply performed the conversion in thought. What he saw on the platform was just what he reported—sesterces, piles and piles of sesterces.

To perceive human beings as heaps of coins requires a distinctive intertwining of slavery, markets, and money. In the ancient Greco-Roman world, these had evolved in tandem, each indispensable to the other. Today, liberal exponents of markets and money disavow these interconnections. Even in a heterodox work in economics, we still find claims to the effect that the invention of money and finance represented "a great civilizational advance."[2] Yet this really will not do. In offering its uplifting fable of civilizing commerce, mainstream thought seeks to expunge the embarrassing commodity that has been fundamental to the story of markets and money—humans in bondage.

$

Questions of money are also questions of truth. In order to function as a means of exchange and payment, or as a measure of value, a monetary item (be it a coin or a bill) must be accepted as the real thing and not an imposter, not a counterfeit. The truth value of money is not merely a conceptual matter. Money's validity must be realized in everyday human practice, in concrete interactions among people. A social epistemology thus accompanies money, a set of symbolic and socio-material practices for determining its veracity. At the origin of Western culture, these practices ran through the enslaved body.[3]

A general equivalent, let us recall—be it a silver coin, a digital inscription, or a note issued by a central bank—requires a guarantee of its integrity; to be universally accepted, it must be recognized as legitimate, as *the* real thing, the incarnation of wealth as such. This recognition can be fraught when new media of payment and exchange are emerging—say, banknotes in societies that have been regulated by coinage, or debit cards when they first appear as substitutes for cash. The same is true in a society in which older means of exchange, such as conventional weights of gold and silver, or iron spits and metal cauldrons, are being displaced by coins stamped by the state. And with this transition, we encounter a fascinating shift in ancient Greece with respect to the testing of money, a shift that inserted the enslaved body directly into the truth regime of money.

During the era in which coinage emerged, the authenticity of a gold coin could be checked by recourse to a *basanos*, a touchstone upon which pure gold, when rubbed, left a unique mark. Over time, the term *basanos* came to refer to the test itself, not merely the touchstone. But the most intriguing semantic shift took place sometime after silver coinage was introduced by the Athenian polis (probably in the late sixth century BCE). Having minted coins, the state also needed to protect against counterfeits, and to provide a public test of authenticity. For a period of time, testing of coins was performed publicly in the agora by a state-owned enslaved person, known as the *Dokimastes*, who received fifty lashes for failure to stay at his post, or for failing to test according to stipulations of the law.[4] A slave's body—always subject to the threat of violence—functioned here as the ultimate guarantee of the integrity of money. The enslaved person who served as *Dokimastes* became a sort of human basanos, and thus implicitly something both animate and inanimate, inhabiting an uncertain zone between the living and the dead. The epistemology of money was thus grounded in the enslaved body and the right of violence against it, in a series that went money → touchstone → slave. This direct link between truth, violence, and the enslaved body facilitated a further, somewhat jarring, semantic shift as the word *basanos* came to designate not a stone for testing coins, nor the test itself, but the act of torturing an enslaved person's body in order to elicit testimony in a legal proceeding. This alteration in meaning thus connected coins and enslaved people as objects whose bodies could be vessels of truth. This was the context in which *basanos* came to denote the use of violence against the enslaved body to *produce truth* in a legal proceeding.[5]

Discussing this semantic evolution, classicist Page duBois writes that such a shift in meaning "is literally *catachresis*, the improper use of words . . . abuse or perversion of a trope or metaphor (OED)."[6] Yet, while abuse (of enslaved bodies) was certainly involved, duBois might overstate the distance between coins and the enslaved body. After all, with the Athenian coinage decree (375–4 BCE), which made the Dokimastes a touchstone for the truth of money, a legal conflation of coins and the enslaved body had occurred: force applied to one, the enslaved body, guaranteed the authenticity of the other, money. Judicial truth and the validity of money were thereby tethered to the enslaved body. We encounter here a chain of substitutions in which the enslaved body could stand in for coins, as it could for truth.

Consider also the following substitution: whereas legal penalties imposed on enslaved people in Greece were frequently paid by lashes on the body, free persons could pay monetary penalties as a substitute. A late fourth-century Attic inscription, for instance, imposed a penalty of fifty lashes on an enslaved person for cutting wood in the sacred precincts of Apollo; a free man, on the other hand, was to pay fifty drachmas for the same offense, an evident substitution of money for the (free) body.[7] Surely these translations between enslaved bodies and money owed something to the fact that enslaved people were bought and sold in the market. Enslaved people, after all, *were* directly exchangeable with coins. And this involved an inherent ontological conflation of (at least some) persons with things—an example of which we saw with Cicero. It may not have been such an abuse of language, therefore, for the meaning of *basanos* to shift from a touchstone for testing gold to the judicial exercise of violence on an enslaved body. This slippage between gold and enslaved bodies discursively mimicked real circuits of exchange. However, these transactional circuits had originated within an overwhelmingly nonmonetary economy. If we want to understand how exchanges became monetized, we will need to explore the economy of violence in the heroic period. Before doing that, however, let us attend to another site in this dialectic of money, truth, and the enslaved body: ancient philosophy.

Tracking the Invisible: Philosophy and the Enslaved Body

Ancient Greek philosophy has an intriguing connection to the emergence of money. It also has a curious connection to enslaved people. Enslaved bodies were, of course, highly visible throughout Athens—in their public labors, in the open-air markets where they were bought and sold, and in the tattoos, brands, and fetters with which their bodies were marked, all signs of their status as chattel property. This public visibility of the enslaved operated, however, to invisibilize their personhood, to render them imperceptible as humans. The enhanced conspicuousness of those in bondage, etched in markings on their bodies, demarcated them from the fully human world of the polis, reducing them to thing-like elements outside the culture-building activities of adult male citizens, including the practice of philosophy. The corporeal semiotics of slavery thereby relegated the enslaved to a twilight zone inhabited by cattle and commodities. "A living piece of property," says Aristotle, the enslaved is "one of the tools" that ministers to the activity of a master.[8] Enslaved people are embodiments of death-in-life, uniting the activity of living labor with the status of creatures who are meant to be socially dead.[9] Yet, this confinement of the enslaved to a zombie domain of death-in-life left traces, clues accessible to the dialectical investigator, which are inscribed in the very rules of intelligibility of the worlds of mind and money.

The enslaved body was inherently scandalous, precisely because it grounded the domains of philosophy and commerce; it ranked among their fundamental conditions of possibility. The scandal did not consist, of course, in the *fact* of slavery, as this seems to have caused little embarrassment at all (with the remote exception of a few intransigent defenders of democratic egalitarianism).[10] Not only was slavery compatible with ancient justice, it was foundational to it, providing an essential precondition for legal truth, as we have seen. Reading Aristotle, it is evident that he considers the submission of enslaved people to masters to be part of the just ordering of our world, equally indispensable to virtue as the domination of men over women and children. The scandal of slavery had to do not with its existence per se, but with the unspoken threat it posed to aristocratic pretensions to cultural autonomy. As Hegel famously demonstrated, the great irony of the master–slave relation is that it harbors a dialectical reversal. In relation to the material world around them, masters are passive beings, reliant on the labors of the people they enslave. The enslaved, on the other hand, develop themselves as social agents in and through these same labors. The master–slave relation is thus the site of a possible reversal in the poles of dependence and independence; it carries the seeds of its own radical undoing at the hands of the enslaved themselves.[11] And this threatens the claims of culture, commerce, and truth to be self-sufficient. After all, philosophy has traditionally assumed that only the true can produce truth, and that only the pure can produce purity.[12] However, the reliance of the world of the masters on the activity of enslaved people represents its dependence on the putatively impure, the domain of people of the body, be they women, enslaved people, or day laborers, whose existence hints at the heteronomy of the world of the masters. The return of the repressed takes here the form of a *return of the oppressed*. This is one reason why classical Greek culture, nowhere more than in Plato's philosophy, sought to banish not just the enslaved but everything that smelled of its presence—women, labor, the body, nature.[13]

Plato's *Meno* is among the most interesting texts in this regard. While enslaved people are frequently mentioned in Plato's dialogues, this is the one case in which an enslaved person actually speaks. While giving him a voice, however, Plato reenacts the social death of the enslaved person by refusing to give him a name, identifying him merely as "boy." This makes it all the easier for Plato to shuttle the boy off the stage and out of the dialogue once he has served to illustrate Socrates' argument.[14] Yet, the repressed returns hauntingly in the final pages of the text, where the philosopher revisits the problem of truth.[15] Socrates here urges his interlocutors not to confuse the chance possibility of having the right opinions about something with possessing true knowledge of it. We may be right about something without having acquired genuine and comprehensive knowledge of it. He then likens accurate opinions not grounded in knowledge to statues of Daedalus that "run away and escape" unless they are tied down. Knowledge, by contrast, is said to be fixed, permanent, locked in place. Opinion, even when correct, is fleeting—indeed, *fleeing*, like "a runaway slave," who "gives you the slip" if left "untethered" (97D–97E). Mere opinions, even correct ones, threaten to escape from us so long as they are unshackled by knowledge. To prevent them from slipping away, they must be tethered: "Once they are tied down, they become knowledge" (98). The pursuit of truth thus requires doing to correct opinions what is done to enslaved bodies—binding them with chains and fetters.

Try though he might to banish them, Plato cannot avoid the conclusion that the enslaved—the one who remains in bondage, the one who cannot escape— is a necessary condition of philosophical truth. This phantom haunts Western culture from its inception, threatening to expose the constitution of the worlds of mind and money in and through the labors of the enslaved. Avery Gordon's insight that modernity is haunted by ghostly images of violence and wounds applies as well to the ancient cultural traditions embraced by the masters of the modern world, which derive from the culture of an antique slave-owning class.[16] Yet, while liberalism disowned its debt to a world of whips and chains, it was Nietzsche's perverse genius to have embraced it. Nietzsche in fact celebrates the domination of the enslaved as indispensable to the noble work of culture building. Railing against democracy, socialism, and feminism, he meets head-on their attacks on slavery: "as if slavery were a counterargument," he writes, "and not instead a condition of every higher culture, an enhancement of culture." Time and again, he affirms aristocratic domination over enslaved people: "Every enhancement of the type 'man' has so far been the work of an aristocratic society . . . that needs slavery in some sense or the other."[17]

Liberalism recoils from this aristocratic affirmation of the indispensability of the enslaved to the regimes of money and philosophy. It knows that such an affirmation undermines its own polite history of Western culture, its claim for the self-constitution of the modern individual through the poetics of mind and exchange, free of blood and dirt, whips and chains. Yet, it cannot evade Walter Benjamin's insistence that "there is no document of civilization which is not at the same time a document of barbarism," a statement that is as true of coins as it is of vases, or texts by Plato.[18] The dialectical archaeology of truth thus requires an excavation of its degraded sites, a reconnection of objects of culture to the bloodied, abjected body-things that haunt the world of refinement. To return to the enslaved body is thus to revisit the spheres of labor and bondage that comprise the truths of our world. Among these essential truths are those of money.

"A Measure of Everything"

Ancient Greece is rightly recognized as the first extensively monetized society in history. Not that markets and commodity exchange were unique to Greece. On the contrary, these were widespread in the ancient world, as were a variety of special-purpose monies, items that performed a range of monetary functions—such as measuring the value of things—without operating as universal currencies. In ancient Egypt and Mesopotamia, for example, payments were frequently made by means of a common standard unit, or measure of value, such as copper, silver, or grain, in which the values of goods or services could be expressed. When two traders wanted to exchange quantities of cloth and barley, for instance, each good might be said to be worth a particular amount of copper. This enabled a comparison of quantities of one thing with another. But copper served here merely as a unit of account, that is, a standard measure that could be used as a reference point to enable trade. Frequently, very little or no copper, grain, or silver actually changed hands in such an exchange. A document from the New Kingdom in Egypt (1550– 1070 BCE), for instance, registers the purchase of an ox by a policeman. It indicates that the price of the ox was fifty *deben* of copper (a little over 4.5 kilograms). But only five deben of the fifty were actually paid in copper; the balance was rendered in other commodities, like oil, clothing, and fat, whose values were expressed in copper. So, while copper *measured* the value of goods involved in exchange, it was not itself the universal *means* of exchange or payment. A similar pattern is observed in Mesopotamia, where various legal codes regulated payments like fines and wages, as well as commodity prices, in fixed weights of silver. But we know from the same documents that grain, too, could be used for payments according to an established silver/grain ratio.[19] Under the dynasty of Hammurabi in Babylonia (1792–1750 BCE), while prices were expressed in silver, most payments were made in barley or corn. Indeed, the Code of Hammurabi (Laws 113–115) refers to payment as "a claim for corn or money." Likewise, in Homer we frequently observe cattle serving as a standard of value, but never as a means of exchange. In all these cases, the items that functioned as standards of value (or units of account) did not figure as a general equivalent that united the functions of means of exchange, measure of value, and means of payment. Nor did they bear visible markings of state authority designating them the sole legal means of payment, as was the case with state-minted coins. In short, special-purpose monies did not operate as the unique socially sanctioned representative of value that moved through circuits of exchange in the way that full-fledged or *general-purpose* money does.[20]

Even where, as in Assyria and Egypt, ingots of precious metal sometimes carried a seal of authority, they lacked universality, coexisting with basic commodities like wool, barley, sheep, and wine, all of which also served monetary purposes. And while the kingdom of Lydia in Asia Minor, in what is now part of western Turkey, seems to have been the first in the Mediterranean world to have introduced coinage bearing an insignia of the state, the absence of small coins there suggests it was not a highly monetized society, since everyday transactions by the demos could only have been undertaken with small units. But among the states of classical Greece, particularly Athens, a unified coinage issued by the state would become fundamental to daily life, mediating incessant exchanges of goods and services. Coins functioned as means of exchange and as *general equivalents*, capable of being traded for everything from olive oil to sex, or for paying government fines. An interesting portrayal of the extent of monetization can be found in Plato's *Republic*, where he describes "all the pains and pangs which men experience in bringing up a family, and in finding money to buy necessaries, for their household, borrowing and repudiating, getting how they can, and giving the money into the hands of women and slaves to keep" (V465). So thoroughly monetized was Plato's society that "finding money" haunted the heads of the household, while women and enslaved people are said to have frequented the market, dispensing money to purchase domestic "necessaries."

We shall return to the *Republic* later in this chapter. For the moment, however, let us observe that Plato's description meshes with compelling evidence for the ubiquity of Greek coins as media of exchange. Most significant here is the archaeological recovery of large quantities of small coins from the classical period, indicating that they were not simply used by the wealthy for large purchases of land, enslaved people, and livestock, but were also deployed in small denominations to facilitate everyday transactions among ordinary citizens.[21] State-issued money in Athens (among other Greek city-states) was to be found everywhere, forming an indispensable element of daily life and provoking insecurities, lest one not have enough of it.

Describing the classical Greek situation, historian Richard Seaford notes the novelty of coined money as "the single, ubiquitous, and *visible* embodiment of universal exchange value," and observes that the Greek polis of the sixth century BCE produced "the first ever words for and thought about *money*."[22] A conceptual revolution was at work here as much as a socio-material one. In societies that are not extensively monetized, measures of wealth involve inventories: lists of discrete items, from cattle to gold chalices, from wheat to enslaved people. Rather than translating all forms of property into the single quantitative index provided by money, such societies require serial lists of qualitatively distinct objects. In the Old Testament, for instance, Solomon's wealth is described by enumerating all the specific things that entered into his daily provisions—flour, meal, cattle, sheep, goats, deer, gazelles, roebucks, and fowl—as well as various items he received on a monthly basis, among them barley and straw for his horses (I Kings 4:22–28). But societies governed by a universal equivalent need merely compute every such item into units of money in order to produce a single sum, a homogeneous lump of wealth—be it drachmas or dollars, or Cicero's sesterces. "From the Greeks onward, we find a new way of speaking and of thinking. Now a person might state the entirety of a household's possessions in terms of money, as no member of a premonetary society would ever do."[23] Not for nothing did Aristotle declare that money (*nomisma*) "is a measure of everything," and that it functions as such by "making things commensurable."[24] But if money is a measure of everything, we have entered a unique set of social relations with a history. And as much as that history involved cultural and intellectual revolutions, it equally pivoted on socioeconomic ones that refashioned aristocratic gift economies and reorganized social life.

Markets Powered by Warfare: Gifts, Reciprocity, and Violence

Homeric Greece, or at least the life of the Greek heroes depicted in the epics, revolved around an aristocratic gift economy.[25] Social status was tied to "competitive generosity," to the ability to bestow lavish gifts on one's peers along with displays of munificence toward those beneath one in the social order.[26] Gift giving was essential to the exercise and display of noble virtue. Guest-friendship (*xenia*) and gift exchange bound people together in a nexus of reciprocal obligation, where receivers owed their benefactors services, assistance, and counter-gifts. Gift-giving systems can certainly be hierarchical ones, reproducing patterns of social inequality. But some critics have mistakenly assumed that these patterns involved a sort of capitalist calculation. They were in fact something entirely different.[27] As much as gifts involved expectations of counter-gifts (hospitality, services, or prized items), the wealthy were driven not to accumulate goods as ends in themselves, but rather to outdo other aristocrats in the extravagance of their generosity. More accurately, perhaps, they were driven to accumulate wealth in order to *disperse* it. Confronted with similar values in the gift-giving economy on the Solomon Islands, one appalled self-styled anthropologist proclaimed such actions "absurd." "The only profit a man can make in a deal in this absurd society is a reputation for generosity," she wrote.[28] Yet generosity—which pivoted on accumulation of wealth for purposes of dispersal—was crucial to social esteem. Alongside valor on the battlefield, gift giving was the key to honor and power. Indeed, oral histories were built upon these exchanges and displays. "No single detail in the life of the heroes receives so much attention in the *Iliad* and the *Odyssey* as gift-giving," writes M. I. Finley, "and always there is frank reference to adequacy, appropriateness, recompense."[29] Similar values pervaded the earliest written histories, so much so that Herodotus, often dubbed "the first historian," exhibited an "obsessive" attention to the bestowal of aristocratic gifts that were "worthy to be seen."[30]

It is often said by anthropologists that societies based on gift exchange are governed by principles of reciprocity.[31] This distinguishes them from centralized systems of *redistribution*, in which the state (or a proto-state) receives contributions, like grain, and reallocates them. Whereas in a redistributive system the circulation of wealth is centrally organized, in reciprocal economies it is decentralized, often revolving around a small number of big men, or "chiefs," and their gifting. To be sure, systems of reciprocity can be highly stratified and tilted in favor of those with greater resources. To get at these complexities, critical anthropology has identified three dominant forms of socioeconomic reciprocity: generalized, balanced, and negative. Generalized reciprocity approximates a system of "pure" gift giving: those who can shall give; those who need shall receive. Balanced reciprocity involves direct exchange (barter) of goods that are considered in some sense to be equivalents. Finally, negative reciprocity entails getting something for nothing, or at least for as little as possible, by means of plunder, theft, and other forms of violent appropriation. As Marshall Sahlins suggests, these three modes of reciprocity are governed by social distance. The closer and more intimate the social bond (e.g., kinship), the more the pure gift giving of generalized reciprocity will prevail. The greater the social distance, the more negative reciprocity (plunder and theft) will be the norm.[32] Where two or more of these modes of interaction are in play, relations between them often become unstable. Indeed, it was characteristic of the archaic Greek world before coinage that a dramatic growth in the sphere of negative reciprocity—particularly raiding and plunder—began to undermine the generalized reciprocity that prevailed within more intimate social relations.

Before turning to those developments, let us note other crucial features of nonmonetary economies based on reciprocity. To begin with, they are *multicentric* systems.[33] Their socioeconomic organization involves distinct spheres, governed by divergent principles and values. A realm in which direct exchange (trade, or balanced reciprocity) occurs may coexist with a domain of negative reciprocity (plunder and theft). Trade and plunder (balanced and negative reciprocity) are permissible only with "outsiders." The sphere of generalized reciprocity will be allergic to such practices. There, within the domain of the clan, tribe, or village community, gift giving will dominate. In the intimate world of the local community, not only are theft and plunder considered evil, but so are efforts to commodify and instrumentalize people and most goods. The bulk of goods move through reciprocal circuits of societal reproduction, preserving and reproducing people and their social bonds in an ethos of mutuality. Rather than things belonging to people, persons adhere to things. People belong, for instance, to the land, the rivers, and the forest. They belong to their ancestors and their gods, to their community and kin, to the shared histories of the living and the dead. Individuals belong to their dwellings and to those of public life—the assembly spaces, sacred trees, temples, and communal sites. In fact, the Homeric adjective indicating that an individual is free, *eleutheros*, actually refers to a state of belonging to others and to the community. To be free is to belong, whereas the unfree lack belonging, like a captured foreigner ripped from her community, with whom the conquerors acknowledge no shared histories or communal obligations.[34] Whereas the unfree inhabit a realm of disconnection, the free belong to a social world in which persons and things are alive with memory and life; they connect groups in the here and now, and they link generations throughout time.

As for aristocratic gift giving, the nature of a prestigious gift was that it had a distinguished history. The most prized shield was worn by a legendary hero in an epic battle; a valued goblet touched the lips of a great king; a treasured cauldron had been passed down through the generations of a noble household. The same was true, albeit on a much more modest scale, for commoners. Land, jewelry, treasured heirlooms, and pieces of clothing—all of these embodied histories and identities. They were no more alienable by the individual than was their own body (a condition that was reserved for enslaved people). For an individual to *belong* to these histories was to be a part of the very material items in which history was sedimented. This is why in societies where important goods are alive with sociality, many possessions are *inalienable*. Even when they change hands, they still belong to their histories and those who embody them. "Inalienable possessions," writes anthropologist Annette Weiner, "are symbolic repositories of genealogies and historical events, their unique, subjective value gives them absolute value, placing them above the exchangeability of one thing for another."[35] I could no more give away such possessions—items of family jewelry or clothing, fertility stones, musical instruments, talismans, or blankets—than I could disown my history, my belonging, my kin relations, my identity. Such items were bound up with life itself. For this reason, they were incommensurable; their histories were specific to persons and groups. They could not be traded because they had no equivalent.[36]

When Achilles declares, "Nothing equals the worth of my life" (*Iliad*, 9:402), he invokes the nonequivalence between life and plundered goods.[37] And, as things that are constitutive of life, memory and identity likewise have no equivalent. They are incomparable, immeasurable—and inalienable. We see this repeatedly in the world of the Greek epics. It is striking that the terms used for possession and ownership in the *Iliad* and the *Odyssey* refer to relationships toward *both* persons and things. This is most clear with the adjective *philos*, whose meaning "ranges from 'beloved' to 'one's own,'" as Sitta von Reden notes. "The heart, limbs, clothes, treasure, wives, husbands, compatriots, guest-friends and the fatherland all belong to the repertoire of *philos* objects, being at once beloved and owned."[38] What is one's own is what is beloved, what is an extension of one-self. Philos objects, precious items to which the individual "belongs," adhere to a sphere of inalienability. Even when gifted, they carry with them their histories and attachments to their donors. The instrumentalization of such things as a mere means (via exchange) to obtain something else is not merely impermissible, it is incomprehensible. Possessing absolute value, such items are radically unique; what has no equivalent cannot be exchanged.

A society of this sort may well have had special-purpose monies, that is, specific goods used to measure value or serve as a means of payment. These would have operated largely in the sphere of trade with strangers. But entire realms of socioeconomic life were cordoned off from such dealings. And even when monetary transactions encroached on relations internal to a community, they did not involve a general equivalent that expressed a singular value framework for measuring the worth of most goods. Money was still marginal and episodic to social life, and Schaps is entirely correct when he states of Homeric Greece that it "not only lacked money; it did not yet conceive of money."[39]

To be sure, goods were exchanged in Homeric Greece (1100–800 BCE, also known as the Greek Dark Age). But within local communities, this predominantly took the form of gift—not market—exchange. Gifts, as we have seen, created and reinscribed social relations and networks of obligation. For this reason, they were memorialized, so that the obligations might be remembered and stable social bonds preserved. In the public recounting of gifts, social ties and obligations were renewed and consolidated.[40] Of course, the social ties reproduced through narration of gifts given and received were often hierarchical ones. After all, esteemed gifts obeyed a ranking system. Prestige adhered to both the possession of specific goods and to the wealth that enabled one to give away gifts, particularly those comprised of precious metal. Consequently, aristocratic gift giving reproduced rank and social difference at the same time that it reknitted networks of reciprocity. And for the poor, obligations to provide flows of wealth to those above oneself—what would later develop into rent and taxes—were modeled on the image of the gift. In the world of the epics, the term *gift* included a disparate set of goods and services, including prizes, rewards, fines, taxes, fees, and even loans.[41] Yet fines, fees, and taxes could easily morph into exactions, just as loans might culminate in debt service and even debt bondage. In all these ways, the "gift economy" could shade into relations of appropriation and class exploitation, especially if intra–ruling class competition were heightened in response to new forms of accumulation, such as raiding and plundering.

It is significant that during the heroic age much of the very wealth that could be dis-accumulated through gift giving was acquired via warfare, raiding, and slaving. Gift economies could thus be deeply imbricated with slavery and debt bondage, as was certainly the case in ancient Greece. Nevertheless, however much hierarchical social relations were reproduced in and through some forms of gift economy, the latter obeyed a social logic foreign to commodity exchange. The appropriateness of expressions of generosity and hospitality among aristocrats, for instance, was not determined by market considerations of equivalence. What was appropriate was governed by historical patterns of reciprocity and by social standing. Similarly, social norms were meant to govern the sharing of booty (goods acquired through negative reciprocity). Yet, these norms might become unstable and contested. And in turning to Homer's texts, we readily detect symptoms of precisely such a breakdown in aristocratic norms—symptoms not unrelated to growing social tensions and class conflicts.[42]

From the outset of the *Iliad*, we encounter a collapse of noble leadership, centered on a crisis over distribution of wealth acquired through war, plunder, and trade. By the eighth century BCE, raiding was an established aristocratic practice for accumulating wealth in archaic Greece. Conducted via longboats rowed by dozens of men, raiders launched surprise attacks in order to capture cattle, enslaved women, and items of precious metal. So routine was such plundering activity that in his *Politics* Aristotle simply describes warfare as "a way of acquiring wealth" (1256b23). In this he echoed Homer's glowing references to noble Odysseus as a "sacker of cities." Turning also to King Nestor of Pylos, Homer describes how he and his fellow Greek warriors engaged in "many raids from shipboard down the foggy sea, cruising for plunder" (*Odyssey*, 3.17–18).[43] So inextricably connected were plunder and trade in the ancient world that markets were literally powered by warfare. Yet as accumulation by raiding grew from about 800 BCE on, it also produced powerful conflicts over distributive norms within the dominant group. Tensions arose between private accumulation and practices of dis-accumulation through gift giving. We get more than a glimpse of these tensions in the epics.

At the beginning of the *Iliad*, we learn that the noble warrior Achilles had been angered by Agamemnon, leader of the Greek war against the Trojans. Having had to part with some of his booty in order to appease gods and men, Agamemnon demands that he be granted Briseis, daughter of a noble Trojan family, who was earlier awarded to Achilles as a war "prize." Achilles' anger over this command drives the epic narrative. "Most acquisitive of all men," Achilles rails at Agamemnon, complaining, "Your thoughts are always set on gain." Withdrawing from battle, he declares, "I have no mind to stay here heaping up riches and treasure for you and receiving no honour myself" (1:119–74). Fueling Achilles' rage is indignation that Agamemnon's acquisitiveness violates customary norms of distribution. A dispute over the sharing of plunder (in the form, let us note, of an enslaved woman) thus discloses a rupture in elite reciprocity. Once booty has been divided, insists Achilles, "it is not right that the army should gather it back again" (1.125–26). Agamemnon has allowed personal accumulation to supersede the reciprocity that binds aristocratic households in a web of mutual obligation. In a telling passage in book 9 of the *Iliad*, Achilles condemns the one-sidedness of Agamemnon's behavior:

> *Like a bird that brings back to her unfledged chicks every morsel she can find, and has to go*
> *without herself, so it has been with me. . . . I have sacked twelve of men's cities from my*
> *   ships,*
> *and I claim eleven more by land across the fertile Troad. From all of these I took many fine*
> *treasures, and every time I brought them all and gave them to Agamemnon son of*
> *   Atreus: and*
> *every time, back there by the fast ships he never left, he would take them in, share out a few,*
> *and keep the most for himself (9.322–30).*

"The crisis of the *Iliad*," suggests Seaford, "is a breakdown of the form of reciprocity . . . controlled by the leader."[44] While the poet dramatizes it in terms of a clash between two godlike warriors, it is clear that a wider social conflict between antagonistic forms of distribution is in play. The crisis sketched in the *Iliad*, which also runs throughout the *Odyssey*, reflected the undermining of more traditional relations by new patterns of war, exchange, and accumulation, which were also creating preconditions for the emergence of coinage.

The Limits of Reciprocity: Colonization, Plunder, and the Slave Trade

Archaic Greece (roughly 700–480 BCE) underwent a protracted expansion in people, settlement, and trade. As population increased, so did the movements of persons and goods. New colonies were established, and new cultural contacts created. With these came an upsurge in raiding and communal warfare, the first records of which date from the late eighth century.[45] All of this drove a series of socioeconomic transformations, culminating in the political revolutions that would usher in both the classical polis and coinage.

While historians continue to debate the scale of the demographic takeoff in the archaic era, there is little doubt that crucial changes in diet and metallurgy propelled population growth, which in turn sent land-hungry people in search of colonies.[46] Fueled though it may have been by a desire for agricultural land, colonization also fostered slaving and market exchange. The capture of women as unfree wives and concubines was nothing new, of course, as the disputes charging the drama of the *Iliad* indicate. And in the *Odyssey*, King Nestor remarks that on leaving Troy, "we stowed our plunder, our sashed and lovely women" (3.170). Recounting his sacking of Ismarus, Odysseus further claims that he "killed the men, but as for the wives and plunder, that rich haul we dragged away from the place" (9.45–47). As colonists established households on land they had occupied, there is little doubt that they also seized local women. But not all the women and children captured would necessarily be incorporated into the household. There was increasingly an option to sell them. Recalling one battle against the Trojans, Achilles brags that he took "droves" of women, whom he "auctioned off as slaves" (*Iliad*, 21.99). And Thucydides, writing in a later period, describes Greek soldiers killing the Corcyraen men they had defeated, while "all the women taken in the stronghold were sold as slaves" (IV.48.4). Later in his *History*, Thucydides narrates a Spartan invasion of Iasus that led to the capture of "a very great booty." The Spartans, he says, turned the town over to Tissaphernes along with "all the captives," who were relinquished for "the stipulated price of one Doric stater a head" (VIII.28.4). These multiple references to the sale of enslaved persons mesh with historical evidence suggesting that early Greek colonists, at least on the Black Sea coast, collaborated with local chieftains in the slave trade.[47] Conquest of land involved not just capture of persons, but also the sale of some as human commodities.

Colonization additionally involved establishment of Greek trading posts. For instance, the early colonial settlement of Pithecusae was founded as a trading station, and the commercial colony at al-Mina served as the base of Greek trade to the East for two centuries (roughly 800 to 600 BCE). To be sure, agricultural produce comprised a considerable part of what Greek colonists sent to these markets. But shares of the booty claimed by raiding parties—from precious metal goods to enslaved people—would have played no small part. The fruits of this plunder were often exchanged for manufactured goods from the East, such as iron, fabrics, metal objects, and precious ornaments. Indeed, Greeks may well have deliberately increased their slaving activities to enhance trade with the East. In the Old Testament, Ezekiel specifically mentions enslaved people "as a typical Greek commodity."[48] Yet, while colonization and raiding opened up new market-oriented activities bound up with slaving, we should not assume this involved the rise of a new merchant class. On the contrary, raiding was a preeminently aristocratic activity. It was wealthy nobles (*aristoi*) who had the resources to build or purchase boats and equip them with both rowers and weapons, and the epics clearly depict them as leaders of raiding parties. In particular, younger sons of aristocratic families were often raiders, just as they were among the most numerous of colonizers. The distinction between warriors and traders is thus a fluid one, revolving on "little but an ideological hairline."[49] So widely accepted was the image of the seafaring noble that Odysseus pronounces, "Most men risk the seas to trade with other men" (*Odyssey*, 9.141), and the whole of his epic tale pivots on maritime misadventures.

Whether heads of households or younger sons, aristocratic warrior-traders propelled the geographic expansion that opened new horizons for raiding, the booty from which fired exchange for Eastern luxuries. Yet, this patrician activity significantly altered traditional aristocratic society, in large measure because goods acquired through raiding (and related trading activity) did not originate in the households (*oikoi*) in which the plunderers had been born. Pillaged goods from new territories could thus readily be treated as treasure acquired *outside* the networks of obligation that defined the household and its agricultural wealth. This may not have been especially significant when slaving and trading were more sporadic activities. But the sustained wave of colonization, which created new settlements and trading centers, removed the young men of the colonies from traditional spaces of aristocratic reciprocity. At sea for extended periods and no longer living alongside the old noble families, colonists and traders advanced more in the world by piling up personal wealth than by relying on customary networks of obligation. Indeed, when establishing constitutions for new poleis, they marked their novel status with more egalitarian laws, at least for those deemed citizens.[50] As a result, the colonies often contributed to the growth of an anti-aristocratic ethos that became increasingly potent after about 700.[51] As new fortunes were made in the nexus of raiding, slaving, and trading, a new fluidity entered the order of rank and power, with lesser lords sometimes acquiring fortunes exceeding those of their former superiors. At the same time, craftsmen and soldiers increasingly entered into market transactions. Throughout Greek society, older noble values and settled hierarchies jostled with new modes of accumulation via warrior-trading. Aristocratic poets of the era can be found complaining that wealth now mattered more than birth.

With these changes came the cultural transformations associated with "the orientalizing revolution." Luxury goods from the East entered the lives of Greek aristocrats on a growing scale, and both traders and migrant craftsmen established new cultural contacts. The myths, rituals, and household goods of the nobility increasingly reflected admiration of Eastern societies, their art, and their highly stratified social orders.[52] Although they were excluded from some of these cultural shifts, particularly the aristocratic symposia, the common folk were not unaffected by the changing patterns of social life. In the words of one historian,

> The man who draws his boat down into the sea and sails it is no longer tied to the man who had
> previously ordered his life across the boundary of his fields. . . . The potter who sells his vases by
> the docks must make what the foreigner wants, not what the basileus [lord] used to demand. . . .
> The mercenary must learn to take orders from any general set over him, not just from the commander of his phratry [extended kinship group].[53]

This was not, of course, a market society in any modern sense of the term, never mind a capitalist one. The vast majority of people were peasants producing most of their own subsistence goods through the labors of their households. Nonetheless, more members of all social classes, including peasant farmers, did enter markets, and the wealth and sensibilities generated there disrupted older patterns of social life, putting considerable strain on traditional forms of reciprocity. Wealth derived at a *spatial* distance from the community augmented the *social* distances between its members. Distancing, as we have already observed, was fundamental to negative reciprocity. It permitted unbalanced transactions, including violent ones. And as colonization, slaving, and the growth of trade networks all developed, wealth based on negative reciprocity began to have ever more profound impacts *within* traditional Greek communities.

Perhaps most significant, these new dynamics of accumulation shook up long-standing relations between rich and poor. To begin with, it seems clear that private ownership of land became more entrenched during this period, and that land was increasingly alienable.[54] Moreover, the general direction of land transfers was from the poor to the rich, implying both growing dispossession, on the one hand, and increased concentration of landed wealth, on the other. Concomitantly, the practice of smallholders honoring the nobility with "gifts" was being displaced by regular payment of rents.[55] By 600 BCE substantial numbers of small peasant farmers were classified as *hektemoroi*, tenants who probably turned over one-sixth of their produce to a lord. These rents had lost all semblance of gifts by the time of Draco's legal codes (probably 621 BCE), which harshly punished the poor for transgressions of the law, including failure to make payments.[56] When rent was too onerous, or other economic hardships intervened, the small farmer, unable to count on the generosity associated with older norms of reciprocity, would have had to contract a debt. But debts incurred in this way were negotiated against the security of their land or their body (or that of one of their kin). Indeed, for the rich, the whole purpose of loans may by now have been as a step toward indebting the poor in order to dispossess them of their holdings. For the peasant, of course, to be displaced and rendered landless could only be a catastrophe. Indeed, dispossession often went hand in hand with enslavement or exile, calamities that Solon was to denounce, as we shall see.[57]

Many of these themes run through Hesiod's *Works and Days*, as the poet narrates how his brother, "foolish Perses," lost his oikos in Boeotia due to an accumulation of *chrea* (debts).[58] Hesiod instructs his brother on the work habits and social behaviors necessary to remake himself as an independent peasant farmer, as well as on appropriate practices of farm management. A presupposition of these is "clearing of your debts" (403). Having accomplished that, he tells Perses, you will need to acquire sufficient money through your labors that "you may negotiate for another man's *kleros* [plot of land, allotment], not another man for yours" (341). That one could negotiate to acquire another man's plot, or he for yours, indicates that land was indeed alienable, and the whole text suggests a growing crisis of impoverishment and dispossession. The poet Theognis would seem to have been referring to precisely such phenomena when he wrote, at some point during the sixth century, "They seize possessions by force, and order has been destroyed/There is no longer an equitable distribution" (677–78).[59] Older forms of reciprocity, or "equitable distribution," had broken down, and now "possessions," particularly land, were being seized by the rich.

This is the context in which *Works and Days* advises the poor man on how to avoid debts and loss of his land. Hesiod describes a social crisis of indebtedness and dispossession. And where relinquishment of land could not discharge debts, the handover of persons *could*—by way of the debt bondage of the debtor or his dependents.[60] Even those commoners who could evade debt bondage, unable to count on the "generosity" of their superiors, had increasingly to resort to greater engagement with the market. It is revealing that Hesiod instructs his brother on how to conduct "seafaring" so that he might get his produce to market (641–45). With communal assistance receding, rudiments of market dependence emerged. This is why, rather than an isolated complaint, Hesiod's poem would have resonated with audiences throughout Greece, expressing a widespread egalitarian sensibility.[61]

The increase in dispossession appears to have been discursively registered in the growing use by aristocrats of servile terms to refer to the poor of Attica, not merely to enslaved people. In the early part of the archaic age, slavery or servility, as we have seen, applied to foreigners, to those captured via war and conquest. Native members of the community, irrespective of wealth, were "free," a term that connoted, among other things, being *undefeated* by outsiders.[62] Now, however, many were being defeated by insiders, and subjugated to them. By the beginning of the sixth century BCE, according to the *Constitution of Athens*, written by Aristotle or one of his students, terms for slavery and bondage were applied interchangeably to the condition of the Athenian-born poor:

> The poor were in a state of bondage to the rich, both themselves, their wives, and their children, and were called *Pelatæ* [bond-slaves for hire], and *Hektemori* [paying a sixth of the produce as rent]; for at this rate of hire they used to work the lands of the rich. Now, the whole of the land was in the hands of a few, and if the cultivators did not pay their rents, they became subject to bondage, both they and their children, and were bound to their creditors on the security of their persons, up to the time of Solon.[63]

It is this historical situation that haunts Hesiod's *Works and Days*. In its treatment of market practices and the crisis confronting the poor, this work contrasts mightily with the Homeric epics. In Homer, remarks critic James Redfield, "the heroes do not buy and sell"—though he quickly adds, "except perhaps to purchase a slave," a vital exception to which we shall return. Odysseus does proclaim that "most men risk the seas to trade with other men" (*Odyssey*, 9.141). But as a general rule, the epics do not portray the aristoi buying and selling, practices that are frequently treated as unheroic. King Nestor, for instance, scorns both traders and pirates, even though, incongruously, he recounts the fortune he attained through plunder (*Odyssey*, 3.80–83, 117–18, 170). Yet, we know that buying and selling, along with raiding and slaving, were well-established noble undertakings by the time Homer's epic poems were written down, around 650 BCE. If, as a growing scholarly consensus has it, Homer largely projected the relations of his society onto a glorious past in ways meant to heroize aristocratic warriors,[64] then his near silence about noble involvement in market transactions would seem symptomatic. It suggests that the poet suppressed evidence of a practice of which he was well aware, but whose effects troubled him or his listeners; it suggests that trade was considered unheroic. Redfield proposes that Homer's avoidance of trade in the epics is "a specific literary strategy—which, paradoxically, implies the importance of trade in the world of the poet."[65] After all, one does not deliberately conceal an *inconsequential* feature of one's world when recasting it in heroic guise. One suppresses something significant that provokes anxiety. And trade, joined to new forms of wealth and the erosion of reciprocity, was just such a troubling phenomenon. To be sure, the epics do interrogate the clash of greedy individualism or hubris (Agamemnon) versus proper noble generosity of the sort that Achilles recommends. But the conflict is portrayed in largely personal terms, as behaviors pursued by individual noble figures, disconnected from social practices of accumulation associated with warrior-trading. Yet if Homer shies away from these realities, Hesiod does not. For this peasant poet, the new social dynamics— and the crisis they wrought on the small producer—are on full display.

Works and Days has been described, reasonably, as an anti-aristocratic broadside against the upheavals deriving from new market relations and practices.[66] The text fairly seethes with rage against the wealthy and powerful. The poet condemns his era as an age of envy, and he denounces "those who occupy themselves with violence and wickedness and brutal deeds," reserving special scorn for those lords who, when acting as judges, had become "bribe-swallowers" issuing "crooked judgments" (238–64). Commentators have observed the similarities between Hesiod's social justice rhetoric and that of the great Athenian reformer, Solon, about a century later.[67] By Solon's time (590s BCE), the social tensions depicted by Homer and Hesiod had erupted into intense social conflict. So profound was the turmoil brought on by popular insurgence that the Athenian aristocracy, seeing no way out, conferred on Solon dictatorial authority to rewrite the laws in an effort to end the crisis and restabilize the polis. Echoing Hesiod, Solon plainly signaled that rapacious practices of exploitation would have to be drastically curbed. "The leaders of the people have an evil mind," Solon warns in his poems, which were recited publicly, and "they know not how to restrain their greed" (4.7–9).[68] He further intones that

> *I brought back to their god-given homeland Athens*
> *many who had been sold, one unjustly,*
> *another justly, others fleeing*
> *from dire necessity . . .*
> *Others here held in shameful slavery*
> *Trembling at their masters' whims*
> *I freed . . . (36.8–14)*

Solon's verses condemn the oppressions afflicting the poor: the concentration of wealth in fewer hands, the displacement of growing numbers of commoners from their lands, and the languishing of others in slavery due to unpayable debts. To be condemned to exile, debt bondage, or chattel slavery also meant exclusion from the political community, and thus loss of communal rights, social belonging, and identity. Crucial to Solon's reforms was the momentous "shaking off of the burdens" (*seisachtheia*), which famously involved elimination of debts and of debt bondage. But the social transformation almost certainly entailed "a more substantial structural change"—the abolition of rents on land, such as *hektemorage*.[69] The result was momentous: the "abolition of the relationship of clientship between peasants and aristocrats."[70] Throwing off their economic bonds, peasants acquired a powerful social, political, and legal independence. The Solonian program thus expressed the dynamics of a plebeian insurgency—"a political struggle that bordered on civil war"[71]—even if the lawgiver stopped at deep-seated reforms rather than a radical redistribution of the land, and even if it would be another four generations before democracy was fully implanted.[72] Notwithstanding these limits, Solon's reforms were a landmark moment in the process that gave birth to the independent *peasant-citizen*—a unique social type that united labor and self-rule, and that comprised the most radical ingredient of ancient democracy.[73]

The scale of the Athenian social crisis that raged in 594 BCE, when Solon was given dictatorial powers, can be gleaned from Plutarch's account, written seven centuries later. While he is surely unreliable in details, Plutarch seems to have grasped the broad sweep of the historical moment:

> *And the disparity of fortune between the rich and the poor, at that time, also reached its height; so that the city seemed to be in a truly dangerous condition, and no other means for freeing it from disturbances and settling it to be possible but a despotic power. All the people were indebted to the rich; and either they tilled the land for their creditors, paying them a sixth part of the increase, and were therefore called Hectemorii or Thetes, or else they engaged their body for the debt, and might be seized and either sent into slavery, or sold to strangers; some (for no law forbade it) were forced to sell their children, or fly the country to avoid the cruelty of their creditors; but for the most part and the bravest of them began to combine together and encourage one another to stand to it, to choose a leader, to liberate the condemned debtors, divide the land, and change the government.*
>
> *Then the wisest of the Athenians, perceiving Solon . . . pressed him to succour the commonwealth and compose the differences.*[74]

We will return to these issues and the rise of democracy later in this chapter. But for the moment one further result ought to be underlined: due to the democratic transformations at Athens, the definition of servility was once more restricted to enslaved people. We saw earlier that by at least 600 BCE, in the midst of dispossession and impoverishment, the lines of servitude had become blurred. With tenant farmers becoming poorer, increasingly indebted to noble men, and even enslaved, relations of servility had been extended to the native born. A variety of conditions of "bondage"—which included, according to the author of the Aristotelian *Constitution of Athens*, the hektemoroi, or rent-owing peasants—had come to overlap with slavery. Indeed, historians note that by now, most of the terms used for enslaved people—among them *doulos, oiketes, therapon, pais, soma*—designated any kind of servant or wage laborer.[75] With the Solonian abolition of debts, rents, and debt bondage, however, such intermediate forms of subordination and subjection were eliminated, and free and servile statuses became sharply differentiated in Athens. While elitists like Plato might continue to use servile terms for all who labored, they did so on contested ground, as democrats were challenging degrading depictions of laboring citizens. Rather than a continuum of forms of bondage that overlapped and bled into one another, Athenian society in its democratic phase knew only freemen—divided, to be sure, by wealth, but still fully free participants in making the laws by which they were governed—as against enslaved people. Non-enslaved women, however, notwithstanding the greater liberties they experienced at Athens compared to other Greek cities,[76] were denied the rights that adhered to their male counterparts. Male social status was now organized around a single binary structure. And given the Solonian decree that no Athenian could be enslaved, servility was aligned with foreignness. To be enslaved was to be an outsider (which is not to say that all foreigners were enslaved). And for the rich, the relaxation of exactions on the Athenian poor meant that the bulk of their surplus product would henceforth have to come from enslaved people.[77] Moreover, if poor members of the community could no longer be subjected to bondage in any form, then it followed that enslaved people would henceforth enter the society principally as commodities purchased on the market.[78] Fundamentally, slavery assumed not only a chattel form, with enslaved people as outright pieces of property, but also a commodity form. And this returns us to the equivalence between enslaved people and money that is central to the story of ancient money.

War, Slavery, and Market Exchange

As Marx suspected, commodity exchange appears to have originated between strangers.[79] Certainly this was true for the Greek society of the Homeric epics. As Finley pointed out, there is not a single example in the epics of a market exchange involving two Greeks or two Trojans.[80] The evidence we have suggests that members of the same archaic communities did not conduct commercial transactions with one another.[81] It is surely no surprise that within a community organized around generalized reciprocity, theft and plunder would be considered antisocial acts. That haggling over equivalents (balanced reciprocity) should also be considered antisocial seems less obvious to those of us raised in a market economy. However, in societies of generalized reciprocity, what one gave to neighbors and kin had nothing to do with their capacity to return an equivalent. Need was need, and it involved a moral obligation beyond the calculus of equivalence. True, support in time of need presumed an obligation on the recipient to reciprocate in the future, if necessary. But this obligation was not subjected to rules of quantitative measure. The principle of commercial exchange—to bargain for trade of equivalents—was foreign to those that regulated this sort of communal life. Indeed, market exchange was considered closer to piracy, which is why it was undertaken with outsiders. Another reason that commercial exchange was kept at a distance from communal life may have had to do with the fact that the principal commodity exchanged with foreigners was often enslaved persons. In fact, linguistic evidence suggests that the concepts of purchase and sale originated in the rights of captors to possess and transfer captives.[82] What could be sold was that which had been seized outside the bounds of the community, and human captives topped the list. Not only was trade conducted *with* outsiders; it often comprised the exchange *of* outsiders.

The ancient Greek world was by no means unique in this regard. Enslaved people appear to have been the earliest goods traded in Neolithic Europe, and the principal item of commerce among the indigenous peoples of the Pacific Northwest. In some societies, enslaved people in fact appear to have been the first acceptable form of private property, particularly where land was not privatized.[83] We find evidence of slave sales in Babylonia and Assyria around 2400 BCE. And further south, in Sumer, temple records indicate the presence of enslaved people by 2700 BCE and of an active market in foreign captives by about 2000 BCE.[84] The commodification of enslaved people was thus a phenomenon familiar to the ancient Middle East for at least two thousand years before the Christian era. As early as 1580 BCE, a large-scale trade in enslaved people had developed across the Indian Ocean—a case that prompted Patterson to remark, "Slavery was intricately tied up with the origins of trade itself."[85] Indeed, outside the ambit of the Greco-Roman world, the evidence strongly suggests that the Arab slave trade that began in the eighth and ninth centuries CE exceeded in size the staggering scale of the Roman trade, which at its height involved 250,000 to 400,000 enslaved people per year.[86] But even though slave markets came later to the Greco-Roman world, by the time of Homer, war, slavery, and market exchange were inextricably connected, and the Mediterranean was home to some of the most active slave markets anywhere. Indeed, all of the enslaved people whose names and histories appear in the *Odyssey* were either purchased, or are the descendants of enslaved people acquired on the market.[87] So closely integrated were warfare and trade that slave dealers in the ancient Greek world trailed behind armies, purchasing their captives.[88]

Let us recall Achilles' boast, with reference to one of his battles against the Trojans: "Droves I took alive and auctioned off as slaves" (*Iliad*, 21.99). As elsewhere, Homer here depicts violence as the primary means of enslaving others, and markets as the place where the victims of such violence—people enslaved as chattel—were sold. Recognizing the decisive role of force in determining personal fate, Heraclitus proclaimed, "War is the father of all and king of all, and some he shows as gods, others as men; some he makes slaves, others free."[89] Throughout the ancient Greek world, violence and enslavement were central to a heroic narrative that pivoted, as we have seen, on the exploits of the aristocratic warrior. To be sure, there were other routes to enslavement. Debt bondage, or the sale of children and kin in order to raise money or acquire food and land, defined alternate passages to slavery. By the classical periods in Greece and Rome, however, both these routes were closed off following uprisings of the demos that won legal protection against the enslavement of citizens.[90] Henceforth, enslaved people in these societies would be foreigners, outsiders seized in war or imported for sale. And with the growth of markets in the Greek world, slavery become predominantly an "economic phenomenon, conforming to laws of supply and demand,"[91] as most captives of war were purchased from troops by slave merchants and transported to market towns for sale.

Recall for a moment Redfield's argument that the omission of buying and selling in the epics is a literary strategy, meant to evade new and destabilizing socioeconomic practices. Redfield acknowledges one exception, though only to effectively ignore it. "The heroes," he tells us, "do not buy and sell—except perhaps to purchase a slave." Yet, rather than exceptional, the buying and selling of enslaved people was one of the most routine of archaic market activities. Redfield evades this by denying that purchase and sale of enslaved people is in fact a market action. Trafficking in women and children, he insists, "does not establish in any important sense a market relation."[92] But this claim simply will not hold. Human trafficking was (and is) quintessentially a market relation. That it might sometimes occur outside geographically settled markets is of little consequence. In fact, descriptions of commercial exchange in the epics often involve the episodic markets that were typical of much early archaic trade—what can best be characterized as a *one-time market*. Homer describes just this, during a pause in the siege of Troy: the heroes turn their eyes to the sea to discover that "ships had come from Lemnos bringing wine, many of them, sent by Jason's son Euneos . . . From these ships the long-haired Achaeans bought their wine. Some paid in bronze, some by gleaming iron, some in hides, some in live oxen, some in slaves" (*Iliad*, 7.473–75).

To be sure, this is trade without a generalized equivalent: bronze, iron, hides, oxen, and enslaved people are all used here to purchase wine. But it is certainly market activity, organized by seafaring traders. Furthermore, we do in fact find clear allusions to settled markets in the epics. The *Iliad* contains multiple references to ports of trade, particularly to towns that specialized in slave markets, including Samos, Imbros, and Euneos's town of Lemnos. The poet says of one captive that Achilles "took him on board ship to well-founded Lemnos and sold him there" (*Iliad*, 21.40). And in the final pages of the epic, Hekabe laments that if Achilles were to capture her sons, he would sell them by "sending them over the harvestless sea to Samos and Imbros and misty Lemnos" (*Iliad*, 24.753–55). Redfield downplays these references, largely because he insists on separating slaving from commerce, and theft from trade.[93] Yet this is to promote a sanitized liberal image of trade and markets, one that evades the overwhelming evidence of piracy, plunder, and slaving as constitutive of early commerce. As one historian of ancient Rome comments, "Pillage and commerce were two complimentary and interconnected methods of exchange . . . it was a long time before the ancient world established a clear distinction between them."[94] Preferring idyllic fables of primitive barter, mainstream economists and historians have elided the profound ties linking markets to slavery.[95] Nevertheless, as we have seen, enslaved people were among the earliest goods traded in countless human societies, and frequently the most significant items of long-distance exchange.[96] Rather than the product of peaceful encounters for mutually beneficial exchanges of basic or luxury goods, markets were frequently born of the violent capture and sale of persons.

This growth of markets in enslaved people prompted Giuseppe Salvioli to declare that enslaved people were the first commodities regularly sold for a profit in the Greek world.[97] While the evidence is sketchy, it does seem that enslaved people were *among* the first commodities bought and sold—and among the most significant. Not only were ancient wars "slave hunts," as Max Weber suggested;[98]

they also fueled some of the most active large-scale markets in the world at the time. In the Greek society captured in Homer's epics, the prevailing aristocratic-warrior ethos meant that slavery was highly gendered. The victors typically killed the men who survived the field of battle, while enslaving the women and children. Warrior elites appropriated for themselves a select number of female and child captives, distributed some as booty, and sold off others for commercial gain, as Achilles brags of doing. In classical antiquity, as across most of human history, enslaved people were disproportionately female, and their primary role was domestic—labor in the home and its fields, including sexual favors for their masters, and the bearing and rearing of the children the latter fathered (both with them and with other women).[99] Over time, however, enslaved adult male, too, became available through commercial markets, and even the epics portray such sales. Homer instructs us that Odysseus purchased his loyal male swineherd, Eumaeus, from Taphian pirates; and the old swineherd later purchased an enslaved male of his own (*Odyssey*; 14:511–14, 15.429–30). We know that merchants trafficking in the "barbarian" regions on the edges of the Greek world carried thousands of enslaved people, many from the Danubian and Black Sea areas, to markets on the main trade routes, like Delos, Corinth, Chios, and Rhodes. Following the end of the Peloponnesian War (414–404 BCE), an extremely active trade in war captives and victims of raids developed at Delos, perhaps peaking around 100 BCE. And by the classical period of the fifth and fourth centuries BCE, public slave auctions were held every month in the Athenian agora, by which time commerce had supplanted warfare as the principal source of enslaved people in Greece.[100]

The pattern was somewhat different in the case of Rome. While slave markets burgeoned throughout the empire, a majority of enslaved people may have been direct captives of war and of predatory raiding by the imperial army, though large numbers were undoubtedly sold off after capture, as Cicero clearly intimates in his visions of sesterces.[101] It is striking that by the second half of the first century CE, chains with manacles were "part of the standard equipment of the Roman soldier."[102] Various snippets of historical evidence on this front are revealing. Following the defeat of Gallic forces in 52 BCE, Julius Caesar distributed one enslaved captive to every soldier in his army. Over one hundred years later, in the Jewish War of 66–70 CE, approximately ninety-seven thousand apprehended Jews are said to have been enslaved by the victorious Romans.

Equally telling, in the subsequent victory procession organized by Titus, son of the emperor, 700 of these enslaved people were paraded as part of the wealth plundered in battle, alongside the animals, and precious objects of gold, silver, and ivory that had been looted.[103] Enslaved people, in short, were plunder; they were objects of wealth, no different in principle from cattle.

Walking with the Feet of Other People: Animals, Possessions, and Enslaved Bodies

> *"Those commodities which are the first necessaries of existence, cattle and slaves."*
>
> —Polybius[104]

Polybius's matter-of-fact description of the commodities most necessary to life in ancient Rome expressed the common sense of his social class. Enslaved people were an essential good, a possession vital to aristocratic comfort in the same way that cattle were necessary to a flourishing agricultural estate. Indeed, enslaved people were of the same category as cattle, a sort of human livestock indispensable to lordly refinement. The conflation of enslaved people with animals also permeated the symbolic registers of classical Greek culture.[105] The only unambiguous term for enslaved person—*andrapodon*—was related etymologically to *tetrapodon* (a being with four feet), which denoted livestock. Literally, therefore, *andrapodon* meant a beast with human feet. And in a military context, the term signified a prisoner, not merely in the sense of a captive, but, crucially, that of "an object acquired as booty."[106] The semantic connection of *andrapodon* to both animals and war loot is arresting. We know that by Homeric times oxen had become the standard measure for the value of commodities, including enslaved persons. We learn in the epics, for instance, that an enslaved woman, Eurycleia, had been purchased for the equivalent of twenty oxen, while bronze armor was valued at nine, and a tripod at twelve (*Odyssey*, 1:490–91; *Iliad*, 6.236, 23.703). Alone among human beings, then, enslaved people were literally equated with cattle. Consistent with this, from the fourth century BCE, one of the most common terms for enslaved person was *soma*, or "body." To designate a person as a body is, of course, to reify them, to strip them of personhood and personality, to represent them as strictly physical beings, simple beasts of burden—ancient zombies lacking consciousness, identity, thought, and reason.

It is customary to imagine that what distinguishes an enslaved person is their legal status as human property. True as this is, it does not go far enough. For law in this regard merely expresses deeper social processes. To be an enslaved person, as we have seen, is to be socially dispossessed, to be humanly uprooted—indeed *de*-rooted, or deracinated. Foundational to slavery is the stripping away of kinship, the deprivation of communal belonging, the destruction of personal identity. Nothing so defines such destruction as the forcible disconnection of people from communities and kin. As Finley points out, of roughly sixty records of private sales of enslaved people in ancient Egypt, not one shows an enslaved adult male being sold with their wife or children.[107] Not only were enslaved people "natally alienated," as Patterson rightly points out—that is, dispossessed of kin relations dating from their birth—but their status also left them at permanent risk of losing whatever precarious bonds they might have forged with children and spouses.[108] While slavery began in the calamity of capture, exile, and sale, the original trauma of social death might be repeated with every subsequent sale. It is illuminating in this regard that the literal translation of the Egyptian word for captive was "living death."[109] Of course, in many societies *members* of the community could be enslaved, too (not just foreigners), particularly those considered to have committed transgressions against their neighbors, including the "crime" of failure to pay back loans, whose result was frequently debt bondage of the debtor or one of their kin. Through such processes, an insider was effectively expelled from membership in their community, becoming an outsider, someone to whom others did not owe communal obligations—and thus someone who could be treated as a thing. In Egypt, as 'Abd al-Muhsin Bakir pointed out, insiders who were enslaved, usually due to their extreme poverty, acquired a status equivalent to legal and social death.[110] One anthropologist of slave societies has remarked that characteristic of all forms of slavery is "the slave's juridical inability to become 'kin.'"[111] Indeed, during the Late Period (first millennium BCE) in Egypt, enslaved people directly owned by the royal treasury were called *nemeh*, or "orphan."[112]

Trade in enslaved people thus involved an intriguing symmetry. In most of the "primitive" societies we have studied, enslaved people were outsiders, and trade in these societies was undertaken *with* outsiders. Trade, slavery, and money were thus all connected in a circuit of alienation; they were constituted in relationships outside of and alien to the societies from which traders came. Slave trading was thus the exchange of (socially dead) outsiders with other outsiders to whom one owed no communal obligations. And money, as the means of conducting such trade, was a medium for these alienated social interactions. It should come as little surprise, then, that in many societies, enslaved people have also served *as* money, or at least as a measure of value. Given their frequent status as the primary items of trade, enslaved people readily became the item by which other goods were measured. We observe this sort of slave-money in a wide range of societies, including many in precolonial and colonial Africa, in the Pacific Northwest of what is now Canada, among the Obydo people of what is now Brazil, and, perhaps most famously, in early Christian Ireland.[113]

The Irish monetary system of the early Christian era pivoted on a dual metric. The most common measure of value was the *sét*, which referred to a head of cattle. Above that, the highest unit of value was the *cumal*, whose literal meaning is "female slave." Fines for bodily injuries were often established in cumal, as were prices for land, even though typically no enslaved people changed hands in any of these purchases and sales. Just as enslaved people were abstracted from their communities—indeed one of the oldest Latin meanings of the verb *abstract* is "to separate or pull away"—so the cumal provided an abstract standard by which the value of other things could be measured. The violent abstraction inherent in slavery thus transformed enslaved-people-as-things into a generic measure of value, into a metric for expressing the value of one thing relative to another. Exchange value, as Marx demonstrated, is expressed in quantity, not quality. On the market, a thing represents an amount of money—not an amount of beauty, nourishment, warmth, et cetera. It is with money, in appropriate quantities, that we can buy the things of life. Money thus acquires the quality of being a measure-in-general (and ultimately of general exchangeability with all things). Its unique "quality" is to embody pure quantitativeness. Clearly, only those human beings who had been dispossessed of the qualities of personhood could serve as money, as measures of abstract quantity. Suggestively, enslaved people shared with coins the fact of being branded, of bearing signs imprinted on their surfaces. It is even said of the Samian prisoners of war captured by Athens in 439 BCE that they were branded with an owl, the very sign with which Athenian coins were marked.[114] Enslaved people and coins, interchangeable in everyday life, shared the characteristic of being emblazoned with insignias of state power.

We see these social processes codified in Roman law, where ownership is defined as *dominium* (power or domination) over a *res* (a thing). It is significant that the word *dominus* originally meant "slave master," not "owner." But as the concept of absolute property was developed, *dominus* came to refer to one who owned anything that could be considered private property. Meanwhile, an enslaved person came to be a res in law, "the only human res," as Patterson notes.[115]

But law here followed the social phenomenology of everyday life in slave society. After all, the same linguistic convention prevailed in Rome as in Greece, where enslaved people were frequently described as *somata*, particularly in documents of sale, and of manumission. Historian Keith Hopkins cites multiple texts in this idiom, including one specifying, "sold to Pythian Apollo, the female body whose name is Pistis" for "a price of four and a half *mnae* [450 drachmas]," as well as a manumission statement that described the freeing of "two female bodies whose names are Onasiphoron and Sotero."[116] Like work animals, enslaved people functioned as bodies that extended the corporeal reach and powers of the slave owner. For Aristotle, what enslaved people share with "tame animals" is that both "help with their bodies to supply our essential needs."[117] Referring to how Roman masters were transported by people they enslaved, Pliny the Elder remarked, "We walk with the feet of other people."[118] So identified were enslaved people with animal bodies that Athenian and Roman laws meant to protect buyers against unseen defects applied to the purchase of *both* animals and enslaved people.[119] As the esteemed jurist Gaius observed, "The statute treats equally our slaves and our four-footed cattle which are kept in herds."[120] With such conflations of humans and beasts of burden in mind, Marx quipped that the slaveholder purchases an enslaved person "in the same way as he buys his horse."[121]

Purchase, of course, was preceded by examination—often by inspection of enslaved people displayed on a platform, known as a *catastra*, of the sort to which Cicero alludes in his letter to Atticus. Roman law required that essential information about an enslaved person be hung on a label around their neck, and it was common practice for the potential buyer to poke, prod, and unclothe the enslaved in order to discern the qualities of the commodity on display. Undressing also operated as a crucial act of degradation, a way of stripping the enslaved of everything that made them social beings. Recounting his "day of slavery," the great Odysseus tells Eumaeus, "They stripped from my back the shirt and cloak I wore, decked me out in a new suit of clothes, all rags, ripped and filthy"

(*Odyssey*, 14:386–88). Enforced disrobing operated as an essential moment in the "secular excommunication" that rendered the enslaved culturally bare.[122] The semiotics of nakedness functioned to negate personhood and the elements of social belonging defined by dress. By eliminating the individual's social skin, masters were empowered to take control of the very identity of the bonded person. So naturalized was this mode of domination that even Seneca, who viewed enslaved people less inhumanely than many of his contemporaries, casually compared buying enslaved people to the purchase of a horse, recommending that the purchaser "pull off the garments from slaves that are advertised for sale, so that no bodily flaws may escape your notice."[123]

Buyers inspected for height, strength, wounds, disease, and beauty. Yet, notwithstanding the appraisal of specific qualities, the enslaved body was in fact being *quantitatively* assessed. As much as it inscribed an order of domination, qualitative assessment of the enslaved person was intended to arrive at a price, a quantitative measure. "No less for buyer than seller," notes one historian, "the slave was his or her price, and thus comparable to any other slave, despite differences of age, sex, origin, appearance."[124] Monetary price was the metric for all enslaved people; each had a cost in a common measure of value, be it units of oxen, pieces of gold, or silver coins. A price having been established and a sale transacted, the change in ownership of the enslaved body might be marked by a brand or tattoo. Just as branding was a claim of ownership, so were chains, as the god Pluto acknowledges in Aristophanes' play *The Frogs* when he remarks, "And branded and fettered the slaves shall go."[125] Slavery was literally written on the body, and it was regularly reinscribed in the course of daily practices of degradation. Nothing more fundamentally distinguished the enslaved from the citizen in classical Greece and Rome than the bodily imprints of power that they bore. If anything symbolized both the exercise of masterly power and the distinction between citizen and enslaved, it was the whip, as it would in modern slavery.[126] But corporeal domination did not end with the whip. Branding, manacles, fetters, neck chains, and slave prisons were all elements of the technology of power, while flogging, burning, and racking figured among its practices.[127] Brutality against enslaved bodies encoded a banality of violence intrinsic to Greco-Roman culture. In his *Memorabilia*, Xenophon describes Socrates asking his interlocutor Aristippus whether in dealing with recalcitrant enslaved people, prudent masters "keep them from running away by putting them in bonds, and drive away their laziness with the compulsion of blows?" To which Aristippus replies, "I punish him with everything bad . . . until I compel him to serve as a slave."[128]

"Until I compel him to serve as a slave": this pithy response encapsulates a whole program of social domination. What is stunning about the exchange is precisely its ordinariness, the utterly mundane quality of a dialogue about the use of "bonds" and "the compulsion of blows." Consider also Aristophanes' comedic commentary on brutality against enslaved people, which enumerates the use of chains, shackles, beatings, branding, whipping, and starvation.[129] *The Frogs* is a particularly striking play in this regard, as it pivots on a carnivalesque inversion, a role reversal in which the god Dionysus appears as a slave, and his slave Xanthias as his master. In order to avoid arrest, Xanthias (misrepresenting himself as Dionysius) offers to give over his slave (in actuality the god Dionysus) for torture. The dialogue that follows returns us to the term *basanos*. Challenged as to the truth of his tale, Xanthias promises, "I'll let you torture [*basanize*] this slave of mine." The judge on the scene replies, "What kind of torture do you suggest, sir?" To which Xanthias responds: "Oh, give him the whole works. Rack, thumbscrew, gallows, cat-o'-nine-tails: pour vinegar up his nostrils, pile bricks on his chest—anything you like. Only don't hit him with a leek or a fresh spring onion. I won't stand for that—brings tears to my eyes."[130]

The absurdity of the final sentences packs a comedic effect. So much so that it is easy to ignore the sheer cruelty of what precedes it—an inventory of instruments of physical torture, whose usage against an enslaved person was entirely routine. Similarly, the use of *basanos* to describe legal torture of an enslaved person makes it easy to forget the earlier connection of the term to the authenticity of money. Yet, symptomatically perhaps, Aristophanes' play itself returns to this question. Act I of *The Frogs* ends with a speech by the leader of the play's chorus. He declares:

> *I'll tell you what I think about the way*
> *This city treats her soundest men today*
> *By a coincidence more sad than funny*
> *It's very like the way we treat our money*
> *Coins that rang true, clean-stamped and worth their weight*
> *Throughout the world, have ceased to circulate.*
> *Instead the purses of Athenian shoppers*
> *Are full of shoddy, silver-plated coppers.*

Having compared the integrity of coinage to the soundness of men, the leader goes on to lament the debasement of money, specifically the substitution of silver-plated copper coins for fully silver ones. Then, he compares debased coinage to the sort of men being celebrated in Athens:

> *Just so, when men are needed by the nation,*
> *The best have been withdrawn from circulation.*
> *Men of good birth and breeding, men of parts,*
> *Well-schooled in wrestling and in gentler arts,*
> *These we abuse, and trust instead to knaves,*
> *Newcomers, aliens, copper-plated slaves.*[131]

Here is a straightforward equation of high-quality money with human nobility. By the last line, foreigners and enslaved people are likened to copper, reflecting a long-standing elitist idiom in which purity of character was linked to the most coveted precious metals, and impurity to the most commonplace metals. Aristocratic discourse allied nobility to gold, and inferiority to copper, with silver occupying an intermediate position—precisely the hierarchy deployed by Plato in the myth of metals in his *Republic*. In the passage above, Aristophanes cleverly adapts the analogy between virtuous character and purity of metal. He modifies the aristocratic schema, however, by making the silver coinage produced by the polis the supreme standard of value, signaling the strength of democratic values at the time. Yet, the poet fears that this high-quality silver coinage, the "gold standard" of a nonaristocratic order, is in the throes of degradation. Linking noble character to silver coins, Aristophanes worries that virtue and money are being simultaneously devalued, "knaves" being celebrated at the expense of "men of good birth and breeding," just as copper coins (with silver plating) are being treated as equivalent to pure silver. More than merely associating the quality of persons with that of money, the playwright also worries that commerce damages the value of both by rewarding greed, rather than virtue. "In everything it's clear that money talks," intones a character in another of his plays,[132] expressing a critical tension in the dialectic of monetization.

While provoking anxieties, monetized relations also elevated the principle of abstract generality as a primary "way of seeing"—the comparison of all (or most) things with money. We see this not merely in Attic comedy, but also in philosophy, where Socrates, a philosopher ostensibly beyond the influence of commerce, nevertheless conflates money and character. This occurs when

Xenophon describes the philosopher's comparison of free men to enslaved in terms of their monetary value. "Have friends like servants their own values?" Socrates asks an interlocutor. "For one servant, I suppose, may be worth two minas, another no less than ten. . . . So I am led to inquire whether friends may not differ in value."[133] Conspicuous here is Socrates' conflation of the pricing of enslaved people—whose value may vary from two minas to ten—with estimates of the value of free men. In his *Republic* Plato famously used the myth of metals—a quintessentially aristocratic grammar—in order to justify inequality and the exclusion of the masses from political decision making. Yet Socrates here elides these premises by *generalizing* the monetary principle and discussing the value of free men by comparison with the metric that applies to enslaved people—monetary prices. Rather than ascribing each group a different value measure—gold for the elite, copper for the masses, silver for the middling sort—Socrates advances here a common measure of the worth of free men and enslaved people. This might seem to introduce an egalitarian element into Plato's philosophy. Yet, this would be an egalitarianism modeled on the commodity form—an abstracted sameness in which people represent different quantities of the same substance (monetary value). Ironically, the critical-utopian charge that is identifiable in Platonic thought derives largely from its attempt to conceive of the "good life" as requiring a society *beyond* the self-interested calculations of monetary acquisition and accumulation, a point to which we shall return. Here, however, Socratic thinking is enmeshed in monetary calculation.

As much as aristocratic thinkers like Socrates resisted the "leveling" effects of democracy, they moved in a social universe inscribed by money, under whose influence philosophy increasingly imagined the world as consisting of universal substances or forms[134]—which also predisposed them to conceptualize persons and things as subsumed by the universal form of money. These are symptoms of a society with a full-fledged universal equivalent, whose metrics infiltrate manifold spheres of everyday life, from the cost of enslaved people to the relative values of friends. But we are getting ahead of ourselves. To fully explore the meanings of monetization, we must revisit the emergence of money itself in ancient Greece.

CHAPTER 2

The Law of the Body

Money and the State

Across human societies, early forms of money have consisted of things that sustain the body (grain, barley, corn, cattle), things that adorn and decorate the body (shells, gold, silver), and things that assist the body in producing the things of life (hand tools of various sorts). Perhaps more than anything else, money has been comprised of foodstuffs, the very fuel of the body. It is no accident, therefore, that we use terms like *circulation* to describe the movement of money through the social organism, just as we use it for the flow of nutrition within the individual body. Indeed, the greatest political economists of the mid-eighteenth century, the French physiocrats, built a theoretical model whose central concept was the "circular flow" of wealth through the economy.[1] Like blood, wealth was said to *flow, circulate,* and *nourish*. The original material and semiotic link between blood and money may be located at this juncture.

In ancient Greece, money had such deep roots in communal practices of food sharing that the common meal has been described as "the first money in our culture."[2] Common meals reproduce the *body politic* by bringing people together in ceremonies for the sharing of food, as well as of memories, recreation, and folklore. It comes as no surprise, then, that money in Greece was often symbolically represented by food and other sources of subsistence, like bulls and olive sprigs.

And in a monetized society, of course, it is often better to receive the symbol than the substance: to have money rather than food. For money in such contexts is the means of access to virtually *all* of life's necessaries. For this reason, it comprises a vital element of the *second nature* through which such societies reproduce themselves; it is part of a human-created web of technologies, practices, and institutions that are indispensable to societal life.[3] All of these social artifacts constitute a sort of *second body* for fostering the daily reproduction of people. And, like tools, technologies, and social institutions, money is a bodily extension that can become autonomous of its corporeal base. In modern capitalism, money becomes an alienated power, one that dominates the reproduction of human life.

Ancient monetized economies were not, of course, capitalist ones. The latter emerge where the reproduction of both laborers and owners has become market dependent, and thus inherently mediated by alienated value forms.[4] Thus, as Marxist philosopher Georg Lukács noted, as much as "Greek philosophy was no stranger to reification," it did not experience these "as universal forms of existence."[5] Even when regularly engaged in market exchange, the peasant producers of ancient Greece were not, as a rule, *compelled* to reproduce themselves by means of the systematic sale of their produce through the market—in large measure because the revolts of the demos had blocked mass dispossession of the poor and the market dependence it creates. Only in the entirely self-reproducing monetary economy (capitalism) does money become a full-fledged substitute for the body, which happens once capital has directly subsumed the bodies of workers to its own reproduction.[6] In capitalist society, money directs and labor obeys. The modern capitalist, as Alfred Sohn-Rethel explained, operates as "producer" of commodities "not by way of labour, not with his hands, not by tools or machines which he operates. He performs it with his money."[7] Money enables this by taking command of the labor of others. Its social power resides in the domination of their bodies (as repositories of labor power). In the fully developed capitalist mode of production, this happens primarily by way of its domination of wage labor. To be sure, it can also occur through command over slave labor. But typically, slave labor in ancient society—unlike plantation slavery in the New World—was not commodity producing, notwithstanding slave-based silver mining in Greece or agricultural slavery in the Roman Empire. On the whole, in the Greco-Roman world, the work of the enslaved—predominantly women—largely produced use values (including sexual "favors") for immediate consumption.

If money had roots in food-sharing rituals in ancient Greece, then we need to track the specific social transformations that made possible its emergence as an increasingly autonomous social power. Food-sharing rituals are widespread across human cultures, after all, and rarely in archaic and ancient societies did they give rise to full-fledged money. It required the specific ways in which generalized reciprocity broke down in ancient Greece to open up the space for new modes of social integration and the emergence of money.

From Food to Metals: The Emergence of Money in Ancient Greece

As the epics demonstrate, food sharing was the basis of reciprocity in ancient Greece. At an ancient *panegyris* (festive gathering), everyone participated in processions, songs, prayers, feasts, and competitions, and all brought an abundance of food to be shared during the *dais* (communal feast). Such occasions were certainly opportunities for aristocratic display, with a great man contributing sheep and oxen, much as a male head-of-house did in the oikos.[8] But these were also egalitarian gatherings of commoners. Even where they took place at the home of a noble man, the focal point was the sacrifice of an animal, typically an ox or a goat, whose flesh and blood were shared by all. Animal sacrifices were deeply sacred acts, involving offerings to nature and the gods, and may have been substitutes for earlier practices involving the killing of persons, even members of the royal family. In this regard, they observed a *social logic of substitution*, with non-human animals being offered to the gods in place of human sacrifices.[9] As I show below, such a logic of substitution is observed in the history of money, along a chain that runs: people → animals → roasting utensils → coins. And this chain of substitutions returns us to the crisis of reciprocity in ancient Greece.

Sacrificial rituals for augmenting the fertility of humans and extra-human nature have been widespread across human cultures, including the Maya civilization of Mesoamerica. In Egypt, Persia, and Mesopotamia, a sacred status was ascribed to bulls, and their sacrifice served as a ceremonial payment to the gods who regulated food supply and human procreation, while also providing meat for communal feasts. In Greek mythology, the god Dionysus, associated with blood, wine, and fertility, is frequently depicted as a bull. Moreover, Greek tragedy may have originated in spring rites meant to celebrate the planting of crops and, crucially, in the ritual killing and eating of a sacred bull.[10] During the City Dionysia at Athens—a five- or six-day festival organized by officials of the polis during the sixth, fifth, and fourth centuries—scores of oxen were sacrificed, and an image of Dionysus was escorted to the theater and placed in the orchestra, while select young men led a prized bull into the theater precinct.[11] And at Magnesia, in Asia Minor, the stewards of the city purchased a bull at the annual fair in the fall, then sacrificed it in the spring as part of a huge feast.[12] As symbols of blood and fertility, bulls were associated with the gods. But in their consumption at the great feasts, their flesh and blood literally flowed through the community, enabling both the physical and social reproduction of its members, and reminding us again of the connection of blood to money. Given their semiotic and material circulation through the community, it is not difficult to see how bulls might come to symbolize wealth in general.

An argument along these lines was first advanced by German historian Bernhard Laum in the 1920s.[13] Laum handily demolished the idea that the origin of money as a unit of account in ancient Greece derived from an item's use as a means of exchange. After all, the inconveniences of using cattle as a medium, passed from person to person, are obvious. Instead, Laum emphasized, first, the sacred character of cattle in Greece, and second, the standardized quantities that governed their ritual use. He observed that various ceremonies required precise numbers of cattle—in the epics they are typically slaughtered in groups of one hundred, twenty, twelve, nine, or four.[14] Payment to the gods was thus made in quantitatively uniform amounts, foreshadowing one of the crucial features of money. In the first book of the *Iliad*, for example, Homer recounts a feast called the hecatomb, where one hundred cattle were offered in a burnt sacrifice:

> *When they had offered prayers and sprinkled the barley-grains, first they pulled back the victims' heads and slaughtered them and flayed them: and they cut out the thigh bones and covered them with fat. . . . The old man burned them on cut firewood, and poured libations of*
> *gleaming wine, while the young men stood by with five-tanged forks in their hands. Then when*
> *the thighs were burnt up and they had tasted the innards, they chopped the rest into pieces and*
> *threaded them on spits, and roasted them carefully, and then drew all the meat off. When they*
> *had finished their work and prepared the meal, they set to eating, and no man's desire went without an equal share in the feast (Iliad, 1.447–76).*

Note that this ritual feast begins with prayers to the gods. After that, the victims are slaughtered and properly prepared for roasting, which is overseen by an elder who pours wine—another symbol of life and of the god Dionysus—over the meat. The young men carry five-pronged forks, utensils vital to the banquet. Next, the meat is threaded onto roasting spits, implements which would eventually become a sort of proto-money. Finally, the men sit down to eat, each receiving an "equal" share.

The idea that everyone at the feast received an equal share can be found frequently in the epics (e.g., *Odyssey*, 19.481). And while the egalitarian sentiments in circulation by the eighth century should not be underestimated,[15] it may be that the equality in question here was a *proportionate*, rather than an arithmetic, one: each individual's portion being relative to (equivalent with) their social standing, with priests and aristoi receiving the largest amounts.[16] A similar description of feasting can be found in the *Odyssey* (3.510–30). Not only does this all look highly ordered, even lawlike; more telling, one meaning of the fifth-century BCE Greek word for law, *nomos*, was distribution. At the root of law in the democratic polis, we thus find the idea of appropriate sharing in a communal meal: the just allocation of food. A just republic is therefore defined as one in which wealth is properly shared. We glimpse here the reason why, from its inception, the democratic norm of justice has been tied to distribution. And, as we shall see, the word for money—*nomisma*—carries this semantic charge as well.

In addition to its long-standing link to distribution, the word *nomos* involved a whole series of connotations that suggested order, way of life, societal norms, and appropriate social relations.[17] The social order in question was shared by both men and gods, who communicated and exchanged gifts with one another. The human side of this equation required sacrifices and feasts, often the responsibility of priests associated with hereditary groups known as *gene* (singular: *genos*). These esteemed private citizens continued to preside over communal rituals even as the democratic polis developed throughout the sixth and fifth centuries BCE, when city-funded festivals came to dominate the Athenian calendar.[18] From Solon's early sixth-century reforms on, religious life and public ritual were increasingly governed by the city-state rather than noble households. The laws of distribution, *nomoi*, were regulated by public officials, working with the priests of the temple, as were the rites observed in sacrifices. Crucially, payments to the gods were matters of sacred custom, governed by civic statutes, not market relations. People did not haggle with the gods; they repaid the debt of life according to community norms.[19] While they did indeed foreshadow money, communal disbursements of meat did not originate in barter or commerce. As much as sacrifices were a sort of payment to the gods, their domain was that of the divine, not the market. They were holy obligations, not exchange values.

Law, Money, the Body . . . and War

Another way that money emanates from the body stems from the body's role as the foundational site of justice. Life and liberty are fundamentally corporeal, involving conditions of human survival and the exercise of bodily powers in the world around us. This is why the very language of justice in the polis is steeped in the idea of a proper distribution of the goods of life. In ancient legal codes more generally, the body is omnipresent, with crimes against the body dominating the law, and with transgressors subject to corporal punishment and confinement. Justice and injustice were written on the body. Indeed, bodily mutilation may have been the most common of archaic punishments.[20] It is equally noteworthy, however, that antique codes also provided for a significant interchangeability of money with the body.

One study of seventeen ancient law collections—including the Babylonian Laws of Eshnunna (ca. 1770 BCE) and Code of Hammurabi (ca. 1750 BCE), as well as the Roman Twelve Tables (450 BCE)—shows the substitution of monetary penalties for corporal punishment to have been widespread, and based on the social rank of the victim. In the Laws of Eshnunna, for instance, if a man causes the death of another man's wife or child, the penalty is capital punishment. If he causes the death of an enslaved woman, however, his own life is not imperiled; instead, he must turn over two enslaved women as compensation. Under the same codes, if a dog or an ox, whose owner has been previously warned, causes the death of a man, the owner shall be fined forty shekels of silver. If the dog or ox kills an enslaved person, the fine is reduced by nearly two-thirds, to fifteen shekels. In the Code of Hammurabi, written two decades later, a lender who beats to death a debtor's male child must turn over his own son to be killed in return. In the event that he kills someone enslaved by a debtor, he must pay the borrower twenty shekels and forgive the loan.[21] In the last case, we observe money's substitution for bodily injury according to the social valuation of the life involved. Where enslaved people were concerned, of course, money and life were always interchangeable. But this monetary principle infiltrated the domain of law and justice in complex ways.[22] We see this especially in the custom of wergild, widespread in ancient Germanic law, in which monetary payments substituted for corporal punishment or death for legal offenses.

This practice of monetary substitution was widespread throughout the ancient world, beyond the examples cited above. Broadly similar arrangements can be observed in the Hittite codes of Central Anatolia (today's Turkey), from about 1400 BCE; the laws set forth in Exodus of the Old Testament; the Law Code of Gortyn (Crete, ca. 480–450 BCE); and the Twelve Tables of Rome, which were almost contemporary with the Code of Gortyn.[23] We also find clear references to such practices in Homer, where Ajax recounts men having accepted payment, rather than direct retribution, for the murder of their brothers and sons (*Iliad*, 9.632–36). These norms for measuring the value of bodies and lives originated at least as much in the domain of law as that of the market.

While it is misleading to see in these ancient codes a long history of "commodification" of persons[24]—largely because none of these "prices" was determined by market relations—it is certainly true that these codes exhibit a set of values attached to persons and their body parts. Indeed, in ancient law, unique "prices" (monetary penalties) were often set for disfiguring, breaking, tearing off, or mutilating eyes, fingers, teeth, bones, and so on. All these body parts acquired monetary values in codes that originated with the state. And it was not just legal penalties that were state regulated. In the Laws of Eshnunna, the itemization of financial penalties was laid out in concert with the determination of wages—that is, the price for "renting" someone's body.[25] The state also decreed prices for food and subsistence goods, the very stuff of corporeal existence. These state-regulated wage rates and prices were certainly money values of a sort, but they were not *market-determined* prices, as commerce was not an autonomous domain of social life. The same was true for the interchangeability of bodies and money in the legal domain, which, unlike the purchase and sale of enslaved people, was not a market process. Indeed, the political economy of the law frequently drove that of the market, with transactions in the latter sphere often adhering to the value ratios determined by laws that governed fines and regulated prices. When individuals were called upon to make payments to the state, goods ranging from barley to copper, and from cattle to silver, were used as

standards for calculating their contributions. These ratios, established for purposes of measuring tax receipts and fines, often infiltrated the domain of commercial transactions. Recall, for instance, our example in chapter 1 of the ancient
Egyptian policeman who bought an ox valued at fifty deben of copper from a
workman, yet paid only five deben in copper, and the rest in a variety of other
goods. Similarly, in 1275 BCE, during the reign of the Egyptian king Rameses
II, a wealthy woman purchased an enslaved Syrian girl at a price equivalent to
373 grams of silver. Yet, none of the payment was made in silver. Instead, a pot
of honey, ten shirts, bronze vessels, and ten deben of copper ingots were handed
over, in order to arrive at the silver price.[26] Here, a standard of value decreed
by an ancient state for calculation of legal fines and tax payments was adapted
to market transactions as a unit of account. To be sure, various forms of money
did emerge as adjuncts to exchange between strangers. However, where centralized governments had developed, money as a measure of value—including
the value of persons and their body parts—was often a largely legal construct.
The "prices" assigned by law to people, their property, or their body parts did
not reflect their purely economic commodification—a valuation through market
exchange—but rather a set of sociopolitical values administered by the state.

To say this is not to deny the role of markets in fostering monetization—
indeed, I have shown precisely such a dynamic in the archaic Greek world from
the age of colonization.[27] But, as I have also shown, market transactions initially
came to dominate *outside* the oikos-centered context of the political community,
particularly in the areas of foreign trade, including commerce in enslaved people. Moreover, in societies in which the "economic" sphere was not substantially
differentiated from the moral-political one, we should not expect them to show
any linear tendency toward full internalization of external market relations. To
be sure, relations between Greek lords and peasants *were* increasingly commercialized in this era. But for lords this involved the use of market exactions, debt
in particular, to appropriate *land*—the foundation of noble wealth and power.
Commercialization thus served to reinforce aristocratic forms of wealth and
power, while pauperizing sections of the peasantry.

Without a doubt, the growth of foreign trade did create space for the development of independent commodity production. But there is no compelling reason why these developments *alone* should have triggered a transition toward the
much more highly monetized forms of life that emerged in the era of ancient

democracy. For that to have occurred, significant sociopolitical pressures must have intersected with and reinforced economic trends. And this was the case for the whole epoch of anti-aristocratic politics—from tyranny to insurgent democracy—as new forms of public expenditure accompanied the centralization of religious, social, and political life around public temples, the agora, and the assembly. All of this, alongside the city-state's assumption of the growing costs of warfare, shaped the context for the channeling of wealth into monetary circuits independent of aristocratic gift exchange. More than this, the democratic polis, like the tyrannies before it, seems to have deliberately visibilized circuits of wealth by introducing symbols of public authority—coins—that displaced aristocratic items expressing private power. Looking at state assessment of legal penalties, for instance, we see a distinct evolution away from fines specified in precious goods and metals and toward penalties measured in amounts of coinage. A similar trend took place with regard to state prizes for games and contests, where monetary awards replaced wreaths and cloaks.[28] And by the fifth century BCE, government officials used coinage for a growing variety of expenditures, including jury pay, funding of liturgies, and payment for attending the assembly in democratic Athens. Beyond making its own payments in coins, the state also required that everyone obliged to pay (or receive) fines do so in coinage.[29] Legal decrees further forbade shopkeepers from refusing coins as payment, upon threat of having their property seized.[30] The polis thus made its coinage legal tender, a state-sanctioned currency that all sellers and creditors were obliged to accept. In a society accustomed to pre-coinage monetary forms, these actions gave coins an enforced circulation. And all of this was reinforced by the state's insistence on conducting its own business with coins, especially by requiring them in payment of taxes and fines.

In important respects, therefore, monetization was a political process as well as a commercial one, as the state promoted transactions in coins as part of the political-economic circuitry of the polis. The association of coinage with Athenian democracy provoked, as we have seen, an aristocratic opposition. And no one articulated elitist antagonism to democracy with such sophistication as did philosophers in the Socratic tradition. Yet, their opposition to democracy was inscribed by the conceptual forms of monetary relations. Socratic philosophy thus mimicked the universalizing drama of the money form—however much it sought to displace money as a regulator of social and political life.

Money, Philosophy, and the Violence of Abstraction

What distinguished the new mathematics and philosophy in ancient Greece was their increasing *abstraction* from corporeal schema. Early mathematics had been grounded in the body. Units of spatial measurement, for instance, were based upon parts of the human anatomy, such as the forearm, which was deployed as a unit of measure in ancient Egypt, and would later be called *cubit* in Latin. We refer to numbers as *digits*, the same term that describes fingers, thumbs, and toes—the body parts used in counting. The division we call a *yard* was derived from the stride of an average-sized adult male.[31] In fact, such bodily based metrics persisted even in overwhelmingly capitalist societies into the nineteenth century, with measures based on foot, pace, and elbow.[32] The early development of fractions, multiplication, and division also seems to have been related to the body and its sources of nourishment. In ancient Mesopotamia, for instance, the state's role in allocating resources prompted it to deploy arithmetic to sort out social problems of distribution, such as how to share out twenty loaves of bread among nine people.[33] The social challenge of collecting and distributing economic resources, particularly foodstuffs, constituted the practical-bodily foundation of much early mathematics.

In deliberately *abstracting* from corporeal schema, Greek mathematics and philosophy distanced their concepts and procedures from the everyday problems of embodied life. To this end, they elevated logical reasoning over practical demonstration. New methods of abstract thinking were cultivated, in which thought moved from one logical axiom to the next without contamination by empirical data. Squares, rectangles, and triangles were to be analyzed in terms of their logically necessary properties, not by way of mundane issues having to do with the layout of agricultural fields. Mind would thus produce its own logical protocols while rising "above" bodily sensation and experience.

Reflecting on the significance of these shifts, Sohn-Rethel argued that they originated in the interrelation between monetization and philosophical abstraction in ancient Greece. Crucial here was his analysis of the *real abstraction* involved in the activity of market exchange. After all, any exchange of commodities requires the participants to abstract from the concrete and specific qualities of the things involved—say, an enslaved woman and twenty barrels of wine—to find a quantitative commonality (e.g., each is judged equal to a quantity of a third thing, such as one ounce of silver). This commensurability is only possible by abstracting from concrete qualities in order to arrive at a quantitative identity. There is, after all, nothing in wine as a use value that corresponds to the useful properties of silver. Market prices thus involve a conceptual and practical abstracting operation that brackets useful properties in search of a quantitative reduction of each along a common metric. It is precisely this that Sohn-Rethel called the *exchange abstraction*. The inner structure of the latter consists in the fact that "the interrelational equation posited by an act of exchange . . . establishes a sphere of non-dimensional quantity."[34] This peculiar sphere of quantity is said to be nondimensional insofar as there is no real, physical dimension in which an enslaved person and twenty barrels of wine are identical. Put differently, their commensurability is possible only in an abstract space, cleansed of all real objects and inhabited simply by mathematical values and relations—and it is in just such an abstract space that the exchange of commodities takes place via the medium of money. The exchange abstraction thus operates in the first instance in a purely logical monetary space, where things are effectively dematerialized so that they might be transformed into mere quantities of abstract (monetary) value. The domain of exchange values thus possesses what Marx described as a "phantom-objectivity."[35] Exchange values are *real*—they move real objects from one hand to another, and make or break personal fortunes—at the same time as they are *nonsensuous*. Twist and turn barrels of wine, enslaved people, or coats as much as we like; we will only encounter their physical (use value) properties. Their values, as pure quantities represented by money, elude our senses—they are phantasmal. Delineating the exchange abstraction thus, Sohn-Rethel suggested that Greek philosophy created a radically new cosmological worldview by formalizing aspects of the social process of exchange in a novel conceptual vocabulary.

Those familiar with Plato's doctrine of truth will recognize the degree to which his philosophy, too, moves through an abstract space. Yet, Plato seeks to demarcate the space of philosophy from that of money, banishing it from the domain of truth. Particularly in his most developed text, *The Republic*, philosophy is so explicitly counterposed to money that the pair can be taken to form "two competing architectonic principles."[36]

Plato sets up this counter-positioning in the first sentence of *The Republic*, when he has Socrates inform his readers, "I went down yesterday to the Piraeus with Glaucon."[37] The Piraeus was the Athenian harbor, the site of an incessant movement of goods and money, as cargo-bearing ships came and went, and as purchases, sales, and business investments were endlessly conducted. It has been suggested that the (private and accumulative) activities characteristic of the harbor were at fundamental cross-purposes with the public duties of citizens to the state.[38] Certainly, Plato's intent in selecting this setting seems designed to contrast these conflicting principles, as he immediately moves to a debate over the relationship of money to justice. The debate occurs with Cephalus, a wealthy citizen whose home the philosopher and his companion are visiting. Socrates quickly inquires as to whether their host inherited his fortune or acquired it through his own pursuits. Cephalus proudly declares that he has largely inherited his wealth, and Socrates intones that he suspected as much. After all, he remarks, unlike those who inherit their wealth (and therefore do not have to engage in acquisition), those who have made their own fortunes "have a second love of money as a creation of their own," and this is a source of corruption. In contrast to the "natural love of money," which everyone has because of its usefulness as a *means* to satisfy wants, these "makers of fortunes" have an unnatural and obsessive worship of money: "they can talk about nothing but the praises of wealth" (330). Already, Plato is intimating that money has a natural role as a means to an end, but that it can also stimulate a perverse and corrupting passion—an unnatural love—when it becomes an end in itself. Yet, Cephalus is not entirely convinced that money ought to be radically demarcated from justice. In fact, he proposes that the man with money can afford to be honest (he has no need to defraud others) and to honor his debts to gods and men. But Socrates is unyielding. "To speak the truth and pay your debts" are not equivalent to justice, he proclaims (331). Indeed, justice cannot be conceived in the terms of a utilitarian calculus. Unlike money, urges Socrates, justice is an end in itself, not a means to an end. And this, as I have suggested, gives a critical-utopian charge to Plato's search for a form of good life beyond monetary calculation. That which is good has no price; it is no means to an end. The good and the true are ends in themselves, requiring no external measure or validation.

Cephalus, however, resists this conclusion. Deploying one example after another, he tries to demonstrate that justice is useful—that it is a means to distinct ends, such as payment of debts, assistance of friends, and the establishment of fair contracts. Each time, Socrates debunks the argument. Indeed, the philosopher goes so far as to insist that the usefulness of justice is that it is not instrumental to *any* external purpose. Justice exists in and for itself, as its own end. "Justice is useful," he urges, only when all other things, including money, "are useless" (333). Justice begins, therefore, where things with specific purposes can go no further, where they have arrived at a limit point. Justice becomes an end in itself naturally, whereas money does so only unnaturally. In this unnatural state, money asserts its nonidentity with all other things; it insists on its primacy over everything else. Coats or boats or enslaved people can be desired for particular purposes; but money as end in itself transcends all particularity—it presents itself as universal, though its generality can only be false. Against this tendency of money toward pseudo-universalization (the essence of the unnatural "second love of money"), Plato seeks to restrict money to a simple means of exchange, something desired only as a means to particulars, rather than for its own sake. Only then, he intimates, can justice flourish as the one true universal end in itself, free of interference by money's false universality. This argument is later rehearsed by Aristotle in his *Politics*, where he contrasts the natural use of money, as a means to finite ends, with its perverse use as an end in itself (which, as I discuss below, he refers to as *chrematistics*). In Marx's terms, Plato and Aristotle describe the circuit $C-M-C$ as natural (where a commodity C is sold for money M, which is then used for the purchase of other commodities). Here, money is used to acquire a use value, a specific good. But the circuit $M-C-M'$—where money is used simply to buy commodities to be resold for more money ($M' > M$)—is unnatural and irrational, as money has become a demonic end in itself. "There is no limit to the end which this kind of acquisition has in view," writes Aristotle. This mode of acquisition never arrives at a natural and rational end; it tends "not for the good life," but away from it.[39] Plato and Aristotle consider money (represented by silver or gold) as a particular thing that is pathologically misapprehended as universal, like justice or truth. But this false universality is a perversion that induces irrational passions and pursuits. For this reason, Plato seeks to limit money to the particular roles of *means* of exchange and *means* of payment. Yet, in trying to get beyond monetary calculation, he proceeds to model justice and truth on the very abstracting and generalizing powers that he discerns in money's unnatural capacities. Thus, while philosophy and money are "competing architectonic principles" in the text, they are also symmetrical. Philosophy takes on the abstracting and universalizing powers of money, the better to vanquish it. Its mimicry of money is on full display when we turn to the crucial books VI and VII of *The Republic*.

Plato's innovation here is not simply the idea of a unifying substance that underlies all things. As Richard Seaford has shown, this counterintuitive idea, which seems at odds with the plurality of things that affect our senses, is widely characteristic of early Greek cosmology, and particularly prominent in the texts of Heraclitus and Parmenides.[40] Plato, however, gives this cosmological notion a heightened idealist inflexion. Early in book VI, he urges that only philosophers "are able to grasp the eternal and unchangeable," unlike "those who wander in the realm of the many and variable" (484). Here we have a clear juxtaposition of the One and the Many, with truth posited as unitary and unchanging in opposition to ordinary experience, which apprehends the world as plural ("the many") and changing ("variable"). Whoever contemplates the "being" of things, according to Plato, must turn away from their becoming and their "multiplicity." The latter features typify everyday, empirical existence, which flounders among the appearances of things, rather than their timeless essences (490). We perceive many things as beautiful and good, he continues, but we fail to attain knowledge unless we grasp the "absolute beauty" and the "absolute good" that transcend any specific iterations of beauty or goodness. These qualities must be "brought under a single idea, which is called the essence of each" (507). Here we have an explicit dualism of essence and appearance, and of the One and the Many, in which truth lies with the former and error with the latter. As in Plato's doctrine of Forms, truth or the absolute does not reside in things as they appear in everyday experience. Truth participates in an eternal, unchanging, and nonsensuous sphere. This is a realm that can be accessed only in thought, through the logic of ideas, rather than via the medium of sensation.

Having laid out his idealist program, which abstracts a realm of pure ideas from the world of ordinary sensation and experience, Plato then turns, in book VII, to mathematics as the science of the unchanging. The true philosophers, he insists, those best qualified to govern the state, should "go and learn arithmetic . . . until they see the nature of numbers with the mind only." Along this route, they will "pass from becoming to truth and being." To see the nature of numbers *with the mind only* is to leave the realm in which "merchants and retail traders" deal with numbers. The latter imagine numbers in relation to actual goods, objects, and coins; their understanding of numbers is contaminated by sense-experience in the world of things. The philosopher, on the other hand, consciously abandons the sphere of sensation in order to "reason about *abstract number*" (525, my emphasis). And here, as I have suggested, Plato's philosophy endeavors to appropriate to philosophy the powers of money as an end in itself.

The quintessence of full-fledged money is to be the universal substance of commodity exchange. Money transcends all particulars; unlike all other commodities, it is the exclusively universal representative of value. It thus embodies the true essence of all things *as* commodities—it is the universality that unites their particularities. Indeed, commodities only realize themselves as money. Outside their expression in money, commodities lack reality and truth *as commodities* (i.e., as goods meant to be bought and sold). It follows that money is the "being" of particular goods, unperturbed by their becoming in space and time, by their volatile movements and price fluctuations. Notwithstanding the chaos of market exchange, money persists as the truth of all things. Money is abstract value, manifest in specific concrete quantities of actual goods, but not reducible to them. Money is not the price of this coat, that loaf of bread, or this automobile. It is the very possibility of particular things *as* numbers (exchange values)—the quality of things that makes the many different numbers (prices) possible. Put differently, nothing could have a particular exchange value if it did not participate in the very ontological possibility of exchangeability. Yet this ontological possibility resides outside the things themselves as use values, and this "outside" property is incarnated in money. Money is the pure form of exchangeability, in the same way that Platonic truth, like the essence of beauty, is a timeless form that resides in a realm separated from the material world of things. "What is absolute unity?" asks Plato. And he answers: it is that which can be "both one and infinite in multitude" (525). Of course, this also describes money, which can assume the appearance of any number (price) without being reducible to any of them, just as truth can pertain to particular philosophical or mathematical arguments without being confined by them. Money and truth are thus infinite in a way that particular prices and truthful propositions are not.

Having, in book I, disqualified money as the architectonic principle of a good society, by the later books of *The Republic*, Plato has projected the universalizing qualities of money onto philosophy. Philosophical truth—be it in the form of wisdom, virtue, or beauty—is represented as the universal substance of our world. More than this, for Plato it is an ideational substance, one that is sharply separated from the world of sense-experience, and of the body and its labors. Yet, here we encounter two rubs. First, the philosophical production of truth has emerged as a counter to the universalizing powers of money. Philosophy mimics money's transcendent properties and emerges only where the latter has already made its imprint on society. Minerva's owl truly takes flight at dusk. Second, money itself is tied to the world of labor. In the ancient case, this notably involved the labor of enslaved people, as was directly evident in the production of Athenian silver in the city's mines. And this double dependency—on money and labor—undercuts philosophy's declarations of autonomy, its claims to produce the truth of our world through mind alone. As Marx would later claim in his *Economic and Philosophic Manuscripts*, the ostensible autonomy of mind is thus an illusion. "Logic is the *currency* of the mind," he wrote, in parody of German idealism.[41] Just as money renders all goods subordinate to it by positing itself as their essence, so Plato's logic, like all idealism, posits the mind's thought processes as the truth of all things. Yet, lurking behind the world of mind, making it all possible, is a social process that logic conceals—the division between mental and manual labor. "From the moment when a division between mental and manual labour appears," declare Marx and Engels, then "consciousness is in a position to emancipate itself from the world."[42] But this "emancipation" is a false one, made possible only by the violence of exploitation, manifest in the surplus product upon which philosophers subsist. Determining the world of the mind, in other words, are the labors of "the motley multitude" (*Republic*, 494), those excluded from the domains of mind and government, whose activity sustains these hallowed spheres. Just as the enslaved person is the secret of ancient money, so is it the secret of ancient philosophy.

Because he was untroubled in his support of slavery, Plato makes the economic dependence of citizen-philosophers entirely visible. In his *Laws*, for instance, when sketching out his preferred social arrangements, he declares, "Farms have been entrusted to slaves, who provide them [the citizens] with sufficient produce of the land to keep them in modest comfort."[43] The same text advises the master class on how to govern this "difficult beast," which should always be addressed with "an order," with whom all forms of friendship should be avoided, and on whom the whip should be freely applied.[44] Once more, we are returned to violence, bondage, and enslaved bodies—bodies that were acquired through war, which had to be fought by common soldiers. The ruling class conceived of the latter by analogy to enslaved people. As much as sacrifice of animals had been at the root of Greek culture, the sacrifice of soldiers was at the root of its wars and empire. And this sacrifice was obtained with money.

Coins and the Polis

With the growth of the polis as the space of public life, sacred ritual increasingly revolved around public temples, many of which were built during the eighth century BCE. With older forms of reciprocity breaking down, aristocrats were pressured to redirect generosity by means of dedications to the temples.[45] A new egalitarian sensibility identified public-spiritedness with redistribution via *public* institutions, over which the demos had increasing influence. To court the goodwill of the gods and of their neighbors, wealthy men were now expected not to host private banquets, but to donate to temples. Growing anti-aristocratic sentiment also brought lavish funeral ceremonies, another form of private display, into disfavor. This change has been described as a shift of redistribution, from gifts-to-men to gifts-to-gods; but equally it was a shift from aristocratic *charity* to the poor, to (rich) citizens' *obligations* to the state, which took the form of temple donations.[46]

As temples became repositories of wealth—and in some cases the first banks in the ancient Greek world—they also took over from private patrons the distribution of wealth to commoners by way of civic feasts. In a society in which the civic and the religious were integrated, temples readily became sites of economic transactions. They sponsored marketplaces and fairs; they issued loans to city authorities at moments of distress; they paid out wages, particularly for labor employed in temple-building projects; and they sold donated objects in order to raise money to fund their diverse functions. In all these ways, temples became focal points for market transactions, while organizing the ritual events at which animals were sacrificed and food shared.[47] Goods that served monetary purposes were thus deeply embedded in an economy of the sacred.

While sacrificial animals were undoubtedly among the votive offerings made by rich men, looking at the epics, we can discern other valuable pre-monetary objects related to communal feasts. In the penultimate book of the *Iliad*, for instance, Achilles convenes an athletic contest to commemorate his beloved friend Patroclus. At various stages of his description of the contest, Homer enumerates the prizes on offer. Predictably, horses, oxen, gold, and enslaved women are among them. But so are metallic goods related to feasting, in particular "a great tripod to stand over the fire," and a cauldron. The poet presents us with precise valuations of many of these goods, expressed in oxen. The tripod, we are informed, was valued by the warriors "at twelve oxen's worth," the enslaved woman "at four oxen," and the cauldron at "the worth of an ox" (*Iliad*; 23:702–5, 886). Note again the role of cattle as a measure of value, as well as the interchangeability of enslaved persons with oxen. Equally significant, the metallic objects offered as prizes—a cauldron and a roasting tripod—are vital components of ritual feasting. In fact, evidence indicates that cauldrons were being used as a regular means of payment in Crete by the eighth century BCE.[48] A growing body of literary and archaeological evidence further suggests that iron roasting spits—known as *obolos*—functioned as a sort of proto-money in several parts of Greece by the eighth and seventh centuries BCE.

Iron spits are significant for several reasons. First, they are metallic objects, as are coins. Secondly, they are items associated with sacrifice and food sharing. Finally, unlike cattle, they were highly portable and could be easily combined into packages of multiple units. The literary and archaeological record exhibits two celebrated examples of roasting spits being used as what appears to be special-purpose money. One comes from the temple of Hera at Argos and concerns a decree from the first half of the sixth century BCE by King Pheidon, who is said to have ordered the replacement of spits by coins. A famous account contends that "Pheidon of Argos struck money in Aegina; and having given them (his subjects) coin and abolished the spits, he dedicated them to Hera in Argos."[49] This textual source received significant confirmation when archaeological excavations at the temple of Hera unearthed a bundle of about ninety-six iron spits.[50] While we cannot discern the motivation for this dedication of spits, we know that similar offerings were made elsewhere. Herodotus, for instance, tells of a large donation made by Rhodopis, a courtesan and formerly enslaved person, in Naucratis. After having become quite rich, Rhodopis is said to have contributed one-tenth of her wealth to the temple by purchasing "as many iron roasting spits" as this part of her fortune could procure."[51] Herodotus implies that he had seen these spits and, apparently unaware of their monetary function, assumed they had first been purchased with money, although considerable scholarly opinion suggests they *were* in fact money—or, more precisely, a special-purpose money. Furthermore, we find bundles of iron spits in aristocratic tombs, presumably as offerings to the gods.[52] Classicist David Tandy has plausibly suggested that spits served "as a sort of value unit" (or measure of value) for trades among commercially minded nobles.[53]

Etymology strongly reinforces this interpretation. The basic silver monetary unit to emerge in the Aegean world was called the *obelos*, a name that reverberates with the word for iron spit, *obolos*. More than this, a coin worth six *obeloi* was called a *drachma*, whose older meaning was "graspful," or "handful." We have seen that iron spits were often bundled together in handfuls (*drachmae*) when they were used as donations to temples. So, this monetary term, too, may well have referred to roasting spits.[54] From the sixth century BCE, we find a variety of precious metal objects being offered in temple donations.[55] These hearken back to aristocratic prizes, particularly metal goblets, oriental tripods, cauldrons, swords, and other weapons—the treasured goods of aristocratic gift exchange. The gifting of such precious metal objects was glorified in the epics and in aristocratic poetry. Yet, these aristocratic circuits of wealth were self-enclosed, encompassing only wealthy aristoi. In fact, aristocratic art and poetry extolled the sphere of truly precious gifts precisely because it was uncontaminated by the presence of commoners. By the eighth century BCE, however, the values of elite culture were under attack by the plebeian or "middling" sort.[56] This makes the appearance of iron spits as a proto-currency quite intriguing. For spits were integral elements of communal festivals in which every citizen partook. Both materially and symbolically, they were thus inclusive rather than exclusive. That they should have been socially validated as a representation of value suggests the evolution of more inclusionary practices within Greek society. Moreover, as we have seen, the democratizing thrust of the period discouraged the rich from lavish exhibitions of wealth, particularly on funerals and burials. As the polis ascended, so luxurious displays of jewelry, fine clothes, and decorative hairstyles declined.[57] It would not be surprising, then, if culturally accepted representations of value came to pivot on metallic objects like spits, which were emblematic of the social solidarity manifest in communal feasts.

The emergence of coinage would thus suggest efforts to *re-embed* wealth and exchange in the wake of a breakdown in older practices of reciprocity. With the erosion of clientelist relations of aristocratic life, the temple-agora-polis nexus arose in part to subordinate wealth to the community as a whole. Coinage emerged, therefore, as part of a project to assert the supremacy of polis-produced tokens of value over transactional spheres dominated by aristocratic luxury goods. Further, as urban temples became the organizers of communal festivities, durable donations not requiring ongoing labor and maintenance (as did animals) might be preferred, if they could later be used to purchase livestock. Additionally, metal objects, like cauldrons and iron spits, might be loaned out when not needed right away. Such items could then circulate as means of payment and exchange because temple or civic authorities would eventually need to buy them back to purchase livestock. As a result, temple goods might have readily acquired a social acceptance as representations of wealth in general. Goods collected by temples could thus circulate as general forms of wealth precisely because sacred institutions were sure to accept them as means of payment. Ultimately, it would not have been a big step for the polis to mint and stamp precious objects—coins—that assumed social validity as means of exchange and payment and as stores of value. But here we need a slight detour, since coins appear to have first emerged in states known as tyrannies. Only by discerning the underlying reasons for this can we appreciate their enduring association with the democratic polis.

Coins, Religion, Law, and the Polis

Herodotus tells us, "The Lydians were the first people that we know of to use a gold and silver coinage and to introduce retail trade."[58] While many of the conclusions Herodotus draws from this origin are dubious, attribution of the invention of coinage to Lydia is not. It is widely accepted among scholars that the first coins, made of electrum, an alloy of gold and silver, were produced by the Lydian monarchy in Asia Minor around 600 BCE. Half a century later, the last of the Lydian kings, Croesus, had the first coins minted from gold and silver. By then or shortly thereafter, a number of Greek city-states, Athens, Corinth, and Aegina among them, began producing silver coins.[59]

What is controversial in Herodotus's account of coinage are his claims that the Lydians invented trade; that poor girls in Lydia "prostitute themselves without exception to collect money for their dowries"; that these prostituted women then—scandalously, in his eyes—"choose their own husbands"; and that Lydians invented idle pastimes like "dice, knucklebones, and ball-games."[60] As historian Leslie Kurke has shown, we have here a network of associations (money → trade → prostitution → female assertiveness → unmanly games) that reflects an aristocratic critique of coinage and its effects.[61] Coinage is hereby counterposed to the heroic virtues of the noble-warrior, however much the reality was one of an aristocracy that increasingly engaged in slaving, trading, and dispossessing peasant farmers. Yet these elite activities had revolved around use of precious metals, largely a monopoly of aristocrats. Coinage overcame this noble exclusiveness by putting stamped precious metals into *general* circulation.[62] Circumventing aristocratic circuits of gift exchange and display, coins gave gold and silver a new promiscuity, allowing them to crisscross through the hands of the multitude. Coinage thus contributed to a wider dislodging of traditional aristocratic grids of power, and this is where its association with tyrants originates.

Tyranny as a political form emerged across the Greek world in the century after 650 BCE. Corinth experienced perhaps the most long-lasting succession of tyrannies (roughly 655 to 585 BCE), but Athens, too, knew tyrannical rule for much of the half century from 560 to 510. Often, tyrants were dissident nobles seeking to break the domination of an elite network of aristocrats. In reconstituting political rule, tyrants not only concentrated powers in their own hands; typically, they also appealed to the people for support, enhancing the rights of commoners in efforts to curb aristocratic influence. Aristotle's summary is instructive: "Tyrants are drawn from the [people] and the masses, to serve as their protectors against the notables, and in order to prevent them suffering any injustice from that class" (*Politics*, 5.1310b).[63] The emergence of such tyrannies seems to have been a product of major social transformations.

First, the growth of poverty, indebtedness, and dispossession was rendering aristocratic rule increasingly intolerable for many of the lower sort. It is instructive that Corinth, where tyranny arose first and endured longest, was also the most commercially developed Greek city at the time. If trade and commercial wealth contributed to social differentiation and class grievances, as I have suggested, then it is no surprise that a popular reaction against noble authority should have come first in a major trading city. Second, with the rise, toward the end of the eighth century BCE, of hoplite warfare, based on a mass of heavily armed troops recruited from the middling sort (*hoplites*), war and politics became more reliant on non-aristocratic groups. The ethos of the new warfare foregrounded mass action, rather than the skill and valor of the heroic individual. As one historian notes, "When these thousands took the field they looked alike. . . . Farmer, artisan, trader and aristocrat stood side by side; and those who stood apart no longer mattered."[64] Hoplites represented perhaps one-third of the men of a city-state at the time, and an aristocrat seeking to break the power of traditional noble households might easily appeal to this group, whose members possessed arms and an enduring commitment to democratization.[65] But as much as aspiring tyrants might mobilize this social layer for incursions against the old power structure, as appears to have taken place at Corinth,[66] these democratically inclined citizens could also launch such upheavals themselves.

Returning to markets and money, we observe that tyrants frequently encouraged the growth of trade and colonization, perhaps as sources of funding for a new kind of state. After all, the new infrastructures of public space and power all came with considerable costs, whether these were used to expand the agora, construct temples, foster urban festivals, create water systems, or finance warfare. But if trade and colonization were to provide the wealth indispensable to emergent forms of governance, they could more readily do so if they were integrated into monetary circuits dominated by state-sanctioned means of payment and exchange. The advantage of coinage is that it can incorporate flows of wealth into monetary forms that are authorized by civic authority and that bear emblems of public office. Coinage is publicly produced at the discretion of civic authorities, not noblemen. Just as politics were increasingly recentered—shifting from the noble oikos and the aristocratic symposium toward the agora and the assembly—so were the circuits of wealth, as coins bearing the authority of the city-state displaced precious metals exchanged between aristocratic households. In addition to assisting political authorities in collecting their "cut," both processes also involved a *visibilization* of power crucial to emergent democracy. As centers of political life, the agora and the assembly undercut the relative invisibility of aristocratic households as bastions of private power, much as coinage visibilized economic transactions. These processes simultaneously involved transformations in religious life.

"In archaic Greece," it has been rightly observed, "religion was the sphere of public activity *par excellence*."[67] But the nature of such activity was undergoing major renovations by the seventh century BCE, as we have observed. The building of temples, the creation of new state-run festivals, the growth of the agora, and the delineation of law created a new public sphere—the collective space of peasant-citizens—meant to displace the power of the aristocratic household. The upsurge in temple building in the late eighth century involved large communal efforts that accompanied the political rise of the demos.[68] By the time of Solon's reforms (the 590s BCE), the polis and urban religion were advancing together, as exemplified in the erection of stone temples, the reorganization of festivals, and dedications of marble statues. All were processes that were extended under the tyrannies of Peisistratus and his sons, who dominated most of the half century from 561 to 510, and which made religion more accessible to all.[69]

Under Peisistratus, the city festivals, known as Panathenaea, were revamped, as was the City Dionysia, which also became the platform for the performance of tragedies.[70] All of these remodeled urban festivals, with their games, processions, sacrifices, and performances, as classical historian Robert Parker notes, were "unthinkable outside the context of the developed polis, with its civic consciousness and pride."[71] As much as reforming tyrants may have reworked the grammar of festivity to legitimate their rule, they could only succeed by adapting their reforms to the growing civic consciousness of the demos. Through the city-state, the demos applied pressure on the rich to publicly contribute tribal dinners to their less well-off colleagues during the Panathenaea and the City Dionysia.[72] Private wealth was thereby rendered accountable to a polis that expressed a new civic consciousness.

This visibilization of power also involved a spatial revolution, and places of assembly, ritual celebration, theater, and market activity were fundamental to the development of the city-state around 600 BCE. Much of this was incarnated in the physical stuff of building materials, as Athens went from being a city of brick to one of marble and limestone. The expansion of the agora and the erection of temples were accompanied by the construction of a new theater of Dionysia to accommodate tragic performances.[73] Such spatial transformations invariably involve economies of human labor and expenditures of wealth to pay wages, and to purchase tools and building materials. After their construction, many of the activities conducted within these public spaces also required ongoing expenditures, from the purchase of meat for festivals to the payment of poets for their performances. Tellingly, the new festivals substituted cash prizes for competitions, making monetary payments to poets in place of precious metal gifts like goblets or cauldrons.[74]

In addition, the preeminent Greek coin—the Athenian owl, first produced around 515 BCE—carried the seal of the polis and was backed by its laws. Monetization was thus as much about new practices related to law, religion, and the state as it was about novel patterns of trade. Nevertheless, the owl was legendary for the purity of its silver content, which in part enabled it to become the first real *world money*, accepted throughout the whole of the Mediterranean trading region (and regularly copied by other states) because of its intrinsic value. Archaeologists have found owls in southern Anatolia, Syria, Egypt, Cyprus, and Afghanistan.[75] Athens's owl coins thus represented a unique fusion of political and economic dynamics: they bore the imprint of a powerful state that could enforce their circulation within its sovereign domain; and they were made of such high-quality silver that they were widely accepted by merchants, state officials, and others far beyond the field of Athenian jurisdiction. They thus represented money's first full-fledged *modular form*, metallic coinage.

Before proceeding, it is essential to pause and underline key facts about the production of the Athenian owl. As we have observed, the enduring value of the coins had much to do with the purity of their silver content, which was consistently maintained across the decades. To acquire general exchangeability in an age of nascent monetization, coinage needed a foundation in earlier forms of wealth, particularly precious metals. However—and this is decisive—for much of its history, the silver that comprised the owls came from Attica's silver mines at Laurium. And these mines were worked by probably the largest concentration of enslaved people to be found in the Greek world—perhaps as many as thirty thousand in the late fourth century BCE.[76] In terms of the activity that produced them, the value of Athenian owls—which created the dominant modular form of money for nearly twenty-five hundred years—was therefore rooted in the *past labor* of thousands of enslaved people. The original world money was tethered to the toil of enslaved bodies. Equally crucial, the reach of this world money owed more to war than it did to trade, more to blood than it did to markets. Like enslaved people, soldiers were acquired through money. And in this connection between soldiers and enslaved people, we are returned to the question of money and bondage.

Coins and Armies

More than one historian has argued that coins were first produced in Lydia in order to pay Greek mercenary soldiers.[77] There is a powerful insight here. Yet, to acknowledge the pronounced significance of mercenary payments in the ancient history of monetization need not commit us to mono-causal explanation. Like every complex historical process, the emergence of coinage involved the interweaving of multiple, reciprocally reinforcing historical "causes" whose results were never predetermined. Such processes have logics of *retro-determination* that can be reconstructed after the fact. Once coinage arose as a multifaceted "solution" to particular historical problems—both political and economic—its emergence clarified tendencies at work earlier and established an after-the-fact path dependency. As Marx observed in this regard, "human anatomy contains a key to the anatomy of the ape."[78] It is, in other words, later forms that illuminate preceding ones. Understood in this way, as part of a complex dialectical process, payment of mercenaries was indeed crucial to the emergence of coined money.

For much of human history, the mobilization of military forces was among the largest of state undertakings. Large-scale warfare requires the recruitment of thousands of soldiers, their provision with weapons and equipment (swords, ships, horses, shields), and their means of provision (food, tents, clothing), along with monetary reserves for wages. Herodotus tells us that the last time the tyrant Peisistratus seized power in Athens, he "hired bodyguards," paying them with revenue raised "from various sources."[79] As the decades proceeded, such mercenary soldiers were employed on ever-larger scales, not just as bodyguards, but as soldiers and sailors for military campaigns. By the time of the Peloponnesian War, between Sparta and Athens (431–404 BCE), both sides were utilizing hired fighters on a substantial scale. One Spartan expedition is said to have contained a thousand troops "persuaded by pay," while the Athenian navy was bursting with mercenaries. The year after the war's end, during the violent class struggles that shook Athens, oligarchs and democrats alike hired armed combatants. This was followed almost immediately by Cyrus the Younger's ostensible recruitment of ten thousand Greek mercenaries in a campaign to win the Persian throne. Even larger numbers of hired fighters from Greece are said to have served in Egypt over a period lasting a century and a half.[80] By then, large-scale hiring of Greek mercenaries—in the thousands or tens of thousands—was common throughout the Mediterranean region, North Africa, and Persia. In fact, one historian has proposed that a "military-coinage complex" was in place throughout the second half of the first millennium BCE.[81] To get a rudimentary sense of the expenses involved and their impact on the supply of coinage, consider that "to support just one legion cost Rome around 1,500,000 denarii a year, so that the main reason for the regular annual issue of silver denarii was simply to pay the army."[82] One historian has suggested that the *only* reason silver coins were issued in the late Roman Empire, where the monetary standard was based on gold, was for military payments.[83]

Returning to ancient Greece, it is easy to grasp the symbiosis between mercenary warfare and coinage. To begin with, it was the nature of the mercenary arrangement that these fighters had to be paid, and it was entirely impractical to pay soldiers on-the-move in cattle, enslaved people, or raw bullion.[84] Coins were readily portable and, if made of high-quality precious metal, as were Athenian owls, comprised readily mobile high-value items. But, of course, soldiers on the move would also spend some of their wages—on food, sex, clothing, and other goods. Not only did this contribute to rural monetization, as peasant farmers often sold produce to troops; it also expanded the circuits of Greek coins. At least equally significant, hired fighters, cut off from kin networks and any means of subsistence of their own, became more dependent upon money than before, and more accustomed to its usage. The claim, made with respect to Rome, that "army life taught soldiers to use money," may be a slight overstatement, but only a slight one.[85] Rome, for instance, increased coin production significantly during the first two Punic Wars (218–201 BCE), and it did so in small denominations that were more amenable to paying soldiers' wages. In all these ways, the Roman army "was a major stimulus for monetization,"[86] as was the Greek use of mercenaries during the first century of coinage.

But what was the status of these men who fought for wages? To modern eyes, they often appear as wage laborers. Yet to the ancients, particularly aristocratic commentators, to sell one's body—and this was the predominant understanding of wage labor—was to be enslaved. The modern liberal distinction between selling one's labor (or, to be precise, one's labor power), as does a wage worker, and selling one's body, like an enslaved person, seems not to be found in ancient texts.[87] Repeatedly, those who work for wages, including mercenaries, are compared to enslaved people. In Xenophon's *Memorabilia*, for instance, Socrates questions Eutherus about his life and background. As a result of war in his homeland, Eutherus replies: "We were deprived of our possessions abroad. . . . I am now compelled to procure my provisions by the work of my body here at home. And, in my opinion, this is better than to beg for something from human beings." Eutherus is thus an independent producer, living off the proceeds of his own labor. Yet, Socrates inquires, ironically to be sure, as to whether there are not advantages to being employed instead as a wage laborer. Since the body ages and wears out, says Socrates, might it not be best to hire oneself out to "one of those possessing a good deal of wealth" and become an employee? Eutherus's response affirms the Socratic position that we find in Plato: "It would be hard, Socrates . . . for me to endure slavery."[88] To work for another, to be employed for wages, is to be enslaved, one who sells their body and places it under the command of a master. Aristotle takes the same position in his *Rhetoric*, where he defines lack of freedom (slavery) as "living under the control of another" (1367a33).

This merging of the statuses of enslaved and wage laborer was widespread in ancient texts, which typically described those working for wages as *doulos*, the most frequent term for a chattel slave, or as *latris*, a term meaning "hired man" or "servant," as well as "slave."[89] This semantic ambiguity must have owed something to the fact that of those who arrived every day at the Athenian market for day laborers, the overwhelming majority were enslaved.[90] Indeed, it was not uncommon in both Greece and Rome for enslaved people to earn wages, which they shared with their masters.[91] In Athens, enslaved people were almost certainly the largest group working for wages, and in Rome some enslaved people, particularly those with a craft skill, received a regular monthly wage from their masters.[92] Thus, when mercenaries hired themselves out for money, they were engaged in an activity that most observers associated with enslaved people, and which seemed to them to resemble slavery. Even several centuries later, under the late Roman Republic, Cicero (106–51 BCE) described the wages of mercenaries as the reward of slavery. Another century on, Seneca defined an enslaved person as a perpetual mercenary.[93] Enslaved people and wage earners shared the condition of being under the control of someone else, a control registered in the surrender of their bodies (and liberties), even if temporarily, for money. These associations continued at least into the early modern period in Europe. Hugo Grotius, a Dutch jurist of the first half of the seventeenth century, for instance, declared that there were many forms of *servitus*. While slavery was "the most ignoble" of these, servile statuses included serfs and *mercenarii* (wage laborers). The latter were described by Grotius as a "perpetual Hireling," bound to a master for the length of a contract.[94] I have elsewhere explored the ways in which wage laborers experienced social death in a different register.[95] But for the moment, it is worth observing that because enslaved people comprised the largest group of wage workers in Athens, this identification of slavery with work for wages was daily reinforced. And this equation worked its way into the very lexicon associated with working for money, as Latin terms associated with wages and trade—think *mercantile* in English—are related to those for mercenaries, as we see in Grotius. As renowned linguist Émile Benveniste noted, "The images of war, of mercenary services preceded and engendered those of work and the legal remuneration attached to it."[96]

This brings us to Marx's insight that "it was in the army that the ancients first fully developed a wage system."[97] Elaborating on this insight in the *Grundrisse*, Marx indicates that he is thinking of both mercenaries and citizen-soldiers in the Greco-Roman world as wage laborers.[98] After all, in the imperial armies of Greece and Rome, citizen-soldiers received pay, as did mercenaries. Athenian democracy sought to cleanse this payment for service of all traces of servility, just as it aspired to do for payments for jury service or for attendance at the assembly. But these efforts encountered stiff resistance from aristocratic elitists, including those in the Socratic tradition. While poor citizen-soldiers were clearly distinguished from enslaved people, aristocrats also sharply differentiated them from patricians, with their noble "virtues." Military wage labor was thus a contested category, combining elements of political freedom and public service with mercenary activity (work for wages), which carried undertones of social degradation. By the early 200s CE, when Rome's imperial army peaked at about four hundred fifty thousand soldiers, military service was unquestionably the primary site of wage labor. The wage system flourished at the nexus of money and war.

"Soldiers and money;" Julius Caesar is said to have proclaimed, "if you lack one, you will soon lack the other."[99] Money bought soldiers, both mercenary and citizen; it purchased the food, weapons, horses, and ships they deployed. And soldiers, as we have noted, in turn spread money throughout rural areas, purchasing food, drink, and more. Money and military power were symbiotically related. We have noted that production of coinage increased dramatically in Athens at the end of the Persian Wars (479–431 BCE),[100] just as it did in Rome during the first two Punic Wars (218–214 BCE). Indeed, by the end of the sixth century, over one hundred mints were at work producing coins throughout the Greek world. By the second century CE, it is estimated that the annual budget of the Roman imperial state was around 225 million denarii, fully three-quarters of which went to pay the wages of the empire's four hundred thousand soldiers.[101]

Military requirements drove the spread of coinage, not only throughout the Roman Republic, Carthage, and the Hellenistic kingdoms established by Alexander the Great, but also in Persia and the Celtic states. In the case of Gaul, coinage was introduced as payment to Celtic mercenaries for service in the Macedonian armies of Philip II, Alexander III, and their successors. Not surprisingly, when they began to strike coins of their own, the Celts used Macedonian and other Greek coins as their models. Tellingly, they did so largely for purposes of financing their own armies as they centralized political power and undertook a concerted program of state building.[102] Among the best-studied cases of the symbiosis of money and state building is Ptolemaic Egypt, which developed from Alexander's conquest in 332 BCE. Following the conqueror's death in 323, Ptolemy became governor (*satrap*), and over the course of more than a century, he and his three successors ruled Egypt without interruption, using monetization to promote state building.[103] Not that ancient Egypt had been unfamiliar with coinage, but its usage had been largely confined to Mediterranean trade and some large luxury purchases. What changed with the Ptolemies was the extent of cash transactions, as monetization joined hands with militarization. Once again, much of the process began with the hiring of mercenaries.

"Soldiers and money," as Caesar said—and so it was with Alexander's wars to secure his hold on Egypt. To absorb the costs of mercenaries and Egyptian soldiers in addition to those of his Macedonian troops, Alexander relied not only on his imperial coinage minted in Macedonia, but also on coins from newly established local mints. Silver coinage was the foundation of the Ptolemaic monetary system, although prestigious gold coins were also used, particularly for military payments.[104] The Ptolemies inherited this monetary system from Alexander, and they continued to use it to wage wars, fund proxies, build armed power, and hire mercenaries. Beyond the introduction of a plethora of new taxes, the Ptolemies also fostered monetization by requiring payment in money rather than kind (e.g., grain), with the exception of levies on land and grain.[105] Production and sale of textiles, fruit, papyrus, beer, salt, and fodder crops were all taxed in money, not in kind, as were real estate sales, transport, and services.[106] Perhaps no levy contributed to monetization more than the salt tax, introduced in 263 BCE. Effectively a poll tax, the levy on salt was applied to all women and men. Its enforcement drove substantial numbers of Egyptians into episodic wage labor, so that they might earn the money (typically bronze coins) needed to pay the exaction. Indeed, "for many inhabitants of Egypt taxation was the only reason for entering the monetary cycle at all."[107]

This should remind us that as much as the development of money is closely connected to trade and markets, there is no automatic process by which these give rise to full-fledged money. Historical accounts that focus exclusively on barter and exchange ignore the decisive role of a new configuration of an institution that has been central to the history of organized violence and warfare—the state. Indeed, there is a compelling truth to historian W. V. Harris's claim that "the economic power of the state is historically the crucial element in the history of monetization."[108]

As the Egyptian case further shows, money can as much be an instrument of imperial rule as one of democratic power. Not only did this involve buttressing the material power of the state; it also entailed the symbolic legitimation of monarchical power. In fact, by 321–20 BCE images of Alexander appeared on Ptolemaic coinage in place of images of gods or symbols of nature's bounty (such as olive sprigs). The identification of kings with the power of gods and nature was indeed a "revolutionary" change, as one historian notes, and it was soon succeeded by an even more unprecedented twist—the appearance of a *living* king, Ptolemy I, on coins minted within Egypt.[109] As much as they were crucial instruments in building new kinds of militarized state-capacities, coins were also components of the representational apparatuses of imperial power.

Thus, while coinage had emerged as an alternative to the privatized circuits of noble power, it was also harnessed to new forms of wealth and power that eluded popular control. War making and colonialism in the ancient world tended to undermine democratic power in those rare places where it had established a foothold. The virtually endless expansion of war and empire involved monetary dynamics that evaded the demos. As Aristotle recognized, unlike the (finite) accretion of particular goods for the reproduction of the oikos (e.g., the stockpiling of grain, horses, or gold chalices), monetary accumulation is potentially infinite. And since the good life cannot be approached via such activity, Aristotle considered the pursuit of money as an end in itself—which he called *chrematistics*—to be unnatural and irrational (*Politics*, 1.9). Here, as we have noted, he intuited the dynamics of what Marx called the general formula for capital, $M-C-M'$. Aristotle's perception of these dynamics of monetary accumulation was possible precisely because of the extensive monetization of classical Greek society. And his analysis indicates the problem that monetary accumulation raised for Greek democracy: that its circuits posed ends (infinite accumulation) at odds with the ethos of the polis. These conceptual and practical forms of abstraction, as described by Sohn-Rethel, are antithetical to politics rooted in the face-to-face interactions of democratic assemblies.

By the era of the Roman Empire, money had become a blatant instrument of war and enslavement—something we intuit in Cicero's conflation of bonded persons with sesterces. Its origins in the democratizing polis had long been buried. After the collapse of the Roman Empire, money did indeed persist, but by no means on the same scale. Only with the emergence of European colonial expansion in the early modern period did monetization surge forward again. And once more, it rose on the tides of war.

Silk Roads and Slave Roads

Even as money, trade, and commerce receded throughout Europe with the disintegration of the Roman Empire,[110] they flourished in the Middle and Far East, from Syria to China. The major beneficiary of Rome's decline, at least in the short term, was Persia, which, in the early 600s CE, seized cities from Antioch to Jerusalem and Alexandria, and expanded trade links across the historic Silk Roads that ran to China. Then, as Persian expansion stalled, a new power assumed dynamically expansive capacities: Islam. Spreading from Medina in 622, Islam rapidly consolidated a political state, bested the empires of Persia and Byzantium, and soon established a geographic reach greater than that of the Roman Empire (doing so in about half the time).[111] Imperial rivalry invariably involves ideological contests. Fittingly, some of the propaganda battles associated with the advance of the Islamic empire have been dubbed "coin wars," for the way in which the contending parties used slogans on coins to spread their messages. I say *fittingly* because the Islamic empire oversaw a tremendous growth of trade, commerce, and monetization throughout Eurasia and North Africa. While markets in the Christian Mediterranean were contracting, the commercial routes of the Muslim world flourished. Luxury goods such as ceramics, silverware, ornamental boxes, and gold and lead ingots poured across seas and down the Silk Roads to and from China throughout the eighth century CE, as the Muslim empire established the largest maritime trading system in the world.[112] As the locus of trade shifted east, so did that of cultural and scientific achievement. Philosophy, science, medicine, and art blossomed across the Arab world, with Baghdad emerging as a renowned center of learning, alongside a number of cities of Central Asia. But as Walter Benjamin reminds us, in class society, all progress in civilization is also progress in barbarism. Accompanying the growth in the arts and sciences was a boom in slaving in Arab regions and parts of Europe. As trade revived across Eurasia, so did the ancient link between markets and enslaved people.

It was the commercial growth of the Muslim empire that fueled new slave trades. The Vikings were central actors here as they journeyed south from northern Europe to trade with the Islamic world. In the course of their voyages, the Viking Rus' seized upon a prized commodity—captive Slavs, from whom we derive the term *slave*. These were joined by enslaved Celts and Scandinavians. By the ninth century, enslaved people auctioned by the Rus' were pouring into Scandinavia, North Africa, Spain, Baghdad, and parts of Asia. At the Muslim court in Córdoba in 961, it is said that thirteen thousand enslaved Slavs could be found. Perhaps 15 percent of the European population consisted of bonded persons in 950.[113] Yet, the trade in Slavs, Celts, and Scandinavians was eclipsed by the trans-Saharan slave trade, which persisted for thirteen centuries. Millions of bonded Africans were transported across the Sahara, while millions more were captured in East Africa in a trade in human flesh whose scale may have exceeded the later Atlantic slave trade.[114] The Arab slave trade from Africa soon eclipsed that of the Roman Empire at its peak, which, as we have seen, may have involved up to four hundred thousand bonded persons every year.[115] It is highly revealing that as the slave trade surged, so did the presence of coins throughout Central Asia.[116] Once more, slaving and monetization grew in tandem. Western Europe soon felt the effects, as Muslim traders set up slaving centers in cities like Marseilles and Rome. While some commentators celebrate the commercial and cultural flourishing of the Italian city-states a short time later, they frequently forget that their renaissance, too, was based on slaving. But before investigating these crucial moments in the prehistory of capitalism, we would be well advised to examine the world's first sustained experiment with paper money.

A Failed Innovation: Paper Money on the Silk Road

In the thirteenth century CE, the Venetian merchant Marco Polo, who lived in China from 1275 to 1292, amazed readers with his descriptions of Chinese money. In his celebrated *Travels*, Polo included a chapter titled, "Of the Kind of Paper Money Issued by the Grand Khan and Made to Pass Current throughout His Dominion." He wrote:

> In this city of Kanbalu is the mint of the grand khan, who may truly be said to possess the secret of the alchemists, as he has the art of producing paper money. . . . The coinage of this paper money is authenticated with as much form and ceremony as if it were actually of pure gold or silver . . . nor dares any person, at the peril of his life, refuse to accept it in payment. All his sub-

jects receive it without hesitation. . . . With it, in short, every article may be procured.[117]

China was already an innovator in many fields. One of the world's oldest civilizations, dating to the second millennium BCE, it was the first state to produce gunpowder, paper, and print. The latter technologies also enabled it to invent paper money. Yet, for many centuries before that, the country had deployed a variety of monetary forms, from leather currency to metallic coins—the latter usually composed of bronze, often in the shape of knives or spades. While bronze coins served as means of exchange for everyday buying and selling, large payments for the likes of bond servants, horses, and manor houses tended to be made in precious commodities such as gold, silk, paper, and silver. During the period of the Five Dynasties (907–960 CE), iron coins were widespread, and in the latter part of the era, silver ingots were cast as coins. Under the Song dynasty (960–1279), China entered into a four-century experiment with paper money, long before such currency was used in Europe. Just as much coinage had been, paper money was at first privately produced, largely as notes that enabled merchants to move financial assets from one region to another without having to transport coins. But state officials soon got into the game, seeing paper notes as a way to increase the money supply at a time when military payments, particularly for the provision of troops, were stretching government expenditure. By 1189 the Jin dynasty had begun directly producing paper currency. So effective was this state-produced paper money that it was copied by the Mongol invaders who established the Yuan dynasty (1279–1368). It would not be long before the Yuan's paper money was imposed as the exclusive currency—a form of fiat money. Committed as they were to this innovation, China's Mongol leaders exported it throughout Southeast Asia, though this did not go especially well.[118]

It was the notes produced under the Mongol emperor Kublai Khan that famously drew the amazement of Polo. So taken by this currency was Polo that he suggested the Khan had come to "possess the secret of the alchemists," enabling him to conjure wealth out of mere paper. In truth, however, China's paper currency was already in the early stages of collapse. The Mongols, creators of an impressive empire, certainly tried to expand the sphere of paper money. Yet the foundations of Chinese paper currency were not amenable to a new monetary form with extensive geographic and economic reach. Largely, this had to do with the temptation on the part of the kingdom's rulers to increase the supply of paper money out of proportion to its backing in precious metals. The result, even by the early 1100s under the Song dynasty, was a persistent devaluation of paper currency. By 1223, the state's notes were circulating at $\frac{1}{150}$th of their original value, and by the last decades of Song rule (1260s and 1270s), they had become worthless, pushing the economy back to a silver standard.[119]

The Ming dynasty (1368–1644) revived the experiment with paper money, and at first, it seemed to do so successfully, as the agricultural economy rebounded and tax collection improved. But as the state kept churning out notes to cover ambitious ship- and canal-building plans and ongoing military buildup, the economy experienced a fifteenth-century version of a credit crunch. So severe was the inevitable collapse that paper notes eventually traded at 0.3 percent of their nominal value. The meltdown of China's paper currency was part of a world depression of the fifteenth century, which I discuss in the next section. Like most of Europe, China did revive in the second half of the century. But by then, the locus of dynamism was shifting west. As other powers ascended, China's influence and power stalled—as did its experiment with paper money. By the second half of the fifteenth century, it appears that China's paper notes had virtually disappeared.[120] As innovative as China's rulers had been in monetary affairs, their reliance on taxes raised on marginal peasant surpluses could not provide the wealth necessary to sustain imperial power or to underpin a new mode of world money. When a genuinely successful paper currency arrived—via the Bank of England in the 1690s—it would be on the wings of a new (and capitalist) regime of empire and war.

Before the Empire of Capital: European Money, Colonization, and Slaving from the Crusades to Columbus

There was, however, little reason to imagine at the time that Western Europe would ever emerge as the locus of economic, technological, and military dynamism. Notwithstanding the earlier successes of the Greek and Roman Empires, for a full millennium, from roughly 600 to 1600 CE, Europe was a laggard. By many criteria, both China and the Islamic world were world leaders in scientific knowledge, cultural production, technological innovation, and economic dynamism.[121] Yet, after its laggard millennium, Europe was to be the site of a new mode of capitalist empire, sustained by a hegemonic form of paper money. This is the story of the next two chapters. For the moment, let us attend to the burst of early modern European colonization and its connections to slaving.

In July 1099, the knights of the First Crusade captured Jerusalem in the name of their Lord. However, ideology and culture are always part of a social-historical ensemble involving forms of production, appropriation, and warfare; and so it was with the Christian assault on the Middle East. From Jerusalem, they quickly extended their reach to Tripoli, Tyre, and Antioch. Even before the first knights reached the holy city, fleets had set out from Venice, Genoa, and Pisa bound for Palestine and Syria. War, of course, has always been an economic enterprise, bringing booty to the conquerors, and the Crusades would be no different. For their role in the siege of Acre in 1100, Venetian adventurers received one-third of all plunder, immunity from taxes, and a church and a market square in every conquered city. After Christian knights were routed in battle at the Field of Blood in 1119, a Venetian fleet arrived in Jerusalem, providing a loan to its Christian leaders. In return they were again promised a church and a city square, alongside a street and annual payments in every royal and baronial city in the Crusaders' kingdom.[122] But the appeal to commercial self-interest was nowhere so blatant as in a widely circulated letter from the French abbot Bernard de Clairvaux. Taking up the call for a Second Crusade in 1145, Clairvaux, who would later be sainted, deployed the idiom of a modern-day investment advisor, imploring prospective Crusaders: "To those of you who are merchants, men quick to seek a bargain, let me point out advantages of this great opportunity. Do not miss them!"[123]

Before the Crusades began in the 1090s, the Italian city-states, particularly Venice, had entered into a new cycle of expansion, largely due to their participation in the medieval trade in slaves. Soon they were extending their reach into North Africa—a harbinger of things to come. By 1180, more than a third of Genoa's trade was with Africa's northern region.[124] Already, foundations were being laid for the great wave of slave-based colonization that would make the modern world. However, we ought not be deceived: the European colonization of the late medieval period took a predominantly feudal form. A failure to recognize this vitiated the historical analysis famously proffered by Henri Pirenne, who saw the Crusades as the launchpad for capitalism.[125] To be sure, late-medieval Europe was the site of a *commercialized feudalism*, one with roots in the corporate trading structures of the feudal towns as well as in the noble estates of the countryside. Yet, the lands colonized by Europeans at this time were most often brought under recognizably feudal forms of ownership and regulation, often involving seigneuries, fiefs, and knight service. This was especially true of the French and Italian colonies in the Middle East. But a number of these elements were also typical of the early Portuguese colonies in the Canary Islands, Madeira, and the Azores—all off the northwest coast of Africa.[126]

Slavery was also a common characteristic of these medieval and early modern European colonies. This was just one feature that would be continuous with the fully capitalist colonization (particularly of the Americas) that emerged powerfully after 1650. Indeed, all great historical transformations involve complex social processes that rework seeming continuities into new social ensembles. Older practices, such as slavery and colonization, get refashioned into new constellations of power and production, just as aristocratic forms were both preserved and transformed throughout the rise of capitalism in England. To the extent that relations and processes that developed within one social form of life and production can later be seen as incubators for emergent relations and dynamics, they must themselves be substantively reshaped.[127] So, as much as we can detect precursors of capitalism in the trading, slaving, and colonizing processes of European states during the late medieval period, the fundamental dynamics of global commerce remained predominantly feudal.

The framework for substantial growth in trade and markets was created across the Mongol "global century," 1250–1350, in which the Mongol Empire stitched together a trading system that oversaw one hundred years of commercial growth and increasing monetization. Large chunks of Europe prospered throughout the Mongol century, the Italian city-states among them, while southern India and China, too, experienced a century-long economic upswing.[128] Lubricating the commercial expansion was silver, which played the role of world money across Eurasia as it flowed from Western Europe, the Near East, Africa, and parts of Asia in exchange for goods from the Far East, such as spices, ceramics, raw silk, and silk textiles.[129] Gold, meanwhile, had become the primary currency of Europe by the fourteenth century, a position that would be further consolidated as Portugal increased its African supplies of the precious metal.[130] But even gold migrated east, albeit not as dramatically as did silver. Government officials from Cairo to London complained about this persistent drain of bullion to the East. Yet, complain as they might, the Euro-Asian economy was structurally imbalanced. Europe's ever-growing demand for Eastern goods required a systematic outflow of precious metals. And here lay a critical vulnerability:

should Europe prove incapable of generating new supplies of silver and gold, the money that lubricated this gigantic trading system would dry up, causing the gears of trade to seize. Precisely this happened in the general economic crisis of the fifteenth century.

The idea of a world economic slump prior to capitalism may come as a surprise, yet there is little doubt that during the first half of the century, "almost all parts of the then-known world experienced a deep recession . . . the absolute level of inter-societal trade dropped, currencies were universally debased, and the arts and crafts were degraded," in the words of Janet Abu-Lughod.[131] Crucial here was a massive contraction of the money supply—in this sense the crisis involved a classic *liquidity crunch*.[132] Mining and silver supplies plummeted across Asia and Europe, severely reducing the latter's capacity to buy goods from the East. The inevitable result was a massive contraction in production and exchange. In China, this was accompanied by a popular turn against paper money, due to a growing mistrust of any currency that lacked adequate underpinning by precious metal. After all, metallic coinage remained the modal form of money. In a Eurasian economy based on bullion, paper currency was ultimately credible only if it was readily convertible into precious metal (in raw or coined form) at stable rates of exchange. As the crisis wore on, this was anything but the case. The initial reaction by the leaders of China's Ming dynasty was to offset their crisis through military and commercial expansionism. The Ming rulers sent invading armies into Southeast Asia, grabbed land in Manchuria, drove military forces deep into Mongol territory, and sent naval expeditions as far as the Red Sea and East Africa.[133] In the end, however, the associated military costs were unsustainable in the context of declining production, trade, and taxes. Shortages of silver and gold guaranteed that the crisis would be accompanied by a collapse of paper money. A period of austerity and retrenchment followed, and while the Chinese economy did eventually revive, things would never be the same. The center of the postcrisis global economy was demonstrably shifting west.

By 1450, a new international constellation was forming around three vital elements. The first we might call the *Columbian moment*: the new burst of Atlantic colonization that began with Portugal's seizure of islands off the northwest coast of Africa, and then extended to the Americas and further parts of both Asia and Africa. The second was the extensive looting of precious metals. Gold was critical in the early going, and modest West African supplies were soon swelled by violent expropriation of treasures from Mexico. Soon, however, New World silver moved to the forefront. At Potosí, in what is now Bolivia, the Spanish extracted mind-boggling stocks of silver. By 1600, this mining town had one hundred fifty thousand inhabitants, and for over a century it churned out half of the world's silver supply. So gigantic were the shipments of gold and silver from the Americas that their value rocketed from just over one million pesos in the early years of the sixteenth century (1503–10) to almost seventy million in its final decade (1591–1600). By that time, the Spanish "piece of eight," a silver coin worth eight *reals*, had become a world currency.[134] The third element of the emerging global configuration was a new wave of enslavement of Africans, which included putting black labor to the cultivation of sugar. European colonizers first undertook sugar production, often by means of slave labor, in Syria and Palestine during the era of the Crusades. Sugar plantations also developed in Sicily and Muslim Spain in the late medieval period. But by the fifteenth century, Portugal and Spain were opening new social frontiers with slave-based sugar cultivation in Madeira and the Canary Islands. In the coming decades, Portugal would extend its sugar-slave complex to Brazil, and Spain to Española (Haiti).[135]

Before long, however, Spain and Portugal would encounter a new imperial rival in Holland. But Dutch hegemony, in turn, soon confronted another challenger. From 1655, the year England seized Jamaica from Spain, its military and colonial undertakings began to surpass those of its Dutch rivals. English dominance would be world transformative, as it reconfigured the three elements described—money, colonization, and slaving—on the foundations of an emerging capitalist mode of production. An epochal shift was in the making, one that would usher in a global empire based on new dynamics of exploitation and a novel form of money. In the fifteenth century, the westward shift of global power might have been masked by continuing and massive flows of New World gold and silver to India, China, and Central Asia. But by the middle of the seventeenth century there could be no doubt: the world order was undergoing profound transformation. Looking back, it is easy to see why. In the words of one historian, "It was Europe's entrenched relationship with violence and militarism that allowed it to place itself at the centre of the world after the great expeditions of the 1490s."[136] Indeed it was. But violence and militarism, as I have intimated, were being reorganized on an unprecedented socioeconomic terrain, one involving new modalities of money and exploitation. With these, a new order of empire was about to be unleashed upon the world.

CHAPTER 3

From the Bones of Princes to the Blood of the Commonwealth

War Finance and the Origins of Capitalism

> *"Great and grave authors pretend that money is the nerve system of war and the republic . . . but it seems to me that it would more properly be named the second blood."*
>
> —Bernardo Davanzati, 1588[1]

The passage above from Davanzati, an Italian translator and economist, is doubly provocative. First, it explicitly links money, war, and the republic. Second, it offers the fecund metaphor of money as the *second blood* of the republic. To be sure, the analogy between the circulation of blood in the human body and the flow of money in the commonwealth was far from new in Europe at the time. We encounter it as early as the fourteenth century in Nicholas Oresme's *De Moneta* (circa 1355), and, as we saw in the example of the eighteenth-century French physiocrats, it remained commonplace over the subsequent four hundred years.[2] But the image of money as a *second* blood is particularly intriguing, for its adaption of the European medieval concept of "the king's two bodies" (to which we shall return) to the phenomenon of money. At work here is a conceptual equivalence between the immortal role of the monarch in politics and the universalizing function of money in the economy. This equivalence is all the more striking because it traces a dialectical tension between monarch and money in the emergence of modern forms of power. A capitalist society cannot accommodate any such equivalence. Personal rule must give way to the impersonal rule of capital; monarchy must yield to the power of money. This chapter delineates the process by which money became the second blood of the commonwealth—and how this was accomplished across oceans of *first* blood.

Before tracing theses circuits of blood, money, and empire, it is worth observing that the metaphor of money as blood was, in fact, to decline in concert with the rise of modern money, colonialism, and the Atlantic slave trade. The more real blood flowed, the more corpses filled the Middle Passage and the killing fields of Africa, Europe, and the Americas, the more did representations of money evade association with blood. Increasingly, money came to be modeled in terms of another, ostensibly clean and neutral, imagery: that of water. Yet, there was blood in this water. The oceans and seas had been turned into veritable killing fields, the domains of war, global commerce, and the trade in enslaved Africans. In these transoceanic circuits of blood and money, we witness the gruesome dawn of capitalist forms of power. This chapter takes the story from the Middle Ages to 1650.

From the King's Second Body to the Second Blood of Money

Let us begin with the idea of money as a second blood, which has its roots in the medieval European concept of the king's two bodies. As historian Ernst Kantorowicz famously argued, centralizing monarchies in medieval Europe fostered the peculiar idea that the king had two bodies: one, physical, temporal, and mortal; the other perpetual and immortal. As much as the mortal king exercised sovereign power, he was in fact the agent of a transcendent and mystical body (a *corpus mysticum*), in which resided eternal powers that passed from monarch to monarch across the ages, outliving every one of them. Notwithstanding the mortality of the king's first body, the second one—the site of sovereign authority—did not perish. Kingship thus endured, attaching itself to particular mortal bodies but never fully merging with them. "He as King never dies," wrote one Tudor jurist, "although his natural body does."[3]

As increasingly sophisticated state machineries developed throughout the medieval age, this notion took on new permutations, especially in light of the enhanced economic capacities of monarchies. After all, wealth was essential to pay for troops and weapons, navies and emissaries, courts and administrative offices, customs officers and tax collectors. Increasingly, the idea developed that those capacities known as the *fiscus*—meaning "basket" or "moneybag" in Latin—were contained in the king's second body. In Roman law, *fiscus* had referred to the emperor's treasury, but in medieval Europe it came to connote all those resources and powers that sustained the treasury—lands and taxes in particular. In developing this concept, European scholars and state officials drew transparently on the Christian idea of the mystical body of Christ, which was said to persist despite the mortality of popes, cardinals, bishops, and priests. Come and go as the latter might, the church persevered as a mystical body, transcending the frail, finite bodies of human individuals. In effect, this idea of the immortal mystical body was secularized by jurists and administrators, among them Baldus de Ubaldis (1327–1400), who wrote that "the fisc is a thing eternal and perpetual . . . the fisc never dies."[4] Note the first steps here toward the *depersonalization* of property and power. The fisc is not the property of an individual; the monarch is not free to sell Crown land or give it away, any more than they can renounce the legal authority of the Crown to impose taxes. Instead, the fisc inheres in the second body of the king, that corpus mysticum later described as the *body politic*. Based on its enduring and impersonal properties, the fisc was frequently imagined as a *corpus fictum*, a metaphysical body attached to a fictitious person,[5] much the way a modern corporation is understood in law today.

What did this conception imply about money? An English judicial ruling made in 1605 serves as an illuminating example. Elizabeth I had recently reduced the amount of silver in the coins her government circulated in Ireland. When an Irish merchant used these new coins to pay an English creditor, the latter rejected them, complaining that they contained less metal than did the coins in use at the time they had entered into their contract. But English justices ruled that the new coins were indeed legal tender and had to be accepted—a judgement that has rightly been described as a victory of *nominalism* over *metallism*.[6] According to the ruling, the value of a coin was not determined by the metal it contained, but by the worth decreed by the monarch: by the de-*nomination* the prince assigned to it. Not only did the Crown possess an exclusive right to produce coins; it also had the power to declare their market value. Of course, kings might proclaim one value and market actors might judge differently. But in law, monarchs governed money. "It appertaineth only to the king of England to make or coin money within his dominion," proclaimed the privy councilors, who then uttered the memorable statement that this power inheres "in the bones of princes."[7] Yet, in which princes' bones—that is to say, in which of their bodies—did power over money reside? The Privy Council, jealous of the personal prerogative of the king, tended to locate it in the monarch as a living person. Yet for parliamentarians and anti-absolutists, this was a dangerous conflation. For them, authority over money could not be a personal plaything of the monarch; this power pertained to a body that transcended the mere personhood of the king.

It is in this regard that Davanzati's dictum is most fascinating. For in referring to money as a "second blood," the Italian economist implicitly tied it to the king's *second* body, the one of which the mortal individual was a mere custodian. Seen in these terms, money is the blood that circulates throughout the realm. It is public blood, the blood of the commonwealth. It nourishes an economic domain that encompasses, but also exceeds, that of the fisc, the properties of the Crown and its right to appropriate (as taxes, duties, and rents) a share of wealth produced by others. Money is thus seen as animating a sphere of economic circulation that embraces *all* commercial transactions among individuals, including but not limited to those involving the fiscal powers and properties of the Crown. It follows that the right to mint coins is a power exercised for public purposes. In minting, the king is exerting powers that reside in his second body, the body of the whole realm, of which he is the head. This is why he might appropriately be said to be secreting a second blood—not the blood that circulates throughout his first (mortal) body, but rather, that which enlivens the *corpus economicus*.

Yet the Privy Council of 1605 did not go there. Instead, its ruling tended to conflate the king's two bodies. In declaring that "money inheres in the bones of princes," it seemed to set no limits to what the monarch might do in this field. However, ominously, this confused the individual feudal powers of the monarch (to rents from his own lands, for instance) with his public fiscal authority to tax, tithe, adjudicate in law, and coin money. Indeed, the political opposition in England from the thirteenth century onward sought to differentiate the fiscal properties and powers of the Crown from the person of the monarch. The conflation of the two was said to lead to tyranny—to personal rule unaccountable to laws, liberties, and established practices. Yet, to insist sharply on the differentiation between public and private had the effect of suggesting limits to the personal powers of the king. The civic sphere tended thereby to become partially autonomous—not merely a kingly body, but a public one, a public thing (*res publica*) that coexisted with the body of the monarch but was not identical to it. So, while dedicated parliamentarians certainly saw the king as *part* of the body politic, they also asserted that the latter contained other components irreducible to the monarch—notably council and Parliament—thus making it a composite body.[8] Here, too, the economic dimension of the body politic loomed large, as is suggested by that crucial term in English political discourse, the *commonwealth*. For, the latter referred both to the realm as a whole and to the economic well-being of the people; it encompassed their common wealth, which was not identical with the wealth of the government.

As we approach the emergence of modern money, therefore, we encounter its extraction from the bones of princes and its transplantation into the blood of the commonwealth. In England, this was accomplished only through the course of intense political conflicts that encompassed the revolutionary upheavals of 1640 to 1689. Central to these struggles was authority over the fisc, particularly the king's powers of taxation. Shortly, we shall look at the many intricate issues—including property, piracy, colonialism, and slaving—that underlay many of these conflicts. But first, it will be illuminating to examine these transpositions through the prism of Thomas Hobbes's discussion of money in his *Leviathan* (1651).

Hobbes is one of the most fascinating figures in the history of English political thought. Imbued with the spirit of scientific materialism typically associated with the Enlightenment, he nevertheless favored a form of absolute monarchy inimical to ideas of rule by the people, or the right of resistance to arbitrary authority. His political theory begins from the premise that individuals are naturally equal and hold identical rights in the "state of nature," yet he deployed this egalitarian principle to distinctly inegalitarian ends, arguing that individuals should forfeit their rights and confer absolute power on a sovereign.[9] Like liberal thinkers generally, Hobbes treated market relations and behaviors as natural and rational, but he advocated decidedly illiberal political arrangements. His embrace of market principles is evident when he tells us, for instance, that commutative justice is really "the Justice of a Contractor; that is, a Performance of Covenant, in Buying and Selling; Hiring and Letting to Hire; Lending, and Borrowing; Exchanging, Bartering, and other acts of Contract."[10] Assuming that market relations are natural, Hobbesian economics do not hearken back to medieval and early modern ideas of just price—where exchange value is to be governed by moral considerations, rather than by market competition. However much his absolutism was at odds with liberal politics, Hobbes was moving with the tide of "bourgeois" economic thought.[11]

We can see this by turning to chapter 24 of *Leviathan*, which bears the intriguing title "Of the Nutrition and Procreation of a Commonwealth." Here Hobbes considers the economic reproduction of society by means of commodity production and exchange. Once again, he combines daring insights about new patterns of social relations with conservative impulses regarding authority and sovereign power. He recognizes, for instance, the emerging commodification of human labor power that is characteristic of capitalist social relations, instructing his readers that "a man's Labour also, is a commodity exchangeable for benefit, as well any other thing." At the same time, he recoils from any notion of absolute private property, insisting that all property ultimately belongs "to the Soveraign Power."[12] His adherence to market economy then directs him to the problem of money and the interchangeability of commodities. He insightfully informs us that market exchange raises the problem of "Concoction," that is, the challenge of "reducing all commodities . . . to some thing of equall value." This challenge is met, he insists, by gold, silver, and money (by which he means coinage). Precious metals solve the problem of concoction—or what we would call *commensuration*—in trade between nations. Inside the sovereign territory of the nation-state, however, coined money operates as effectively as raw bullion (gold and silver) when it comes to measuring the value of all goods and services, since it "passeth from Man to Man, within the Common-wealth." In this way, coined money nourishes all the organs of the "Artificiall Man" we call the body politic, in a manner similar to the circulation of "natural Bloud" in the organic "Body of Man." However, because the circuits of coined money are confined to the *national* space of the commonwealth, gold and silver bullion are necessary when nation-states undertake to "stretch out their armes . . . into forraign Countries; and supply . . . whole Armies with Provision."[13] In short, the second blood constituted by coined money flows only as far as the king's second body extends territorially. Beyond that—on the international stage of war and global commerce—world money rules in the form of silver and gold bullion.

"Money, Money and Still More Money": Feudalism, War, and the Rise of Capitalism

From about 1500, waging war on a dramatically larger scale became the central preoccupation of all European governments. This had to do with ruling-class responses to the general crisis of the feudal mode of production during the fourteenth century. Let us briefly sketch the dynamics involved.

Following the disintegration of the Roman Empire (formally in 476 CE) under the combined weight of overexpansion, social and regional revolts, and "barbarian" invasions, decentralized military lordship was to gradually emerge as the pivot of social organization. This occurred only through a protracted period of fragmented armed conflict, and the failure of the Carolingian Empire (800–888) to reconstitute imperial power in Central and Western Europe. Those who prospered in this period of instability and breakdown were those who excelled in war, raiding, and plunder. Eventually, "the plunderers settled down as landlords" and went on to form the core of feudal ruling classes.[14] The feudal aristocracy was not just an arms-bearing class, pledging military support to a monarch; it was a class *constituted* through war and a specific sort of war economy. In the early feudal period across Western and Central Europe, "the pursuit and intensification of warfare revitalized an economy based on forcible capture and pillage," in the words of French historian Georges Duby.[15] Warfare was the key to seizing tracts of land and concentrating weapons, knights, and resources. Occupation of land also involved the conquest of peasant communities, which were then subjected to systematic pillage in the form of regularized rents, services, and obligations (such as marriage fines), rather than the episodic plunder of a marauding warrior class.

After 700 CE, the classic socioeconomic relationship between lord and bondsman crystallized, where surplus product, and/or surplus labor, was appropriated by members of a decentralized lordly class. Yet these relations could not solidify until the Carolingian Empire (formally consecrated by Pope Leo III in 800 when he crowned Charlemagne in Rome) disintegrated in 888. Around the year 1000, in the absence of a powerful imperial monarchy, we observe "the birth of a new social system . . . with the classic structure of two elements: seigneurial demesne and peasant tenures."[16] The center of the feudal arrangement was the lord's manor, which was both a unit of landed economy and of political domination. As a social-geographic entity, the manor comprised four types of land. First was the lord's demesne, the produce of which was appropriated directly by the lord, and which was worked by his serfs (who owed specific amounts of labor and other services), as well as by enslaved people and hired wage laborers. Next came the customary land worked by unfree peasants, who effectively belonged to the lord. These bonded tenants owed labor services on the lord's demesne (which might be commuted to cash rents), were required to pay a variety of fines (such as entry fines in taking up a tenancy; chevage, for the right to live outside the manor; and merchet, for permission to marry), and were bound to the rulings of their lord's manor court in any issue concerning their tenancies. The third form of landed property consisted of free holdings, whose occupants were required to pay rents (usually lower than those of servile tenants) and sometimes to provide services. But they were free of many other obligations, and had the right of access to the king's courts. Finally, there were extensive common lands, which were the property of the community and were available to all its members for grazing animals; gathering wood, straw, and berries; and for hunting and fishing. For smallholders, in particular, common rights could be the key to the continued survival and reproduction of the peasant household.

In England of the late thirteenth century, perhaps three-fifths of the population consisted of unfree persons.[17] These unfree peasants found themselves in a class relation with lords (seigneurs) who were fragmented across multiple territorial units, each based on a manor house, castle, or monastery, and each operating its own courts and armed forces. Lordly domination thus involved a relatively decentralized network of power—to be sure, a defining feature of European feudalism. For this reason, among others, it is unhelpful to simply characterize precapitalist Europe as belonging to something called "peasant society."[18] We forfeit an enormous amount of historical specificity if we treat ancient China, medieval Europe, the great civilizations of Mesoamerica, and much of the ancient Greco-Roman world—indeed most precapitalist societies with settled agriculture—as simply variants of a nearly universal social form called "peasant society." Crucially, such an approach loses sight of the specificity of the feudal form of domination, since, in Hilton's formulation, "it is the lordship which is specific to feudalism."[19] The territorial basis of lordship, as we have seen, was the lord's manor: a political and military unit, as well as an economic one. It was this fusion of economic, political, and military powers into decentralized units, organized around landed production by peasants, that constituted the specificity of feudal lordship. Indeed, even when serfdom disintegrated in much of Europe in the centuries after the Black Death, lordship did not. The lords' economic powers and manor courts continued to operate after peasants had slipped servile bonds.[20]

This is why the *parcellized sovereignty* of classic feudalism is integral to its social form, in which local lords and bishops exercised extensive legal and military powers, while pledging military support (initially in the form of the feudal levy—the direct provision of knights, soldiers, horses, and weapons—which was incrementally displaced as time went on by financial contributions) to defend the territory and common interests of the association of noble families that comprised the feudal state.[21] So confined was this ruling class that from 1160 to 1220, there were just over 150 great lords (or magnates) in England.[22] To be sure, monarchies overarched this system of manorial power. But these were rooted, often precariously, in an alliance among aristocratic households that centralized limited political and military responsibilities for defense of the realm and adjudication of intra-aristocratic disputes. There was nothing of the centralized state power of ancient Persia, China, or Rome to be found in feudal Europe. Indeed, feudal monarchs often disposed of such limited economic and military resources that they barely exceeded those of the wealthiest landed magnates.

There is a real sense, therefore, in which the feudal state in its classic form was a sort of mutual protection racket among militarized "big men," who retained small armies of their own while simultaneously exploiting peasant households. To be sure, this was codified ideologically as a system of deference, homage, and obligation to those above one in the social order—of peasants to lords, and of lords to kings. Everyone below the monarch was thus a *vassal* of those above.[23] But in practice, the powers of monarchical states were significantly limited, at least by both ancient and modern standards. In their immediate domains, individual lords had their own manor courts (and sometimes their own gallows), and they made local law with next to no oversight. They appropriated directly from their peasants with little regulation from above, and they marauded and pillaged with a considerable degree of autonomy. Beyond this, monarchical power was hemmed in by the international power of the Catholic Church—not only the dominant ideological institution of the era, but also an enormous property owner with its own courts and diplomatic offices, and the principal arbiter in European interstate relations. The extent of church power can be gleaned from the fact that in 1086 it appropriated one-quarter of all the landed revenues of England, a share that appears to have been typical across most of Europe.[24]

The capacities of the feudal state were shockingly limited. In 1171–72, for instance, the total revenues of Henry II of England seem to have amounted to just over twenty-one thousand pounds, not much more than the household revenues of a large lord or church official. It perhaps comes as small surprise to learn that the two key "departments" of government "were the chamber in which the king slept and the wardrobe where he hung his clothes."[25] The state, in short, was not much more than a large noble household, able to call upon aristocratic support in times of war.

Feudalism would thus seem to have been a highly unpropitious social ground for the emergence of modern states. Yet, because of its internal contradictions as a mode of production, once it entered a period of sustained crisis, militarized state building became the dominant political dynamic—albeit one whose inherent features pressed toward the transcendence of feudalism itself.

There is no doubt that the European feudal mode of production possessed an internal vitality. For about 250 years, from roughly 1000 to 1240 CE, the amount of land under cultivation, the social surplus product (rents and tithes), and the population grew persistently, the latter roughly doubling in England between 1100 and 1300. Especially around 1150 or so, the process of reclaiming uncultivated land for farming proceeded rapidly. New villages sprung up as the agricultural frontier was extended, and new revenues flowed to the lords. In England, perhaps a million acres of woodland, heath, moor, and fens were brought into productive use.[26] The feudal system also showed a *weak* tendency toward technological innovation, manifest in its use of animal traction and water power, in particular. As a result, while agricultural productivity grew, it appears generally to have lagged behind population increase, lacking anything comparable to the capitalist tendency toward systematic technological revolutions of the means of production.[27] As output and surpluses expanded, the feudal economy also fostered growth of market exchange, monetary transactions, and urban development.[28] Yet, by the mid to late thirteenth century (perhaps around 1230–40 in France, for instance, and maybe 1280 in England), this growth wave had exhausted itself.[29] The centers of growth shifted to those towns whose merchants could profit through the growth of the Eurasian economy that emerged during the Mongol century (1250–1350). But agrarian growth had reached an impasse.

Because the *primary* dynamic of feudal economic growth was an extensive one—by means of increasing the amount (or extent) of land under cultivation—it produced diminishing returns, as ever more marginal land was farmed. Less fertile land requires greater inputs of labor per unit of output; put simply, more effort is necessary to get the same product from inferior soil. As a result, after roughly two and a half centuries of growth, agricultural productivity declined, each unit of newly reclaimed land supported fewer mouths, and new feudal surpluses shrank. Declining growth also reduced demand for urban and rural manufactures and dampened any tendency toward technological innovation. Technical improvement in cloth production, for instance, faltered after about 1300.[30]

Crucial here is that the feudal mode as a whole did not encourage sustained and continuous investment in the productivity of labor on the land. The latter is known as *intensive* growth, and in an agrarian setting it is stimulated by investment per hectare in use of manure, improved tools, scientific crop rotation, and so on. The priority of *political accumulation* for lords (to which we return shortly) meant that military investment in men and arms often trumped investment on the land. At the same time, the poverty of the peasantry set real limits to their capacities for reinvestment of wealth. While there may have been a slow rise in agricultural productivity in Europe between about 850 and 1150 (something by no means agreed upon among historians), this began from a decidedly low base, and its rise was arrested at an extremely low peak.[31] Furthermore, there was no systematic imperative for urban merchants to invest in manufacturing industries, either to increase their scale or to improve their technologies.[32] Inevitably, then, feudal expansion came to a halt, diets deteriorated, malnutrition mounted, and populations became highly susceptible to disease, resulting in demographic crises like the Black Death (1346–53), which wiped out tens of millions, and whose effects lasted for generations. Not only did life expectancy fall, but more than a century after the Black Death (that is, by about 1470), most European villages were only half as populous as they had been in 1300. Across this era of contraction, between 20 and 30 percent of all human settlements disappeared in Germany, while in England we find at least two thousand abandoned rural settlements.[33] Regression on this scale crushed manorial revenues, which plummeted in the century after the Black Death by as much as 70 percent.[34] The feudal mode of production had entered into a downward spiral of plummeting output, falling surpluses, and population decline, comprising what has been called "the great medieval depression."[35]

But while the feudal mode of production experienced a systemic crisis across two centuries or more (roughly 1240 to 1450), individual feudal lords had strategies for mitigating the private effects of collapse, as did allied aristocratic groups, sometimes on regional and national levels, if they could organize cohesively. These strategies centered on what Robert Brenner has described as *political accumulation*.

Given the feudal mode's internal constraints on sustained expansion, Brenner points out, there was an inbuilt tendency for lords to construct "larger, more effective military organization" in order to clamp down on peasant resistance to heightened exploitation, *and* to forcibly encroach on the resources of other lords. All-out attacks on village communities had severely limited prospects, however, given the capacities for peasants, particularly in times of falling population, to flee to the estates of other lords, or to rise in rebellion—which could occur in insurrectionary fashion, as in the French Jacquerie of 1358, or the English Peasants' Revolt of 1381. Given these constraints on efforts to squeeze peasants, lords frequently turned on other lords, the result of which "was a generalized tendency to intra-lordly competition and conflict," something that made it necessary to accumulate ever more military resources, beginning with land and retainers.[36] Consequently, as Duby noted, once Europe had entered a period of feudal crisis, "war became a semi-permanent state of affairs."[37] Ironically, this was to give European states considerable advantages after 1450.

Intra-lordly military conflicts might take the form of civil wars within the territories of a kingdom, or of wars between kingdoms, such as the Hundred Years' War (1337–1453) that pitted England against France. The ultimate objective of such confrontations was the conquest of foreign lands—including the peasants that went with them (and the surplus product they could produce)—to be incorporated as new territories into the marauding states, and whose proceeds were to be shared like war booty. This, of course, was Hobbes's case of stretching the state's "armes into forraign Countries." But conflicts on this scale required that nationally based nobilities should band together and endow monarchs with sufficient military and financial resources to wage longer wars in larger spaces. Rather than episodic, war had become effectively permanent, requiring that monarchs mobilize larger armies, technologically improved weapons, greater financial resources, and the augmented political and administrative powers these involved. Political accumulation in a context of feudal decline and war, as Brenner notes, thus required more powerful, centralized states: "Warfare was the great engine of feudal centralization."[38]

But war could not be waged without money. Larger armies, new weaponry (such as cannons), new arts of fortification, and unending conflict all greatly raised military costs.[39] When Louis XII of France (who reigned from 1498 to 1515) inquired of the Venetian ambassador how best to defend his kingdom and advance the exploits of his army, the latter replied, "Most generous King, three things are essential: money, money and still more money."[40]

Three things, indeed. During his reign (1413–22), Henry V of England had spent more than two-thirds of the royal budget, plus most of the revenue from his lands in France, on his army and navy, and in financing war-related debts. Nearly two centuries later, during the last five years of her reign (1598–1603), Elizabeth I directed three-quarters of her budget to war-related expenses. In this regard, there was nothing exceptional about England. During a similar five-year period (1572–76), the Hapsburg dynasty devoted more than 75 percent of its revenues to defense and war-induced debts, as did the French monarchy.[41] Yet the capacities of European monarchies to cover escalating military costs were strikingly restricted. In England, for instance, the revenues available to Henry VI in the 1440s were equivalent (in constant terms) to what Henry II deployed nearly three centuries earlier. Even when we come to the horizon of the English Civil War (1642–51), we discover that the tax revenues of the Crown were essentially unchanged over the preceding three hundred years.[42] Incapable of significantly expanding financial capacities and resources, states across Europe confronted incessant fiscal catastrophes driven by mounting war costs.[43] The result was an unending series of crisis measures—emergency borrowing, forced loans, debasements of the coinage, debt repudiations—that undermined the longer-term financial viability of the monarchies involved. Indeed, for two hundred years after 1485, most European states repeatedly struggled to finance permanent debts brought on by the costs of war. Even the Spanish Crown, recipient of 40 percent of all the New World silver plundered between 1503 and 1660, came away from its military campaigns deeply indebted.[44] In this context, any state that could establish a stable system of war finance was thus sure to accrue an enormous advantage.

This breakthrough was to be made by the English state after 1689. It was incarnated in the Bank of England, formed in 1694. But the road to this break-through was neither smooth, nor inevitable. It would require a prolonged period of upheaval (1640–89) to usher in deep social transformations through which new forms of *impersonal power* displaced older forms intimately linked to person-alized rule.[45] In the process, new modalities of money emerged in direct associa-tion with war, colonialism, and slavery.

§

According to Marx and Engels, the construction of a new kind of state machin-ery—one bound to the dynamics of capital—entails a twofold reorganization of political power. Modern civil society, they wrote, "must assert itself in its external relations as nationality and internally must organise itself as state."[46] In its relations with other states, in other words, capitalist power must con-dense itself as a national entity, capable of mobilizing the force of the nation as a whole under its sovereign command. To do this, however, it must also be able to "organise itself as state," and this requires that it subordinate all competing political powers under the sovereign rule of a centralized apparatus of govern-ment and administration.

As historians recognize, the transformations of the English state under the Tudor monarchs (1485–1603) involved crucial moves in just this direction—toward political centralization and the subordination of contending sources of power. The most dramatic events involved its "external relations as nationality." The effect of the Protestant Reformation (accelerated by Henry VIII's demand for papal support for his divorce) was to eliminate political interferences by the foreign power of the Church of Rome, and of bishops and prelates loyal to it. As early as 1516, prior to the formal break with Rome (1532–34), Henry VIII had asserted, "Kings of England have never had any superior but God alone."[47] This declaration of government's supreme authority on earth constituted the prelude to a revolution from above, establishing the indivisibility of the sovereign power of the nation-state. Henceforth, an English subject was to have a singular loy-alty: to the English state. The intellectual underpinnings of this revolution in political consciousness are expressed in the preamble to the 1533 Act of Appeals, written by Thomas Cromwell, then the most powerful counselor to Henry VIII:

"This realm of England is an Empire, and so hath been accepted in the world, governed by one Supreme Head and King having the dignity and royal estate of the imperial crown of the same, unto whom a body politic . . . be bounden and owe and bear next to God a natural and humble obedience."[48]

Here we discern an assertion of unitary power ("one Supreme Head") and the novel claim that England alone comprised an empire. Rather than refer to English rule over others, like the Scots or the Irish, this declaration stakes a claim for the total ("imperial") rule of the English state over the *English* people. No longer was sovereign power to be shared with an external authority, like the Church of Rome, with its vast monastic properties and its own courts and diplomatic offices; no longer were English priests and prelates to have loyalties divided between church and state. But more than this, the king was also to no longer have *internal* rivals among the great lords. To this end, Tudor monarchs systematically curtailed the military and political powers of the nobility. The power of violence and war was henceforth the domain of the Crown and its state apparatuses. "The greatest triumph of the Tudors," writes social historian Lawrence Stone, "was the ultimately successful assertion of a royal monopoly of violence both public and private."[49] State power was now unitary and indivisible. "The essential ingredient of the Tudor revolution," according to another historian, "was the concept of national sovereignty."[50]

In Marx's terms, the English monarchy had now embarked on the process of organizing "itself as state" internally, while asserting itself "in its external relations as nationality." However, at this stage—that of the "Tudor revolution"—imperial claims remained largely internal. As much as the Tudors dramatically established their political autonomy as the sovereign representatives of the nation-state, their full-fledged imperial powers—their ability to "stretch out their armes . . . into forraign Countries"—remained highly constrained. As celebrated historian Christopher Hill suggested, only with the Dutch War of 1652–54 do we encounter "the first state-backed imperialist adventure in English history," which was quickly followed by many more.[51] However, during the century and a quarter between the English Reformation and the First Dutch War, powerful new relations between property, the market, and the state laid the basis for a unique sort of capitalist colonialism—and with it, for new forms of bourgeois money and finance.

Age of Plunder: Enclosure, Dispossession, and Agrarian Capitalism

Early English colonialism had three distinctive features, the combination of which contributed to the consolidation of capitalist social relations in England. The first was the relative weakness of the Crown in military and colonial affairs in the early period, which brought private interests directly into war finance. The Crown's weakness was displayed especially clearly throughout the decisive conflict with Spain, which broke out in 1585 and continued for eighteen years. Disposing of annual revenues of roughly three hundred thousand pounds, Elizabeth I was in no position to lead a military confrontation with the dominant imperial power of the time. Unsurprisingly, the queen for years resisted those urging an aggressive posture toward Spain.[52] As much as a relatively weak state would later be a deficiency to imperial ambition, at this stage it fostered the emergence of new forms of bourgeois power—and this would provide a source of strength by bringing bourgeois fortunes directly into the financial affairs of the state.

This is why, secondly, the Spanish War of 1585–1604 was commanded by private capitalists—merchants, landed gentry, prosperous sea captains. This has led to the apt description of early English colonialism as a system of *privateering*. Two examples from the war with Spain illustrate the point. Francis Drake's 1585 expedition to the West Indies is the stuff of English lore, yet the queen supplied only two of his twenty-five ships. The rest were provided by private investors looking to profit from the looting of Spanish vessels. Two years later, of the twenty-three ships in the English military expedition to Cádiz, eleven were launched by a consortium of London merchants, and four by traders from Plymouth, while two belonged to the lord admiral, and six to the queen.[53] War was thus *directly* bound up with private investment and profit making. Investors in military expeditions expected to claim "prizes"—particularly commodities such as wine, olives, raisins, figs, oils, and nuts—plundered from Spanish and Portuguese vessels.[54]

The third distinctive characteristic of early English colonialism was the central role of the landed gentry in privateering, trade, and colonization. It has been estimated that about half of the peers of England invested in foreign trade between 1575 and 1630, a practice unparalleled in continental Europe. Landowners were also major investors in joint-stock companies devoted to trading and establishing plantation colonies. Indeed, members of the landed gentry showed a distinctly capitalist commitment to long-term investments that might not yield a profit in the short run.[55] With the establishment of plantation colonies in Ireland in the second half of the sixteenth century, gentry investors once again played a critical role.[56] Not only were trade and plunder "inseparable in the sixteenth century";[57] both also involved collaboration between merchants and landed gentlemen. Yet, if England's landed gentry was unique in its commitment to trade, plunder, and colonization, the question remains: "Why was it, in this country and at this time, that the gentry broke with the most persistent tradition of their class throughout western Europe?"[58] To answer this question requires examining the transformation of large English landowners (aristocracy and gentry) into a class of agrarian capitalists—in other words, that we investigate the history of early modern plunder at home, which laid the basis for colonial plunder abroad.

$

The crisis of the feudal mode of production in Europe—or the "great medieval depression"—of the thirteenth and fourteenth centuries produced a series of divergent societal trajectories. In much of the eastern part of the continent, the bonds of serfdom were reimposed on a considerable scale, quite intensely in Bohemia and Prussia.[59] In other areas, notably France, absolute monarchies powerfully centralized political authority while preserving peasant property as the basis of state revenues (via taxes). In much of the Netherlands and the Italian city-states, highly commercialized merchant republics evolved on the basis of expanding markets for foreign trade. Here, merchants' capital predominated, but often without transition to a full-fledged capitalist mode of *production*.[60] Such a transition did, however, occur in England, where it was predicated upon late medieval/early modern transformations in the countryside that ushered in agrarian capitalist social relations. To be sure, there are important historiographic debates about both periodization and social causes of this transition. But when it comes to the actual emergence of agrarian capitalism in the late medieval/early modern period in England, much of the best historical scholarship is in accord.[61]

In terms of periodization, there seems little doubt that "the long fifteenth century (1350–1520)" is decisive.[62] And if there is one phenomenon that markedly stands out during the early stages of this period, it is the rise of a stratum of rich peasants, often referred to as *yeomen*, who were crucial to the emergence of capitalist farming. The flip side of the yeomanry's rise was the development of a huge layer of effectively landless poor peasants whose conditions of life increasingly resembled those of an agrarian proletariat. There is considerable truth in one historian's claim that "it was the consolidation of the yeoman oligarchies that decisively changed the realities of village life."[63] But we ought not to forget the other side of this process: the proletarianization of the rural poor.

The collapse of population brought on by the Black Death and other epidemics had radically shifted the social and demographic context in which lords and peasants encountered each other. With the potential workforce effectively halved, lords now found themselves at a comparative disadvantage. Given the shortage of labor, wages steadily rose. Perhaps more significant, if they hoped to retain or attract tenants, lords had few options but to relax obligations, lighten services, and offer attractive rents. Those feudal bonds that had persisted gradually dissolved: "Between 1350 and 1450, serfdom largely disappeared from English Manors."[64] The result was the famous golden age of the peasantry, characterized by declining rents and services, rising wages, and the disappearance of the remnants of serfdom.[65] Poor peasants generally found life easier, while middling and richer peasants frequently thrived. The latter could often lease more and better properties. A whole layer of them began to rent lands that formerly comprised the manorial demesnes.

The motivations for lords to stop directly managing their demesnes were probably quite straightforward. To begin with, using servile labor was less and less viable, given the erosion of feudal bonds and the ability of tenants, where labor was scarce, to flee to other manors or to the towns in search of better conditions. At the same time, working the demesnes with wage labor was decidedly costly, given the rising wages brought on by a shortage of workers. For these reasons, it would have been attractive to convert this land to rent-paying copyholds and leaseholds, so long as appropriate tenants could be found. And in case after case, this is what we find—lords leasing out their own estate lands, either in blocks to a number of better-off peasants, or sometimes in their entirety to a single well-off tenant. Perhaps 25 percent of the cultivated area of English manors was so rented in the decades around 1400.[66] Frequently, this also involved a conversion of land from arable (crop growing) to pasture (livestock grazing), the latter of which required fewer tenants and less labor. Crucially, pasturelands needed to be enclosed, which meant a radical transformation in the social geography of English life, as the open-field system so central to peasant life went into decline.

Here, a few words are in order about the phenomenon of enclosure. In its narrowest sense, the term implied a spatial alteration based on the erection of hedges and fences. But the term more typically referred to a multifaceted process of societal transformation by which unenclosed farms (open fields), linked to common lands, gave way to an increasingly enclosed and privatized agricultural system, dominated by large-scale commercial farms that employed wage laborers. Seen in these terms, enclosure also meant the spatial consolidation of lands, as peasants and incipiently capitalist farmers swapped, or bought and sold, strips of land to create a single contiguous unit in place of dispersed plots. More crucially, it meant the *engrossment* of lands, whereby prosperous farmers bought up or took over leases on plots previously held by neighbors or lords. Both spatial enclosure and engrossment involved sweeping social change in traditional open-field communities, where peasants had regularly crisscrossed one another's fields, moving between the scattered strips of land they worked, as well as to and from the wastes, forests, and fields that comprised the community's common lands. Typically, villagers had shared access to land belonging to their neighbors, including the right to guide animals across them at certain times of the year. As much as it was the land worked by a specific household, then, an open field was also shared; it was not held in severalty, that is, under the private dominion of an individual. With enclosure, this relatively cooperative ethos of open-field communities gave way to more individualized and privatized social and spatial relations.[67] Hand in hand with privatization went differentiation, since enclosure was also "a method of increasing the productivity or profitability of land."[68] Those who enclosed tended to profit more than—and, as time went by, often at the expense of—less prosperous members of the community more attached to its communal practices. As enclosure (privatization) and engrossment (the expansion of individual holdings by richer farmers) proceeded, a consistent pattern emerged, after 1348, of a declining number of tenants throughout the English manorial economy. Large farmers were acquiring more land; poor farmers were losing it.[69]

In the early going, much enclosure and engrossment was piecemeal. A survey of enclosures, largely in the Midlands of central England, showed that many were for one to eight acres. This, alongside other evidence, also indicates that yeomen "were probably the most numerous of all piecemeal enclosers."[70] Small as these enclosures may have been, over the course of generations, their effects were world-altering. By the first half of the sixteenth century, perhaps 45 percent of the lands of England had been enclosed.[71] And large yeomen farmers were the principal beneficiaries, working lands of up to two hundred acres in arable regions, and as much as five to six hundred acres in grazing areas.[72] By most sensible criteria, they could no longer be considered peasants. Increasingly, they were commercial farmers, investing in enclosure, livestock, marling, and other "improvements," and producing specialized agricultural commodities for the market, while frequently hiring wage laborers and encroaching on the rights and properties of their poorer neighbors.

As enclosed sheep walks and cattle granges appeared where open fields, marshes, and publicly accessible wastes had once stood, wealthy farmers with larger herds of sheep and cattle frequently "overstocked" the commons, exceeding customary practices and intruding on the access of the poorest. The related decline of open-field systems and the erosion of wastes and commons meant that life became more precarious for cottagers and poor peasants, whose personal plots were inadequate to household subsistence. Without communal land on which to graze animals, gather wood and straw, hunt, fish, or pick berries, their household reproduction was imperiled. In all these ways, dispossession of the rural poor advanced while land accumulated in the hands of a small layer of rich peasants. To take a single example, at Cheshunt in Hertfordshire in 1484, one-third of the manor tenants held 70 percent of the land. By this time, as Wrightson remarks, "The English 'yeomen' had emerged."[73]

The process had become significantly more advanced by 1522, when Henry VIII's government ordered a wealth assessment in order to prepare a new tax. The assessment revealed that the county of Rutland contained 302 owners of land. But nearly half of this group owned property worth merely one pound sterling per year. In other words, rather than landowners in any meaningful sense, these were semi-proletarian members of rural society who owned a cottage, small house, and/or a plot of land too tiny to sustain a household. At the other end, 43 percent of the land was owned by 4 percent of the landholders. The village of Babergh, in South Suffolk, presents an even starker case. There, about 60 percent of those named in the survey—or 1,375 out of 2,277 people—had no property at all. Further, of the 902 who were assessed as "landowners," 620 of those held land that generated only one pound per annum.[74] Less than 10 percent of the local population held the overwhelming bulk of the land. By the 1520s, then, an enormous process of social differentiation had transpired. No longer could the peasantry be spoken of as a single social class; instead, it had differentiated into an emerging group of capitalist yeoman farmers, on the one hand, and a growing layer of peasant-proletarians, clinging to a cottage and/or a miniscule strip of land, on the other.

It is worth emphasizing here that the *motives* that at first impelled yeomen in this direction need not have been specifically capitalist ones, even if they contributed to a subsequent transformation in that direction. Peasant life within feudal society involved production primarily for consumption—that is, for direct domestic subsistence—not for the market, even if periodic sales of surpluses did take place. Nevertheless, peasants were almost always inclined toward *petty accumulation* of land and livestock.[75] In part, this sort of accumulation was an insurance against lean years. Petty accumulation protected against times when dearth, drought, and other hardships might impose a *dis-accumulation* of resources built up in the past. Beyond this, the ability to provide for children by way of land, livestock, or cash induced households to accumulate beyond their annual needs so that their offspring might thrive. In no way could these be said to be capitalist forms of accumulation, as they did not involve the buildup of land and equipment in order to more efficiently produce commodities for the market in competition with other market-driven producers. Instead, the logic of petty accumulation was to store up resources for purposes of reproducing the domestic household and its descendants. However, once market-driven pressures came to the fore, the social logic of petty accumulation could mutate in capitalist directions.

Before outlining that process, let us examine a single case of an aggressive yeoman encloser, as revealed to us in the manor court records from Hevingham Bishops in Norfolk.[76] The individual in question is Robert Bisshop, a large tenant who descended from a well-established family in the manor. In July 1529, Bisshop was fined for having enclosed land near the "lord's great enclosure," a forty-acre parcel of pastureland that he himself leased. In October of that year, he was accused of having converted the land in his illegal enclosure to pasture. By August 1530, we hear of Bisshop being charged with refusing to let "poor tenants" graze their animals on the great enclosure for reasonable payment, a right which was customary and was written into Bisshop's lease agreement. By July 1533, four years after the original charge, manor records show that Bisshop had still not taken down his illegal enclosure.

This case is intriguing because it demonstrates just how aggressive a yeoman farmer could be in relation to the customary rights of the poor tenants.

It suggests that social differentiation was generating conflict between capitalist farmers and increasingly impoverished, semi-proletarianized cottagers. Also suggestive is the aggressiveness with which Bisshop defied the local lord, maintaining an enclosure that the latter declared illegal.[77] As time went by, however, lords increasingly allied themselves with this aggressive and "improving" yeomanry, particularly as they themselves moved to enclose on a large scale.

As much as wealthy peasants were the original drivers, landlords soon grasped the advantages that enclosure, engrossment, and eviction might bring. The key was to break free of traditional copyhold agreements—so called because documentary evidence of these customary arrangements, which often contained inheritance rights to the land for children, was held in the copy rolls or legal records of the manor house. In the late fourteenth century and the first half of the next, copyhold could be undone by moving customary tenures into the demesne. This transpired not only because much land had been made vacant by the massive collapse in population, but also because of peasant flight from estates where lords attempted to impose conditions of serfdom and/or high rents. At the manor of Forncett in Norfolk, as early as 1378, a quarter of all customary land had been appropriated by the lord.[78] Early on, these lands were let out as leaseholds simply to attract tenants, though many lords may have hoped to later convert them back to servile tenures. But by the 1520s, leaseholds became hugely advantageous for landowners as population growth resumed.[79] As prices rose and demand for land mounted, landowners could regularly raise rents. Increasingly, this meant leasing out land at market rents (not customary ones) that accorded with what the wealthiest yeoman farmers could pay. At the same time, those small to middling tenants who could not keep up with rising rents and land prices were progressively squeezed. By the sixteenth century, roughly seven-eighths of the free tenants held fewer than twenty acres of land, the minimum necessary for household subsistence.[80] Meanwhile, those wealthy farmers who were accumulating land in order to more efficiently specialize in commercial production were more and more compelled (by rising rents and competition from other yeoman farmers) to invest to raise the productivity of farm labor. Lords, too, now had a competitive incentive to spend on their estates—by way of enclosure, drainage, irrigation, and more—in order to attract the most prosperous tenants able to pay top market rents.

Through these processes, both wealthy farmers (producing for the market) and landlords (making the investments that would attract them—and their rents) were becoming *market dependent*. For farmers, the incomes they earned required them to meet standards of productivity that would produce agricultural commodities at competitive market prices. In the case of landlords, high rents could be charged only if long-term capital investments (in surveying, enclosures, irrigation, draining, fertilizing, and so on) had been made on land and farms that met the standards of agricultural improvement. Instructively, some of the earliest English tracts on surveying land and improving agriculture date from this period, such as Anthony Fitzherbert's *Husbandry* and *Surveying* (both published in 1523), or Thomas Tusser's *A Hundred Good Points of Husbandry* (1557). Land was now to be surveyed, mapped, and enclosed, while planting, seeding, manuring, and the like were to adhere to best competitive practices.

Improved farms offered commercial advantages. But the consolidation of such farms, in order to raise revenues and attract prosperous tenants, required aggressive action. A commercially minded lord might increase entry fines (levied when a new tenant took a holding), and deny tenants customary rights, such as grazing animals on hills and wastes, or growing crops on parcels of the demesne.[81] He could overstock wastes and commons with his own livestock. He might also shorten leases so that rents could be raised with each renewal (a practice known as "rack renting"). As population started rising around 1520, and prices followed course a few decades later, these tactics could pay off handsomely. At Whitby, Sir John Yorke doubled the rents on his estates in the 1540s. And over a fifty-year period (1530–1580), the price that could be charged for small parcels of land quadrupled at Hevingham manor.[82] In an increasingly competitive environment, landowners moved vigorously to expand the land they held as leasehold (lands that could be rented out). If their demesnes had already been converted, then enclosure of open-field and common lands was often the next step, sealing the fate of the small peasant. In all this, the "improving" lord was considerably assisted by the social differentiation of the peasantry, which, according to Hilton, "destroyed the internal cohesion of the medieval rural community," thereby making it much more difficult to mount coordinated peasant resistance.[83]

The agrarian history of England suggests that more land was enclosed between 1600 and 1760 than during any other period—more even than during the great wave of parliamentary enclosure of the eighteenth century. Throughout this era, large sections of the gentry and aristocracy used their considerable social power to do on a larger scale what the yeomen had done piecemeal from roughly

1380 to 1520: enclose and engross to an extent that imperiled the survival of the poor peasants. In the process, they were transforming themselves into capitalist landowners—a class that invested in the productivity of the land in order to attract commercial tenant farmers who used wage labor to produce for the market, while charging market-determined rents. Moreover, peasant dispossession was generating a class of propertyless laborers at a faster rate than they could be productively absorbed. During the period from 1560 to 1625, for instance, England's vagrant population grew twelve times over, a clear indication of the extent of displacement that was underway.[84] It is this set of social relations, based around the triad *landlord/capitalist—tenant farmer—wage laborer*, that we have in mind when we describe England by the time of the revolution of the 1640s as a society based upon *agrarian capitalism*.

But the transformation of the English landed classes into capitalist landowners would not have assumed the form or observed the pace it did without the phenomenal plunder of church lands stimulated by the English Reformation. We have already touched on the significance of the Reformation for the construction of a unitary and sovereign English state. It would be naive, however, to neglect its economic impact.

Consider that in 1535, the yearly net revenue of the church was probably close to £400,000. The king, on the other hand, would have netted at best one-tenth that amount from Crown lands, and he took in perhaps £100,000 in total annual revenue, or about a quarter of what the church earned.[85] So, it is not surprising that as Henry VIII waged war and burned through his tax revenues of the 1520s, he should look covetously at the wealth of the church. With war costs mounting, the state's fiscal situation became so desperate that in 1529 Henry repudiated the loan he contracted in 1522. Five years later, his chief minister, Thomas Cromwell, began his first assault on church wealth, transferring to the Crown a series of payments worth about £40,000 per annum. Then in 1536, as the king's dispute with Rome raged, an uprising swept much of northern England, involving noble and gentry opposition to Cromwell's centralizing policies, as well as clerical resistance to the break with Rome, and peasant movements against enclosures. When this Northern Rising collapsed, Henry and Cromwell moved quickly, hanging key opponents for treason and confiscating the properties of those who had surrendered, as well as many monasteries and great abbeys. Through these expropriations, the Crown added another £100,000 to its yearly income, an amount equal to the annual royal revenues at the start of Cromwell's ministry a mere five years earlier. But the king and his chief minister were far from done. In 1542, 700 Irish monasteries were suppressed. Three years later, an act gave the king the power to seize other church institutions, which netted him approximately 90 colleges, 1010 religious hospitals, and over 2,000 chapels and chantries.

It is possible that these hugely enhanced revenues and properties might have funded moves toward a more autonomous, centralized state. But Henry VIII was caught in the crossfire of war, and this led him to squander what he had plundered. The king commenced war with Scotland and France in 1543, and concluded peace three years later, having expended the weighty sum of £2 million on his campaigns. Even the extraordinary taxation of 1540–47, which raised £650,000, could cover merely one-third of these costs. To dig out, the king sold Crown lands, particularly those seized from the monasteries. Altogether, the government took in another £800,000 in this way—enough to stay afloat and to pay back foreign loans. But in surrendering huge tracts of land (and the revenues they provided), the king was undermining the long-term financial independence of the Crown.

What the king lost, the prosperous commercial gentry gained. For it was they—and this includes those younger sons who had thrived as merchants, manufacturers, lawyers, and state officials—who bought up the bulk of these manor estates. The Crown's great plunder was thereby shared out, benefiting the most commercially minded sections of the landed class. More than this, a much more fluid and dynamic land market emerged from these years, with landed property changing hands at rates that were extraordinary for the time. Equally significant, layers of "new men" entered landed society, including wealthy clothiers, merchants, and prosperous yeoman farmers, all of whom could be found busily buying up Crown lands.[86] The combined result of these processes was a stunning growth in the number and the combined wealth of the landed gentry. By 1565, the proportion of Norfolk manors held by gentry households had jumped to three-quarters, up from merely half just thirty-five years earlier.[87]

If wealthy yeoman farmers had been the principal agents of agrarian change for a century and a half after 1370, they were now increasingly overtaken by landed gentlemen. Enclosure moved into a higher gear, and capital investment on the land assumed grander dimensions. Twice as much enclosure took place in the seventeenth century as in any other, eclipsing both what had come before and what would occur later. As we have noted, between 1600 and 1760, nearly 30 percent of all English lands were enclosed.[88] So active was the land market that perhaps one-quarter of all the land in England changed owners (often many times) between 1500 and 1700, becoming concentrated in ever-fewer hands. "The gainers in this process," observes one rural historian, "were the great landowners and the gentry, the losers the institutional holders, crown and church, and the peasants, perhaps in roughly equal proportions."[89] For the small tenants, the end point of these processes meant displacement from their lands—via eviction, increased fines on renewal of leases, enclosure of the commons, and rack renting—to the point where up to three-quarters of all land was gathered into the hands of large landowners. With the great wave of enclosure by act of Parliament between 1760 and 1830, the destruction of the English peasantry was thereby completed. But the tipping point had been reached much earlier, as the following table illustrates.

Table 2.1: Number of Landless Laborers in England and Wales, 1086–1640

Date	Population (millions)	% of peasants not tied to a manor	Number of landless peasants
1086	1.1	6	66,000
1279	3.3	10	330,000
1381	2.1	2	42,000
1540–67	2.8–3.0	11–12	308,000–360,000
1600–10	3.75	35	1,312,500
1620–40	4.5–5.5	40	1,800,000–2,200,000

Source: R. Lachmann, *From Manor to Market*[90]

Clearly, a certain caution must be exercised with figures such as these. But there is little doubt that they capture the essential trends. By 1640, something in the neighborhood of four in ten peasants were no longer connected to a manor—nearly quadruple the proportion of a century earlier. And of these, about two million were entirely landless. These people had been thoroughly proletarianized, alongside millions more who, clinging to a cottage and whatever common rights remained, survived through sub-subsistence farming supplemented by wages. The following table gives some sense of how rapidly proletarianization advanced:

Table 2.2: Proportion of English Peasants Employed as Wage laborers, 1096–1688

Date	Percentage of peasants employed as wage laborers
1086	6
1279	10
1381	2
1540–59	11
1550–67	12
1600–10	35
1620–40	40
1688	56

Source: R. Lachman, *From Manor to Market*[91]

The rise of capitalism was a transformative social process, not a single event. Nevertheless, we can say with some confidence that by the middle of the seventeenth century, English society was a predominantly agrarian capitalist one.[92] Feudalism and the classic manorial economy were dead or dying, and with them the traditional peasantry. Large-scale, market-oriented farming now dominated economic life, revolving around commercial farms worked by wage laborers in the employ of capitalist farmers, who rented from a commercialized landowning class. It is important to add that many wage laborers were contracted as servants in husbandry, not as ideal-type "free laborers" (a point to which we shall return in the next chapter). Indeed, between 1574 and 1821, servants comprised between one-third and one-half of the agricultural workforce.[93] Similar forms of indentured labor figured in manufacturing industries in the guise of apprenticeships. In this regard, as in many others, rapidly growing industries in the countryside and the towns were developing in symbiosis with capitalist reorganization on the land, and in conjunction with bonded forms of colonial labor.[94]

It is crucial to note the ways in which all of these metamorphoses involved profound monetization of relations between people, and between individuals and the land, and how all of these expressed the rise of a social world governed by abstract space. To begin with, land had now been substantially commodified: its value was no longer registered in terms of communal memory and belonging, but in terms of market rents and prices. Older peasant practices had involved the re-creation of social space through annual perambulations, where members of the community walked the boundaries of the parish, the village, and its components, orally recording boundaries, common rights, and practices. With their bodies, they traced their shared belonging to the land and its custodians. Within these customary practices, which, to be sure, had their oppressive features, land was integrated with people; it expressed their histories and communal relations. Enclosed land, on the other hand, was bounded, measured, and monetized; it was set off from all but its direct owners, extracted from communal and customary relations. Against the concreteness of bodies and collective histories, enclosed land asserted the dominance of money and abstract measurement. A piece of land was so many acres, capable of producing a crop worth so much per acre. Mapping, which was virtually unknown in the English countryside before 1500, captured this reorganization of land into units of abstract space—areas bereft of actual people and their histories of belonging. Commodified land was open to the highest bidder, meant to be used to generate the largest monetized surplus product possible. That it had been the site of familial histories was irrelevant to the monetary calculus governed by prices, profits, and rents. Enclosed and commodified land was governed by the geometricized knowledge of abstract shapes and spaces. In seeking to reduce everything to "number, weight and measure," Baconian reformers of the seventeenth-century mimicked the quantifying rationality of the market, where everything is measured in terms of the monetary logic of *abstract number*. And the Newtonian conception of abstract space would only take this intellectual project to a higher, more rigorous level.[95]

With the rise of capitalism, money intermediates virtually all economic transactions—rent payments, crop sales, the purchase of consumer and capital goods, borrowing and lending, payment of wages. The yardsticks of the market invade the transactions of everyday life. Money governs who gets land and food, and who gets dispossessed. With this comes the colonization of life by the abstract, quantitative metrics of commodities and prices. More than this, however, such a socioeconomic order reorganizes the experiential dimensions of life, recalibrating them according to the social physics of abstract space and time. One geographer has described this as the "victory of decorporealization," since the body is no longer the regulator of spatial and temporal rhythms.[96] Instead, the body is now subordinated to the phenomenology of money and the market, and reconceptualized in the categories of mathematized space and time. Decorporealization means that land is not tracked by real feet on a perambulation, but only via the price signals of the market. What guarantees connection to the land is not communal memory, but the (alienated) social synthesis of money. At the most fundamental of levels, monetization is thus a victory of the abstract over the concrete.

We see all of this at work in the Cromwellian conquest of Ireland, to which we shall turn in the next chapter. There, William Petty, a social Baconian reformer and pioneer of political economy, undertook in the 1650s to survey twenty-two Irish counties. The lands of Irish peasants and their landlords were thus subjected to the rule of number, quantified and placed on grids, the better to expropriate and enclose them. Petty's famous Down Survey subjected Ireland not just to a spectatorial gaze, but to the quantifying logic of money—all of it backed up by troops and terror. The world was indeed seen anew: through the lenses of profit and dispossession.[97]

We should be clear now as to how England's landed class came, uniquely in Europe, to figure as pioneers of trade, plunder, and colonization. This was a class that had been reshaped along capitalist lines. When one social critic complained in 1550, "Merchauntes they become lords/and Lordes useth marchaundyse," he captured the unique social integration of large merchants and manufacturers in England with the gentry, as well as the immersion of landowners in the world of commerce and commodities—the world of "marchaundayse."[98] Large English landowners comprised a class accustomed to plunder (by way of enclosure and eviction of peasant holders), to accumulation, and to capital investment in the countryside. It was no great stretch to extend those practices to the seas and beyond.

Trade Wars: Conquering, Colonizing, Slaving

By 1550, the English gentry had defeated the great uprisings against enclosure and eviction that swept much of the country the previous year. The rebellions of 1549 were so widespread and insurrectionary that they have fairly been described as "the closest thing Tudor England saw to a class war."[99] These protests, whose center was Norfolk, drew on manifold social and religious grievances. But anti-enclosure riots were at the forefront of the disturbances.[100] The insurgents tore down fences and hedges, grazed animals on the wastes, and demanded restoration of customary rights along with reductions in rents and exactions. Had they succeeded, they might well have "clipped the wings off rural capitalism."[101] The rebels' defeat, however, paved the way for the plundering class to turn outward in the first great wave of English colonization.

Members of the English gentry first sought to transplant agrarian capitalism to Ireland. Beginning in 1565, plans were made to clear native inhabitants off their lands and make way for English colonizers, many of them soldiers. Colonization and the seizure of land were so intertwined that the words "colony" and "plantation" were largely interchangeable.[102] To their proficiency as enclosers, English colonizers added expertise in the use of armed force. In 1574, they massacred all six hundred or so inhabitants of Rathlin Island, before wiping out a couple of hundred supporters of Brian McPhelim O'Neill and his family at a Christmas feast later that year. Massacre as official policy was decreed by Humphrey Gilbert, English colonel for Ireland, when he ordered that "the heddes of all those . . . which were killed in the daie, should be cutte off from their bodies" and laid outside his tent, in order to terrorize all of the Irish who should come to see him.[103] Conquest, dispossession, plantation, and terror were joined as integral elements of a program for settler colonialism. And while the success of the colonial projects of 1565–76 was mixed, they established a pattern of conquest that came to fruition most thoroughly in the Americas (and by the 1650s in Ireland itself). Indeed, English families involved as "adventurers" in Ireland frequently went on to establish plantations in Virginia.[104] In this they were following the lead of Gilbert himself, who planted the first English colonial outpost in North America at Newfoundland in 1583.

Among the distinguishing features of the late-sixteenth- and early seventeenth-century occupation of Ireland was the conquerors' emphasis on commercial agriculture and their use of "improvement" as a legitimating device. Sir John Davies, lawyer, writer, and colonizer, was among the chief architects of English imperial rule in Ireland. In a 1610 letter to the Earl of Salisbury, he laid out the legal and moral case for seizing Irish lands:

> His Majesty is bound in conscience to use all lawful and just courses to reduce his people from barbarism to civility . . . they [the Irish] would never, to the end of the world build houses, make townships, or villages, or manure or improve the land as it ought to be; therefore it stands neither with Christian policy nor conscience to suffer so good and fruitful a country to lie waste like a wilderness, when his Majesty may lawfully dispose it to such persons as will make a civil plantation thereupon.
>
> . . . for half their land doth now lie waste, by reason whereof that which is habited is not improved to half the value.[105]

This document is fascinating in its use, more than three-quarters of a century before John Locke's *Two Treatises of Government*, of the ethos of improvement as a moral defense of colonial plunder. Irish lands are said to be "waste"—the very claim Locke would make for indigenous lands in America—and therefore an index of "barbarism." Of course, this claim had already been developed as a rationale for enclosure with respect to common and "waste" lands in England itself. But its extension to settler-colonial contexts was momentous, signaling as it did that agrarian capitalism would be joined to a global project of colonial conquest.[106]

However, none of this could be accomplished without first overcoming Spain, whose monarchy had created "the largest overseas empire the world had ever seen."[107] Direct hostilities began in May 1585, when crews of English ships were arrested in Spanish harbors and their goods confiscated. Immediately, English merchants began petitioning their government for letters of reprisal authorizing them to use armed vessels in pursuit of *private* retribution—via capture of Spanish ships and their goods. By the summer, the first of such private war parties took to the sea, followed shortly thereafter by Francis Drake's expedition to the West Indies. Over the next eighteen years, until the war's end in 1603, hundreds of naval war parties were launched. During just three years at the height of the conflict (1589–91), over two hundred private ships set sail in search of plunder.[108] These voyages were effectively piracy, albeit with state sanction, and gentry investors were key to their fortunes.[109] Until the 1650s, privateering of this sort was the essence of English naval conflicts around the globe. To be sure, the state was a partner in these expeditions and set some terms of engagement; but it was nonetheless locked into a business arrangement with private investors in the pursuit of *state* policy. As I have noted above, in Drake's Caribbean raid of 1585, the queen provided just two of the twenty-five vessels. This was imperial warfare as public-private partnership.

In these ways, early English colonialism traced distinctly different patterns to the west and to the east. Where the latter was concerned, commerce dominated, often based around large trading concerns (such as the Levant and East India Companies) controlled by London's great city merchants. To the west, in contrast, trade was accompanied by settler colonization and the development of plantation economies. Lesser traders and merchants from outside the privileged networks of the city elite played prominent roles in the colonization of the Americas, frequently in league with gentry investors. As we approach the English Revolution of the 1640s, it is these "new merchants" who come to the fore as the most dynamic commercial capitalists.[110] Moving beyond the merely mercantile business of carrying goods from one market to another, these new merchants began investing in commodity production in emerging planter colonies—and eventually in slavery. As Brenner remarks, the new traders broke from the practices of the great city merchants and the likes of the East India Company, who "would not take the risks or make the new types of investment in plantation production that colonial trade demanded." For the mercantile elite, this came at the considerable cost of losing out in the competitive struggle with new merchant groups. By the 1620s, for instance, all of the original companies formed for colonial trade with the Americas had collapsed because of the reluctance of big merchant capital from the city to invest in labor and means of production. Henceforth, "accelerated colonial development . . . was carried out by an entirely different set of traders."[111] The American colonial traders who rose to prominence after 1620 charted a new course based on directly supplying labor by financing the voyages of indentured servants, whose contracts of indenture were then purchased by planters. It would not be long before many of them also financed slave ships and provided investment funds for agricultural and agro-industrial production.[112]

The new breed of merchant, however, could rarely afford to operate on their own, and typically needed partners from the landed classes in order to finance investment on the scale necessary. And they readily found gentry capitalists eager to collaborate. In fact, roughly half of England's peers of the realm invested in trade between 1575 and 1630, with nearly twelve hundred members of the gentry and nobility putting capital into joint-stock companies specializing in overseas commercial ventures.[113] Particularly in the early decades, landed gentlemen tended to take the financial and organizational lead. Thus, however much they were primed for plunder, the gentry also led the shift from privateering to settlement and landed investment.[114] A major figure in colonial activity like Sir Humphrey Gilbert could soon be found elevating the acquisition of land above mere plunder.[115] Such gentry colonizers showed a notably capitalist aptitude for long-term investment. Taking surpluses that originated as rents and agricultural profits, they eagerly put forward capital for colonial projects that might take some years to show a return.[116] Their practices in this regard were surely influenced by the handsome profits they had made at home from enclosure and improvement, which demonstrated that land was a prize commercial asset.

Plantation colonies—in contrast to exercises in commercial plunder, such as those carried out by the East India Company—required the organization of a labor force. Here, the English ruling classes were again pioneers. Starting with the "surplus" population in Britain generated by enclosure and dispossession from the land, they constructed a transatlantic labor supply system based on indentureship— as we have seen, a practice that had a long history in Britain.[117] Service in husbandry was a rite of passage for many young adults from rural households: a majority of agricultural wage laborers in early modern England would have spent time as servants, bound to a master for a year at a time. And under the law, any unmarried and propertyless person under the age of sixty could be forced into service.[118] Similarly, in English manufacturing many apprenticeships involved indentured service of up to seven years. But a *transnational* indenture system—and the veritable industry in the export of bonded laborers from Britain to the New World that it involved— required the huge reserve army of labor that emerged with primitive capitalist accumulation on the land.

In fact, seventeenth-century England outperformed all competitors in this area. Though its population averaged under five million, the country shipped out seven hundred thousand migrant laborers across the century, around half a million of whom went to Britain's New World colonies.[119] To export one-seventh of the population—and a substantially higher percentage of the young adult population—is extraordinary. It spoke to the scale of the mass dispossession brought on by primitive accumulation, and to the rapid increases in labor productivity associated with agrarian and emerging industrial capitalism. The business of exporting laborers on this scale required substantial investments, including in clothing and transportation. Substantial, too, were the profits earned by those who financed this labor-export trade. These profits on the export of laborers were effectively advance deductions from the surpluses that migrant workers would generate during the three to five years, sometimes more, in which they were bound to plantation service.

Mass export of labor underpinned England's early success at colonial settlement and plantation production. Indeed, one of the reasons England leapt so far ahead of the Netherlands in colonial production and trade during this period had to do with this export of "white" indentured labor—the precursor of the large-scale buying and selling of enslaved Africans.[120] By 1700, the English had established seventeen colonies in the Americas, encompassing roughly 100,000 square miles and containing a population of around 400,000. France, with a domestic population four times larger and a colonial land mass twice as large as England's, had settled only 70,000, while the Dutch Republic had fewer than 20,000 New World settlers.[121] As a consequence, Dutch colonialism remained trade-based, while the English bounded ahead in the production of plantation commodities. As much as the Netherlands had prospered through the global expansion of merchant capital across networks of international trade, it failed to make a meaningful transition to a global system of commodity production using bonded labor.[122] For a prolonged period, Dutch merchants led all of Europe in the noxious trade of buying and selling enslaved Africans, though England eventually surpassed them in this bloody business as well. But England ran rings around its European competitors in the development of slave-based *production* in the New World. Contrary to those formalisms that counterpose capitalism to slavery and bonded labor, the historical relation was just the opposite. The world's first full-fledged capitalist power was in fact the most massive trader and exploiter of enslaved labor.

We shall return below to the unique nexus of war, colonialism, and slavery pioneered by the first fully formed capitalist nation-state. But in order to appreciate why Britain catapulted itself into the front ranks of slave trading and slave-based commodity production, we first need to revisit the political transformations associated with the revolutions of 1640–60, which laid indispensable foundations for global capitalist development.

A Beheaded King and a New Empire

The story of the English Revolution has been told, and told well, many times.[123] For a few years, after executing the king, its leaders abolished monarchy and the House of Lords—moves that they reversed by 1660, since killing the king (first body) to save the King (second body) seemed too much an invitation to subversion and popular tumult. But crucial (bourgeois) revolutionary accomplishments would have to be preserved, even as monarchy was restored, as they were pivotal to the new order of things. In a nutshell, these involved abolition of the king's arbitrary legal powers, elimination of the last remnants of monarchical jurisdiction over lordly property, and destruction of the rights of peasants. Through these measures, agrarian capitalists were emancipated from constraints imposed from above and from below. A series of legal changes proved decisive accomplishments of the 1640s. First, the legal powers of the monarchy were massively curtailed with the abolition of the King's Star Chamber, High Commission, and Council in the North. Taxation without the consent of Parliament was decreed illegal. The Triennial Act required a new Parliament to be elected and convened every three years, making impossible the Stuart practice of refusing to call one for years upon years, sometimes decades. Bishops were expelled from the House of Lords, and government was now overwhelmingly accountable to the landed gentlemen assembled in Parliament. Equally critical was the abolition of feudal tenures and the Court of Wards, moves that made private ownership absolute and unconstrained by legal obligations to the Crown. In these ways, as Christopher Hill observed, "landowners were set free from the incidence of arbitrary death duties and their land became a commodity which could be bought, sold and mortgaged; thus, long-term capital investment in agriculture was facilitated."[124] Then a series of acts from the late 1640s struck blows against peasant ownership by undermining the security of both copyhold and freehold agreements, and thereby facilitating yet more enclosure and eviction.

If the revolution dealt shocks to internal opponents of the new capitalist order, it also prepared attacks on England's external enemies. Under the rule of Oliver Cromwell and the generals (1646–58), England's new rulers aggressively expanded their global reach by building up shipping, trading, slaving, and colonization.[125] The Navigation Acts of 1651, for instance, required that all goods produced and traded by the English and their colonies be carried in English ships. This was a transformational move against Dutch dominance in world trade and shipping, provoking the first of a series of wars in 1652–54. Rather than a battle waged by privateers, this Anglo-Dutch war was, as Hill noted, "the first state-backed imperialist adventure in English history."[126] For this purpose, between 1651 and 1660, over two hundred ships were added to the British navy. At the same time, a government-initiated conquest of Ireland was afoot. The 1652 Act for the Settlement of Ireland authorized the seizure of two-thirds of Irish lands and their transfer to settler-colonists. Notwithstanding the massacres that ensued, the conquerors failed to meet this target. But the expropriations were massive nonetheless, and Ireland became the first example of English settler colonialism. It would not be the last.

As much as England's rulers sought to capture much of Dutch trade and shipping, they equally coveted Spain's American possessions. War with Spain soon became Cromwell's order of the day. While frustrated on some fronts, his troops managed to seize Jamaica in 1655, a victory that proved momentous. The Navigation Acts had already required that people enslaved to English colonies be sent in English ships. Now, having inflicted military defeats on the Dutch and seized Jamaica, the English cornered even more of the slave trade: their ships hurdled in excess of 350,000 Africans to New World slavery during the latter half of the seventeenth century. In the meantime, the Royal African Company, chartered in 1672, proceeded to ship 60,000 Africans to the Americas in the 1680s alone. As the African trade boomed, indentured servants from Europe were increasingly displaced by enslaved Africans. In 1650, for instance, there were roughly 100,000 English settlers in North America and the Caribbean, and only a few thousand enslaved Africans. Fifty years later, there were 260,000 English settlers alongside fully 150,000 enslaved Africans. Barbados underwent a spectacularly rapid metamorphosis. In the twenty years after 1640, the number of enslaved Africans on the island increased fifty times over.

Both economic and political considerations drove this shift to African bonded labor. Rising wages in England from 1660 reduced the flow of indentured servants and drove up their price, just as New World planters were experiencing greater needs for labor power. And joint insurrectionary conspiracies by servants and enslaved people in Barbados and Virginia added a sociopolitical impetus for separating "races" (first by creating them) in order to break their sense of shared interests.[127] For these reasons and others, by 1700 three-quarters of all arrivals to these regions came from Africa.[128] In the first decade of the eighteenth century, British ships carried more than one hundred thousand enslaved Africans. Henceforth, until the trade was abolished in 1807, the English held their place as Europe's reigning slave traders.

In the next chapter, we'll take a closer look at the interrelation of capitalism and plantation slavery. For the moment, it is instructive to note how utterly entangled English capital was with the business of slavery. A case in point is Maurice Thomson, whom Brenner refers to as "the greatest colonial merchant of his day."[129]

Born around 1600 to a prominent household in Hertfordshire, England, by 1617 Thomson was in Virginia, where he accumulated an estate of 150 acres. Virginia planter he may have been, but soon he was also a Caribbean trader, a colonizer, a shipper of enslaved people, and an interloper in the East Indies. In 1626, he equipped three ships, bought sixty enslaved people on the West

African coast, and delivered them to a St. Kitts planter. On their return voyage, these ships contained twenty thousand pounds of tobacco. A few years later, we find him interloping in the fur trade in what would later become Canada. By the late 1630s, Thomson was conducting some of the most successful raids yet on Spanish possessions in the Americas. And in 1642, he was financing the Earl of Warwick's privateering activities, which resulted in his becoming a major landowner in Barbados, where he established a sugar works. From 1649, he was financing Cromwell's plunder of Ireland, for which he was promised over sixteen thousand acres of Ulster land. Slaving, trading, plundering, and managing plantation production were thus interconnected activities, each feeding the other—and most profitably so. By 1634, Thomson sent out the largest shipment of tobacco yet seen in Virginia—some 155,000 pounds—representing one-quarter of the year's total export. Of course, his record shipment of tobacco from his Virginia estates had been produced by slave labor, as were the products of his plantations throughout the Caribbean.[130]

By 1647, Thomson had become a prominent voice representing merchant-planters in London. By then, it was clear that robust use of state power was essential to the advance of English colonialism. Soon he became a major influence on Cromwell's trade and colonial policies, profiting enormously, as we have seen, from the lord protector's invasion of Ireland. Moreover, Thomson may actually have authored the Navigation Act of 1651; he was definitely "the right hand man of Cromwell's Western Design," the project intended to seize large parts of Spain's possessions in the Americas.[131]

While the scale of his influence was unique, in many ways Thomson was typical of many hundreds of merchant-planters who plundered, traded, bought and sold enslaved people, and exploited bonded labor in order to produce world market commodities like tobacco and sugar.[132] His case also highlights the ways the English state directly inserted itself into global exchanges between commodities, money, and enslaved Africans. The blood of the commonwealth now traversed transatlantic circuits—and flowed through the bodies of enslaved Africans. Within those bloody circuits, new forms of finance were gestating.

CHAPTER 4

Blood in the Water

Colonialism, Slavery, and the Birth of Modern Money

"In that quiet room with its oak wainscoting and Turkey carpet, its shelves of ledgers and almanacks, it would have been difficult for these two to form any true picture of the ship's circumstances or the nature of trading on the Guinea coast. . . . Picturing things is bad for business, it is undynamic. It can choke the mind with horror if persisted in. We have graphs and tables and balance sheets of corporate philosophy to help us remain busily and safely in the realm of the abstract."

—Barry Unsworth, *Sacred Hunger*[1]

A s we follow the trajectory of English capitalism after 1650, we find ourselves on the edge of a global vortex. Colonial storms, conjured up through war, plunder, and slaving, were collecting hurricane force. Warships had driven the Dutch out of England's Baltic trade, from its East Indian exploits, and from New Amsterdam. Jamaica had been filched from the Spanish. Enslaved Africans were being crammed into English ships and sold into New World slavery on scales previously unthinkable. Immense winds of plunder and slaughter were gathering, preparing a new order of imperial power.

121

Looking back two centuries later, Marx enumerated the forces that unleashed these tornadoes of destruction: "Colonial system, public debts, heavy taxation, protection, commercial wars, etc., these offshoots of the period of manufacture swell to gigantic proportions during the period of infancy of large scale industry. The birth of the latter is celebrated by a Herod-like slaughter of the innocents."[2] But before the 1690s, two of these elements were not yet in place: public debt and heavy taxation. Without these, a financial system appropriate to capitalist war and colonialism could not be consolidated. Lacking this—and the new form of money it required—Britain would be unable to establish its hegemony as the world's first global capitalist Goliath. Money had still to be extracted from the bones of princes.

Sacred Hunger: Gold, Money, and State Finance

As Hobbes recognized in *Leviathan*, published the same year the 1651 Navigation Act was enacted, world money—the money accepted as payment between nations—consisted of precious metals. "Gold and Silver," he wrote, "being (as it happens) almost in all Countries of the world high-valued, is a commodious measure of the value of all things else between Nations."[3] In a European world economy increasingly characterized by the global movement of goods, an international means of payment was crucial. In the absence of a national currency that could function as international money, as had the Athenian owl, global payments relied on precious metals, be they in the form of bullion or high-quality coins.

In the sixteenth century, the acquisition of gold became the obsessive aim of European colonial policy. By the 1470s, Portuguese mariners were reaping the stuff along Africa's "Gold Coast." Meanwhile, Spain, the first European power with extensive colonies in the Americas, displayed a devotion to gold (and soon after to silver) that can only be described as maniacal. "Gold is the most excellent, gold is treasure, and who has it can do whatever he likes in this world," wrote Columbus. "With it he can bring souls to Paradise."[4] It was the craze for gold that first induced "the discoverer" to deploy indigenous peoples as slaves, just as it inspired his earlier fixation on selling them in Europe.[5] Yet, as Adam Smith would later argue in *The Wealth of Nations*, this "mercantilist" devotion to precious metal is fetishistic. It confuses the thing (precious metal) with the activity—labor—that brings it into being. It mistakes a *result* for a cause. As Smith could easily see by the second half of the eighteenth century, wealth accrues ultimately to those who succeed in raising the productivity of labor, capturing markets in the process, not those who pursue money as an end in itself. Win the battle for markets in goods, and money will flow your way. Spain's leaders, like Portugal's monarchs, were led astray in seeking to build up great hoards of gold rather than investing to raise the efficiency of labor. Almost a century before Smith's great text, pamphleteer Charles Davenant had made a similar point. "Affluence of money," he urged, may simply induce a "lazy temper." After all, "it is not the taking in a great deal of food but it is good digestion and distribution that nourishes the body." However, it was precisely this—good digestion and distribution—that had been scandalously neglected by the rulers of Spain. Disregarding labor and manufactures, they had allowed New World riches to pass through their country undigested, without having provided any "spirits, strength, or nourishment."[6]

By the 1580s, Spain controlled vast New World territories, along with trading posts in India, Africa, the Philippines, and beyond. Its inflows of silver and gold were staggering. To all appearances, its imperial power was unrivaled. Yet already it was reeling from massive financial crises based on imperial overextension and the weakness of domestic production. Before the decade was out, upstart England would defeat the Spanish Armada. By now, crises were endemic. Portugal deserted its ally in 1640, while Catalonia set down the road of revolt. The manic pursuit of precious metals had come up empty, prompting talk of a "curse of gold."[7]

Certainly, England's rulers, too, were fueled by what one writer, in 1686, called "the sacred hunger of gold."[8] But generations of English experience with boosting profits via investment in agriculture, trade, and manufacture had instilled practices of "improving" the means of production. And by establishing plantation colonies in the New World, by building up a protected shipping industry, by investing in colonial trade and production—and by backing all of this up with unrivaled military force—England was moving into first place in the new imperial order. One ominous indicator of this is that between 1697 and 1702, as a new financial order was being established, the monetary value of enslaved people exported from Africa exceeded that of gold.[9] It was now the means of producing wealth—enslaved labor power—not the metallic means of payment, that was central to New World fortunes. Nevertheless, prior to the 1690s, England's rulers were financially constrained from fully unleashing English imperial power. These constraints would be burst only via revolution in state and finance.

$

The problem of financing war and colonialism had reemerged with Oliver Cromwell's aggressive imperial policies. To carry through the conquest of Ireland and Scotland and the First Dutch War (1652–54), Cromwell sold off Crown lands and the estates of royalist opponents, along with dean and chapter lands. Even then, he was forced to raise taxes.[10] Taxation, however, encountered resistance. Cromwell's regime, resting as it did on an army rooted in the lower and middling strata, was not sufficiently a government *of* the ruling class for the latter to readily accept new taxes. This was its fatal flaw, and a paramount reason that the Stuart monarchy was restored in 1660 with the crowning of Charles II. Yet, Charles's regime, too, failed to win the confidence of England's dominant class. This had much to do with the tendency of the Stuart monarchs to subordinate the king's second body, the *body politic* (and its *fisc*), to its mortal first body, with its passions and whims. Failure to respect the independence of the second body as the impersonal sphere of bourgeois property led the king into debacles such as the infamous Stop of the Exchequer.[11]

The Stop involved a suspension of debt payments on the eve of another war with the Dutch in 1672. Charles unilaterally stopped payments on debts totaling over £1.3 million plus interest, an enormous sum at a time when the average annual income of the Crown was around £2 million. Much of this debt was owed to goldsmith bankers, private financiers who took in deposits (for which they usually paid 6 percent interest) and then lent out a share of these deposits to the king (at an interest rate of 10 percent or more). Yet, persistent debts from *past* wars severely hampered the Crown's ability to wage wars in the *present*. Charles and his advisors inevitably gave priority to new wars and renounced past debt payments (including those accrued from two previous wars against the Dutch). At first, the Stop was said to be for one year, but it was twice extended. In 1677, the government finally agreed to resume payments. But over the next dozen years, only about half the interest owed (and none of the principal) was paid. Then, in 1690, once more at war, Parliament agreed to again stop paying these debts. With little hope of ever seeing repayment, the creditors sued the Crown in the Court of the Exchequer.

In and of itself, the Stop of the Exchequer and the regular skipping of payments were anything but unusual; indeed, European monarchies were famous for such maneuvers. However, the English state was different. It was in the midst of transformation into a *bourgeois monarchy*, and the claimants insisted it adhere to a corresponding regime of property and power. Moreover, until it could ensure investors that it would invariably honor its debts, the English Crown could not establish a new regime of state finance. Charles II and his advisors had managed to significantly expand the market for government debt by selling "tallyes of loan," which were essentially interest-bearing bonds meant to be repaid out of future tax revenues. These bonds, which came to be known as "treasury orders," could not be cashed on demand. But they did circulate as means of payment.[12] If the government had been able to sell treasury orders to a larger public, rather than merely to goldsmith bankers, it might have paid much lower rates of interest. Yet, the viability of a large, liquid market in state debt required the abiding confidence of financial markets in the integrity of government borrowing. So long as the monarch insisted on sovereign immunity before the law—which amounted to its right to renege on contracts—its credit would be suspect. Precisely this—sovereign immunity versus contractual obligation—was at the heart of the legal dispute over the Stop of the Exchequer.

It is not necessary to follow the details of what has become known as the Case of the Bankers as it went through hearings, preliminary decisions, and appeals over many years. The crucial thing is that the judges of the Court of the Exchequer and the appeal court ruled that the bankers had a legal right to sue the Crown. Grasping the heart of the issue, the chief justice of the King's Bench stated, "The king himself . . . hath obliged himself to make such payments. . . . it is not so much the judgment of the courts as binds the property, as the obligor himself." This was a radically new doctrine. The king was being treated here like any other contracting party, an "obligor" who is *subject* to the law, not above it. In the domain of contract, the monarch, the incarnation of sovereign power, was henceforth identical with a private individual. The chief justice highlighted this when he proclaimed, "Indeed it would be a hard thing to say that the court of Exchequer can relieve the king against the subject, and not help and relieve the subject when he produces a legal title against the king."[13]

This is most clearly a judgement on behalf of the sanctity of property and contract. In a society organized around property rights grounded in monetary and financial transactions, the Crown, too, is obliged to honor its contractual agreements—a position we shall see again in John Locke's analysis of money. For the courts to place the monarchy above the obligations of contracts would imperil all its public obligations; it "would destroy all annuities, rent-charges, and other payments which the crown is obliged to make."[14] To be sure, under pressure of war, Parliament did later renege once again on its obligations to the bankers; and the bankers ultimately accepted a final settlement amounting to about half of what they were owed. Nevertheless, the bourgeois principle had been established by the courts: in financial matters the Crown was to be treated like any other party to a contract. The state was to be subsumed to impersonal power—to the compulsions of money and the market. Its powers did not exempt it from market obligations. The "second blood" of money having been depersonalized, the king resumed his first body just like everyone else.

But the Stuart monarchs were not prepared to observe these obligations, and this is what sealed their fate. Their demise had little to do with the actual performance of the economy. In fact, the Cromwellian matrix of war, colonialism, and slaving prospered after the Stuarts were restored in 1660. Enclosure and agricultural improvement continued apace; colonial investment thrived. Soaring shipments of British manufactures to the North American colonies financed massive British imports of slave-produced goods like tobacco, cotton, and sugar. It is certainly true that from the 1660s to 1700, English manufactures exported to Europe rose by 18 percent. But exports of similar goods to the colonies burst forth by 200 percent over the same period, clearly accelerating the pace of industrial development. As New World populations and production ticked up, English colonists imported textiles, clothing, metals and metal goods, hand tools, paper, sugar-making equipment, and more, greatly stimulating English manufacturing.[15] In this environment, the big trading companies flourished like never before. The East India Company may have doubled its capital between 1660 and 1668, but it was outdone by the Hudson's Bay Company, whose assets tripled, and by the Royal African Company, which quadrupled in size during the same period.[16] No, it was not a faltering economy that doomed the Stuarts. What sealed their fate in the economic domain—and here I barely touch upon the crucial arena of religion and foreign policy—was their handling of finance and taxation.

The very expansion of trade described above enhanced the king's revenues from the customs and excise taxes. And as we have seen, the Stuart monarchs turned increasingly to London's growing financial markets to raise loans. Ominously, growing commercial revenues buttressed by loans allowed James II, who ascended the throne in 1685, to dramatically increase the size of his army without having to seek additional funds from Parliament. Yet, this raised the specter of a monarchy independent of the key centers of bourgeois power: Parliament and financial markets. In short, the threat had returned of a monarchy that might raise personal power (the first body) above the powers of money and Parliament (the second body of the commonwealth). Bourgeois monarchy—the subordination of the Crown to agrarian capitalists in Parliament and financial capitalists in the market—would not be secure so long as the Crown could assert personal over public powers, by way of financial autonomy from Parliament, a growing king's army, and a pro-Catholic religious and foreign policy—all of which fueled fears of absolutism. And so, another monarch would have to be toppled, though this one was allowed to keep his head.

The revolutionary upheaval of 1688–89, which brought William of Orange to the throne in the guise of "liberator," was overdetermined by Stuart refusal to accept a bourgeois system of finance that was fully autonomous of the king's first body—one that obeyed the rules of the market in money. Even after the Stuarts were gone, the Stop of the Exchequer remained a traumatic point of reference for financial and monetary debates throughout the 1690s, pitting the rights of private property against those of the Crown.[17] And throughout the 1680s, it was the irreducible backdrop to bourgeois opposition to the Stuart monarchy: "The Stop of the Exchequer, a contemporary tells us, caused greater consternation than did the appearance of the Dutch fleet at Medway. There was a crisis of confidence in 1682, the year of the attack on the City's Charter, a disturbance of credit in 1685. . . . There were many reasons why the City welcomed its Liberator, under whom £1,300,000 was at last repaid to Charles II's bankers."[18]

A fully capitalist monetary system could not be constructed until money was extracted from the bones of princes and transplanted into the blood of the commonwealth. To accomplish this involved depersonalizing money, making it the property not of royal persons but of Hobbes's "artificiall man," that social construction we dub the commonwealth. Money would have to transmogrify. It would have to migrate from one body to another, from the royal corpus to that of the impersonal body politic. Yet, money's extraction from the bones of princes proved a violent business. It required that kingly bones be fractured, so that the blood of money might flow like never before through the oceans of the world economy.

War Finance and the Birth of Bank Money

William of Orange landed in England on Guy Fawkes Day, 1688, with eleven thousand foot soldiers and another four thousand on horse. He did so at the invitation of seven of the most powerful men in Britain, who also offered him the British throne. As James Stuart fled to France, the elite of the country's landed gentlemen, great merchants, and manufacturers swiftly rallied behind the invasion force. Mighty though William may have been, England's rulers had learned their lessons and immediately set about taming his kingly power. Parliament assigned the new king an annual income of seven hundred thousand pounds, much less than had been granted to Charles II or James II, making it impossible for him to pay an army or wage war without seeking Parliament's authorization to raise funds. One courtier complained in the House of Commons that the king was being kept "as it were at board wages," but that was exactly the point.[19] A leash having been placed on the monarch, Parliament was again ready to wage war.

Predictably, the bloodshed commenced in Ireland, where rebellion had broken out once more. Nearly fifty thousand troops were sent to crush the Irish rebels. This was necessary to preserve the colonial project. But the endgame was to break France, England's real imperial rival. Spain had previously been vanquished under Elizabeth, the Netherlands under Cromwell and the Stuarts. If England was to achieve imperial hegemony—dominance of world trade and colonization, military supremacy in Europe—then France, with its powerful absolute monarchy and a population four times greater, would have to be subdued. For twenty of the next twenty-five years, the two nations waged an epic struggle for European supremacy (the Nine Years War of 1689–97 and the War of the Spanish Succession, 1701–14). Decisive to victory was England's alliance with the Dutch, Spanish, and Austrian states. And what held the alliance together was money.

Everywhere in Europe, it seemed, England's rulers were subsidizing troops and sending money. For the first three years of the war (1689–91), the government paid for an average of nearly ten thousand soldiers in the Dutch Low Countries. The elector of Prussia received an annual subsidy of £20,000 to send troops to

Flanders to fight alongside the English. By the time of the War of the Spanish Succession, fully 52,000 troops were being funded in the Low Countries, two-thirds of whom were foreign. Portugal and Savoy were brought—or perhaps bought—into the alliance in 1703, at the cost of annual subsidies of £150,000 for Portugal, a tad more for Savoy. The latter's yearly subsidy was then hiked by £50,000 in 1705, and another £100,000 a year later. In the late stages of the war (1710–11), the English state was paying to keep 171,000 troops and their officers in action across Europe—almost 114,000 of whom were of foreign origin.[20] And this was just the beginning stage in England's "Second Hundred Years' War," which began with the Glorious Revolution of 1688. For the next century, the pit of military spending seemed bottomless, as wave after wave of troops was armed, fed, and sent to theaters of combat, while warships were built in the thousands. In terms of capital investment, nothing in the early eighteenth century compared with building a warship. A large multistory cotton mill cost around £5,000 at the time. Meanwhile, a first-rate battleship required an expenditure of up to £39,000. Altogether, the British navy had an investment of around £2.25 million in its ships during the first half of the century—at a time when the total capital investment in the 243 woolen mills in the West Riding equaled a little over £400,000.[21] "Until the rise of the modern factory," writes one historian, "the building and equipment of a fully armed warship remained the largest, most concentrated form of investment in material goods that either the state or private entrepreneurs could undertake."[22]

"Money, money, and still more money," indeed. In 1691 the English government was spending £3 million for military purposes. Within four years the figure had reached £8 million. Yet, tax revenues over those same years averaged just £4.5 million. As always, the gap would have to be covered by borrowing. And now, in the context of the new bourgeois monarchy, an innovative structure of debt-based war finance could emerge—and with it the foundations of a capitalist banking system.

Enter the Bank of England, which was formed for a single purpose: to fund war with France. At the start, this meant providing the government with a hefty loan. Even its most farsighted founders could not have grasped the revolution in monetary arrangements the bank's loan would trigger. But as war became effectively permanent for a century after 1689, so did the need for war finance. It was thus as an instrument for *permanent* war finance that the bank transformed England's financial architecture.

It all began innocuously enough. Within months of the declaration of war against France, the government was engaging in all the typical forms of state borrowing against future tax revenues (by means of Exchequer tallies, and navy and victualing bills, in particular—the details of which need not concern us here). All involved the contracting of loans (usually from goldsmith bankers) with which to pay bills, and the promise to repay creditors once tax revenues arrived at the Exchequer, the British treasury. These promises to pay were risky assets, however, given the long-standing propensity of cash-strapped governments to defer repayment, and even to default. To make matters worse, investors typically prefer financial instruments for which an active resale market exists, should they want to cash out, yet government debt instruments were relatively illiquid at the time. As a result, they tended to decline in value (i.e., they were discounted when holders sold them off) and, knowing this, potential creditors expected a higher interest rate to counter the danger of depreciation. Yet, high interest rates locked the state into larger borrowing costs, precisely when they desperately needed to bring them down. The government thus endeavored to raise funds in other ways, such as lotteries and the sale of annuities, which provided regular payments, often for life, in return for a lump sum contribution. But these were stopgaps, often no more economical than loans from goldsmith bankers, and as the expenses of war kept rising, so did public deficits. It was to escape these traps that in May 1694 the government finally accepted a proposal from William Paterson, a Scottish merchant and financier. Paterson offered to gather subscriptions for a large perpetual loan to the state, the subscribers to which would be incorporated until 1706 as the Bank of England, with the authority to take deposits and to circulate paper instruments like notes, bills, and checks. The government having agreed, Paterson and his partners delivered it a £1.2 million loan. Unwittingly, all parties had embarked on a revolutionary experiment in banking and state finance.

The rapidity with which this occurred had everything to do with a government unremittingly desperate for money. Within a month of delivering the initial loan, the bank was asked for £300,000 more. Soon its directors were also remitting money to Flanders to pay the troops and cover their supplies. By March 1696, barely more than eighteen months after its incorporation, the bank's loans to the government had more than doubled, surpassing £2.7 million. Then, in December of that year, the bank absorbed £800,000 of government tallies (at discount), taking more state debt onto its books. "Constant pressure was put on the Bank to meet urgent calls for the Army," writes one historian, and each time it rose to the occasion.[23]

Nothing in the act that created the bank, nor anything in its charter, suggested it would become the most revolutionary innovation in monetary practice since the invention of ancient coinage. But it did—because it stumbled on the means by which to monetize public debt. Turning government debts into money would become the foundation of modern finance, and of money's second modular form.

Two essential features of its early loan made the bank truly innovative. First, for the first time in English history, a loan to the state would be made largely in paper currency (banknotes and bills), rather than in gold and silver coins. Second, those who subscribed to the loan—that is to say, those who bought interest-bearing shares in the bank—would be able to cash out at any time simply by selling their shares (their part of the loan to the state) on the developing stock market. Because a paper currency arrangement like this was so novel, the government insisted that the bank maintain a £200,000 gold reserve to back up its bills and notes, believing this would reassure the public as to their solidity. As essential as this metallic reserve was, it was the circulation of a *privately produced* paper currency based on *public* debt that revolutionized the production of money.

No actual cash changed hands, therefore, in the bank's loan to the government. Instead, it handed over bills that paid interest, alongside notes that did not. In return, it received Exchequer tallies—wooden tokens representing as-yet-uncollected tax revenues. These had been used since the fourteenth century and could be transferred in payment of debts and taxes.[24] The government proceeded to use the bank's interest-bearing bills and notes to pay for military goods and services. Those who received them thus displayed confidence (a) that the bank would redeem them for silver or gold coinage if requested; (b) that the government would pay the bank the interest on its loan (at a rate of 8 percent); and (c) that for both those reasons, others would accept the bank's paper promises as means of payment. Then in 1698, the government started to accept the bank's paper instruments in payment of taxes. This was decisive. After all, anyone expecting to pay taxes could now receive banknotes and bills with full confidence that they and others could always dispose of them as tax payments to the state. In practical terms, this made bills issued by a private bank full-fledged money, even though they did not formally become legal tender for another 135 years. And it meant that the bank's bills and notes became an indispensable part of the money supply.

Year after year, decade after decade, as it provided more finance to the Crown, the bank acquired enhanced powers: to issue notes as legal tender (first to the treasury and then more generally); to enjoy a monopoly on the issue of such notes; to have the forgery of its notes subject to the death penalty, just like the king's coinage; to have its property exempted from taxation; and to serve as the official agent for the exchange of bills issued by the Exchequer. No longer simply an investment trust for a public loan, in just a few decades the bank had become the pivot upon which both public and private finance turned. It was the principal lender to the state and the supplier of liquidity to the financial system as a whole.

Let us underline what this means. A private financial institution, the Bank of England, was issuing IOUs based on government debt and backed by future taxes. These paper IOUs then circulated as the *privately* produced money of the realm. Moreover, the social validity of these (privately produced) public debt notes was determined by impersonal markets, not the king's mints. The financial viability of these IOUs to the government depended, first, on the willingness of private investors to buy a share of the bank's loans to the state—that is, to "purchase" the public debt notes the bank was selling by investing in its shares. This required, secondly, investor confidence that the Crown would honor its debt payments to owners of bank stock. Everything rested, after all, on the government's use of its tax revenues to honor these debts. In the spirit of the Case of the Bankers, the Crown was now being held to the same market rules as any individual borrower. The state was thus becoming "more abstract and disembodied,"[25] governed by the disciplines of bourgeois power. And these were determined in the depersonalized sphere of financial transactions, where Bank of England stock changed hands in the same way as the shares of the East India or Royal African Companies: according to assessments of risk, credibility, and profitability. Private financial markets had inserted themselves as the foundation of public finance. Henceforth, the making of money would be inextricably tethered to market processes and dynamics.

All of this made it possible for the government's promises to pay, represented by bills and notes issued by the bank, to circulate as money. This meant that certificates of government debt were functioning as cash. Perhaps it did not look quite this way, so long as interest-bearing bills predominated among the paper instruments issued by the bank. Recipients of these could have said they did so because the potential profit outweighed the risk. But notes were the key to the emerging financial architecture of English capitalism, and they soon sidelined interest-bearing bills, which were not issued subsequent to 1716, barely more than twenty years after the bank was launched. Since they did not pay interest, Bank of England notes did not circulate as investments. They were, however, readily received as means of exchange and payment, and were held as stores of value. What, then, was the basis of these banknotes? In the first instance, they represented nothing more than the credit of the government. But this credit was now validated in private financial markets. Ultimately, these notes were good so long as the government made its debt payments to the bank. Any move by the state to default on its loans would have immediately driven down the value of bank shares and the notes tied to them, and it would have created a flight to other stores of value, such as gold and silver coins or bullion. But so long as government honored its debts, and so long as financial markets upheld the good credit of the government, a banknote that represented nothing more than a loan to the government could circulate as a universal equivalent for all goods and payments. The foundation of bank money was thus the *future* revenues of the state; and notes issued by the bank represented a fiduciary money built upon public credit.

This temporal shift in the foundation of money is at the heart of the revolution in finance that generated money's *second modular form*—just as it is linked to new practices of speculation, and the bubbles and crises that derive from them.

The Athenian owl had been based upon past labor, that of enslaved people in the Laurion silver mines. Bank of England notes, however, carried an index of future labor, not past work. They denoted a slice of social wealth (derived from labor) that would find its way to the state in the form of taxes. To be sure, the bank agreed in principle to exchange its notes for silver or gold coin. Yet, the bank's precious metal reserves amounted to merely 12 to 15 percent of its money stock. In practical terms, its commitment was viable only insofar as most people did *not* exercise this right. In the circular flows of economic life, paper currency revolved on the government's use of future tax revenues to meet the interest payments on its *past* debts.[26] A failure of government to honor that commitment— precisely what had been at issue with the Stop of the Exchequer two decades earlier—would now have induced a rush to exchange banknotes for gold and silver, which would have quickly become unsustainable.

What backstopped banknotes, at least within the domestic economy, was "the sound functioning of the fiscal system."[27] And whether the functioning was "sound" was determined by private investors acting in impersonal financial markets. All of this was, of course, a work in progress, one that proceeded by fits and starts, including a profound monetary crisis in 1696–98. Nevertheless, as England's rulers imposed the disciplines of financial markets on the Hanoverian monarchs, they also granted them, subject to parliamentary consent, the powers of taxation required to finance a century of war. An unwavering commitment to honoring its debts thus allowed the British state to establish sovereignty over the disposal of military force. This was a dramatic shift from the situation a mere twenty-five years earlier, at the end of the Third Dutch War in 1674, when the accounts of the Customs and Excise branches, which made up four-fifths of state revenues, were a full year in deficit. So fragile at that time was confidence in the government's commitment to pay back its debts that tallies—wooden markers of loans to the state—were being resold at a 30 percent discount. Wages of sailors and dockworkers in government service were up to a year and a half in arrears.[28] These problems did not derive principally from administrative inefficiency; they had more to do with battered confidence in the Stuart monarchy's commitment to its debts, and with the reluctance of Parliament to grant taxes that might encourage absolutist tendencies toward monarchical independence. Parliament, the political institution of England's landed gentlemen, merchants, and manufacturers, had first to trust that the Crown honored the dual constraints imposed on its authority by Parliament *and* the private market. Only then was it prepared to authorize a sufficient—indeed, a sufficiently growing—flow of taxes. And that flow of tax revenues was what inspired public confidence in the financial pledges of the state. A basis in paper pledges grounded in *future* taxes from future labor thus comprises the foundation of bourgeois finance, and of money's second modal form.

This is not to deny that credit instruments, such as private and public debts, had assumed a strategic role in the financial system. Bank of England notes were, after all, a form of *private credit money* backed by the state. These were augmented by notes issued by country banks alongside a variety of forms of private credit money, such as bills of exchange. It was an enormous innovation in monetary affairs for the most credible IOUs, those of the Bank of England, to become a universal equivalent. But these did not float independently of the world of labor and production. Rather than mere fetishes of the imagination, these notes were grounded in the political economy of public credit. Like shares in the bank, which made the original war loan possible, banknotes were underwritten by that share of the national wealth taken by government in taxes. A basic confusion is thus in play when eminent political theorist J. G. A. Pocock writes that with invest-ment in the national debt, "property . . . has ceased to be real and has become not merely mobile but imaginary."[29] A similar critical failure is at work when literary critic Patrick Brantlinger says of early modern English finance that "the economic base, or mode of production" of modern societies resides "in the form of a financial abyss rather than of a positive, material economic force."[30] For, dematerialized as credit monies and other financial instruments appear to be, they remain intricately hitched to the world of bodies and their labors—and of the connections of these to the state. To decipher this, however, involves critical work of *defetishization*. Let me demonstrate this at the most rudimentary level: that of taxation.

$

A considerable merit of studies on the political economy of British taxation is the attention they direct to what *underpinne*d the national debt. Rather than resid-ing upon an abyss, state finance in Britain rested atop a tremendously efficient machinery of taxation.

It is often forgotten that the early loans made by the Bank of England were guaranteed by government commitments to finance their interest payments out of specific revenue funds. Those who subscribed to the original £1.2 million loan, for instance, were promised a tax-free "perpetual Fund of Interest" derived from the ships' tonnage and liquor duties.[31] The £300,000 loan of February 1695 was secured against Customs duties. In fact, until the American War of (1775–83), the share of government borrowing that was *not* specifically funded from government revenues declined steadily across the eighteenth century.[32] Bourgeois state as this now was, not a single interest payment was missed. And the revenues for these payments came from somewhere beyond the void.

Unless we recognize this, the entire financial and monetary revolution after 1689 appears, as it did to some contemporaries, as a work of alchemy, a mere con-jurer's trick. After all, long-term public debt rose from around £2 million pounds in 1688 to £834 million in the 1820s. This is an astronomical increase, and it sent crit-ics into paroxysms of panic about monstrous debt consuming the whole of society.

The trick with a perpetual debt, however, is that investors must simply receive their expected interest payments on a regular basis (and also that they should be able to easily sell the securities they hold based on that debt). This requires that government has the actual revenues—deducted from national wealth—with which to make those debt payments. Most decidedly, they did. By the time of the Napoleonic Wars (1803–15), the British state was taking in thirty-two times as much in taxes as it had under Charles I.[33] This was the "positive, material economic force" that made possible a rapidly growing permanent public debt. It is why Marx identified "heavy taxation" as one of the elements of primitive accumulation. Figure 4.1 gives us a first clue as to how this new financial system operated by tracing the tremendous growth in the government's tax revenues after the 1680s.

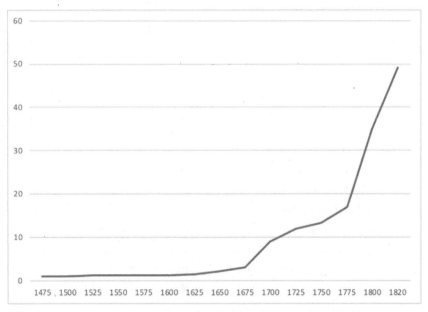

Figure 4.1: Growth of English State Revenues, 1475–1820 (as expressed in £00,000 of government spending per year, measured in constant prices 1451–75)

Source: *British Parliamentary Papers*, vol. 35; data prepared by P. O'Brien and P.A Hunt, in European State Finance Database: http://www.esfdb.org/table.aspx?resourceid=11192

It is worth stressing, as well, that the English were especially heavily taxed. By the first quarter of the eighteenth century, they were paying more than twice as much as were the French per capita. By the 1780s, they were paying nearly three times as much.[34] Clearly, then, the representatives of the English ruling class who assembled in Parliament did not oppose taxes. But they would authorize them only to a regime that demonstrated accountability to financial markets, the investors who dominated them, and their class representatives in Parliament. Figure 4.2 illustrates the British trend with respect to taxation per head. Again, we observe that the crucial transition occurred late in the seventeenth century.

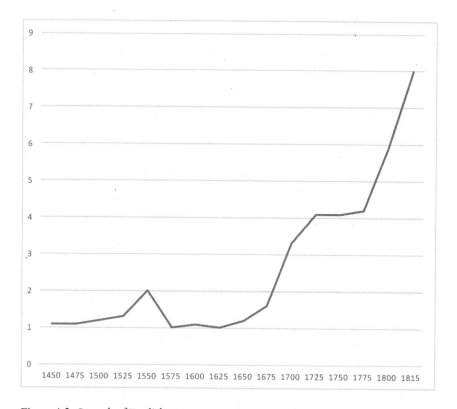

Figure 4.2: Growth of English State Revenues Per Capita, 1451–1815

Source: *British Parliamentary Papers*, vol. 35; data prepared by P. O'Brien and P.A. Hunt, in European State Finance Database: http://www.esfdb.org/table.aspx?resourceid=11192

Increasingly, the state's tax income was derived from the customs and excise taxes, rather than levies on landed wealth.[35] These revenues were granted in large measure because they were funding capitalist expansionism, not courtly extravagance. It was war, the foundation of foreign trade and colonization, that drove the ever-rising budgets of the state. Throughout the eighteenth century, current military expenditures plus spending on debts from past wars consumed between 75 and 85 percent of total public expenditure.[36] By any reasonable definition, this was a *fiscal-military state*.[37]

Of course, bank money brought new instabilities in its wake. As I have shown, there is a speculative element involved in any financial instrument whose foundation is *future* wealth. Since the future is inherently unknowable, risk and uncertainty enter into the very modular form of modern bank money. Of course, this is inherent in all fantastic wagers on the future, from the Dutch tulip mania of the 1630s to England's South Sea Bubble three-quarters of a century later (to which I return below). But modern bank money, only loosely constrained by precious metal, can fuel such speculative ventures. There is an inherent risk that paper money can proliferate out of all proportion to the past labor (precious metals) or the future labor (in the form of anticipated government revenues) that are its vital underpinnings. It was precisely this that happened to Chinese paper money, which regularly went through massive collapses in value. Lawmakers were thus concerned to contain overproduction of paper currency, as well as financial manias. They also had to reckon with the fact that the mass of the population still lived and moved in an economic universe dominated by coins, not bills and notes. To build confidence in the new monetary and financial arrangements of the late seventeenth century, political figures not only endeavored to lock in government's responsibility to honor its contractual obligations. They also sought to ground bank money in gold, because of both its popular acceptance and its role in international payments. Insistence on the contractual obligations of the monarch and the need to anchor money in precious metal figure prominently in the interventions of that most bourgeois of philosophers, John Locke, during the raging debates about money in the 1690s.

Newton to Locke: Coins, the Death Penalty, and World Money

Revolutions proceed through crises. The same was true of the monetary revolution associated with the Bank of England. In fact, within a year or two of the creation of the bank—in the midst of an escalating war with France—the country was staggered by a near collapse of the monetary system. The bank certainly played a role in resolving this crisis, but so did a massive overhaul of the coinage that involved John Locke, Isaac Newton, and the death penalty.

England had long endured a scarcity of coins, and this only became worse with the rise of capitalism. Embedded in the first modular form of money, the monetary system of early modern England was utterly reliant on metallic coinage. Yet, as the economy grew rapidly from the middle of the sixteenth century, and as marketization rapidly escalated, scarcity of money became acute. One historian estimates that demand for coins soared 500 percent between 1540 and 1600, while the supply grew by just a shade more than 60 percent.[38] Throughout the 1620s, some of the most perceptive economic writers of the time—Thomas Mun, Gerard de Malynes, and Edward Misselden—all addressed the shortage of money, generally focusing on the need for a favorable balance of trade to attract silver and gold that could be minted into coins.[39] Given the dearth of cash, the people of England increasingly resorted to credit to conduct the commerce of everyday life. This involved everything from a working-class household's debt with the butcher to sales credit, loans, and circulating bills of exchange among merchants and manufacturers. One economic historian suggests that in the first half of the seventeenth century, eleven times as many transactions were conducted by credit as by coins.[40] Yet, while credit oiled the wheels of commerce, it could not substitute for legal tender. Few credit instruments had wide circulation, and final payment still had to be made with metallic coins. Paper monies, too, a variety of which were in circulation, rarely served as means of final payment until Bank of England notes achieved that status around the middle of the eighteenth century.[41] Facing a shortage of coins from the middle of the seventeenth century on, manufacturers often produced monetary tokens of their own—normally in small denominations like half pence—for payment of wages, and to lubricate local markets. Town councils also got into the act in order to stimulate economic activity. Tokens usually mimicked coins in being round, but could be made of anything from leather and copper to tin and lead. By the 1660s, over thirty-five hundred token manufacturers appear to have been active in the City of London alone.[42]

This was a fragile monetary system, stitched together by webs of credit, bills, and notes that lacked legal tender status, joined to a proliferation of localized tokens. In good times, it might hold together clumsily. But it was prone to dislocations. And nothing dislocates like war.

The supply of armies in foreign lands, as Hobbes reminds us, required payment in an accepted form of world money. In the late seventeenth century, that meant gold and silver bullion, or coins minted from those metals. As the war with France expanded after 1689, so did England's army and navy. Fighting as they were in foreign lands and waters, it was necessary to remit money across borders. England's massive subsidies to its allies required additional cross-border remittances—a sort of payment for mercenaries. As state expenditures rose by 50 percent in the course of a mere three years (1691–92 to 1694–95), so too did outflows of silver and gold. Meanwhile, as precious metals flowed outward, *inflows* slumped as the war disrupted trade patterns and cut into Britain's earnings from exports. A growing gap thus developed due to war-induced drainages of silver and gold, on the one hand, and declining inflows due to disrupted trade, on the other. To make matters worse, England's silver coins had been significantly degraded over the decades, as clippers trimmed away small quantities of metal and then returned the clipped coins to general circulation. By the early 1690s, coins contained perhaps 20 percent less silver than their official weight dictated. As a result, they were accepted in foreign markets at a 15 to 20 percent discount below face value. Yet, this meant that even more silver and gold—15 to 20 percent more—had to be shipped out to pay for war.

All of this was further compounded by the fact that the English mint, for reasons I leave aside, undervalued silver by pricing it below the market rate. This eliminated any financial incentive for individuals to bring in the metal for minting, since it could fetch a higher price elsewhere. English holders of silver were thus incentivized to ship it overseas for sale and/or conversion for gold. This put the monetary system in a fatal loop. As exports of silver made the desperate shortage of money even worse, this only encouraged the practice of clipping silver coinage—which was a simple matter before coins with milled edges became common—so as to melt down even more of the stuff for export. London goldsmiths estimated in 1690 that silver was being shipped from London to metal dealers in Holland and France at a rate of nearly fifty thousand ounces per month.[43] Worse, the more silver a coin contained, the more likely it was to be hoarded and/or melted down for export, since degraded coins did fine as means of everyday exchange and payment, encouraging people to hold back the highest-quality ones. Consequently, only the oldest and most worn coins tended to stay in circulation. By 1695 many English coins had lost as much as half of their silver content due to clipping and long-term wear.[44] Inevitably, as export and clipping of silver exacerbated the severe shortage of coinage and combined with the economic dislocations brought on by war, prices soared. At this point it was obvious that the English monetary system was on the verge of a disastrous collapse brought on by war finance, rocketing overseas remittances, and an epidemic of clipping. This was the urgent context for the Great Recoinage of 1696.

$

Parliament had been investigating and debating the state of the coinage since 1691. Many commentators, including William Lowndes, secretary of the treasury for more than a quarter century, advocated a devaluation of English coins that would acknowledge their diminished silver content without altering their nominal value. A devaluation along these lines would have meant the British pound being represented by about one-fifth less silver. In the pamphlet literature on the issue, Locke emerged as the preeminent critic of this strategy. He advocated instead for a recoinage of silver at the prevailing legal standard—that is to say, with its metal content restored to its former level. In early 1696, Parliament adopted the policy of the "Locke party": calling in all English coins in stages and reminting the entire coinage to restore its previous metallic content as established by law. I will examine Locke's theoretical arguments against devaluation shortly. But first let us consider the role of Locke's friend, Isaac Newton, in the overhaul of the English monetary system.[45]

In the early stages of the recoinage, and amid the parliamentary furor over clipping and counterfeiting, Locke secured Newton's appointment as warden of the London Mint. Three years later, he was promoted to master of the mint, a position that he retained until his death in 1727, and one that made him a wealthy man. While these were typically patronage appointments requiring little real service, Newton assumed his duties with gusto, particularly his obligation to seek out and prosecute those guilty of counterfeiting and clipping coins, both capital crimes. Armed with the death penalty as his ultimate weapon, the great physicist went on an obsessive campaign against clippers and counterfeiters. He organized a network of spies and personally traveled to inns, taverns, and prisons, often in disguise, to pursue forgers. And having nabbed them, he did not let up. As one apologetic scholar conceded, Newton "was disinclined to mercy."[46] Indeed he was. During his first three years at the mint, Newton imprisoned more than one hundred alleged clippers and counterfeiters. And in his first year alone, at least fifteen people were executed in London for coinage-related crimes.[47] Had state terror been enough to reform the coinage, Newton might have carried it off single-handedly. Alas, more was required, including a revolution in the technology of minting, and raising the purity and uniformity of the coinage—another area in which Newton proved himself a fervently devoted master of the mint.

Locke, too, was an advocate of *thanatocracy*, to use radical historian Peter Linebaugh's apt term for a state that rules through capital punishment.[48] He fully shared Newton's deadly animus toward clippers, declaring they did more damage to England "than all the forces of our enemies could do"—and this at a time when the country's soldiers and sailors were dying at the hands of the French.[49] He joined to this animus a cruel determination to inscribe the rule of capitalist markets on the bodies of the poor. This might mean hanging in the case of clippers, or whipping children and abducting them from their impoverished parents—all of which he advocated. The philosopher's brief on the Poor Law, prepared in 1697 for the commissioners of Trade and Plantations, is a case in point. As political theorist Neal Wood noted, "Little of Christian charity or compassion for the less fortunate can be found in this unusually harsh document."[50] Instead, Locke proposed that boys and girls caught begging outside their parish without a pass should be seized and placed in workhouse "schools," where they were to be "soundly whipped and kept at work till evening." Children between ages three and fourteen with parents on poor relief were to be removed to workhouses. Anyone caught begging outside their parish with a counterfeit pass was to have their ears cut off on first offense and to be transported to the colonies on second offense. Locke's proposals heap abuse on the poor, denouncing them as "begging drones," "idle vagabonds," and the like.[51] As in his political philosophy, the state that protects the liberties of property—for that is the true Lockean commitment—is seen as doubly threatened. From below, it is endangered by the rabble, represented in this case by clippers and counterfeiters. From above, it is vulnerable to the machinations of government officials inclined to manipulate the currency. Just as Newton had devised a strategy for suppressing the menace from below, Locke's interventions in the recoinage debate tackled the threat from above.

It is often imagined that Locke's campaign to restore the full silver content of the coinage represented a kind of fetishism of precious metals. It is sometimes claimed that this prevented the philosopher from grasping that the nominal value of, say, an English shilling need not have corresponded perfectly with a specific amount of silver.[52] But this is to misunderstand the *social* basis of Locke's argument, which pivoted on the need for all economic transactions and contracts to be underpinned by a stable measure of value. Anyone who enters an economic contract, be they a wealthy landlord or a day laborer, does so on the assumption that the monetary amounts stipulated will not be arbitrarily altered by government, he argued. To revise the value of the coinage, as the secretary of the treasury proposed to do in recommending a reduction by 20 percent of the silver content of English coins, is to act as if "the mint should coin clipped money."[53] Any such alteration in the value of coins—be it by government contrivance or illicit clipping—blatantly "defrauds" individuals and, by disrupting value relations, sows "confusion" in the market. Just like Charles II's Stop of the Exchequer, devaluation violates the tacit consent that underpins contracts and thus constitutes an "injury done to the public faith"—that is, to the confidence of economic agents in the reliability of monetary valuations, from the prices of goods and properties to the sums set out in contracts.[54] Locke has here made public confidence, or "faith," in contractual obligations decisive. It is true, he readily concedes, that the actual amount of silver designated by the word *pound* or *shilling* is a convention, not something given by nature. But once this "imaginary value" is established "by general consent," then trust in it "is the great bond of society."[55] To arbitrarily alter a value established by consent is to rupture the social contract that binds people in a political community.

Locke's opposition to revising the metallic content of money thus had little to do with his being mesmerized by the "intrinsic value" of silver or gold as things in themselves. He clearly recognized the conventionality of specific monetary denominations. What he opposed was the idea that any agent, be it the state or the clipper, has a unilateral right to change established economic ratios. It is, for Locke, as if one party should try to change the terms of contracts after rents, prices, and rates of interest have been agreed. By preserving the metallic standard of the coinage, government publicly declares that values established by consent are independent of the whims of monarchs and statesmen, and that they should rest upon the impersonal forces of the market. To be sure, this position favored the interests of landlords (whose rents are usually locked into long-term contracts), or those who have lent money at interest. Similarly, it disfavored renters and borrowers, for whom devaluation would mean being able to pay back less precious metal (although the same *nominal* amount of money) to fulfill their contracts. Yet, as much as he clearly favored certain interests, Locke's argument was of a more general nature. He was seeking to safeguard property, money, and market relations by grounding them in social relations that are constituted *prior* to government and political society. For him, the state is meant to protect these pre-political relations—not to alter them.

Locke added a further wrinkle by arguing that the impersonal power of the market is enacted most decisively at the global level. To be sure, clipped or devalued money can function within the boundaries of national territory, as when the king accepts it for taxes or the landlord for rent. In an enclosed, autarkic economy, nominalism—the conferral of the name *shilling* or *pound* on whatever amount of silver we choose—might be viable: "And this perhaps would do well enough, if our money and trade were to circulate amongst ourselves, and we had no commerce with the rest of the world."[56] But there is no reason, insists Locke, to believe that economic actors in foreign markets will accept less silver from us for their "salt, wine, oil, silk," and so on, simply because we rename our coin at a higher value than in the past.[57] For any economy "that hath open commerce with the rest of the world," what governs the value of money is "the universal trade of the world."[58] Asserting that world market relations are dominant over nation-states, Locke affirmed the priority of world money, a priority that was practically demonstrated in the operation of high-quality gold and silver as means of international payment.[59] Locke's underlying assumption was that governments have no more right to interfere with the natural laws of money than they do with inherent rights to property. In his political-economic writings of the 1690s, as political philosopher George Caffentzis notes, Locke thus located "in the universality of money (not in the pretensions of domestic 'projectors' or 'divine monarchs') the driving logical and social force of his day."[60]

By identifying the universality of money, or what Marx will call *world money*, as of a higher order than the state, Locke implicitly identified the capitalist world market as the cornerstone of modernity. He thereby broke from the conceptual framing of money as a creature of the nation-state, insisting that money is governed by "the universal trade of the world." Rather than the blood of the commonwealth, Locke identified money as the *blood of world commerce*. In so doing, he intuited that bourgeois society must ultimately be understood as a global totality, and world money and the world market as its most concrete, universal incarnations.

It is this insight that defines the "Locke party" of the 1690s, a current that included Isaac Newton, who became a Whig member of Parliament in the immediate aftermath of the Glorious Revolution of 1688–89.[61] Of course, the cosmopolitanism of this Whig camp was an entirely bourgeois one. Indeed, it was defined by an unflinching commitment to English colonialism and the slave trade. The young Locke, for instance, was among the earliest investors in the first British company devoted to slaving, the Royal Adventurers into Africa, which was given a monopoly on the English slave trade. Then, after the Adventurers were succeeded in 1672 by the Royal African Company, Locke bought four hundred pounds of its stock in 1674, an investment he increased by another two hundred pounds a year later.[62] Newton, made wealthy by his years at the mint, would follow his friend's lead, becoming a considerable investor in the South Sea Company, which acquired the famous monopoly, the *asiento*, on the sale and transport of enslaved Africans to Spain's New World colonies.

If slavery did not perturb these great English liberals, neither did colonialism, as is evident in Locke's 1696 appointment to the new Board of Trade and Plantations, in which body he quickly established himself as the driving force.[63] To the consternation of one of his biographers, Locke wholeheartedly promoted colonial domination (and denial of the right to self-government) in England's American colonies and in Ireland.[64] In fact, Locke's commitment to both colonialism and slavery extended back to at least 1669, when he served as secretary to the Lords Proprietors of Carolina, in which capacity he ardently recommended slavery for the new colony—perhaps unsurprising in light of his personal investments in the trade in enslaved Africans. Members of the Locke party were also among the most fervent supporters of England's wars for imperial power, whose finance was the very raison d'être of the Bank of England—itself effectively a Whig institution, and one in which Locke was also an early investor.[65] Here again we return to the integral link between money and blood. If capital does indeed come into the world "dripping in blood and dirt," as Marx urged, then so did its intellectual companion, liberalism, in the form of its most famous English exponent. And this Lockean nexus of money–slavery–colonialism was at the heart of liberal political philosophy in England.

Money, Power, and Enslaved People: Locke on Persons as Things

To suggest that this nexus is at the heart of Locke's political philosophy is not merely to refer to the facts of his biography. It is also to point toward crucial arguments developed in both his political economy and his political theory. In particular, it is to claim that rather than rights in general, classical liberalism is constructed as a defense of the *rights of property*—including to property in persons.

Without a doubt, the facts of Locke's biography predisposed him to support for slavery. We have already noted his direct investments in slaving. Similarly, the first English colony in Carolina—created by Locke's patron, the First Earl of Shaftesbury—not only became embroiled in conflicts with indigenous peoples, but also enslaved them. In fact, one historian suggests that colonists in South Carolina became "*the* Indian slave traders of the North American continent."[66] Shaftesbury, who is credited with a major influence on Locke's political development, quickly invested in this trade in enslaved Indians. It is especially instructive that by the mid-1670s, the colonists were "portraying their slaves as captives taken in just wars."[67] This defense was little more than colonial apologetics, offering a veil of legitimacy for a project of violent displacement of indigenous peoples. After all, the classic "just war" theory urged that only wars of self-defense against aggression were morally legitimate. It was obviously disingenuous to suggest that New World colonizers were innocently enslaving people as they defended themselves against unprovoked aggression. There were, however, wars between colonizers and indigenous peoples to which they could point, even if there was nothing "just" about them. When it came to enslaving Africans, the just war argument was blatantly absurd. After all, the Africans bought and sold by the Royal African Company—in which, let us recall, both Locke and Shaftesbury were investors—had not been at war with Englishmen. Yet this did not deter Locke, when designing a constitution for Shaftesbury's new colony, from recommending that slave owners in Carolina should have "absolute power and authority" over their enslaved Africans.[68] How did he justify this position?

Let us answer this by beginning with Locke's famous opposition to the "patriarchal" argument for the origin of government, according to which earthly power derived from God's bestowal of authority to Adam as the first man. This line of argument, advanced by Robert Filmer, served as a defense of monarchical absolutism. God gave sovereignty on earth to Adam as the first man, the original patriarch, Filmer had insisted, and all kingly power descended from that godly gift.[69] As an anti-absolutist—that is, a writer concerned to protect the rights of men of property against arbitrary authority—Locke needed a different account of property and power. After all, to grant that all political authority descended from God's bestowal of kingly power on earth to Adam seemed to make any defiance of monarchs sinful. Yet, if power did not derive from God via Adam, this raised the subversive prospect that all persons were equal before God; that God had not created any original distinctions among persons. But Locke was certainly no egalitarian.[70] What Locke needed, therefore, was an alternative account of legitimate power and inequality among men. The attempt he makes in his *First Treatise of Government* (composed in 1681) is intriguing, as Locke counterposes to the Adamic account a "new way" to power, derived from money. Social power, he argues, attaches itself to those who dispose of money on a large scale. This is so much the case that a West Indian planter might have "318 Men in his Family without being Heir to *Adam*." While some of these people will be sons and friends, the majority will be "bought Men and Maid Servants" along with "Soldiers under Pay, or Slaves bought with Money." So, there is a source of earthly power—money—that does not go back to God's creation of the world. With money (which he innovatively linked to labor and property in his *Second Treatise*) men can buy the services of others. Money thus buys men, just as it purchases goods, and Locke has no compunctions about domination of such persons, instructing us that the Master's "Title to the Power . . . whether over Slaves or Horses was only from his Purchase" (*First Treatise*; 11.130, 131, 130).[71]

"Only from his Purchase": this is the key to Locke's political theory and his political economy. Confronted by the apparent contradiction of a liberal individualist who condones enslavement, one commentator has suggested that Locke had "a kink in his head" when it came to American slavery.[72] True. But there is a systematic logic to this kink: it is the *ratio* of the monetary abstraction, a logic that reduces all that can be bought to objects of ownership, to possessions. It is the commodity-economic logic of emergent capitalism, extended across the board. Money detaches goods, including *humans*, from concrete sentience and chains of individual meaning, inserting them in a network of abstraction, of quantitative equivalences. Items of monetary value lose their qualitative being in order to appear as mere quantities of exchange value. So committed was Locke to the rights of property acquired by money that he had no difficulty extending the commodity logic of reification to persons, who now effectively became things. How else to explain the apparent ontological confusion of his *Second Treatise*, which claims the "Turfs my Servant has cut" as the product of "*my* labour" (5.28, my emphasis)? For Locke, once I have bought the servant (as slave), or the labor power of a wage-earning "drudge," their work and its products belong to me, the purchaser. Because money is ostensibly an extension of my body, it embraces all that I purchase, making me master of them. Money even makes *persons* mine, either permanently or temporarily. Via the magic of money, my bodily powers now extend to the bodies of others, enabling me to "walk with the feet of other people."

Locke may indeed have been a possessive individualist, as C. B. Macpherson famously proposed. Without doubt he was a theorist of *possessed individuals*.[73] Locke did not flinch, after all, before the fact that money had acquired demonic properties—his "new way" to power—that conferred dominion over, even ownership of, persons.[74] How else do we explain his investments in the trade in enslaved Africans? By the 1680s, the alienated logic of the monetary abstraction that saturated the philosopher's thought had widely pervaded English society. We see it at work in John Bunyan's hugely influential allegorical work, *The Pilgrim's Progress* (1678), with its depiction of Vanity Fair, a place where "all such merchandise [are] sold, as houses, lands, trades, places, honours, preferments, titles, countries, kingdoms, lusts, pleasures, and delights of all sorts, as whores, bawds, wives, husbands, children, masters, servants, lives, blood, bodies, souls, silver, gold, pearls, precious stones, and whatnot."[75]

Locke not only accepted these powers of money; he endorsed them. And this enabled him to justify commercial slavery in defiance of the principles of natural liberty he elsewhere advanced. It is entirely possible that Locke was so dedicated to monetary power that he failed to see that when it was extended to power over persons, it produced a state of slavery that violated his own liberal principles of the "natural liberty" of persons. Yet, this is another way of saying that rights of property and the powers of money were foundational to his liberal principles, and undercut his other commitments. The drift of Locke's argument, therefore, is to establish a new, modern defense of slavery, grounded in the power of money, and not merely in the just war doctrine that he incoherently invoked. In the argumentative logic at work in Locke's *Two Treatises of Government*, it was entirely reasonable that "servants, lives, blood, bodies, souls" should be bought and sold in much the same way as were houses or pearls. And they were—on ever-growing scales, as monetary power was extended across the oceans, sweeping millions of Africans into its vortex.

"Traffickers in Human Blood": *Atlantic Slavery and English Liberalism*

> *But is it not notorious to the whole World, that the Business of Planting in our British Colonies, as well as in the French, is carried on by the Labour of Negroes, imported thither from Africa? Are we not indebted to that valuable People, the Africans, for our Sugars, Tobaccoes, Rice, Rum, and all other Plantation Produce? And the greater the Number of Negroes imported into our Colonies, from Africa, will not the Exportation of British Manufactures among the Africans be in Proportion; they being paid for in such Commodities only?*
> —Malachy Postlethwayte, 1745[76]

Had they been able to look back a century or two later, most early English colonizers would have been surprised by an eighteenth-century colonial empire that resembled "a magnificent superstructure of American commerce and naval power, *on an African foundation*" as Postlethwayte puts it in another passage from the text quoted above.[77] To be sure, the vast majority of them displayed no qualms about the *trade* in captured Africans. But few of these early "adventurers" imagined colonies built on the *labor* of enslaved Africans. Yet, this was the ultimate logic of what the purchasers were doing; they were, after all, selling bearers of human labor power. An exclusive focus on the triangular trade—British goods to Africa, enslaved Africans to the New World, New World goods to Britain— can tend to leave us in an abstracted sphere of exchange. Yet, New World goods had first to be produced. And it was increasingly the labor of bonded Africans that did the producing. By attending to the New World labors of enslaved Africans, we are directed to the commodities they produced and the fortunes they created for their owners.

As we have already observed, early modern Europeans initially plundered Africa and the New World largely for gold. For a long time, enslaved people were a secondary matter. The 1660 charter of the Company of Royal Adventurers, which enjoyed monopoly trading rights in Africa, stipulated that it comprised "under-takers in discovering the golden mines and the setting of plantations there."[78] Sixty years later, agents for the Royal African Company were still focused on gold, but enslaved people had become a principal commodity for procuring it. Only in the eighteenth century did the value of enslaved people exported from Africa exceed that of gold. Yet, even then, enslaved Africans were for the sellers primarily a *means* to gold. Humphrey Morice, England's greatest slave merchant of the 1720s, regularly instructed his slave captains to turn their "Cargoe of Goods and Negroes into Gold" as quickly as possible.[79] We shall meet Morice again in his capacity as a governor of the Bank of England.

Colonization required settlers. There was no way to establish outposts, forts, trading stations, mines, and plantations without on-the-ground colonists. Even if indigenous people were to be mobilized as forced labor—and colonizers tried this on a much larger scale than historians have often appreciated[80]—Euro-peans would still be needed as soldiers, supervisors, artisans, and so on. In fact, New World colonizers needed Europeans for further purposes: as cheap labor, imported "drudges" who came under the guise of servants. These "white" ser-vants came from a variety of groups—poor children taken from their parents, convicts, defeated Irish rebels, kidnapped youth, and poor people willing to sign contracts as bonded ("indentured") workers in exchange for food and passage to the Americas. And for the first generation or two of colonization, inden-tured servants from Europe were the largest source of immigrant labor to the American mainland and the Caribbean. Indeed, by 1650 enslaved Africans still accounted for just one in three migrants to the English Americas. And in some areas, reliance on European servants would last considerably longer. Through-out the eighteenth century, as many as two-thirds of Pennsylvania's immigrants may have been white indentured laborers.[81] Eric Williams was thus largely right when he asserted, "Unfree labor in the New World was brown, white, black and yellow; Catholic, Protestant and pagan."[82] But that began to change, and change rapidly, from about 1660. Henceforth, unfree labor in the Americas would be overwhelmingly African.

There are multiple reasons for the overriding shift to the purchase of enslaved Africans. A critical one is that British wage rates appear to have risen in the second half of the seventeenth century, thus reducing economic incen-tives for the poor to emigrate, and raising the costs necessary to induce those indentured servants who did so.[83] There is also some evidence to suggest that around the same time, mortality rates began falling for those arriving in the New World, making enslaved people more economically attractive to planters, who could now expect more years of "returns" on their investment.[84] In addition, with the formation of the Royal African Company in 1672, British colonies began to receive a larger supply of enslaved people. When we look beyond strictly economic calculations, there are also indications that planters felt the need to differentiate (white) servants from (black) enslaved people in order to undermine threats of unified resistance. Racially demarcating bonded African labor decidedly enhanced social control, in part because it created a gulf between different orders of poor laborers, thereby undermining their solidarity.[85] So, as the integrated plantation emerged as the most economically viable colonial system of production, so did the Africanization and racial differentiation of the workforce. From the 1660s, we enter a new era in European colonization of the Americas, one resting not only on escalating purchases of enslaved Africans, but also on systematic racialization of them.

As we should by now expect, the Glorious Revolution gave a powerful fillip to the British slave trade. Again, this had to do with war. Following every war from 1688 to 1763, Britain's share of the Atlantic slave trade expanded alongside its colonial and commercial activities. Although the Atlantic slave trade lasted four centuries—from the 1440s to the 1830s—two-thirds of the Africans sent to the New World were shipped between 1698 and 1807.[86] And during that century or so, no nation transported more enslaved people than Britain, and no nation did so more efficiently and profitably. Using calculations of "total factor productivity," economic historians have shown that traders with the Royal African Company were at least one-third more efficient than those who worked out of French slave ports. Logics of measurement, efficiency, and profit per unit of investment enabled RAC traders to carry 50 percent more enslaved people per ton (ship size) and twice as many enslaved people per crew member as did their French rivals.[87] The English capitalist push for efficiencies did not falter when it came to the sale of human captives.

This returns us to Locke, and to persons considered as things. In 1767 at Whydah, in the Dahomey region of West Africa, an enslaved person could be bought for 25 guns, 40 iron bars, 16 anchors of brandy (about 133 gallons), 200 pounds of gunpowder, ten long cloths, and so on.[88] These were commodity exchange ratios, which are simplified when money becomes interchangeable with any good. Nonetheless, that leaves a problem: how to calculate the relative values of enslaved people, who came in different shapes, sizes, ages, and sexes. Here, slave traders developed standardized metrics. Portuguese and Spanish slavers used the term *pieces* (*pieças*), or "pieces of Indies," to this end. One "piece" referred to a fully developed male seven palms high (about five feet tall), still relatively young and in good health. Younger or older males, women and children, those of less robust stature or poorer health would then be measured as fractions of a full "piece." This abstract measure—the piece—thus made every enslaved person commensurable and provided a common measure for pricing, measuring of cargoes, and so on. We can see this logic of reification at work by looking at two 1725 slave shipments to Buenos Aires by the English South Sea Company. In one case, that of the ship *Syrria*, 437 enslaved people were supplied, assessed as equal to almost 326 pieces. The *Asiento*, on the other hand, delivered 278 enslaved people, but according to the official tally provided nearly 209 pieces. So, while 645 enslaved Africans were sold from these two ships, traders received money for slightly fewer than 534 full pieces, concrete persons having been translated into abstract units.[89]

The same quantifying abstraction underlay the procedure of British slave traders who entered each enslaved person they purchased into their ledgers with successive numbers, as if they had purchased units of the same thing.[90] In the US South, about which I shall have more to say in chapter 5, slave traders used a metric scale based on a "number one" enslaved person (similar to a full "piece"), a second-rate one, and so on. They could then adjust for "defects," such as a filter on the eye, which, in the estimation of one nineteenth-century slaver, would subtract between twenty-five and forty dollars from the price for an enslaved girl. Through these procedures of standardization and differentiation, "traders turned people into things and then into money."[91]

Perhaps nothing illustrates the brutality of reification more dramatically than the infamous episode of the *Zong*. The basic facts of this case are clear enough.[92] In September 1781, the slave ship *Zong*, under the command of captain Luke Collingwood, departed from the Guinea coast of Africa for Jamaica carrying 440 enslaved Africans and 17 white crewmen. Naval incompetence and indescribable cruelty resulted in more than sixty Africans perishing en route, alongside seven crew members. In addition, many more enslaved people became ill. Realizing that the latter were "damaged goods" unlikely to fetch much in the Jamaican market, Captain Collingwood decided to take advantage of the owners' insurance contract, under which enslaved people were insured for thirty pounds sterling per head. With this in mind, he ordered that 133 Africans be tossed to their deaths in the sea, intent on claiming that sickness and shortage of water made this a necessary emergency measure—even though steady rain during the two days that preceded the executions of the last twenty-six enslaved people had provided eleven days of full water allowance (and twice that many days at half-water allowance). When the owners' insurance claim was presented to the underwriters in London, the latter refused to make payment, forcing a Guildhall court case in March 1783. Without even leaving the court to deliberate, the jury found against the insurers, ruling that they had an obligation to compensate the slave ship owners for the "property" lost at sea. However, the underwriters appealed this judgement to the Court of King's Bench, where Lord Mansfield heard their case. Mansfield ordered a new trial—but not because of the murderous behavior of Collingwood and his crew. Instead, he questioned whether the circumstances aboard the *Zong* truly constituted a case of "necessity." The morality of the action was not at issue before the court, nor was a legal charge of murder. Solicitor General John Lee, who appeared on behalf of the *Zong*'s owners, had boldly declared during the trial that under English law "it has been decided . . . that a portion of our fellow-creatures may become the subject of property. This therefore was a throwing overboard of *goods*." Mansfield basically concurred: "Though it shocks one very much, the case of slaves was the same as if horses had been thrown overboard."[93]

Let us bracket the question of cruelty toward animals. What stands out here is that enslaved Africans were "the subject of property"—legal possessions, commodities. This is the Lockean principle writ large: that an owner has "absolute power and authority" over what he has purchased with money. When it comes to monetized goods, including persons, owners have claims over them comparable to their rights to life and liberty. Through money, "our fellow creatures may become the subject of property"—or, more accurately in non-legalistic terms, *objects* of property. Indeed, what is most striking about eighteenth-century English debates over the slave trade is that the dominant liberal position was to *expand* the trade by ending the monopoly of the Royal African Company and opening it to all. Rather than the rights of the enslaved, what bothered eighteenth-century liberals were the restrictions placed on the freedom to buy and sell enslaved Africans.

From the standpoint of these liberal critics, the revolution of 1689 changed things for the better. That very year, Parliament passed an act that allowed traders outside the Royal African Company to buy and sell enslaved people. Interlopers had always been a nuisance for the RAC, but now new entrants could legally practice the trade in exchange for a 10 percent duty on all their exports to Africa, payable to the RAC. Known as the "ten percenters," the new players quickly came to dominate the trade, shipping seventy-five thousand enslaved people in the first decade after the business was opened, more than four times the number carried by RAC ships.[94] Still, the free traders were not satisfied. They saw no reason that any payments should be due to the company, and so they agitated for an end to all its privileges. The RAC responded by hiring the political economist Charles Davenant and the novelist Daniel Defoe to produce propaganda on its behalf. Yet, the tides were moving in favor of the free traders. And, with no apparent sense of irony, they publicly equated the RAC monopoly with slavery. The existence of trading monopolies represented "the Badges of a slavish People," declared one pamphleteer, while a Bristol trader proclaimed that "Monopolies in Trade . . . were always esteem'd the greatest Badges of Slavery and Oppression."[95] Slavery was thus defined as any hindrance on an Englishman's right to trade . . . in slaves. Once again, enslaved Africans were possessions; and possessions had no rights, unlike their owners. Under the impact of these liberal arguments, the English slave trade was deregulated in 1712; forty years later the RAC was defunct. In "freeing" the trade, the new entrants thereby also enormously increased the number of Africans sold into bondage. Between 1700 and 1807, British traders exported roughly two and a half million Africans to New World slavery.[96] The victory of liberal free traders meant dramatically more capture, trauma, enslavement, and death for Africans—a horrific increase in blood for money.

Among the liberal slavers who spearheaded this "victory" were two wealthy and influential Whigs prominently associated with the Bank of England: Gilbert Heathcote and Humphrey Morice. Heathcote, a director of the bank for forty years, its governor for five, and a member of Parliament for the better part of three decades, was said to be the wealthiest commoner in England when he died in 1733, with an estimated worth of seven hundred thousand pounds. In concert with his brothers, Heathcote was heavily involved in the colonial trade with Jamaica (and later with the East Indies), agitated on behalf of free trade in African slaves, and was a modest slaver himself.[97] Much more heavily involved was Humphrey Morice, "the foremost London slave merchant of his time," who became a director of the bank in 1716 and its governor in 1727–28. This slave merchant, too, was a member of Parliament, holding a seat from 1713 until 1731. Morice's slave ships accounted for nearly 10 percent of London's capacity in the slave trade, transporting close to twenty thousand Africans to the New World.[98]

We shall explore the relationship between slavery and English banking shortly. But before proceeding, let us return to the case of the *Zong*. Because the enslaved Africans on the ship were insured as commodities, one commentator has suggested that they comprised goods with *imaginary value*. With insurance, says literary theorist Ian Baucom, simply to imagine exchange "is to have created the value." Value was generated, in other words, as soon as the enslaved people were imagined as *sellable*. Under an insurance contract, therefore, the economic values of enslaved people were constituted not through an actual exchange but simply through the (imaginary) possibility of one. It follows, declares Baucom, that the value debated in the court proceedings concerning the *Zong* was constituted through the circuit "money–imagination–money" (rather than Marx's famous general formula for capital, money–commodity–money). Insurance, he insists, provided the "novel epistemology" for the capitalist commodity form, which enabled the imagination "to bring a new world of objects and values into existence." Once this epistemology is in place, once this social imaginary is consolidated, "an actual, literal exchange is no longer necessary."[99] The problems here are manifold. To begin with, long since the rise of modern insurance, billions of *actual* exchanges continue to take place on a daily basis. Yet, it is hard to see why this should be so if the value has merely to be imagined to be realized. Moreover, this goes far beyond the role of insurance, since prices are assigned to goods in stores, in menus, or online—all prior to being sold. All these also acquire values in the imagination, irrespective of insurance. But most crucially, the underpinning role of plantation labor to the traffic in enslaved people entirely vanishes in Baucom's account. The fixation on imaginary value ignores the vital fact that the market values of enslaved people tracked the values of the commodities they produced. Investment in an enslaved person was governed (in market terms) by the values—in sugar, cotton, rice, coffee, tobacco, and so forth—that a "piece" could produce *through its labor* over the course of a normal productive life span.

Rather than imaginary, the values of enslaved Africans were materially grounded in generalized slave labor, that is, in the output that could be reasonably expected from an average enslaved person at average productivity over an average working life (with appropriate price adjustments being made around this norm based on size, age, strength, etc.). When enslaved people were used as collateral for debts—which was incredibly common—what the borrower put up was "collateralized labor," or, more accurately, collateralized future labor.[100] The lender accepted this collateral precisely because an enslaved person represented *labor power*, potential work. To be sure, this futural element built into the purchase of an enslaved person involved an inherent element of risk (the enslaved person might die young, the products of their labor might not fetch an adequate price, etc.), but such risks are associated with every capitalist investment. There was nothing imaginary, however, about the labor of enslaved people in the fields, about the use of violence to discipline and intensify that labor, or about the commodities that slave labor made available to global markets. As Postlethwayte understood in the passage that opens this section, "the Business of *Planting* in our British Colonies, as well as in the *French*, is carried on by the Labour of *Negroes*, imported thither from *Africa*." The whole "magnificent superstructure of American commerce and naval power" was thus constructed "on an African foundation," one that certainly created a social imaginary that informed the categories of race and empire. But it was one grounded in plantation labor and geared to global commodity production.

Colonial Slavery and British Capitalism

For much of the eighteenth century, many of the largest business enterprises in the world operated on the plantations of the Caribbean. By 1775, most enslaved people in the West Indies worked in groups of more than two hundred in "factories in the field" that integrated agricultural and industrial tasks to produce tobacco, sugar, cotton, coffee, and other commodities destined for export markets. By comparison, even sixty years later, the average British cotton mill employed about 175 people. The largest sugar plantations had enslaved workforces of over five hundred and usually included boiling houses, distilleries, curing houses, and large storage facilities. Looked at in financial terms, a late-eighteenth-century sugar plantation might represent a capital investment of more than £30,000 pounds—and some were more than double that amount— at a time when a water-powered cotton mill would have cost £5,000 at most, and even a multistory mill powered by steam would have required £10,000 to £20,000.[101] The New World plantation of the eighteenth century thus involved large-scale mobilization of labor and capital to produce commodities for global markets. C. L. R. James was on point when, in an appendix to his masterpiece, *The Black Jacobins*, he wrote:

> When three centuries ago the slaves came to the West Indies, they entered directly into the large-scale enterprise of the sugar plantation, which was a modern system. It further required that they live together in a social relation far closer than any proletariat of the time. The cane when reaped had to be rapidly transported to what was factory production. The product was shipped abroad for sale. Even the cloth the slaves wore and the food they ate was imported. The Negroes, from the start, lived a life that was in essence a modern life.[102]

Notwithstanding all of this, many scholars remain committed to the view that plantation slavery in the Americas was noncapitalist. For instance, following on the analysis of Eugene Genovese, historian Peter Kolchin has argued that plantation slavery could not be considered a capitalist formation, because "the market was conspicuously absent" in relations between masters and enslaved people, unlike in those between capitalists and wage laborers.[103] The questions raised by such reasoning are manifold; however, in lieu of an extensive critique of this position, I here restrict the discussion to two points of key theoretical importance.[104]

First, let us consider an argument made by economic historian Jairus Banaji in the 1970s, in which he pointed out that Marx uses the term "mode of production" (*Produktionweise*) in two distinctive ways—one referring to the immediate labor process, and another describing epochal *systems*, or social forms, of production. The latter, he rightly insisted, is the more complex and developed concept, as it is meant to grasp the "laws of motion," or the dynamic social processes, by which a specific form of production is reproduced across historical time. What is critical to capitalism is that individual units of capital reproduce themselves by appropriating surplus value through production of commodities—and essential tasks related to that production—in a context of market competition. This requires that these units match or better the average costs (and times) of production, which are expressed in market prices. While capitalism may well show a historical tendency toward wage labor as the predominant *immediate* relation of production, this need not be the only form of commodity production and surplus value appropriation. This is why Marx could describe cotton-producing plantation slavery in the US South as generating "surplus value," and why creative Marxists, such as Rosa Luxemburg, could analyze "capitalist accumulation with forms of slavery and serfdom." Rather than a formal equation of capitalism with wage labor, capitalist production is theorized here as a complex and dynamic system in which capital reproduces itself by appropriating surplus value from a diverse set of commodity-producing workers.[105]

A second theoretical observation is in order. In a very different tradition from Banaji, so-called political Marxists have made *market dependence* the definitional feature of capitalism.[106] By this they mean that in the capitalist mode of production, both producers (workers) and appropriators (capitalists) are dependent on the market for their survival. Workers rely on the market to find buyers of their labor power in exchange for a wage, which they then use to buy the means of life; while capitalists must purchase all the inputs required for production—raw materials, machines, labor power—and must sell their finished good or service on the market in order to pay these costs (and reap a profit). Members of both groups thus rely on the market to reproduce themselves economically. Moreover, competition dictates that, as a rule, goods and services can only be sold at or below competitive market prices. This compels capitalists to meet or exceed average times and costs of production in order to reap a profit at prevailing prices. Working with this view of capitalism as systematic market dependence, John Clegg has concluded that "Antebellum plantations were capitalist . . . for the simple reason that land and slaves could only be acquired through markets, typically on credit. Only a profitable plantation could afford these inputs, and if a planter failed to produce cotton at a competitive cost he would be threatened with foreclosure."[107]

With these insights in mind, let us return to the site of production. The large integrated plantation based on gang labor was the centerpiece of colonial slave production. The term "integrated" refers to the coordination of calibrated agricultural and industrial tasks within a unitary process of producing finished commodities. This plantation model developed first in Barbados in the 1650s, then spread to Jamaica and the Chesapeake region of the United States in the early 1700s. By the middle of the eighteenth century, these units of plantation production would come to play a decisive role in the Atlantic economy. However, before the integrated plantation could sink roots, the problem of labor discipline had first to be solved. The management of a hundred or more enslaved people involved significant challenges with respect to coordination and domination. The more difficult of these was domination, as it required creating a stratum of white "overseers" prepared to solve "the problem of discipline through the application of terror," as Atlantic historian Trevor Burnard put it. This, he argues, required turning men with military experience—who had themselves been subjected to ruthless discipline and corporal punishment, like the lash—into the administrators of plantation violence.[108]

The brutal industrial despotism of the integrated plantation was racialized from the start. Indeed, the social mechanisms did not exist for subjecting European workers to this degree of systematic workplace violence. In her history of tobacco production in the Chesapeake, Lorena Walsh shows that the labor regimes introduced by planters collided sharply with the customs of English workers with respect to holidays, food, and the pace of work. Deploying enslaved Africans, they felt, gave them greater leeway to increase the number of workdays, add night work, put women in the fields, and intensify the pace of work.[109] Much of this involved the extension of working time—a quantitative increase in labor hours, or what Marx called increases in *absolute surplus value*—rather than greater productivity per hour worked.[110] So successful were planters in implementing this system that plantation management also provided a model for factory organization and industrial discipline in both Britain and North America.[111] Precisely because this regime degraded customary expectations of (relatively) freer migrant laborers from Europe, the disciplinary technologies of the plantation tended to separate Europeans and Africans according to conditions of work and life. Thus, it is perhaps unsurprising that the white overseers were not only assigned to new practices of supervision and violent discipline of enslaved people, but also brought into local militias as protection against foreign invasion and slave rebellion.[112]

Historically, industrial organization and labor discipline have been crucial to capitalist output and productivity. In the case of the English factory system, before output and productivity could be systematically raised, despotic control over labor had first to be established.[113] And so it was on the slave plantation as well. Once the new regime based on gang labor was consolidated—or developed in hybrid combinations of gang and task labor, as in tobacco farming[114]—the productivity of slave labor rose significantly. Over the period 1674 to 1790, for instance, plantation productivity in Barbados doubled, much of the increase coming in the first thirty years of the eighteenth century as the gang labor system was perfected. Comparing it to North American agricultural production based on "free labor," three historians conclude that the slave plantation was "a dynamic and parallel route to higher per capita output," though much of this may have had to do with large increases in hours worked per year.[115] But beyond increased work hours per enslaved person, there was also a strong trend toward increased productivity per enslaved person (that is, in their output per hour). In the US South, for instance, the average daily amount of cotton picked per enslaved person quadrupled between 1801 and 1862, which translates into rising output of about 2.3 percent per enslaved person each year.[116] These leaps in the productivity of slave labor were not unique to the United States. By the nineteenth century, slave productivity in Cuba, Brazil, and the US South displayed sustained vitality. In this era of the "second slavery," steam power, the vacuum pan, mechanized sugar mills, the cotton gin, and revolutionary new means of transportation, notably the steamboat and railroad, were systematically developed, all of which contributed to more vigorous growth of plantation output in both sugar and coffee.[117] Slave-driven plantation production was also consistently profitable: one well-documented study suggests an average rate of profit of 10 percent for the British West Indies as a whole between 1749 and 1834.[118] It may be an exaggeration when one historian writes, "No economic activity in the Old World could match the productivity possible on New World plantations."[119] But there can be no doubt that, in Marxian terms, New World slavery comprised a dynamic surplus value-producing sphere of global capitalist accumulation.

Yet, if plantation slavery was a vigorous element in a capitalist world economy, this does not entirely vindicate the claims of Eric Williams's *Capitalism and Slavery* (1944). Pioneering book though it was, Williams overstated the link between plantation profits and the Industrial Revolution in England. And he was overly deterministic in suggesting that British abolition of the slave trade in 1807 (and then of slavery itself in 1833) was due to declining economic viability of the plantation system in the face of rising industrial capitalism. However, the shift of British capitalism's center of gravity toward manufacturing industries (and related changes in trade patterns) may indeed have facilitated the abolition of the slave trade, and then of slavery itself in the British Empire.[120] Moreover, Williams posed vital questions concerning slavery, colonialism, and the rise of capitalism that have too often been neglected or dismissed outright, and his identification of modern racism as rooted in slavery was prescient.[121] Recent scholarship inspired by Williams has also convincingly demonstrated that while plantation slavery "did not cause the industrial revolution," it did play "an active role in its pattern and timing."[122]

If there is any agreement among historians about the Industrial Revolution in Britain, it concerns its "takeoff" between 1760 and 1820.[123] And while the growth of the home market must be seen as a central driver of this process, there can be little doubt that it was considerably accelerated by colonial exports. During the last two decades of the eighteenth century—a crucial moment in the industrial takeoff in Britain—almost 60 percent of increased industrial output was exported.[124] And exports to Africa and America led the way. At the beginning of the century, just as the large integrated plantation was emerging, merely 10 percent of British exports went to those regions; by the end of the century it was 40 percent. During the critical third quarter of the century (1750–75), nearly two-thirds of Britain's increased exports derived from expanding sales in Africa and America.[125] Most importantly, manufacturing industries were prime beneficiaries of export growth, as fully one-third of British manufactured output went to foreign markets during the first three-quarters of the century, with Africa and America once more in the forefront.[126] In a critical industry like iron, 40 percent of the growth in output was export-driven in the 1760s.[127] Finally, a considered estimate suggests that in the period 1775–1815, a quarter or more of fixed capital formation in Britain came from domestic reinvestment of profits from the triangular trade.[128] While Williams overstated the contribution of triangular trade wealth to British industrialization, there is still much to be said for his insight about the crucial interconnections of slavery, colonial trade, and industrial capitalism in Britain.

These interconnections pivoted, of course, on money and finance. Both the slave trade and plantation investment revolved around expanding networks of transatlantic credit.[129] To begin with, cargoes of enslaved people were turned over to sales agents, or "factors," in towns like Kingston, Jamaica. Rarely would a factor be able to sell enslaved people for full price up front. Instead, planters would typically make a cash down payment supplemented by a sequence of bills (promises to pay) falling due on a series of future dates. The factor would take his cut (some of it in IOUs) and then remit an interest-bearing bill of exchange to the slave merchant based in Liverpool, Bristol, London, or another slave port.[130]

Foreign bills of exchange—by which merchants based in one country could make payments in local currencies in another—developed in the late sixteenth century. Essentially, these bills enabled merchants to borrow in one market against cash surpluses they held in another. This might allow a London-based trader to make a payment in francs in Paris based on cash reserves they held in pounds in London. All that was necessary was that another trader would like to borrow some of their pounds. Bills of exchange thus facilitated elaborate networks of global credit. They enabled trade and payments in circumstances in which merchants did not have immediate access to the currencies they needed. By allowing our London trader to make a payment in France based on what was effectively a check drawn on pounds in a London bank, bills of exchange fostered trade where local currency was unavailable. More than this, however, such bills soon became transferable, so that a promise to pay could be passed through a long chain of transactions as means of payment before being finally retired. Through these instruments, for example, an IOU that merchant A (perhaps a London-based dealer in enslaved Africans) held from merchant B (say, a slave trader in Jamaica) could be remitted to a wine dealer in Portugal, who might then use it to repay a debt in Amsterdam, and so on. In this way, the bill of exchange became a depersonalized financial instrument, no longer dependent upon the personal credit of one trader with another but, instead, moving through a largely abstract international credit system. In the Atlantic slave trade, the bodies of enslaved Africans thus became the material foundation for a global system of financial credit. Congealed within these transatlantic bills of exchange was the blood and sweat of New World slaves. Also crystallized there was the blood of war. In fact, the Thirty Years' War (1618–48) stimulated the first great explosion in the volume of bills of exchange transacted, as such bills enabled a merchant to buy provisions on behalf of a government for an army fighting in foreign lands.[131] But, it was the massive growth in the transatlantic slave trade immediately after those decades of war that drove global credit transactions to an even higher level, reminding us again of the intricate interconnections among war, slavery, and global finance.

Indeed, this is a sphere in which we ought to acknowledge Williams's insights into the connections of large British banking houses, especially Barclays and Baring Brothers, to the slave trade and West Indian plantations. Two members of the Barclay family were active participants in the slave trade, one of them the owner of a large Jamaican plantation.[132] Moreover, Baring Brothers not only had roots in the business of transatlantic slaving, but also served as foreign banker to the United States government in the early nineteenth century, selling bonds from the Consolidated Association of Planters of Louisiana on international markets. Through their sale, secured by planters' estates and the enslaved people they owned, Baring Brothers "turned lands and slaves into paper—paper that was readily convertible into gold, " as one historian puts it.[133] The metamorphosis of blood into money had become a cornerstone of global finance.

Financial Revolution, Talking Coins, and Bourgeois Self-Mastery

The period of the Bank of England's creation has frequently been referred to as one of "financial revolution." It might also be described as the original era of financialization, both in terms of material transactions and the social imaginary. As banknotes proliferated and stock markets expanded, new financial instruments captured the popular imagination. One observer worried, in 1694, that traders were increasingly preoccupied with finance rather than conventional business: "Now almost their whole Discourse is of Lottery-Tickets, Annuities, Bank-Bills, &c. and in contriving how they may draw their Money out of Trade, to put it upon some of these late Funds."[134] Too often, financialization of this sort is treated as entirely a cultural transformation, simply the product of new imaginings and novel epistemologies.[135] Yet, as one economic historian has remarked, the "transferable and negotiable claims" that were embodied in shares of early trading companies (such as the East India Company and the Royal African Company) were claims upon "the stocks of fixed capital embodied in the thousands of oceangoing vessels" and on "the stocks of inventory capital carried in their cargo holds."[136] Yet, even this is to mystify. For the term *inventory capital* functions to occlude, to invisibilize the *human* cargoes compressed into ships' holds. To be sure, the imagination was very much involved in identifying share certificates in trading companies as financial commodities capable of being purchased like flour or beer. But these symbolic conjurings were bound up with real social-material transactions, with circuits of capital, labor, and human bodies.

It might seem that things changed once the commodification of public debt became central to financial markets. After all, the heart of the financial revolution of the century after 1694 was the sober and ostensibly orderly London stock market, where trading consisted primarily of the buying and selling of shares in a handful of large joint-stock companies, including the Bank of England, the New East India Company, and from 1711, the South Sea Company. All these firms were heavily involved in lending to government. Their capital consisted, significantly, of shares in the national debt, which was in large part what investors purchased when they bought their stock. Yet, as we have seen, shares in the public debt were not evidence that property had become "imaginary." Markets in government debt were underpinned by a very real political economy of taxation—that is, deductions from the wealth generated by the production and exchange of commodities. In fact, throughout the century of financial revolution, English tax revenues rose much more rapidly than did national income—and ultimately it was this that made debt finance possible.[137]

To be sure, financial markets were expanding, and this owed much to the increasing liquidity of shares, which insured that no investor would be obliged to hold company stock or certificates of government debt when they wanted to cash in. By the early eighteenth century, a buyer could always be found in London's stock market. It has been estimated, for instance, that about five thousand people owned government-related stock in 1694, a number that doubled by 1709, then quadrupled to forty thousand by 1719.[138] By that point, government debt was thoroughly depersonalized; it was generic rather than specific, its price resting not on the personal ties between the monarch and goldsmith bankers, but on prices determined by thousands of market participants. This was a boon to the state, as a mass market for its debt meant considerably lower interest rates.

With these novel financial instruments and practices came new modes of behavior, fresh anxieties, and emergent sensibilities, including aesthetic and cultural forms. Recall that paper claims to a share of forthcoming corporate profits or as-yet-uncollected taxes are futural in character—they represent *fictitious* assets, values that are yet to be created, and might not come to pass. A culture of speculation and risk thus accompanied England's financial revolution, as investors had to calculate investments based on assessments of *possible* values and profits. This reactivated long-standing apprehensions about the dangers of "imaginary wealth," and concerns that society was now unmoored from stable foundations.[139] Much of this sense of uncertainty was negotiated by way of information exchanged and sales conducted in coffeehouses, through the dissemination of financial market information in newspapers, and by the exploration of new and increasingly unstable identities in novels, broadsheets, periodicals, and the like. The new bourgeois public sphere represented by the coffeehouse, the newspaper, and the novel was a thoroughly financialized one.

What was happening in coffeehouses and the stock exchange was one thing, and certainly of interest. But parallel processes of commodification and monetization affecting the poor were lived in very different registers. From the sixteenth century onward, as we have seen, enclosure and dispossession had pushed millions from the land, many of whom moved from parish to parish in search of alms and wages. Draconian legislation was regularly passed to regulate, supervise, and punish these "vagrants," "rogues," and "drudges."[140] When they pilfered and stole to survive, their bodies were again subjected to the monetary calculus—their punishment governed by the "value" of the crime. In the court records for London's Old Bailey in January 1715, writes Peter Linebaugh, "We observe a relationship between 10d. and a whipping, between 4s.10d. and a branded hand, and between large sums of money and hanging."[141]

By the eighteenth century, money was also increasingly deployed as an incentive to apprehend ostensible vagrants. A 1713 law offered constables two shillings for every person turned over to a justice of the peace, an amount that was increased to five shillings in 1744. The 1744 law also doubled the reward (to ten shillings) for the snatching of "rogues and vagabonds."[142] Monetary values were thereby attached directly to the bodies of the poor. They now had prices on their heads, even if not so dramatically as did convicts and indentured servants, who were routinely bought and sold, as were wives from about 1740. Analyzing wife sale, E. P. Thompson pointed out the ways in which its "symbolism was derived from the market," noting that this social transaction "borrowed the forms of the malt, cheese or butter market, and subsequently . . . those of the cattle market or horse fair."[143] And when it comes to the selling of convicts and servants to America, it is revealing that England's first Contractor for Transports to the Government was "well versed in the management of human cargoes," having earlier acquired experience in the slave trade.[144] As I have shown elsewhere, the poor experienced the expanding regime of wage labor as a demonic system in which their bodies and freedom of movement were regularly relinquished for money.[145] From rewards for apprehending vagrants, to wife sale, to the selling of convicts, to the wage system, "the methods set out to handle the movements of the wandering poor entailed monetary transactions at every turn."[146]

Let us recall the reification at the heart of the market in human laboring capacities. It was not just fines and penalties that inscribed the power of money on poor bodies. Wage labor itself did that. After all, the survival of a wage worker depends on selling body and soul to an employer—over and over again. The worker, writes Marx, "sells at auction eight, ten, twelve, fifteen hours of his life, day after day, to the highest bidder . . . to the capitalist." As a result, the life energy of the worker becomes a commodity that is "made over to another."[147] Wage earners are thus obliged to treat themselves (or at least their working energies) as a thing, a commodity, in order to earn that other thing—money—that makes life possible in a capitalist society.

It thus comes as little surprise to discover that the social imaginary overflowed with images of persons as things and as money—and of things and money as persons. In *Capital*, volume 1, Marx asks us to imagine that "commodities could speak."[148] At least sixty literary texts published in eighteenth-century England allowed them to do precisely that.[149] In works such as *The Adventures of a Pin*, *The Adventures of a Cork-Screw*, *The Adventures of a Black Coat*, and dozens more, commodities narrated their lives. The appetite of the reading public for such texts was insatiable: "Other speaking objects," writes Christopher Flint, "include a settee, a sofa, a bedstead, a pulpit, a reading desk, a mirror, an old shoe, a smock, a waistcoat, a wig, a watch, a ring, an umbrella, a gold-headed cane, a sedan, a pincushion, a thimble, a top, a pen, an old pocket Bible, and a stagecoach." Particularly intriguing are tales of talking money, which included guineas, shillings, banknotes, rupees, sovereigns, and pennies.[150] All of these are fables of travel, adventure, misfortune, and uncertainty. Of course, precisely this was also the story of millions of working-class lives in an age of displacement, migration, and fear of calamity. Whether by relocating for service in husbandry, moving to London in pursuit of work, or emigrating to the Americas as a servant, the poor were on the move as never before. The random, indefinite, sometimes dangerous circulation of a coin or a banknote thus mimicked the precarious movements of working-class people. People who moved *in search of* money might thus readily identify themselves *with* money, the very object they pursued. It is a short leap from there to imagine money that talks. Identification with money was about more than the fact that the poor had monetary prices on their heads, though it definitely included that. It was also about lives that felt as uncertain and perilous as that of a coin moving from pocket to purse, from ship hold to lockbox.

In 1710, Joseph Addison published the earliest story of talking money, relating the adventures of a shilling with "a wonderful inclination to ramble." In the course of its escapades, the coin is exchanged for meat, bread, a book of plays, sex, and brandy, and is given as wages to a soldier. It eventually falls into the hands of a clipper, only to be melted down and reminted, presumably in the Great Recoinage of 1696.[151] But no novel of a talking coin was as successful as Charles Johnstone's *Chrysal: Or the Adventures of a Guinea* (1760), which went into its third edition within two years and was expanded into a four-volume work (from two) in 1765. "I can see your thoughts," the gold coin tells its readers, announcing that it also has "a power of entering into the hearts of the immediate possessors of our bodies." Here we have a classic dialectical reversal: the possessor of the coin turns out to be possessed *by* it. As much as one seems to control the body of a coin, it in fact grips our souls. "When the mighty spirit of a large mass of gold takes possession of the powers of the human heart, it influences all its actions," the coin explains.[152]

Few writers engaged the issues of money, commodification, and possessed individuals more obsessively than Daniel Defoe, known best for his novel *Robinson Crusoe*. Published anonymously, as were all his major writings, *Robinson Crusoe* went through four editions in 1719 alone and continued to sell well throughout the century. It was lauded by Jean-Jacques Rousseau in his *Émile* (1762) and went on in edited versions to become "one of the most popular children's books ever written."[153] Much of the text, as in most of Defoe's novels, revolves around migration and travel. The protagonist (and this applies to *Moll Flanders* and *Colonel Jack* as well) travels in search of money and fortune, but also in search of self—in particular, a self that can prosper in a world dominated by the cash nexus. Yet, ventures after money—which for the unfortunate often involve thieving, prostitution, lying, and deception—are all too often self-destructive. Defoe tracks possessed individuals, moving haphazardly through the world much like the coin that randomly finds itself in a pocket, a butcher's hand, or a ship captain's lockbox. His writings display an anxiety of entrapment by money and the market. Defoe frequently bemoans how the pursuit of money distorts and deforms us—even calling it a "drug." And Crusoe, abandoned on his island, asks of a box of coins, "What art thou good for?"[154] Of course, he knows very well that money sets the rules of the game in our society. And Defoe, who himself endured bankruptcy and was incarcerated in London's Newgate Prison, was intent on establishing his bourgeois respectability, as were the central characters of his novels. Amid hunger, homelessness, crime, and brushes with the law, Defoe discerns moments where his protagonists might turn over a new leaf, where they might put their money to honest use. And this is the task set before his characters: to carve out an honorable independence in a world dominated by money. Having been money's slave, they must acquire self-mastery in market society.

There is clearly a gendered dimension to Defoean self-mastery in the world of money. To begin with, he typically portrays money itself as feminine. In his *Review of the State of the English Nation*, he introduced money's "younger Sister," named "Lady Credit," as a "coy Lass," whose mysteries must be divined if the (male) individual is to be successful in "courting her." Lady Credit is both necessary to the wealth of the nation and dangerous to those "who lose her Favour." Yet, the paradox of credit is that she woos those who have no need of her. "Punctual honourable dealing" keeps one always in her good graces, in part by reducing dependence on her.[155] The goal is thus masculine autonomy, and in the world of money, keeping Lady Money and Lady Credit in check by taming one's passions and whims, particularly the desire to "ramble."[156] If independence is a quintessentially male virtue for Defoe, dependence on money is feminine. It means being prey to one's passions, rather than disciplined and self-regulating. It means not only being dominated by money, but actually reduced to it. As he wrote in *Moll Flanders*, a woman on her own "is just like a bag of money or a jewel dropped on the highway, which is prey to the next comer."[157] To be without money, and thus prey to the vagaries of the market, is to be dependent, feminized, and enslaved.

Crucially—and this is a point that has not received adequate attention in the literature—mastering oneself is often accomplished in Defoe by way of becoming an actual *master over others*. In transcending enslavement to his own passions and to those sisters, Money and Credit, Defoe's characters often turn slave master. Self-mastery thus has its dialectical twin, for Defoe, in lordship over bonded persons. Internal bonds are removed by way of external bondage—by literally shackling others. Let us recall that Robinson Crusoe had himself been enslaved. Yet, he does not hesitate to sell a human being who had befriended him and assisted his escape; to enslave another (to whom he gives the name, "Friday") on his Island; to buy European servants and enslaved Africans for his New World plantation; or to pursue full-fledged slave trading in his long journey to personal freedom and prosperity. Where Crusoe erred, Defoe instructs us, was in choosing the rambling life of the slave trader over the settled existence of the planter, one who uses enslaved people productively, rather than engaging in risky slaving expeditions.[158]

We observe similar dynamics in *Colonel Jack*, which Defoe published in 1722, three years after *Robinson Crusoe*. In the novel, a young waif, who has spent his childhood and adolescence thieving and picking pockets, is captured by kidnappers and sold into servitude in colonial Virginia. Bondage provides a certain rite of passage, however, and he eventually gets promoted to the role of plantation overseer. As an overseer, he not only earns the respect of his master but, ultimately, his own estate, worked by European servants and enslaved Africans. In the transition from slavery to mastery, he is "made a man," crucially by learning to use the whip on people enslaved on plantations, who must be "ruled with a rod of iron, beaten with scorpions," yet shown occasional mercy.[159] In contrast to Hegel's dialectic, in which it is the enslaved person who, through labor, achieves spiritual growth and self-mastery, dialectical transformation occurs for Defoe on the side of the master, through his work of domination over enslaved people.

Defoe's novelistic sympathies with slavery were no mere literary conceit. He, too, was an investor in the Royal African Company, for which his first patron, Sir Dalby Thomas, had been an agent-general. In a series of pamphlets, including *An Essay upon the Trade to Africa* (1711), *A Brief Account of the State of the African Trade* (1713), and *A Plan of the English Commerce* (1728), he stridently defended the trade in bonded persons. And for years he used his *Review of the State of the English Nation* to advocate on behalf of the trade and in support of the slaving activities of the South Sea Company, in particular.[160] The latter case is particularly interesting, as it returns us to the rise of modern money and the Bank of England.

Slavery, the South Sea Bubble, and the Bank of England

The South Sea Company was launched in 1711 as yet another instrument for financing government war debt. It originated from the desire of the new Tory prime minister, Robert Harley, to retire considerable short-term debt (nine million pounds) that had accumulated during the ongoing War of the Spanish Succession (1701–14). For political reasons, Harley mistrusted the Whig directors of the bank and sought to create a rival to it while also ridding himself of a financial headache. He had no idea that his new company would soon be a financial rage.

Under the terms of the South Sea Act, those holding this nine million pounds in state debt could exchange it for shares of the newly incorporated South Sea Company, which was given a monopoly on British trade to the South Seas. Such a debt-for-equity swap had already been undertaken by the Bank of England in 1697, when it engrafted eight hundred thousand pounds of short-term government bonds in exchange for bank stock.

Soon after the South Sea Company's inception, the war with Spain brought into British hands the *asiento*, by which the Spanish government had conferred on merchants exclusive rights to supply enslaved people to Spain's American colonies. Now, the British government controlled this privilege. The Tory government quickly vested it with the South Sea Company. Under the terms of the agreement, the company was contracted to deliver annually up to forty-eight hundred "pieces" to Spanish America for a period of thirty years. Inspired by the profits to be made in the slave trade, English investors now flocked to the Company. Its shares, which had been floundering in the £70 to £80 range throughout 1712, commenced a sustained rise, reaching £97 in June 1713.

With these developments, English public debt was more directly tied to slave trading than ever before. In 1714, its first full year of slaving, the South Sea Company transported 22 percent of all enslaved people carried on English ships, a proportion it more or less maintained for several years. As it shipped and sold bonded Africans, it prospered handsomely. The company found new investors, recorded strong profits, and watched its share price rise to £100 by May 1715, and £115 in 1718.[161] Every member of the royal family subscribed to its stock, as did the lord chancellor and the speaker of the House—all anticipating the profits of trade in enslaved Africans. Defoe, too, saw great fortune in slaving, extolling the company's operations as a boon to the Royal African Company since they would provide "an Opportunity of Vending great Numbers of *Negroes* to the *Spaniards*."[162] The South Sea Company had now joined the Bank of England and the East India Company as a pillar of England's financial markets. Yet, it was the fortunes of war that had brought these profits of slaving. War's misfortunes might equally undo them. And in 1718, after a clash with the Royal Navy, Spain terminated the company's trade with its colonies. This was the turning point, the beginning of the company's decline. Yet, many historical accounts, reluctant to acknowledge that the South Sea Company rose on the backs of enslaved Africans, ignore or downplay its loss of the *asiento* in explaining its demise.[163] Instead, they focus entirely on its financial machinations of 1719–20 (to which I turn in a moment). However, it was only as its core business—slaving—declined that the South Sea Company resorted to financial shortcuts. As economic historian Carl Wennerlind rightly notes, "It was only towards the end of 1718, when the company's access to the slave trade was terminated . . . that the company looked to John Law's financial wizardry in Paris for ideas on how to make its stocks appreciate without an underlying revenue source."[164]

The next phase—that of financial machination—began with a plan to absorb all of the public debt not held by the Bank of England or the East India Company. Once again, the company would receive payment for taking on government debt, and it would issue company stock in return to holders of that debt. Now it was just a matter of the company devising financial schemes to push up its share price, which jumped to £335 on April 27, from £288 merely two weeks earlier. Rising share prices easily enticed investors to convert their government debt into company stock. Emboldened by its increasing stock price, the company then offered a new round of public debt conversion, this time merely requiring of buyers that they put down margin payments of between 10 and 20 percent of the full share price. Feverish buying, much of it on margin, now kicked in, and the stock hit £950 at the beginning of July. A full-scale mania was in swing, and it spilled across the market. In the climate of financial euphoria, new companies were conjured into being and their shares "hawked up and down Exchange Alley," notwithstanding that many of them were "quite blatantly swindles."[165] By this point, the bubble was also being inflated by foreign speculation, which had been hugely stimulated by the Mississippi Bubble sweeping French markets.[166] Once this stage had been reached, the South Sea Company was probably purchasing its own stock in order to keep the wave rising. It then brought things to the bursting point by "lending on stock": namely, loaning money for further share purchases against its existing stock (or mere *promises* to buy that stock) as the collateral. In effect, it is as if you let people borrow from you on the "security" of the IOUs they already held with you. In other words, it is as if you were to extend more credit to people based on the fact that they already owe you money. In this house of mirrors, ludicrously overvalued stock was backing purchases of additional inflated shares. By early August 1720, the company had lent over £11 million on the security of its own stock, or pledges to buy it.[167]

All bubbles burst, and it was now just a question of when. In late August, the share price entered a slide. Then, the company's primary banker, the Hollow Sword Blade Company, collapsed when its creditors wanted real money, not IOUs. A full-fledged panic ensued. In the month leading up to September 24, South Sea stock plummeted from £820 to £370. By early December, it was at £191, having lost 80 percent of its market value in just over three months. Wealth was being savaged, fortunes lost—including a staggering £20,000 by the "disinclined to mercy" master of the mint, Isaac Newton.[168] Even Defoe, ever the financial enthusiast, began to doubt the new culture built around "Lady Credit."[169]

There was one potential savior on the horizon—the Bank of England—and it held all the cards that mattered. In October 1722, after tough bargaining, it agreed to purchase £4.2 million worth of South Sea Company stock in return for £200,000 per year in annuity payments. In other words, in return for ongoing payments, the bank absorbed the bulk of South Sea Stock and provided cash to owners of the stock, thus calming the market and providing the company's stockholders with a return on investment. This was a blatant financial rescue by the bank, which stabilized things and expanded its capital base, while reducing that of the company by £4 million.[170] The South Sea Company hung on, continuing to trade in enslaved people for another decade, but the Bank of England no longer had a serious rival. It had become the uncontested pivot of England's financial system. When war returned twenty years later, again with France, so did the government's need for massive emergency funding. Once more, the bank, and the bank alone, was the decisive instrument of war finance.

In 1742, the bank extended an interest-free loan of £1.6 million to finance the latest war, receiving in return a twenty-one-year extension of its charter. Four years later, it agreed to fund nearly £1 million in Exchequer bills, and to lend an additional £1 million against the land and malt taxes. Another £3 million in departmental debts was financed in 1749. Over the decade, financial markets calmly bought up a £25 million addition to the national debt, nearly all of it administered by the bank.[171] Underlying all of this was the circulation of banknotes, which the market validated as money on par with gold coins (guineas) long before the state did. Legal recognition of this would have to wait for Lord Mansfield's acknowledgement, in 1758, that banknotes "are as much money, as guineas themselves are."[172] But here, the courts simply recognized what private market actors had long ago affirmed.

Money was now a privately generated credit medium, grounded in the national debt, but validated in financial markets. As economist Glyn Davies notes, "For the first time in history money was being substantially created, not ostentatiously and visibly by the sovereign power, but mundanely by market forces."[173] Moreover, as we've seen, money's essential structure was now futural—resting primarily not on past labor (embodied in gold or silver) but on future wealth in the form of as-yet-uncollected tax receipts that would be used to pay interest on public debt. Of course, it shared this futural structure with all the paper instruments traded on markets. A stock purchase, after all, amounts in the first instance to a wager that the money invested will entitle its holder to a cut of future corporate profits (what we now call a dividend). This is also why financial bubbles, like that surrounding South Sea stock, are an endemic feature of the futural form of capitalist credit markets. Notwithstanding the obsessive efforts of market analysts at prediction, the future is inherently uncertain and unknowable, and capitalist markets regularly overshoot—especially when they are encouraged to do so by financial institutions, speculative fevers, central bank policy, and so on.

To ease anxieties about the volatility and instability of bank money and credit instruments, government insisted that banknotes remain tied, however tenuously, to gold. For reasons we have seen, this tie was especially important for global finance, where world money was necessary to the conduct of international trade and payments. But bullion also played a considerable role in anchoring the domestic monetary system. Indeed, one of the reasons Parliament decided in 1696 to recoin at existing weights and values, as Locke recommended, may have been to reinforce *paper* money. In so doing, it reassured those who received banknotes (linked to the public debt) that they might always cash them in for coins, which would embody unchanging quantities of silver or gold. In the eyes of recipients, therefore, the tying of bank money to stable amounts of precious metal appeared to be a protection against devaluation.[174]

This comprised much of the domestic rationale for the so-called "gold standard" in Britain. Specie—money in the form of metallic coins—did not actually anchor the financial system, even if most poor people used coins rather than bills. Instead, the financial system (consisting of markets in government debt, stocks, and other paper instruments) revolved around banknotes and credit monies issued by country banks, along with private credit monies, like bills of exchange, circulated by firms. At the beginning of the eighteenth century, the value of banknotes in circulation amounted to between £1 million and £2 million. By century's end, £15 million in Bank of England notes flowed through the economy, alongside another £10 million issued by country banks, which operated locally.[175] As the monetary system transitioned to this modern credit money, specie served increasingly as a "legitimating device," rather than as means of exchange and payment.[176] Gold reserves projected the image of a system resting on the solid foundation of precious metal, even if the real gravitational center was elsewhere. To be sure, the Bank of England kept significant stocks of gold and silver coinage as a reserve, in the event of a public loss of confidence in notes. But at times of war and financial distress, convertibility of notes for specie was frequently suspended. Indeed, when war with France broke out in 1797, the suspension of convertibility was to last nearly a quarter century (1797–1821). Yet the financial system soldiered on with a paper pound. When convertibility was resumed, the government also accepted what the markets had long ago decided by making gold, not silver, the metallic basis of the pound.[177]

This "gold standard" was also meant to have a disciplinary function by linking the creation of credit money to a physical stock of gold. This, it was argued, would constrain the production of bank money by enabling holders of notes to cash in for gold whenever the supply of the former became excessive. We see this rationale in the parliamentary *Bullion Report* of 1810, which recommended that the bank's notes should be convertible to gold. Concerned about a 45 percent growth in the volume of notes between 1798 and 1809 to cover the costs of war, the authors of the report argued, "No safe, certain, and constantly adequate provision against an excess of paper currency . . . can be found, except in the convertibility of all such paper into specie."[178] It would be another decade before the state adopted the main recommendation of the report, which it reaffirmed in the Bank Charter Act of 1844. However, the operation of this ostensible gold standard, which became international during its heyday (1821–1914), was much more complicated than theory suggested. Rather than a more or less automatic market mechanism, it also involved coordinated action by central banks, albeit not on the scale of central bank action today. Nevertheless, central banks operated a sort of managed gold standard, led by the Bank of England, in which interest rates, lending, and the supply of money were deliberately manipulated.[179] Yet, the link to gold remained, and it constrained what central banks could do much of the time (outside of war, when conversion to gold was frequently suspended). The legal tie to gold did more than enforce deflationary financial discipline when the production of credit monies had gone too far. It also enforced *wage deflation* during periodic depressions, thus providing for the discipline of labor. By constraining borrowing, higher interest rates had the effect of reducing purchases and investment across the economy, which translated into growing unemployment and downward pressure on wages. Adherence to the gold standard thereby imposed monetary discipline upon labor, reinforcing the power of employers over the working class. And such wage deflation, it was hoped, would ultimately restore profitability and new investment—since lower wages eventually make it viable for some capitalist to restart production and undertake new business spending. In this crucial sense, the gold standard, while it did not govern the production of money, served as an effective instrument of class war against labor.

The conflicting imperatives that characterized money's second modal form were expressed in its hybrid combination of metallic and credit monies, which produced enduring contradictions. As Marx realized, the Bank of England was called upon to serve two masters: the capitalist *credit system*, with its range of paper credit monies that lubricated business and accelerated accumulation; and the gold-based *monetary system*, which required on-demand convertibility of credit money into coins and bullion, and could thus bring the economy to a crashing halt during a panic. A credit and banking crisis, in which people rushed to convert all paper currencies into the most secure form of money—gold— would inevitably induce a drain on the Bank of England's reserves. In response, the bank would react by raising interest rates in order to draw gold back into its orbit (either through attracting direct deposits of gold, or of cash that could be used to buy gold). The reflux of gold to the bank would eventually cut short the monetary crisis and reimpose wage discipline on workers, albeit at the cost of exacerbating the economic crisis, since higher interest rates would discourage borrowing to spend and invest—even though the latter is exactly what a capitalist economy needs to get out of a slump. Under the classical gold standard, to quote Marx, "as soon as credit is shaken . . . all real wealth is supposed to be actually and suddenly transformed into money, into gold and silver—a crazy demand, but one that necessarily grows out of the system itself." The gold standard thus imposed "a metallic barrier" upon the progress of the capitalist economy, a form of craziness grounded in the second modular form of money.[180]

Yet this was a distinctively bourgeois form of craziness, since adherence to the gold standard inflicted social discipline on the working class in all the ways described above. This is an essential reason why major capitalist powers clung to gold in the early stages of the Great Depression of the 1930s—the other major reason being that gold functioned as world money. Eventually, they all found themselves compelled to abandon these "golden fetters," but this abandonment came belatedly and reluctantly.[181]

It would not be until the late decades of the twentieth century that capitalism fully overcame this metallic barrier. For about a century after 1870, global capitalism revolved around a gold standard, or a gold exchange standard, linked to credit money. But throughout its first phase, the classical gold standard also allowed the British pound to serve as a representative of gold, which gave it a unique function as world money and bestowed upon the Bank of England a dominant role in coordinating international finance.[182]

The directing role of the Bank of England derived, of course, from its imperial supremacy, established during the course of the "Second Hundred Years' War" (1689–1815). The global dominance of the British Empire enabled the pound to function as world money for nearly two hundred years. But just as the pound ascended on the wings of war, its descent, too, would be war-induced. This time it would take another Thirty Years' War—comprising the two World Wars of 1914–45—to reorganize the regime of world money.

CHAPTER 5

Imperial War, Imperial Money

The Dollar's Rise to Global Dominance

"The dollar is our currency, but it's your problem."
—US Treasury Secretary John Connally, 1971

I t has been said that "one of the things that makes a nation a nation is its currency."[1] Consider in this light two of the earliest forms of money in the United States: Virginia's tobacco receipts, and notes based on mortgaged land. The first, tobacco money, became legal tender in 1642 and persisted for nearly two hundred years. The second, currency issued by land banks, originated in South Carolina in 1712 and would soon be found in eight more American colonies. The first, of course, is a receipt on the product of slave labor, and the second is backed by lands appropriated from indigenous peoples. Across these monies, therefore, run traces of concealed sources of American capitalism: slavery and settler colonialism.

Typically, the historical study of money in the United States is posed in terms of a number of binary oppositions: paper money versus metallic coins; debtors versus creditors; state banks versus central banks. Undoubtedly, all of these oppositions are significant and important. But as explanatory matrices,

177

they all elide fundamental questions of violence, expropriation, domination, and labor. They wash blood from money. This chapter reframes the origins of US currencies, beginning instead from their roots in war and subjugation.

Coined Blood: Scalp Bounties and the Violent Economy of Indigenous Displacement

> *"You white people get together and measure the earth and then divide it."*
> —Too-schul-hul-sote, indigenous "dreamer"[2]

Land is, of course, foundational to capitalism everywhere. Primitive accumulation pivots on the theft, enclosure, and parcelization of the earth. But in the Americas, the metamorphosis of land from communal to private property was accomplished by centuries of war. Looting, scalping, raping, pillaging, shooting, burning villages—all the techniques of organized slaughter abetted settler colonialism. This New World marriage of war and economy was consummated through the displacement and elimination of indigenous peoples. "Territoriality is settler colonialism's specific, irreducible element," notes one scholar. "Settler colonialism destroys to replace"; its goal is the destruction of indigenous society and its replacement by settler colonies.[3] To ground money in land banks, as did South Carolina, Pennsylvania, New York, and other states, was to root it in soil drenched with the blood of indigenous peoples.

Discussing banks based on real estate, Benjamin Franklin referred to their currencies as "coined land."[4] But before it could be coined—turned into a form of money—land had first to be privatized and commodified. And this was accomplished by way of what military historian John Grenier calls *extirpative war*. To extirpate, according to the Oxford English Dictionary, is to "eradicate or destroy completely." Indeed, the Latin root is the verb *exstirpare*, meaning to rip out from the roots. Precisely this was the nature of the "Indian Wars" upon which the US state and economy were founded. This foundational violence was most frequently waged by militarized settlers, marauding groups of land-hungry Europeans. If anything, this heightened the murderous violence, as "rangers" and armed settlers had no respect for rules that were presumed to limit the targets or the tactics of military violence. Grenier's description of the

Indian Wars of 1607–1814 is apt: "For the first 200 years of our military heritage, then, Americans depended on arts of war that contemporary professional soldiers supposedly abhorred: razing and destroying enemy villages and fields; killing enemy women and children; raiding settlements for captives; intimidating and brutalizing enemy noncombatants; and assassinating enemy leaders."[5]

An inflection point arrived with the French and Indian Wars (1755–64), part of the Seven Years' War between Britain and France. As much as this conflict catapulted Britain to unrivaled global supremacy, it also consolidated unrelenting hatred toward Indians among Americans who fought alongside the British. War against indigenous peoples now became systematic, at the very time the independent commodity-producing society of the US Northeast was being subsumed into agrarian capitalist development. Settler colonialism now consolidated itself in the form of *settler capitalism*. All "primitive" accumulation of capital, as Marx reminds us, is based on the violent dispossession of people from the land.[6] In the United States, this sort of primary accumulation was carried out by means of military expropriation of indigenous peoples, and became more intensive, extensive, and methodical following the French and Indian Wars.[7] It was in this period that Virginia set out to seize lands as far west as the Mississippi by driving indigenous nations into the US interior, and when the Carolinas turned to a much more aggressive expansionism. As part of these processes, American troops destroyed the power of the Cherokee Nation in a campaign of indiscriminate carnage.[8] The American revolt against Britain in 1776 only intensified these trends.

During the American Revolution and after, federal military forces moved to the forefront of "Indian removal," taking over the role previously assumed by armed settler groups. In 1779, George Washington ordered his troops to undertake "the total destruction and devastation" of the Iroquois Confederacy.[9] Forced relocation, bribery, exploitation of debts, and tribal animosities would all be tools to this end, deployed strategically by President Jefferson in a campaign of ethnic cleansing in the early 1800s.[10] Monstrous chapters were written with the Louisiana Purchase (1803). Then, the War of 1812 against Britain drove militarized expropriation to ever-higher levels, creating the conditions for General Andrew Jackson's murderous rampages through Georgia, Alabama, and Florida (1812–25), the conquest of Texas beginning in 1825, and that of New Mexico, Arizona, California, Nevada, Colorado, and Utah across the 1840s, followed by the systematic "cleansing" of the West after the Civil War.[11] By 1887, indigenous peoples in the United States had been dispossessed of nearly three billion acres of land, or more than 98 percent of the land mass of the continental United States, in one of history's most colossal and merciless processes of primary capitalist accumulation.[12]

The commodification of land was sealed in violence against indigenous bodies. And that violence, both material and symbolic, was directly monetized in the form of scalp bounties. Rewards for Indian scalps appeared in American colonial laws beginning in the 1670s. Massachusetts and South Carolina were among the most aggressive promoters, with the former offering ten pounds sterling for a scalp, about ten times the maximum day wage of a laborer. Even "pacific" Pennsylvania got into the act, regularly increasing scalp bounties as years went by.[13] This grim commerce also excelled at something slavery pioneered: the reduction of persons to monetary sums. In the case of scalp bounties, this entailed a New World *corpse economy*, a morbid exchange between money and severed human body parts—scalps.[14] Indeed, the currencies issued by colonial land banks were literally secured by *redskins*, as American settlers dubbed the bloody corpses they left to rot after scalps had been claimed. Land bank currencies were thus not merely coined land; they were also coined blood. And the same applied to most other monies issued by colonial states. A large number of colonial currencies, after all, were debt notes issued for war finance. And these debts were paid off with land sales once indigenous peoples had been pushed out of their environments. "In the final analysis," remarks one commentator, "most Americans saw currency for what it was: a measure of the value of land . . . that states would sell once the shooting stopped."[15] It is instructive that America's first major financial crash in 1792 was triggered by the defeat of the United States Army by Little Turtle and the Indians of the Western Confederacy in what is now northwestern Ohio. Since military defeat meant no new lands—and thus no land sales to pay off war debts—it immediately induced economic panic.[16]

These deep social connections between Indian wars, slavery, and early American banking are starkly revealed in the life history of America's first president, George Washington, and of his friend Thomas Willing, probably the wealthiest man in Philadelphia from the mid-1790s through the War of 1812. These two men were not merely rapacious individuals. They were also "personifications of capital," to use Marx's term—individuals who personally embodied the social dynamics and behavioral norms of emergent capitalism.

In late 1755, Willing wrote from Pennsylvania to his cousin in London, inquiring about investing two thousand pounds in Bank of England stock. Often described as America's first banker, Willing was fed up with the lack of vigor with which his colony's leaders waged war against indigenous peoples. In the absence of a more aggressive military policy, he turned his eyes to England's bank of war finance. A mere four months earlier, this future president of the Bank of North America (1781–91), and then of the Bank of the United States (1791–1807), had advertised for sale "a parcel of likely servant men and boys"—bonded laborers from Ireland, Germany, Wales, and England. It would not be long until enslaved Africans imported from the West Indies were added to his sales catalog.[17]

Biography rarely encapsulates the sweep of history with such clarity. Yet, in Willing's case, banking, military contracting, slaving, and support for war against indigenous peoples were bound together in a personal trajectory that traced the path of capitalist development in colonial America. At the 1795 wedding of Willing's daughter, attendees included a who's who of America's elite, including its sitting president, George Washington. If the first president had achieved glory on the battlefield, it was in large measure thanks to gunpowder, cannons, and thousands of arms provided by Willing to the troops Washington commanded against the British.[18] The friendship between these powerful men also highlights the social connection between Philadelphia bankers and Virginia planters that underlay early American capitalism, a connection that was forged ever tighter through war and war finance. And for Washington personally, it was war that enabled his acquisition of land, and his entrée into the world of plantation production.

It seems fitting that the future president found his original profession as a surveyor, since military displacement of Indians generated a huge demand for the mapping of expropriated land. Like many in his trade, Washington found time to snatch up speculative holdings for himself, purchasing a thousand acres in the Shenandoah Valley in 1750. Then, before the decade was out, his marriage to Martha Custis made him one of northern Virginia's largest landowners. To these estates he added twenty-five thousand acres, grabbed as reward for military service, much of it against indigenous peoples in the French and Indian Wars. Continued war service brought him forty-five thousand acres more in 1773. Yet, none of these lands were worth much without labor. And on Virginia's large estates, the work was done by enslaved people of African descent. Always the social climber, Washington was not one to brook the practices of his class. At his death, the United States' first president owned 277 bonded persons.[19]

Washington excelled in the two practices foundational to planter capitalism: indigenous displacement and African enslavement. We have observed his 1779 presidential instructions that the US Army should march on the Iroquois to bring about "the total destruction and devastation of their settlements." His officers complied, destroying at least forty Iroquois towns.[20] Just over twenty years later, Congress created the US Land Office, which financed real estate purchases. Measured in terms of its loan book to borrowers, the Land Office would soon be the world's largest bank.[21] As Indian wars and indigenous displacement took on continental dimensions, the United States rushed "like a comet into infinite space," as one federalist critic put it.[22] Land was now being coined on a scale Franklin would have found inconceivable. Yet, the inner secret of coined land and of American capitalism's rush into infinite space was, as scalp bounties remind us, *coined blood.*

Revolution, War Finance, Capitalists, and Con Men

War pivots on finance. And it also breeds new forms of it. The American War of Independence against Britain was no exception. Revolutionary quartermasters, colonels, and treasurers in the colonies sought weapons, provisions, horses, and basic supplies on a tremendous scale. During the winter of 1777–78, American soldiers consumed almost 2.3 million pounds of flour and nearly as much beef. In the month of May 1778 alone, the army's horses ate two and a half million tons of hay and a quarter-million bushels of grain.[23] Arranging the logistics of war economy was the order of the day.

Inevitably, this pushed public credit to the fore, since wartime supplies were needed *before* they could be paid for. As they gathered weapons, food, ammunition, and supplies, colonial officials frantically issued promises to pay at a later date. These pledges, as we have seen, were ultimately backed by land that would be seized "once the fighting had stopped."[24] But many bills would come due long before then. To manage this, two-thirds of the cost of the Revolutionary War was funded by the use of bills of credit.[25] To the good fortune of the Americans, a market in these promissory notes developed among investors in Paris and Amsterdam willing to bet on a victory for the colonial rebels (and on the land seizures that would accompany it). America's government could thus receive cash up front in return for debt notes.

Massachusetts issued its first war bonds in May 1775. The following month, the Continental Congress started printing a national paper currency, known as continentals. Treasury Secretary Alexander Hamilton was soon to propose a national bank with powers to print notes, coin money, receive deposits, and make private and public loans. A decade later, this proposal would come to fruition with the creation of the First Bank of the United States in 1791. But even without a national bank, the Americans found means of war finance in the form of "floods of paper money," as future president John Adams was to put it.[26] By the time the shooting had stopped, Congress had issued $226 million in notes, while an additional $100 million in paper currency had flowed from the states.

Americans had already demonstrated a unique fondness for paper money, much to the dismay of the imperial metropole, which repeatedly prohibited it (in laws of 1720, 1741, and 1751).[27] But the Revolution scaled a new summit. Paper money would reign supreme in the United States for the next fifty years, notwithstanding widespread fetishism of precious metals as the only "true" money. And with proliferating paper currency came intensified monetization and precocious financialization. As in the ancient Greco-Roman world, war was a medium for monetizing social life—first, through the huge demand for *market* goods like provisions and weapons, and second, through wages paid to soldiers, many of them recruited from largely self-sufficient farms. A feedback loop developed in which government bought up foodstuffs for soldiers and horses; young men spent their army pay; and farmers, under pressure to pay off land loans or to acquire more land, pushed foodstuffs to the market. Meanwhile, rocketing demand for agricultural goods drove up wartime prices, just as wages rose due to labor shortages, brought on by the absence of farm boys due to military service. As monetary transactions expanded, so did financial institutions. As early as 1794, when four chartered banks could be found in the whole of the British Isles, the United States already hosted eighteen. By 1825, the United States had nearly two and a half times as much banking capital as did England and Wales. Riding this precocious financialization, bank assets as a share of aggregate US output rose steadily from 1785—hitting levels in the 1820s comparable to those that many countries reached only in the 1990s.[28]

This postrevolutionary surge of banks and paper currency provided fertile ground for an astonishing rise in the number of swindlers and con men, of the sort later depicted in Herman Melville's novella *The Confidence Man* (1857). Specialists in constructing "pawnshops for promises," con men regularly bilked small investors in a plethora of get-rich-quick schemes.[29] In so doing, they contributed to the mistrust of paper money that was such a powerful force in US financial history. Heading the pack of early nineteenth-century experts in the art of the con was Boston-based Andrew Dexter Jr., who began building his paper money machine in 1804. Dexter chose Rhode Island, the mecca of paper money, for the launch of his innocuous-sounding Farmers Exchange Bank. From there, he churned out tens of thousands of notes, which he sent as far from their source as possible, thus delaying, if not preventing, their redemption for specie.[30] En route, he set up several more banks, including one in Detroit and another in Pittsfield, Massachusetts—each an instrument for the production of baseless banknotes. Amazingly, Dexter's pyramid scheme thrived for five years before it all came crashing down. By the time it did, in 1809, the Farmers Exchange had issued over $760,000 in notes, backed by a mere $86 in specie.[31]

The panic associated with Dexter's meltdown was one element in a larger reaction against paper money and national banks. So intense was the early nineteenth-century revulsion against paper money that it also brought down the First Bank of the United States (BUS), which had faced hostility from its inception. Created in 1791 as a component of Alexander Hamilton's program for an activist state promoting capitalist development, the Philadelphia-based BUS was modeled on the Bank of England.[32] From the start, powerful Virginia tobacco planters opposed Hamilton's national bank. Immersed in an economy where they controlled finance as well as production of a global export commodity—tobacco—these planters mistrusted any shift of financial power out of the Old South. Republicans like Thomas Jefferson inflected this opposition with anti-centralist rhetoric, and in 1801 they created the US Land Office as an alternative. Then, in the wake of monetary scams and financial panics, an awkward coalition of agrarian populists, financial capitalists outside Philadelphia's Chestnut Street, and working-class radicals all turned their enmity on the bank and the very idea of central banking. By 1811, the BUS could not muster enough support in the Senate to get its charter renewed. With the elimination of the BUS's power to regulate banking, new banks could now multiply like weeds.

In a single legislative act, Pennsylvania created forty-one new banks in 1814. Three years later, Kentucky wished forty banks into being, with a nominal capital of ten million dollars—though in truth, they had not a coin in their treasuries. These were soon known as "caterpillar banks," as they were said to gobble everything in their path. A country that had 114 banks in 1811 boasted 256 five years later. Despite official bullionism, the United States was blatantly a country of footloose paper currencies, a mecca of easy money. The more than two hundred banks to be found in 1815 reported a combined $82 million in capital, only one-fifth of which was backed by silver and gold.[33] By this time, canal companies, railways, blacksmiths, and various academies were also issuing a dazzling array of notes that circulated as money. American capitalism had set off down the road of fragmented finance. Yet, down that road also lay the potholes of scams and panics that regularly provoked anti-banking fevers, and a fetish of precious metal.

Indian Hunting, Market Populism, and the Rise of Wall Street

No sooner had the First Bank expired than support for a strong central bank was renewed, following the trauma of the War of 1812—which saw the British burn down the White House, provoking a financial panic during which banks suspended conversion of notes into specie. With public expenditures running two to three times higher than government income, it required substantial sales of interest-bearing Treasury notes to finance the war. Accepted as legal tender for all government transactions, including taxes, these notes became a crucial part of the money supply.[34] In 1816, shortly after the war's end, Congress approved the launch of the Second Bank of the United States, though it remained little more than an accessory to the Treasury, the real central bank at the time. But the Second Bank soon found itself with half of all bank-held specie, and it began to assume many of the coordinating and regulating functions of a modern central bank. However, its history was plagued by crises, scandals, and intensifying political opposition. Particularly during the tenure of Nicholas Biddle as BUS president (1823–36), with the United States in the throes of intensifying capitalist transformation, the bank became a lightning rod for social grievances against moneyed interests and Washington officials. The acclaimed Indian killer, Andrew Jackson, shrewdly mobilized these sentiments on his road to the presidency, fostering a *market populism* that extolled economic individualism while condemning monstrous bankers and bureaucrats. Dynamic capitalist development in the United States was thereby joined to a fragmented, decentralized, and largely unregulated banking system.

It must be underlined that monetary fragmentation did not significantly hinder capitalist accumulation in the United States. There has been a widespread tendency, particularly since the onset of global financialization in the 1970s, to treat finance as the prime mover of capitalist development, a view that all too easily meshes with neoclassical conceptions of capitalism as a "money economy" fueled by individual property rights.[35] Such perspectives miss the vital sources of capitalist growth in labor, exploitation, and accumulation of means of production. For it was as a powerful machinery for harnessing human labor that the US economy thrived in the decades after 1800, notwithstanding its highly localized financial system.

A growing body of research has demonstrated that this phase of vigorous capitalist growth had fundamentally agrarian roots. Far from "revolutionary" market forces overturning a "conservative" economy and culture based on land,[36] American capitalism developed *on the basis* of landed production. Where dispossession of indigenous people had been largely completed, the transition from independent farming to agrarian capitalism occurred in large measure *through* household production, rather than via its eradication, as had been the story in Britain with the expropriation of small tenants. In the US case, family farms were rendered market-dependent via the effects of land prices, mortgages, and market pressures. Farmers were increasingly compelled to produce monetizable cash crops in order to make debt and mortgage payments to government and banks, and to purchase farm implements and household goods. All of these capitalist relations subjected petty commodity producers to the imperatives of the market. By the 1830s, farmers in the Ohio Valley, drowning in debt, were in a state of insurgence against banks in general, and the Second Bank of the United States in particular.[37] If it is true, as historian Jonathan Levy asserts, that "after 1870, mortgage debt pressured farmers into growing the product that brought in the most cash" in states such as Kansas, Minnesota, Wisconsin, Nebraska, and the Dakotas, it is also the case that in Ohio and areas of the Northeast this transition had begun decades earlier.[38]

Well before the outbreak of the Civil War, a market-integrated, commodity-producing agriculture held sway in the dominant regions of the US economy, generating monetized surpluses and increasing demand for manufactured goods.[39] This in turn stimulated the large-scale industrial manufacture of shoes and textiles, especially in Massachusetts; the development of water-driven mills and cotton-spinning machinery; the concentration of urban populations; and the expansion of roads, turnpikes, and canals—to be followed by steamboats and railroads.[40] While powerful internal transformations propelled these developments, European wars again intervened—this time the conflicts of 1793–1815 provoked by the revolution in France—enabling US shipping to emerge as the world's premier mover of world goods, and enticing European investors back to American markets.[41] American growth further heightened the country's attractive power to immigrants. Population soared from 3.9 million in 1790 to 9.6 million twenty years later, just as capitalist industrialization pushed the number of cotton mills from fifteen to eighty-seven in the space of four years, at the same time as the quantity of spindles increased tenfold. Beginning in the 1790s, the corporate form of organization emerged in the North, soon becoming widespread. By 1861, American states had incorporated over twenty-two thousand enterprises, making the United States the original "corporation nation."[42] The precocious rise of the corporation also fostered the growth of finance, as joint-stock firms took out loans and issued equities, bonds, and other securities. This was the stimulus for a wave of new banks, whose numbers jumped from four in 1791 to 250 by 1816.[43] Banking in the United States was thus a major beneficiary of a feverish process of social and geographic expansion of commodity production and trade, alongside the corporatization of American business. None of these processes was unduly hindered by the fragmented character of US banking.

It would be easy to imagine that the localism of US banking owed much to peculiar forms of finance in the Southern slave states. But, as much as the market in enslaved people lent distinctive features to finance in the South, banks there were tightly connected with both Northern and British mercantile groups. In fact, given that cotton was the world's most widely traded commodity by the 1830s, banking in the South was a force for financial integration, not fragmentation. The same was true for the commerce in enslaved people.

Enslaved people were the largest capital investment in the Southern economy, and slave trading was a powerfully rationalized business. Bonded persons were widely used as collateral in debt transactions, from the purchase of shares in Louisiana banks to the contracting of a mortgage. In the Louisiana parish of

East Feliciana, enslaved people secured 80 percent of antebellum mortgages.[44] In addition to collateralizing investments, enslaved people comprised one of the commodities most actively bought and sold across the South, and banks were keen to provide funds to businesses engaged in buying and selling bonded persons. In the case of the Bank of North Carolina, perhaps two-thirds of its loans were made to slave traders.[45] Significantly, those states in the Deep South that imported the most enslaved people—and thus had the most active markets in bonded persons—were also the most monetized. So much did slave markets foster banking that by 1840, Louisiana, Mississippi, Alabama, and Florida were circulating more bank money per capita than any other US states.[46] In this respect, as in many others, there was nothing premodern about the Southern economy.[47]

As indicated, Southern slave-based banking was thoroughly integrated into financial markets in the eastern United States, as well as the global market based in London. Baltimore's premier merchant bank, Alexander Brown & Sons, eventually the nation's second-largest mercantile exchange, connected investors in Liverpool, London, South America, Africa, and beyond to the purchase and sale of cotton and enslaved people.[48] Lending in the Mississippi Valley Cotton Belt was dominated by the Second Bank of the United States, thus incorporating slave and cotton finance into the monetary circuits of America's de facto central bank.[49] Many banks originating in the South, like the Consolidated Association of Planters of Louisiana, issued loans backed by collateralized enslaved people (loans financed by selling bonds to Baring Brothers of London).[50] Slave trader Jean Baptiste Moussier, working out of New Orleans, partnered with a Virginia bank to build an interlocking slave-trading network that featured branches in New York, London, Le Havre, and New Orleans.[51] Banking in the American South was thus integral to international capital flows that dealt in financialized instruments secured by enslaved bodies.

Notwithstanding its regional specificities, therefore, Southern finance was not the source of the uniquely fragmented character of US banking. More significant was the way in which intra-elite regional conflicts converged with popular grievances against the "market revolution." The latter was articulated into a market populism that channeled subaltern protest into the political insurgency of Andrew Jackson.

With Philadelphia bankers controlling both the First and Second Banks of the United States, financiers in cities such as New York, Baltimore, Boston,

Richmond, and New Orleans frequently bristled at the privileges conferred on their competitors in the City of Brotherly Love. They eagerly joined the chorus declaiming the monopoly powers of Philadelphia bankers, a chorus that grew amid the heightened social tensions over gender, race, and class inequality that accompanied the "market revolution" of the early nineteenth century.[52]

Andrew Jackson would be the ultimate beneficiary of the anti-elite sentiments of this period. The first presidential candidate of non-gentry background, Jackson was the offspring of rough-and-tumble Scotch-Irish immigrants who populated the Carolina backcountry. Theirs was a culture of patriarchy and white supremacy, and Jackson himself owned fifteen enslaved people by the time he was thirty. An abject failure as a planter, merchant, and land speculator, the violent and short-tempered Jackson found his calling as a killer of indigenous people. The War of 1812 was a turning point for the Indian hunter, as it was part of a pivot by the United States toward more concerted practices of conquest, expansion, and ethnic cleansing. Jackson played a decisive role here, massacring indigenous peoples while seizing a fifth of Georgia and three-fifths of Alabama in the process—twenty-three million acres in all.[53] Presidents Monroe and Adams would now turn Indian eviction, dispossession, and relocation into systematic state policy.[54] But it was Jackson's conquest of Florida (1813–18)— which he snatched in a frenzy of slaughter from the Creeks, the Seminoles, and defiant African Americans (as well as the imperial claims of Spain)—that raised militarized displacement to unprecedented heights, while cementing his political reputation. When a group of congressional leaders turned against him for effectively declaring war against Spain on his own, Jackson rode to Washington and rallied supporters to reject resolutions condemning him, galvanizing the movement that carried him to the White House in the election of 1828. Blatantly anti-Indian aggression and belligerent continental expansion were now the order of the day, symbolized in the decision of the new state of Mississippi, created on the ancestral lands of the Choctaws, to name its capital "Jackson."

Jackson's violently anti-indigenous sentiments were entirely wanting in originality. Even his wedding of bellicose expansionism to an anti-elite discourse that targeted the Second Bank of the United States lacked inventiveness. After all, hostility to banks was emblematic of democratic politics in the first decades of the nineteenth century. Farmers struggling with mortgages, working-class radicals protesting exploitation of labor, and Jeffersonian Republicans displacing their qualms about slavery—these groups and others singled out banks for special reproach. The six new states that joined the union between 1816 and 1820—Indiana, Maine, Illinois, Mississippi, Alabama, and Missouri—all adopted comparatively democratic constitutions (subject to predictable racial and gender exclusions). They also all noticeably constrained banking.[55] No doubt, Jackson's hostility to bankers was genuine. But it was also shrewd politics, for it enabled him to channel subaltern grievances of farmers and workers—who were undergoing the pressures of capitalist transition—into an expansionist program of indigenous displacement that glorified the virtues of the white male yeoman farmer and artisan. Class antagonisms could thus be mobilized against entrenched privilege of the sort represented by the Philadelphia bankers who dominated the Second BUS, while glorifying a market individualism based on white male producers. The strident campaign Jackson waged against the Second BUS during his second presidential term (1833–37), which included withdrawing all its federal deposits in 1833, effectively destroyed the institution, whose charter was not renewed in 1836. Yet, as much as this appeared as a victory for popular forces, the destruction of the bank was in fact largely "a blow at an older set of capitalists by a newer, more numerous set. . . . Destruction of the bank ended federal regulation of bank credit and shifted the money center of the country from Chestnut Street to Wall Street."[56]

In addition to shifting the center of financial power, the demise of the Second Bank, like that of its predecessor, opened the floodgates to pell-mell creation of new banks and new paper monies. There was an irony here, since Jackson was a "hard money" man, as manifest in the "specie circular" he and his Treasury secretary issued in 1836, which directed federal land agents to accept only silver and gold in payment for relatively large parcels of public lands. Yet, an expanding US capitalism could not function on the limited monetary resources of gold and silver bullion and coin. So, having destroyed the effective central bank of the United States, the hard-money president unwittingly oversaw a manic proliferation of paper, much of it produced by so-called wildcat banks, operating on next to no capital and prey to counterfeiters (that is, when they were not generating funny money themselves).

A total of 379 banks had produced paper money by the time Jackson made his concerted moves against the Second Bank in 1832. The number leapt to 596 in 1836, the year renewal of the bank's charter was denied, and it jumped again to 711 in 1840.[57] By 1860, some seven thousand different banknotes could be found circulating in the United States, courtesy of one thousand six hundred state banks. Traveling alongside those were up to four thousand counterfeit issues.[58] There may be some poetic license in describing the United States as a "nation of counterfeiters" at this point. But it is certainly fair to say that waves of frauds, scams, and wildcat banks, and a dizzying proliferation of paper money generated profound anxieties. Rather than providing a trusted means of exchange and social interaction, money inspired abiding uncertainties about financial institutions, bankers, politicians, the salesperson in the shop, and the medicine man and his elixir. A society overflowing with people (and currency) that pretended to be something other than what they were nourished epistemological doubt. As in Melville's *The Confidence Man*, everyone's identity seemed in doubt, never mind the veracity of their stories or the authenticity of the wares they peddled. Systematic suspicion appeared to be an entirely rational attitude.

It is all too convenient, however, to conclude that the market magically conjured up a dynamic order out of this financial chaos. In reality, it was the antebellum US state that produced financial order, by providing a greater degree of monetary regulation than most historians have appreciated. True, American capitalism lacked a typical central bank at the time. But the independent Treasury fulfilled many of its functions. We have already seen the decisive role of Treasury notes during the War of 1812; and these were also widely deployed in response to the Panic of 1837 in order to stimulate the economy, and later, to cover deficits incurred during the Mexican-American War (1847). In providing monetary stimulus during panics and in financing wartime deficits, the Treasury performed key central bank functions. Congress authorized such practices in both 1840 and 1846, when it passed Independent Treasury Acts as an alternative to sanctioning a national bank.[59]

Notwithstanding the regulating role of the Treasury, financial fragmentation had more than a few defects. Not only was it a complicated business to properly assess the relative values of hundreds of different banknotes, but the plethora of largely unregulated banks also fostered scams and frauds. The latter contributed to speculative bubbles and painful panics like the 1837 crash, and its successor twenty years later.[60] Moreover, market populism's hostility to central banking and capitalist developmentalism—which promoted state-supported infrastructure, like roads, canals, and railways—was far from optimal for the common interests of capital. A bureaucratically centralized state capable of military defense and expansion, the management of economic crises, the construction of transport infrastructure, the domination of labor, and the suppression of oppressed groups is very much in capital's general interests, so long as its interventions do not impinge upon the rights of property and the "liberties" of business. Such a state is an integral aspect of the capital relation, expressing and managing the forms of alienation unique to capitalist society and the conflicts it generates through institutions of impersonal power. Excessively fragmented state powers are generally suboptimal to this project, and they carry the risk that conflicts between regionalized part-sovereigns can become militarized.[61] This was to be the story of the United States in the 1850s and 1860s, when aggressive expansionism on the part of the slavocracy provoked armed conflict. And from that conflict was born a new centralization of money and power.

Blood on the Fields: Civil War and the Making of American Money

"Success in crushing the rebellion and maintaining the Union is much more a financial than a military question."

—Ohio Senator John Sherman, 1863[62]

War makes states, just as it makes money. In the American case, it was the Civil War (1861–65) that "nationalized" the state and the banking system—a metamorphosis that began, predictably, with war finance.[63]

On April 13, 1861, Fort Sumter fell to Confederate soldiers from South Carolina defending the slavocracy. Full-fledged war was now unavoidable. Within weeks, President Lincoln ordered up 83,000 troops for the army and navy—numbers that would soon represent mere drops in the buckets of blood. When Congress met in July, the president requested "at least four hundred thousand men and four hundred millions of dollars."[64] No US government had ever imagined something on this scale, never mind implemented it. At the time Sumter fell, Lincoln commanded 16,000 troops. He was now requesting 250 times as many. Before 1861 was out, he would have 600,000 soldiers in uniform. Six months later he would add half as many again—all prior to the self-recruitment of nearly 200,000 African Americans into the Union Army.[65] As new troops swelled the ranks of the army, war costs skyrocketed. During Lincoln's first fiscal year, which closed on June 30, 1861, US government expenditures totaled $67 million. A year later they had climbed to $475 million, topping out at $1.3 billion in 1865—a level they did not reach again for over fifty years.[66]

While the Union government managed to improve and augment its revenue collection, taxes could not possibly keep pace with the mushrooming costs of war. Lincoln's tax revenues comprised only about one-quarter of what his government spent. The rest had to be covered by borrowing (selling bonds), or by printing money and declaring it legal tender. And even this required significant increases in taxes, since bonds can be sold only if creditors believe in government's capacity to makes its interest payments. But war could not have been waged, never mind won, without innovative debt instruments and new forms of money. And these were underwritten by a tremendous expansion of state powers.

It has rightly been said that two critical acts of 1862 "advanced the national government's powers far beyond what had ever been ascribed to it before."[67] One, the Revenue Act of July 1862, enshrined federal powers of taxation, laid the basis for income tax, and radically expanded the powers of the federal government—all critical to the maintenance of the state's credit in money markets. But it was an earlier bill, the Legal Tender Act of February 1862, that had inadvertently launched a revolution in money and finance.

From the early days of the Civil War, the Union had been issuing Treasury notes as a means to raise funds. One version of these, known as demand notes, did not pay interest and was used widely as currency for everyday payments. But the Treasury secretary, Samuel Chase (another gold and silver bug), resisted making these notes legal tender. Doing so would have made paper equivalent to bullion, fully usable in all monetary transactions, and would thereby have eliminated many difficulties of war finance. Unwilling to take this course—which would eventually become inevitable—Chase instead clung to the idea of gold as real money. In selling his Treasury notes, therefore, he insisted that banks buy them with specie. Yet, this meant no legal expansion of the money supply. All it meant was that gold moved to the government from the banks, with the latter holding Treasury notes in return. In not making its notes legal tender, the government failed to increase the circulating medium with infusions of state credit money. The results were predictable: within months of war, commercial bank purchases of Treasury notes had exhausted their supplies of gold. With gold disappearing, government suppliers went unpaid, and Treasury notes were heavily discounted in money markets (since, in the midst of a gold shortage, sellers would accept amounts of gold much smaller than the face value of their notes). Something had to give.

Once again, war dictated monetary innovation. If the war was to be prosecuted, the sacred status of precious metal would have to be sacrificed, and paper made as good as gold—simply by fiat of the state.[68] Unpalatable as this might have been to many politicians, it was either that or the collapse of war finance. Introducing debate on the Legal Tender Act on January 28, 1862, Representative E. G. Spaulding declared the bill "a war measure." He continued, "In carrying on this existing war . . . it is necessary to exercise all the sovereign power of the government to sustain itself."[69] Contra Jefferson and the republican tradition, this meant the constitutional right of the federal government to create fiat money. In a further repudiation of the Jeffersonian vision, the war state ushered in an unprecedented enhancement of federal power. Supporting the Legal Tender bill, Radical Republican Thaddeus Stevens intoned, "If no other means were left to save the Republic from destruction, I believe we have the power *under the Constitution and according to its express provision*, to declare a dictator."[70] And if Congress possessed the right to appoint a dictator in times of national emergency, it most certainly had the authority to create a national currency. And so, the famous notes known as greenbacks were born, backed by nothing more than the state's promises to pay—but enforced as legal tender by an act of government.

Lincoln signed the Legal Tender Act into law on February 25, 1862. All individuals were required to accept both the $100 million in new greenbacks the government was furiously printing, as well as the existing $50 million in demand notes. While greenbacks had a predecessor in Treasury notes, their scale gave them a colossally greater impact. Treasury notes had been of marginal importance, fluctuating in volume between $3 million and $20 million. Before the war was over, more than $450 million in greenbacks were in circulation. Alongside those went $300 million in national banknotes, which were backed by US government bonds. At one level, the US government now had something equivalent to the currency issued by the Bank of England—legal tender notes backed by the credit of the state. But whereas pound notes were legally convertible into gold, Lincoln's government went a major step further, in imitation of British wartime practice, by prohibiting convertibility of greenbacks for specie—a suspension that would in fact persist for seventeen years, long past the end of the conflict. The United States was thus operating with fiat money, pure and simple. Nevertheless, as the *New York Times* reported on April 14, 1862, greenbacks were immediately accepted with "universal confidence" and "esteemed in all respects the equivalent of gold." Four weeks later, the paper announced that the new legal tender notes had won acceptance as "universal currency."[71]

Many commentators were befuddled as to how this could be so. In May, the *Economist* declared the success of the greenbacks to be incomprehensible. Yet Karl Marx, observing the situation from London, was not in the least surprised. The triumph of "the paper operations of the Yankees," he wrote, derived from three social factors: confidence in Lincoln's government and its cause; the desperate need for currency in the US West; and the Union's favorable balance of trade.[72] He might have added that the latter—a result of the North's advantage in international trade—was a product of the vitality of its agrarian and industrial capitalism. In 1860, for instance, 110,000 manufacturing enterprises were active in the North, compared to 18,000 in the South. The South possessed no machine shops that could build marine engines for its navy, while during the war the Union constructed 671 warships, 236 of them steam-powered vessels. Its industrial base enabled the North to manufacture 1.7 million rifles; the South produced barely any. Rather than being sent into disarray by civil war, the Northern economy surged industrially, as Congress provided massive land grants to launch the Union Pacific and Central Pacific railways. Railroad expansion stimulated domestic steel production, and the first commercial steel using the Bessemer process appeared in 1864. Output in industries such as iron ore, machine tools, wool, and lumber jumped two to three times between 1861 and 1865. And while the Southern economy sputtered, productivity rose in the North in both agriculture and manufactures, a key reason that "Northern soldiers were probably better fed and supplied than any army in history."[73]

An expanding economy supplied the army *and* underpinned war finance, via taxes and secure borrowing. Indeed, the industrial and commercial power of the North (and its capacity to raise taxes) conferred on it the capacity to finance war with fiat money. Even a tripling of the money supply from 1860 to 1865 did not create monetary instability. In the Confederacy, on the other hand, the more than $1.5 billion in notes ("graybacks") pumped into circulation plummeted in value rapidly—not only because they were not legal tender, but also due to economic dislocation and financial disorder. By 1864, one Confederate officer related that graybacks had "ceased to have even a nominal value."[74] In some respects, the North's victory was sealed on its factories and farms, its railway lines and steel mills. Notwithstanding strategic bungling and political hesitations on the part of the Union, its economic resources enabled it to wage war for as long as proved necessary. As financial scholar Bray Hammond observed: "In the North an industrial system gave assurance of the necessary production of supplies, and required mainly a reform in the system of payments. In the South, a reform of the system of payments would accomplish nothing, the means of production being at want."[75] That industrial system was the economic foundation of Northern victory. In political-military terms, however, it was the self-emancipating activity of African Americans, including the "general strike of the slaves" and the entry of two hundred thousand black troops into the Union Army, that would prove decisive.[76] But whereas black insurgency would be broken in the Reconstruction era, the key wartime monetary transformations that underwrote military success would persist, sometimes in modified forms, in the capitalist economic expansion that followed Union victory.

These transformations required, however, that the banking system be "nationalized," and the state banks brought to heel. The federal government would thus have to become the regulator of the American financial system. Lincoln pushed this process in a letter of January 19, 1863, which advocated "a uniform currency"—rather than the cacophony of hundreds of contending bills and notes—to be supplied by a new system of federally constituted banks. This letter, intriguingly, was a reply to the "workingmen of Manchester," in which the president felt obliged to assert the vigor with which his government was developing the state powers necessary to win the Civil War.[77] The real heavy lifting on the banking front was done, however, by Ohio Senator John Sherman.

Nothing fosters state centralization like war, and it was not long before Sherman laid out a program to nationalize and centralize government authority. The Ohio Republican steered through the Senate a bill inaugurating a system of national banks, pronouncing, "The policy of this country ought to be to make everything as national as possible, to nationalize our country."[78] Commitment to defeating the Confederacy now made political and economic fragmentation anathema. And Sherman happily took the lead among the centralizers. When many state banks continued to print their own notes rather than switch over to greenbacks, he launched a tax offensive against them. When his initial 2 percent tax did not bring the state banks to heel, he pushed through legislation raising it to 10 percent. The government was now dictating what would and would not function as money. Determined to annihilate the notes issued by state banks, Sherman invoked constitutional powers. "It was the intention of the framers of the Constitution," he urged, "to destroy absolutely all paper money, except that issued by the United States."[79] Early the next year, as the 10 percent tax on currency-issuing state banks took effect, large numbers of these banks quickly nationalized themselves, relinquishing their own currencies and agreeing to exclusive use of greenbacks and national banknotes.[80] American finance thus revolved around two national currencies, both issued by government—United States notes (greenbacks) and national notes tied to government bonds. American money was now genuinely the product of the national state.[81]

Not Yet World Money: The Dollar, Gold, and the Creation of the Federal Reserve

If American money was now national, it was still a long way from being *global*. For the dollar to become a principal currency of international business, multiple transformations would be necessary—economic, political, and institutional. Over the half century that followed the Civil War, these would all be put in place. Yet the processes of change were typically piecemeal and confused, sometimes outright ludicrous. Having created a national fiat money, America's rulers now tried to get rid of it by restoring convertibility of banknotes to gold. Yet so ham-fisted were the efforts that it took them nearly fifteen years to pull it off.

Immediately after the Civil War, the government began retiring and destroying greenbacks, just as economic growth turned up and state revenues leapt higher. The money supply thus contracted, while demand for money rose in response to the rising volume of transactions. The result was predictable: as the money stock declined by about 7 percent a year, so prices dropped by 8 percent annually from 1866–68.[82] Declining prices are almost always disastrous under capitalism, as investors and individuals postpone purchases and investments in order to take advantage of the lower prices expected next week, next month, next year. The economic effects were worst in the South and West of the United States, which were cash-starved long before hostilities between the Union and the Confederacy had ended. These regions strenuously opposed the resumption of dollar–gold convertibility and frequently advocated for silver to become an additional component (sometimes the primary one) of the money supply. Yet, notwithstanding widespread public hostility, the party of resumption eventually prevailed, though it was not until 1879 that the convertibility of dollars for gold came into effect.

The ruling-class push for resumption owed something to a concern that government fiat money might get recklessly out of control—with the stuff being churned out at a rate that would fuel price inflation. But the most farsighted capitalists had an additional concern. They knew that while a state might impose whatever it liked as legal tender within its borders, it had no such authority in world markets. In short, they understood, to recall Hobbes's words, that there had still to be some "measure of the value of all things else between Nations."[83] It followed that if the United States was to be a top-tier player in international markets, it needed a currency that carried global legitimacy, one that might become a recognized instrument of global finance.

We live in an age that is bedazzled by finance. It is essential to remind ourselves, therefore, that what brought about the internationalization of the dollar was a dynamic process of capital accumulation in industry, agriculture, and transportation. Agricultural expansion remained vital to these developments after the Civil War, although it was now increasingly integrated with finance and burgeoning manufacturing industries. During the 1870s, farm acreage grew by 44 percent. This extensive growth dovetailed with increases in the productivity of agricultural labor to generate often-staggering rises in output. "Between 1866 and 1886 the corn produced in Kansas rose from 30 million bushels to 750 million. In 1880 the wheat crop of North Dakota was not quite 3 million bushels. In 1887 it passed 60 million. These figures had no historical precedent."[84] Between the end of the Civil War (1865) and the 1898 Spanish-American War, US wheat production jumped by more than 250 percent, and the output of corn by over 220 percent.[85] All of this was tied, of course, to industrial transformations of the landscape: canals and waterways, steamboats, the telegraph, and—most dramatically—the railways. Over the course of the 1850s, the national railroad system more than tripled in size, from nine thousand miles of track to thirty thousand. And no city benefited more than Chicago, by this time a hub of railways, grain trading, meatpacking, and finance.[86]

The expropriation of land from indigenous peoples also lay at the heart of Chicago's rise. On the backs of that dispossession came a half century of truly remarkable growth beginning in the 1830s. Again, military conflict was crucial. During the Crimean War (1853–56), US wheat exports to Europe soared; Chicago's wheat shipments tripled. The city's board of trade had been organized in 1848, the same year that telegraphs reached the city, enabling rapid dissemination of price information and deeper financial integration with New York, the most important business center in the country. The city's evolution into a railway hub expanded all its networks of industry and commerce, and by 1852, two rail lines linked Chicago to New York. Then, the Civil War worked its economic transformations. The Union Army's insatiable appetite for oats and pork kindled huge rises in production and exchange of these goods. As demand soared, Chicago's nine largest railroad companies joined with the city's Pork Packers' Association to develop the mammoth Union Stock Yard and Transit Company. Building thirty miles of drainage, and siphoning half a million gallons of fresh water per day, the consortium operated ten miles of feed troughs. This industrial system covered sixty acres of city land and funneled one hundred tons of hay (as well as corn) each day to five hundred pens. These titanic increases in the production and exchange of grain, animals, and packed meat also excited a plethora of speculative trades, as financiers gambled on the ups and downs of prices. This was the origin of futures trading, as the Chicago Board of Trade pioneered markets in financial pseudo-commodities based on bets about future prices (a development to which we shall return). Fittingly, it was in 1865, the year the Civil War ended, that the CBT introduced standardized rules governing futures trading.[87]

Complex financial markets developed in tandem with so-called *financial banking*, which enabled businesses to procure loans backed by securities—primarily stocks—rather than simple promises to repay, such as promissory notes or commercial paper. In the decade after 1896, loans by New York banks and trust companies secured by stock exchange collateral jumped by over 200 percent, rising three times as fast as loans tied to an enterprise's commercial paper. Within a few years, roughly 60 percent of the loans made by New York banks were backed by negotiable securities.[88] Not only did US capitalism witness, as we have seen, the most widespread adoption of the corporate form; it also developed some of the most intricately structured financial markets in the world.

What was emerging in the United States, as illustrated in the case of Chicago, was a dynamic symbiosis between agriculture and manufacturing, in which finance served as a leavening agent. Between 1869 and 1883, the American economy grew faster than ever before, at a rate of about 9 percent a year. Railroads were at the heart of this boom, with more than one hundred sixty-two thousand miles of track laid in the forty years after 1860.[89] By 1890—twenty-five years after the end of the Civil War—US capitalism produced more steel than did Great Britain. And a decade later, its *total manufacturing output* had also overtaken that of Britain. Meanwhile, the American economy had entered a phase of furious concentration and centralization of capital. Huge conglomerates emerged, like the Standard Oil Trust (1892), the US Steel Company (1901), and General Motors (1908). By 1902, there were nearly one hundred industrial firms with capitalizations in excess of ten million dollars—a size that was extraordinarily rare just a decade earlier. So overweening was the power of giant corporations that by 1909 nearly two-thirds of all manufacturing workers labored for fewer than 5 percent of all industrial enterprises.[90]

The dynamism of post–Civil War American capitalism and its growing financial sophistication positioned the US economy for a jump to global status. Booming exports of manufactures and semifinished goods delivered a favorable balance of trade virtually every year after 1873. But this rise posed significant questions about the US monetary order. Among other things, global power in capitalist society works through *world money*. Capitalism involves a hierarchy of monies—from those with the most limited range of exchangeability (e.g., tokens accepted only at a particular store) to those of universal equivalence—in which the more limited have less social force than the most general. In Great Britain under the gold standard, for instance, country banks issued their own currencies backed by the private notes of London banks and Bank of England notes, while using gold reserves as reserve assets. London banks, in turn, held a combination of Bank of England notes and gold, while the Bank of England's official reserves consisted entirely of gold. Gold thus sat atop the monetary pyramid in Britain; and as world capitalism went to the gold standard, the yellow metal became the ultimate expression of world money. This is not to say that gold was the medium of everyday commerce; banknotes and coins typically played that role. Rather, gold was the measure of world value as well as its embodiment (as the store of global value). It was the means of comparing national prices and earnings and, thereby, of globally measuring what one nation-state owed another in the course of world trade and investment flows (tallied via each state's balance of payments with every other). Great Britain had fixed the price of an ounce of gold at £4.247, while the US government set its value at $20.671.

This determined a rate of exchange between dollars and pounds based on gold. Each major currency had a gold value, which provided for straightforward conversions of one currency into another through the medium of gold. "It was almost as if the gold-standard world possessed a single international money," remarks one historian.[91] There is in fact no "as if" about it. Gold *was* the ultimate means of payment in international transactions—the only one that was fully universal.[92] Assessing the role of gold in 1870, the majority report of a US congressional committee pronounced, "For all purposes of internal trade, gold is not money . . . but for all purposes of foreign commerce it is our only currency."[93]

However, at the end of the Civil War, the United States was not on the gold standard: it had a pure fiat money until 1879.[94] And even after its return to gold, strong forces continually pressed for a silver standard, or a bimetallic standard (gold and silver). Indeed, the Silver Purchase Act of 1890 remonetized silver by requiring the government to undertake regular purchases of the metal as a way to augment the money supply. Yet, bimetallic standards are inherently fraught, as developments in private markets shift the relative values of each metal away from their official government values. This inevitably leads to a drain of one metal at the expense of the other, as speculators exploit deviations of market prices from the official rate of conversion (which is often set in law) between the two metals. If the market price for silver is worth 5 percent less than the government rate, for instance, then investors—including foreign ones—will trade silver for gold at government windows (and pocket the extra 5 percent in gold). In the 1890s, this would have meant a persistent drain of gold away from the United States, moving it, sooner or later, to a silver standard for its currency as gold reserves declined. However, those sections of American business that were eyeing a jump to global status knew that their project required a dollar tied exclusively to gold.

The urgency of committing the dollar to gold became more pressing in 1871, as the international gold standard gained momentum. Having militarily defeated France, German Chancellor Otto von Bismarck took his newly unified state onto gold. This quickly forced France onto the gold standard, as well. In rapid order, four other European nations converted to gold, as did Japan, India, Russia, and Argentina throughout the 1890s, followed in the next decade by Austria-Hungary, Mexico, Brazil, and Thailand. As the gold standard became genuinely international, Britain, its originator, established itself as the center of world finance. Indeed, governments and investors the world over had more confidence in the pound's convertibility into gold than they had regarding any other currency—a confidence that was supremely practical, given Britain's leading position in the global economy.

From early on, British capitalism had developed surpluses above its own domestic investment needs, and much of this could be profitably loaned to international borrowers. In addition, it had an empire for the circulation of its currency, and dominions that could be bullied into buttressing sterling when necessary. If London was the center of global finance, this also meant that its gold standard was the de facto foundation of world money—and thus, crucially, that gold was now the basis of war finance. For any government entering the late-nineteenth-century scramble for empire, or even simply building its armed forces for defense against aggressors, gold was essential as payment for weapons, ships, armored vehicles, aircraft, provisions, cotton and linen for uniforms, and iron—increasingly the world's key industrial material. It is no accident, therefore, that the internationalization of the gold standard occurred in the decades leading to the First World War, when military budgets were soaring amid colonial scrambles. Total military expenditures for Britain, Germany, Russia, Austria-Hungary, France, and Italy more than tripled between 1880 and 1914, as the imperial powers lurched toward war. Observing these trends, while his own country engaged in a pell-mell military buildup, one astute Japanese analyst wrote: "Bismarck said there are only two things: iron and blood. I, on the other hand, believe that there are only iron and gold."[95]

This substitution of gold for blood goes, of course, to the very heart of the argument I have been developing. As the blood of the modern state, gold was the medium of imperial life. It thus underwrote the sorcery of death-as-life—necropolitics—practiced by states as war machines.[96] Gold, the means of war finance, had become the circuitry of world power. As lifeblood of the military commonwealth, it was the instrument for making real blood flow across the world's oceans and battlefields.

Cognizant of this, US President Grover Cleveland warned Congress in 1893 that a monetary system orbiting around silver would mean the United States could "no longer claim a place among nations of the first class."[97] Congressman Josiah Patterson of Tennessee expressed the same idea, in the parlance of everyday ruling-class bigotry: to move to a silver standard, he pronounced, would position the United States "not with the enlightened nations of Christendom, but side by side with China, with the republic of Mexico, with the republics of Central and South America, and every other semicivilized country on the globe."[98] Adoption of the gold standard became the measure of all things wholesome—civilization, global standing, war, and empire.

To be sure, the gold standard served important domestic functions. Among other things, it limited just how expansionary central banks could be with the money supply, since the requirement to convert currency to gold upon demand constrained profligate tendencies, real or imagined. (For instance, an excessively rapid expansion of currency might provoke a bank run that could exhaust the gold reserves.) But most importantly, with the emergence of an international gold standard from 1873–90, global capitalism had acquired a singular form of world money—and American capitalists were intent that their system should revolve around it. After passage of the Silver Purchase Act of 1890, which threatened to move America off gold, they spearheaded a campaign to secure the supremacy of the yellow metal. As much as they invoked domestic reasons for this, American business leaders were also insistent about its necessity for war finance. America's extensive global investments, explained Treasury Secretary Lyman Gage, required "a well-supplied war chest with an impregnable credit"—and impregnable credit meant a dollar as good as gold.[99]

In fact, war once again proved a turning point. In 1898, US capital turned its sights on Spain, a colonial power in terminal decline. Offering little real resistance to American military aggression, Spain handed over its colonies in the Philippines, Guam, and Puerto Rico, while Cuba was made a US protectorate.[100] American capitalism was now asserting itself as the rising imperial power of the era. But it still needed to establish itself as a heavyweight in the sphere of world trade, investment, and finance. Twenty-four months after Spain was vanquished, the Gold Standard Act of 1900 was passed. The dollar was now officially tied to gold and backed by a $150 million gold reserve at the Treasury.[101] Expansionist dreams had carried the day. But they were far from exhausted.

While consolidation of the gold standard would be critical to the projection of power abroad, so would the institutional capacities to manage crises and panics. In fact, with the latter in mind, corporate America had been promoting a US central bank since the early 1890s, as the transition to mammoth firms exacerbated tendencies toward overproduction. The growth of output prompted by giant corporations, deploying new productivity-boosting technologies, pushed prices into a downward movement. Between 1875 and 1896, for instance, US prices dropped by an average of 1.7 percent each year.[102] Compounding these trends were financial crises like that of 1893, in which four hundred banks collapsed, all of which reinforced the big business campaign for a central bank with powers of countercyclical crisis management.[103] But progress toward central banking was slow, in part because some sections of capital distrusted any state initiative that seemed too readily influenced by popular forces. Then the Panic of 1907 struck, rocking markets and severely damaging the international reputation of America's financial system.

The crisis broke out in October of that year, with a run on the Knickerbocker Trust Company, which then suspended all cash withdrawals (whether currency or gold). Within days, as panic spread, major banks in New York and Chicago did the same. Overnight, companies could not meet payrolls, and commercial and personal credit dried up. Cash was now at a premium, with some brokers receiving up to a 4 percent surcharge on every dollar they provided.[104] As individuals and financial institutions hoarded cash, interest rates on stock exchange *call loans*—overnight loans secured by shares—leapt to 70 percent. Hoping to alleviate the panic, Treasury Secretary George Courtelyou pumped $25 million into New York banks. He may as well have been fighting wildfire with a water pistol. Only when stock prices had dropped sufficiently was the downturn arrested by the appearance of large inflows of gold from European investors (looking to take advantage of falling share prices). Six months later, Congress authorized the Treasury to create up to $500 million in emergency currency to relieve future panics.[105] But progress toward fashioning a central bank remained erratic. And when it was finally accomplished with the Federal Reserve Act of 1913, it was too late to address the trauma that seized global financial markets with the outbreak of world war in August 1914.

Global Slaughter, the Second Thirty Years' War, and the Triumph of the Dollar

"In Europe they mobilize armies and navies. In America we mobilize bank reserves."

—Minnesota Senator Knute Nelson, August 1914[106]

By the time war erupted, the US economy had become the world's largest, responsible for one-third of global industrial output—nearly as much as that of Britain, France, and Germany combined. Yet, notwithstanding its industrial heft, America was a lightweight in world financial markets. There, Britain reigned supreme. When countries needed to raise money, they sought out British pounds, which were effectively as good as gold. Even the German mark and the French franc received more use as a means of international payment than did the dollar. Certainly, some countries tapped US markets for loans, though rarely were the bonds issued in New York denominated in dollars, given the US currency's lack of global reach.[107] But this mismatch between industrial and financial power would not last. The game-changer, once again, was war—and war finance.

In fact, America's rise to financial supremacy would take a mere six months of war. And this time, gold would work in its favor.

One after another, the belligerent states of 1914 were forced to suspend gold convertibility, as the demands of war finance exhausted their supplies. France, Germany, and Russia did so in August, the first month of the conflict. The reason was basic: gold was the most universally accepted means of paying for the weapons, raw materials, and foodstuffs essential to sustaining armed forces. Warring states would no longer part with the precious metal except for the purchase of war materials. Each and every soldier and sailor had to be trained, equipped, clothed, fed, and transported to bases and fronts. They needed to be supported by armored vehicles, ships, and planes. Once the shooting started, for instance, France required up to two hundred thousand shells daily, nearly seventeen times its prewar output.[108] Given the scale of mobilization, which went on for nearly five years, the primary combatants were starved for cash, while America, which would wait three years before entering the conflict, was flush with loanable funds. This is why Minnesota Senator Knute Nelson could declare, "In Europe they mobilize armies and navies. In America we mobilize bank reserves." And this time America's leaders, intent on achieving global status, refused to be pushed off the gold standard. That would be the difference maker.

Adhering to gold was far from easy. As Europe moved to war in late July 1914, its governments feverishly stockpiled bullion. To do so, they began selling their US financial assets, like stocks and bonds, and cashing in the dollars they received for US gold, which was immediately shipped across the ocean (or sometimes to Canada, in the case of Britain). During the final week of July, $25 million in gold was drained from America's reserves in this way. This seemed bad enough. But the drain had actually started earlier, with $9 million in gold exports in May, rising to $44 million a month later. Altogether, $83 million worth of US gold had been siphoned to Europe, even *before* the shooting started. Worse, in 1914 European investors owned $4 billion worth of US railway stocks alone—all of which could be liquidated and turned into gold in due time.[109] Of course, the American government could take the dollar off gold for the duration of the war, but this posed two problems. First, America was not at war (and would stay out of the fighting for three more years), and war was the only accepted rationale for suspending dollar–gold convertibility. Second, notwithstanding its entry into the conflict, Britain was committed to maintaining the gold standard in order to preserve the unique role of the pound as a world currency, and that of London as the center of world finance. For the United States to close the gold window would be an admission that it could not compete with sterling as a world money, setting back New York's emergence as a site of world finance. All of this compelled America's leaders to cling to gold. Expressing a growing bourgeois consensus, Benjamin Strong, first president of the Federal Reserve Bank of New York, vowed to make the dollar "an international currency" by building "confidence in the redeemability of dollars in gold at all times."[110] Among other things, this also implied a growing global role for American banks, and to this end the Federal Reserve Act authorized US national banks with at least $1 million to set up foreign branches, a privilege of which the largest quickly availed themselves.[111] Yet, the global expansion of American banks rested on the stability of the dollar. And as gold exited the United States in record amounts, that stability seemed precarious.

Treasury Secretary William McAdoo had a plan, however. He would shut down Wall Street, rather than see the United States go off gold. This would close off the main avenue by which European investors could sell their American stock holdings for gold. If European investors had nowhere to sell their US financial assets, exports of US gold could be considerably constrained. So, he arranged for the New York Stock Exchange to close its doors on July 31, 1914. And closed it would remain for the next four months.[112] At the same time, McAdoo knew that in shutting down Wall Street, he was simply buying time. Eventually, the market would have to be reopened. The key was to pump out exports, particularly of grain and cotton, to European states desperate to feed and clothe their troops. This would stop the gold outflow, since the belligerents would need the precious metal to pay for American goods. By autumn, US exports were booming, the value of the dollar was ticking upward, and European states were hurrying to New York to borrow money. Gold was no longer flowing out, while foreign money was pouring in. By the time the United States entered the global conflagration in 1917, foreign governments had raised more than $2.5 billion in wartime funds by selling *dollar-denominated* securities in New York.[113] The dollar had now displaced sterling as the global currency of choice. By the early 1920s, interest rates were lower in New York than in London, which encouraged governments and investors to continue to do business there. At long last, American capitalism had mastered money's second modal form— central bank currency backed by government debt and redeemable in gold.

$

By most measures, America had become the premier capitalist economy in the world by 1915. But its formal ascendance to *imperial hegemon*, the power that dominates global politics and economics, would not transpire for another thirty years. This reminds us that the organization of hegemonic power involves complex social processes. Between immediate events and the *longue durée* of centuries, argued French historian Fernand Braudel, there occur cycles or conjunctures that work themselves out over a decade or a quarter century.[114] The thirty-year period consisting of the two World Wars (1914–19 and 1939–45), in whose interregnum occurred a global depression, might be seen as just such a conjuncture. Only out of the turmoil of trench warfare, blood-soaked fields, revolutions and civil wars, fascism, and the atom bomb would there emerge a new global hierarchy based on American power—and the US dollar.[115]

It is incumbent to say a few things here about the *total wars* of the first half of the twentieth century. These were conflicts characterized by the industrialization of killing, the use of machine technology—tanks, modern battleships, bomber aircraft, chemical weapons, and the atom bomb—in order to murder and destroy. To rework Walter Benjamin's expression, we have here the eruption into world history of *mechanically reproducible death*.[116] More than sixteen million people probably perished in the first global conflagration, vindicating Rosa Luxemburg's verdict that "shamed, dishonored, wading in blood and dripping with filth—thus stands bourgeois society."[117] Reflecting a decade later on "the nights of annihilation of the last war," Benjamin contemplated the ominous mobilization of means of destruction that reshaped the earth: "Human multitudes, gases, electrical forces were hurled into the open country, high frequency currents coursed through the landscape, new constellations rose in the sky, aerial space and oceans thundered with propellers, and everywhere sacrificial shafts were dug in Mother Earth."[118]

The shock registered by the brutalities of total war unsettled and traumatized its combatants as well as its victims. Even a dedicated imperialist like Winston Churchill registered its dreadful features in a speech given after World War I. "The Great War differed from all ancient wars in the power of the combatants and their fearful agencies of destruction," he declared, continuing, "Every effort was made to starve whole nations into submission without regard to age or sex. . . . Bombs from the air were cast down indiscriminately. Poison gas in many forms stifled or seared the soldiers. Liquid fire was projected upon their bodies. Men fell from the air in flames, or were smothered, often slowly, in the dark recesses of the sea. . . . Europe and large parts of Africa and Asia became one huge battlefield."[119]

Twenty years later, the science and technology of destruction had become frighteningly more powerful as the Second World War exterminated at least sixty million people, fully 3 percent of the world population. And now a second feature of total war—the systematic killing (genocide) and displacement of civilian populations—came fully into its own, producing the industrialized death camp (Auschwitz), and giving rise to the new human categories of refugees and the stateless.[120]

Total war was "the largest enterprise hitherto known to man," wrote Marxist historian Eric Hobsbawm.[121] It required colossal efforts to coordinate food production and distribution, armaments manufacture, rationing of goods, worldwide transportation and communication, financial management, mobilization of "manpower," patrol of the oceans and the skies, movement of troops, and orchestrated destruction and killing on a planetary scale. In the interregnum between the two concentrated periods of global slaughter, capitalism underwent its most devastating slump, the Great Depression of the 1930s, reminding us why millions came to reject a system that seemed capable of nothing but murder and economic hardship.

The story of the Depression has been told many times. The drama is usually associated with the great stock market crash in New York, beginning in October

1929.[122] In fact, "business was in trouble long before the crash."[123] Profits and output had started to turn down prior to the meltdown on Wall Street. But the latter thoroughly destroyed personal fortunes and traumatized the financial system. Four thousand banks collapsed in the United States. By 1933, US gross national product had dropped by nearly a third, and one person in every four in the labor force was unemployed. The American economy was particularly hard hit by the slump, but it was far from isolated. Seventeen other countries saw bank panics and collapses, and one after another, each went off the gold standard. The United States ended gold convertibility for domestic purposes with the Gold Reserve Act of 1934, though it retained the yellow metal for settlement of international transactions.[124] Trade protectionism and currency devaluations induced a massive contraction in world trade, which underwent a decline of more than a third by 1932. Plummeting prices, particularly for raw materials and agricultural commodities, hammered nations like Canada, Argentina, and Australia. After more than five years of persistent decline, it seemed the bottom had been touched. Output and investment started to grow, unemployment eased a bit. Then, in 1937, the bottom fell out once more.[125] But this new slump would not drag on like that of 1929–35. What ended it was war—total war to be precise, and human carnage on a planetary scale.

That capitalism should thrive on destruction comes as no surprise. The frantic production of tanks, fighter aircraft, jeeps, battleships, millions of rifles, and millions of uniforms—and the iron, steel, electrical goods, and more that all these required—catapulted economies out of depression. As economist John Kenneth Galbraith observed, "The Great Depression of the thirties never came to an end. It merely disappeared in the great mobilization of the forties."[126] Yet, it was not just troops who were mobilized; so was capital. And as with the troops, it was the state that did the mobilizing. World capitalism revived, in other words, on the back of a *state-directed* war economy.

Following the decade of depression, the American gross national product grew by 65 percent from 1939 to 1944. Industrial production expanded more rapidly than during any other period in US history. Driving all of this was military demand: production of war goods catapulted from 2 percent to 40 percent of all output over the same five-year period.[127] By 1943, the US government was initiating 90 percent of all investment, and the arms sector was generating half of all output.[128] Factories were humming, and farms were working flat out to meet military demand.

But as much as war revived world capitalism, its effects were highly uneven. And there was no greater beneficiary of this unevenness than Uncle Sam. To begin with, the United States did not enter the war until late 1941, more than two and a half years after the rest of its allies. Yet, while it remained outside the conflict, it nonetheless profited from it—producing ever more goods for its European trading partners, and providing them loans. Even when it did enter the brutal fray, the United States did not experience the massive physical and industrial decimation that accompanied the human slaughter elsewhere.

Japan, for instance, lost one-quarter of its factories and a third of its industrial equipment as a result of the carnage. Italy's steel industry saw a quarter of its capacity destroyed, while Germany suffered damage to 17 percent of its stock of fixed capital. Meanwhile, one-tenth of France's industrial stock was wiped out.[129] While economies like these were ravaged by war, the United States boomed. At the commencement of hostilities in 1939, the US economy was about one-half the combined size of those of Europe, Japan, and the Soviet Union. Six years later, when war at last ended, it was larger than all of them combined. By that point, the United States accounted for half of global industrial production and held almost three-quarters of the world's supplies of gold. Lifted ever higher on oceans of blood, the United States now dominated the international economy. And the dollar was its unrivaled world money.

The Great Boom, Vietnam's Unraveling, and Global Fiat Money

Once the bombs had stopped falling, the losers' countries occupied, and the victors' lust for conquest (temporarily) satisfied, world capitalism entered a sustained quarter-century expansion (1948–73). The contrast with the previous period—three decades of war and world depression—could scarcely have been starker. To be sure, there were cyclical fluctuations across the Great Boom, with periodic domestic recessions. But overall, global capitalism experienced a period of high growth rates, robust profits and investment, low unemployment, expanding world trade, and generally rising living standards. This "golden age" for Western economies had its brutal undersides of course: imperial interventions, racist violence, the Cold War arms race, an intensified regulation of gender and sexuality. Yet, Western economies just kept humming.

World manufacturing output quadrupled between the early 1950s and the early 1970s, while world trade in manufactures leapt ten times higher. The stock of plant, machinery, and equipment per worker more than doubled, driving labor productivity forward at record pace. Food production rose more quickly than did world population, with grain yields doubling over a thirty-year period. Rates of economic growth hit record highs in every major capitalist nation, with the exceptions of Great Britain and the United States.[130] As labor militancy was contained and pro-business policies consolidated, the era of high profits created the space for governments to expand social provision ("the welfare state") without compromising capital accumulation. A myth of social harmony triumphed, according to which capital, labor, and the unemployed could prosper together in a new managed capitalism. John Kenneth Galbraith, not known for recycling conventional wisdom, suggested, in his 1958 book *The Affluent Society*, that since the problem of wealth-creation had been solved, the social challenge was now to manage affluence and share the wealth.[131]

Although often described as the "Keynesian era," the boom had considerably less to do with the influence of British economist John Maynard Keynes than is often supposed. What fueled expansion was not deft fiscal and monetary management so much as the maintenance of high rates of profitability. Through a complex algebra—whose variables included the impacts of wartime destruction of capital, the stimulating effects of permanent arms budgets, the mobilization of new technologies, the containment of labor insurgency, and the reconstitution of reserve armies of labor[132]—capitalism seemed to have found a new growth trajectory that would forever eliminate crises and depressions.

Floating atop the boom, coordinating its flows, was the almighty dollar. After climbing into the top tier during the First World War, the supremacy of the greenback became incontestable after the second global conflagration. Dollar hegemony was enshrined when Western leaders gathered at Bretton Woods, New Hampshire, in the summer of 1944 to hammer out a new monetary regime.[133] Contrary to a present-day myth, this conference was anything but a harmonious gathering of responsible leaders seeking the common good. Bretton Woods was another exercise in great-power politics, with the United States refusing proposals from Keynes, the British representative, in order to impose dollar supremacy. The global economy would henceforth revolve around the dollar as the world's primary reserve currency. All major currencies would be pegged at fixed rates to the dollar, which in turn was to be tied to gold at a ratio of thirty-five dollars to an ounce. Like the British monetary system, this was a gold exchange standard. The dollar was to be the basis of monetary payments, albeit with the understanding that central banks could exchange the latter for gold. To stabilize the global structure, exchange rates of other currencies would be held fairly steady to the dollar by the use of capital controls, which would prevent so-called "hot" flows of money. The major powers also agreed to finance a new institution, the International Monetary Fund, empowered to provide loans in the event of currency crises should a member country encounter severe balance-of-payments difficulties.

Ironically, in light of what would later transpire, the main challenge to this arrangement in the early years of postwar boom was a dollar *shortage* in Europe. By mid-1947, the United States was running a twenty-billion-dollar export surplus—goods that could only be paid for by America's trade partners with dollars or gold, each of which was in short supply due to their massive concentration in US hands. Without an outflow of dollars to Europe and Japan to support international trade and capital flows, the dollar-based system risked seizing up. The conundrum was at first evaded when the American government announced the Marshall Plan and its program of aid to Europe. But it was the decision to rearm Europe, and to provide military aid to this end, that really turned the tide. And this decision crystallized into strategic policy direction when war commenced in 1950 on the Korean Peninsula. This policy was accelerated in the face of the election of left-leaning governments in France and Italy, worker revolts in countries like Japan, and fears that the end of war would induce another wave of working-class and socialist insurgence. As arms spending soared, and the American state shifted to "Military Keynesianism" at home and continuous military assistance to allies abroad, an outflow of dollars lubricated the gears of the world economy.[134] But US corporations were soon to augment these outflows by increasing their offshore investments in order to build multinational operations and thereby profit from sales in rebounding European economies. The "solution" initially provided by militarism was now amplified by corporate globalization. The result was a consolidation of the new regime of world money, as a persistent US balance-of-payments deficit (driven by overseas military spending and aid), alongside foreign investment, generated the dollar liquidity essential to the smooth working of the world economy. Yet, so long as America had a surplus on its merchandise trade, foreign-held dollars were welcomed as payment for US-produced goods.

But this postwar balance would not last. It was no longer the case, after all, that the United States mobilized bank reserves while others mobilized armies. As the imperial hegemon, America was paying for troops and tanks, bombs and aircraft, and for ever more expensive ballistic missiles. Simultaneously, it was exporting dollars to maintain foreign bases, and to feed, clothe, house, and pay wages to soldiers overseas—all costs that rose with the escalation of the war in Vietnam. In 1964, America's debts to foreign central banks exceeded its gold reserves for the first time in the postwar period, due to a balance-of-payments deficit that stemmed from Vietnam-driven foreign spending. Official government figures estimated that overseas military spending by the United States equaled $3.7 billion during the following three years (1965–67). Yet these figures excluded a $2.1 billion outflow due to military grant agreements—consisting of military goods and services paid for by the American government and delivered as gifts to client states—during these years.[135] These "gifts" would grow by more than a billion dollars by 1971, when the dollar crisis erupted. By that point, US military outlays abroad exceeded its foreign sales of armaments by almost $3 billion, with some analysts estimating that the foreign costs of empire amounted to $8 billion per year.[136] The dollar outflow—and the weakening position of the greenback that accompanied it—was thus directly connected to the costs of war and empire. To be sure, the US state believed in the necessity of such imperial expenditures. But, the empire itself appeared to be in decline at the time, nowhere more so than in Vietnam, where it was losing the war despite ongoing military escalation. As the rest of the world watched the gyrations of the dollar and the humbling of America's war machine at the hands of Vietnam's national liberation movement, the US empire underwent a credibility crisis.[137] A vice president of Citibank insightfully informed a Congressional committee in 1970, "Hegemony, not liquidity, is what the dollar problem is all about."[138] While that may not have been the whole story, it was a crucial part of it.

Underlying this challenge to hegemony was American capitalism's relative economic decline. While the US government spent extravagantly on empire, its domestic economy performed much more sluggishly than did the very economies that had seemed so weak and broken in 1945. America's listless progress can be seen in growth rates of the "capital stock" in manufacturing—the accumulation of plants, machines, and equipment. During the critical fifteen-year period from 1955 to 1970, US capital stock in industry grew by 57 percent. In Europe, it grew twice as rapidly (116 percent), while in Japan it rose an incredible nine times faster (500 percent). By 1972, American business had spent several years at the bottom of the rankings of industrial nations for reinvestment of corporate earnings.[139] The United States was thus among the least dynamic of the major capitalist economies. As a result, it now began to lose markets, especially for manufactured goods, to up-and-coming rivals. To make matters immeasurably worse, the so-called Great Boom was winding down, ordaining the downfall of the Bretton Woods system.

The decline of the Great Boom was driven by the overaccumulation of capital and a downward movement in the general rate of profit that commenced around 1968.[140] But like all economic slowdowns, the effects were borne unevenly. This time, having lost ground to its main competitors, American capitalism endured some of the harshest blows, among them a full-fledged dollar crisis.

As early as 1960, while Europe and Japan recovered, the reserves of dollars held overseas exceeded America's supply of gold. Had all those dollars been converted for the precious metal, the United States would have been abruptly forced off the gold exchange standard. Instead, US governments enforced a series of stopgap measures, some of them at odds with the spirit of Bretton Woods. As early as 1961, Americans were prohibited from holding gold outside the country. Then, European governments were strong-armed into contributing to a Gold Pool, and pressed to refrain from converting dollars to gold. Shortly after, American residents were barred from collecting gold coins. But none of these ad hoc moves could offset the structural trend: the United States was now importing more goods than it exported, and shipping out billions to finance overseas military spending, while covering the shortfall with a currency in which its trade partners were drowning.

It was one thing for the United States to have a deficit in its overall balance of payments; but this was now joined by a deficit in merchandise trade. By 1969, the American economy was running a four-billion-dollar shortfall on trade in consumer goods. And two years later, its *overall* trade balance turned negative.[141] The world was now awash with billions of dollars that many of its holders simply did not need. So long as they bowed to US pressure and abstained from demanding gold, America's trading partners were accepting useless IOUs in exchange for the real goods and services they supplied to the United States. And by exchanging inconvertible IOUs for goods and services, as one economic analyst noted, the US was effectively appropriating "from the dollar receiving countries an equivalent amount of their surplus value for its own use."[142] To make matters worse, the era of escalating war in Vietnam was also one of steadily rising price inflation. The real buying power of the dollar—the actual material goods it could purchase—declined persistently. To hold dollars was thus to hang on to a depreciating asset, one that could buy less and less. French President Georges Pompidou openly grumbled about having to use as a global measure of value "a national currency that constantly loses value."[143] The dollar was no longer as good as gold—but it could still be redeemed for the precious metal by foreign central banks. Notwithstanding US threats, foreign governments and investors rushed to do just that. By 1968, more than 40 percent of the US gold reserves had left the country.[144] On a *single day* in March of that year, some four hundred million dollars was presented for conversion.[145]

As the precious metal exited its vaults over the course of 1968, the American government ceased providing gold to *private* dollar holders at the official price of thirty-five dollars per ounce. But the real bombshell exploded in 1971. On August 15 of that year, President Richard Nixon slammed shut the gold window. No longer would the US Treasury provide bullion for dollars, even to foreign central banks. The foundations of Bretton Woods had collapsed. Initially, this move sent shock waves through government and financial circles. Told that Nixon was contemplating going off the gold exchange standard, one Treasury official "leaned forward, put his face in his hands, and whispered, 'My God!'"[146] Yet Treasury Secretary John Connally was prepared to play hardball. When warned by Federal Reserve President Arthur Burns that other nations would retaliate against the United States' unilateral move, Connally replied: "Let 'em. What can they do?"[147] Very little, as it turned out.

The initial effect of the US abdication of gold convertibility was to volatilize currency values. The Bretton Woods system of fixed exchange rates between currencies crumpled as the United States bullied its trade partners—particularly Germany and Japan—into revaluing the deutsche mark and the yen. (The former appreciated by 13.6 percent; the latter by nearly 17 percent.) This was simultaneously a devaluation of the dollar—one that was meant to assist American exports and the balance of trade, as US-based goods would now be cheaper in Germany and Japan (since every dollar for which a US good was sold would require fewer deutsche marks and yen). Over the first two years after Nixon closed the gold window, the dollar declined by 25 percent relative to the yen, deutsche mark, British pound, and French franc.[148] For a time, there was an effort to restabilize currencies at a new series of fixed rates of exchange. But with ever-larger global flows of funds, particularly of dollars held outside the US (known as *Eurodollars*) that eluded control by central banks, every attempt to fix exchange rates broke down, as speculators bet against currencies they perceived as overvalued, while gambling on those they expected to rise.

In earlier days, governments might have used capital controls to block the movement of speculative finance in and out of currency markets. But those days were long gone. The stunning growth of the Eurodollar market (to which we return shortly) meant that billions moved in a monetary space outside the sphere of state regulation. The buying and selling of currencies now became a world growth industry. In 1973, the daily turnover in foreign exchange (forex) markets amounted to $15 billion; by 2007 it had grown more than two hundred times, to $3.2 trillion per day. Meanwhile, the daily turnover in nontraditional forex markets also exploded, reaching $4.2 trillion in 2007.[149] With financial movements this massive, there was no way that governments could set the value of currencies. Having abandoned a world money anchored to gold, capitalism found itself in a new era of *floating* exchange rates—which changed every day under the influence of massive flows of finance across global markets. So unstable were monetary values that one world leader referred to the new monetary regime as "a floating non-system."[150] And this nonsystem, as I have argued elsewhere, fostered a proliferation of new financial instruments—particularly financial derivatives—that were meant to hedge the risks associated with volatile money, but that actually had the effect of heightening instability by producing even more complex means of speculation. The global financial crisis of 2008–2009 was in part a dramatic expression of these very volatilities.[151] Lurking behind this monetary instability was the reality of a dollar that had become a global fiat money.

It is important to emphasize here that *fiat* refers only to the ability of the state to enforce the acceptance of its currency—not to impose its value. The latter is determined in the long run by the relative productivity of the capital within the nation-state in question. And this is approximated by the rate of exchange a national currency maintains with others (and with the world of commodities).

The inherent paradox of a currency that serves as world money is that it is both a credit money produced by a single nation-state *and* a global means for measuring value and making international payments. The system works most effectively when the imperial hegemon spends extensively outside its borders—thereby furnishing the system with liquidity—while also maintaining decided advantages in the production of vital goods and services, so that holders of the world money require it for ongoing transactions. This was the story of the dollar for the quarter century from 1945 to 1970. But once the United States lost its decisive strength in world manufacturing, dollars became little more than inconvertible IOUs accumulating in the hands of its major trading partners. Henceforth, the outflow of dollars in order to police world capitalism became an economic liability. This is what produced the run on US gold reserves—better, after all, to get gold for your dollars if you don't need American-produced cars or electronics. Yet the run on US gold could only be a stopgap. By the summer of 1971, gold was exiting the United States at a rate of thirty-five billion dollars per year. Sooner rather than later, America's gold reserves would dry up. Nixon's decision to close the gold window simply recognized the inevitable. Foreign governments objected vociferously to America's unilateral abdication of dollar convertibility, to which Nixon's Treasury secretary retorted, "It's our currency but it's your problem."[152] Indeed it was.

Reconstituting Imperial Money after Gold

The overwhelming assumption during the 1970s was that the US dollar was in unambiguous decline. On the Left, this was generally joined to the view that the downfall of the dollar was a manifestation of the breakdown of the American empire.[153]

Nearly half a century later, it is clear that such predictions were skewed. Yes, the dollar-gold standard collapsed, and the global economy endured a decade of profound turmoil. But something quite novel—and with which theory has generally not caught up—emerged in its place: *imperial fiat money*. Consider that, more than four decades after it was taken off gold,

- the dollar is used in 85 percent of all foreign exchange transactions;
- it is the medium in which the world's central banks hold nearly two-thirds of their currency reserves;
- it is the currency in which over half of the world's exports are priced;

- and it is the money in which roughly two-thirds of international bank loans are denominated.

In short, notwithstanding its detachment from gold or America's enduring and massive payments deficits, a reconstituted dollar dominates the world economy. And with that domination we find ourselves in the age of the *third* modal form of money—one in which a national fiat money, untethered to any sort of physical commodity, operates as world money. I refer to this as *global fiat money*.[154]

We can readily understand this changed modality by returning to the earlier discussion of Bank of England notes. These, as we observed, were essentially private monetary instruments based on government debt. What prevented them from being pure fiat money was the bank's obligation to redeem them for gold or silver at a guaranteed rate. During wars, however, the Bank of England often suspended convertibility, just as Lincoln's government did during the Civil War. Throughout those periods, money was backed by nothing more than state debt and the government's injunction that these currencies had to be accepted as legal tender (the latter making them fiat monies).

What distinguishes the period after 1973, when Nixon announced that there would be no return to a gold-based dollar, is that inconvertible fiat money was made permanent. The emergence of this third modal form has sometimes been described as the de-commodification of money, which is both formally correct and substantively misleading. Officially, the dollar is no longer exchangeable with gold at a fixed rate guaranteed by the US state. In this sense, we have moved beyond commodity money. At the same time, however, the dollar can be readily exchanged for gold or any other commodity at prevailing *market* rates. In this sense, the dollar is entirely convertible with gold (as it is with any other commodity). What is described as the "de-commodification" of money thus actually refers to its de-anchoring from a *fixed* rate of exchange with gold. Rather than money becoming inconvertible, then, it is more accurate to say that it has become destabilized in a regime of floating exchange rates.

Nevertheless, the shift to a floating regime for world money was a system-altering transformation, and it continues to pose significant theoretical challenges for critical political economy, not least because the complete de-linking of world money from a fixed commodity is without precedent. For instance, one mainstream economist, writing in the late 1970s, argued that "commodity money is the only type of money that, at present time, can be said to have passed the test of history in market economies . . . it is only since 1973 that the absence of any link to the commodity world is claimed to be a normal feature of the monetary system. It will take several more decades before we can tell whether the Western world has finally embarked, as so often proclaimed, on a new era of non-commodity money."[155] Those several decades have now passed, and non-commodity money rules the world. All critical and radical theory is obliged to come to terms with this metamorphosis. Yet, it must be said that many efforts to make sense of this mutation in world money have been distinctly incapacitating.

Perhaps the most significant of these is a decidedly unhelpful position often associated with deconstruction and poststructuralism. Recall two texts with which I have taken issue in previous chapters. One intoned that "the economic base or mode of production" of modern societies is "a financial abyss." Another urged that finance "is a particularly interpretive and *textual* practice."[156] In the same vein, a recent work declared that "money is in itself nothing but representation."[157] Whether acknowledged or not, all of these formulations are responses to the severing of fixed convertibility of the dollar for gold. Ostensibly freed from any referent (such as gold), money is proclaimed to be purely *self-referential*. Rather than epitomizing something else, national currency is said to reflect nothing more than itself, leading us into a monetary house of mirrors.

These analyses are products of an influential line of commentary on the post-1973 era that has diluted critical thinking. I am referring, in particular, to "economic" analysis that has gone under the banner of postmodern criticism, emblematized by Jacques Derrida's *Given Time*, whose central arguments about money and (post)modern economics have been widely reproduced. Derrida informs us in that text that we now live "in the age of value as monetary sign." He does not mean this in the commonplace sense that all money has a symbolic form—as coin, paper currency, or digital inscription. Derrida intends us to understand that money represents *nothing but itself*, that there is nothing that sustains it or to which it refers. It follows that capital (accumulated money and its effects) is infinitely self-reproducing because it issues "from a simulacrum, from a copy of a copy (*phantasma*)."[158] There is no "real" here; there is no sphere of labor and capital to which money is tethered. We are simply inside the simulacrum, trapped by an image capable of endlessly proliferating. Derrida's argument dovetails with the pronouncements of postmodern theorist Jean Baudrillard who, in addition to declaring that the First Gulf War did not happen, has also proclaimed that we live in a "virtual economy emancipated from real economics," one that has arrived at "the end of labor. The end of production. The end of political economy." In this virtual economy without labor or production, "money is now the only genuine artificial satellite," endlessly orbiting around itself.[159] While it might be tempting to pass over ludicrous pronouncements of this sort, their pervasive and disabling influence demands critical engagement. After all, if these were accurate depictions of our world, then it would make very little sense to be concerned about sweatshop labor, precarious work, or bonded migrant laborers, as these would comprise outmoded references to a now-obsolete world—one that vanished with the end of labor, production, and political economy.[160]

Equally unhelpful is the Lacan-inspired claim that, as much as we are all exploited by it, money in fact "does not exist."[161] Weirdly, this argument dovetails with right-wing libertarian attacks on modern "funny money," so-called because it lacks a commodity basis. Referencing the pledge on a British five-pound note that "the Bank of England promises to pay the bearer on demand the sum of five pounds," one pundit asks, "Five pounds of *what?*" The answer, post–gold standard, is entirely circular. Since the Bank of England is not offering a fixed exchange with gold or any other commodity, all it can really do is replace one five-pound note with another.[162] Of course, this commentator ignores the simple fact that the note in question is legally validated by the state as exchangeable for five pounds worth of any market good, including gold. It has, in other words, *infinite* convertibility in the world of commodities, which is no small thing for a hungry person.

A central problem with such analyses is that they tend to describe the post-1973 monetary order in terms of a *dematerialization* of money. These tendencies have been strengthened by the digitization of money, which resulted, by the early 2000s, in actual cash composing merely 3 percent of the money stock.[163] Yet, intangible money still has *material* force. To think otherwise is to adopt a philosophically naive view in which something must be tangible and/or visible to be material—a position that would make gravity an immaterial force.[164] Running through such interpretations, as I have argued elsewhere, is a mode of thought that uncritically reproduces the fetish character of commodities and money by taking the immediate form of appearance of a phenomenon—in this case non-commodity money—as the basis for knowledge claims. Yet, in an alienated social world, things appear in forms that systematically mystify their grounding in human practical activity. The responsibility of critical theory is to de-fetishize by deciphering the practical foundations of mystifying social phenomena, including money, in alienated forms of social praxis—not least because this opens the possibility that they might be transcended by way of *dis-alienating* praxis.[165]

In invisibilizing the world of production and reproduction, the positions I have been canvassing abdicate the work of critique and eliminate any coherent basis for a transformative politics.[166] By occluding the world of labor, analyses of this type obscure the immense expansion of wage labor on a world scale over the neoliberal period (since the late 1970s). The global paid working class effectively doubled over about a quarter century, from roughly 1.5 billion to 3 billion wage workers.[167] At the heart of this *great doubling* was the drawing of hundreds of millions of newly dispossessed laborers in Asia, especially China, into capitalist production.[168] Indeed, the new forms of money and finance we see today are integrally related to this expansion of capital accumulation and the working class on a world scale. To note this, however, is not to invite radical theory to pretend that nothing has changed, and that all is well with inherited concepts. These are major challenges—ones we cannot shirk as we build comprehensive accounts of the changed and changing shape of late capitalism.

At the same time, it is equally unhelpful to treat such changes as simple negations. Particularly disabling in this respect are ostensibly Marxist accounts that conclude that in the absence of commodity money, the classical laws of motion of capitalism are no longer in play. In this perspective, across the twentieth century—and particularly since 1973—capitalism has been in "managed decline" as a consequence of the detachment of money from gold.[169] This, however, is to confuse transformation with decline. Rather than decipher the historical renovations of late capitalism, such positions confuse mutations with *exits* from capitalism's laws of motion. In place of explicating system-wide transformations, which would involve working through the dialectics of continuity and discontinuity they exhibit, such positions instead declare that the latest stage does not conform to a frozen image of an earlier one. In so doing, such analyses abdicate the dialectical injunction to grasp phenomena in their *becoming*.[170] As an organic system, capitalism is in incessant motion; it repeatedly sheds one historical form in its movement into another. And since the starting point for dialectical theory is that which has *actually happened*, rather than formal models, our challenge is to illuminate as best we can the actual social-historical process.[171]

World Finance and Imperial Debt

Let us instead explore the ways in which global fiat money expresses a specific matrix of international capitalist relations. Put in the analytical framework we have been developing, this requires a delineation of the multidimensional configuration of classes, states, empire, war making, and world finance characteristic of the post–Vietnam War era. If the dollar has been reconstituted as a new modal form of world money, this speaks to a dynamic nexus of capitalist power in which an imperial fiat money can operate as the regulator of a *historically specific* arrangement of the capitalist mode of production on a world scale. To be sure, all such arrangements are inherently contradictory; they manifest fractures and fault lines (some of which I discuss below). At the same time, imperial fiat money has been sufficiently functional as to regulate the global reproduction of capital. With this in mind, let us return to the historical situation after 1973.

Writing about the post-1973 advent of "pure paper money," radical geographer David Harvey observes that when money supply is "liberated from any physical production constraints . . . the power of the state then becomes much more relevant, because political and legal backing must replace the backing provided by the money commodity."[172] There is a valuable insight here. After all, what backs the US dollar today is not gold, but government debt (US Treasury bills and bonds, in particular) *and* government fiat, the state's declaration that a given currency is legal tender. Of course, this is not entirely new. Nevertheless, even the British pound, which also rested atop state liabilities, was simultaneously governed by the "metallic barrier" described by Marx, particularly in its functions as world money. Convertibility of pounds to gold limited the production and circulation of private credit money, from notes created by country banks to corporate IOUs. During a crisis in credit markets, holders of IOUs and banknotes would rush to exchange them for gold—the highest and most universal form of money. As much as a Bank of England note was a claim to a share of *future* state taxes that would repay its borrowing (and thus "anchored" by fictitious or futural capital), such notes were also officially linked to *past* labor in the form of bars of gold or metallic coins. This dual temporality of money tied notes based on future wealth to existing products of past labor (gold bars and coins). Within the hierarchy of money, gold loomed above pound notes, as became clear every time a panic induced a stampede for the precious metal. Bank of England notes thus possessed a hybrid structure characteristic of money's second modal form, linked as they were to future returns on loans to the state, which could generally be converted into gold as product of past labor.

What is distinctive of money in its third modal form is that, released from its formal ties to gold, it obeys neither of its former masters: not the credit system nor bullion. With the constraints imposed by the latter now removed, we move in a world of full-fledged credit money. "In contemporary economies, then," economist Duncan Foley points out, "a fictitious capital, the liability of the state, rather than a produced commodity, functions as the measure of value."[173]

When I receive a US dollar, I accept a note based exclusively on future payments derived from government revenues. Of course, since the state has made this note legal tender, within the United States I am obliged, like everyone else, to take it as a means of payment. This gives the dollar a universal validity within the national economy. But why should US government debt be a functional basis of *world* money? Why, in other words, should foreign central banks and international investors find an exclusively debt-backed dollar an acceptable and legitimate means of regulation and coordination of world payments and finance?

One tempting answer is that the United States has largely forced the dollar on the rest of the world. And this cannot be entirely disregarded. After all, the United States reaps an enormous advantage in being able to provide "decommodified" money for the world's goods and services. Over $500 billion in US currency circulates outside the United States, for which foreigners have had to provide an equivalent in goods and services. In addition to well over half of all dollars circulating outside the United States—and thus representing cost-free imports to the US economy (that is, IOUs that are never cashed in)—as of the late 1990s, three-quarters of each year's new dollars stayed abroad.[174] Equally significant, by early 2018 foreign governments had accumulated $6.25 trillion in US Treasury securities. Dollar-receiving countries, in other words, unable to convert their dollar holdings into a higher form of money—like gold—have often used them to purchase American government debt, as well as other US assets. In essence, they have loaned back to the US state the very dollars Americans have spent to import goods and services, or to purchase foreign assets. The effect of this arrangement is to exempt the United States from a balance-of-payments constraint. Rather than having to boost exports or cut imports (and domestic consumption) in the event of sustained deficits in its payments with the rest of the world, the United States can simply issue IOUs that are redeemable primarily for its own government debt.[175] This is indeed an "exorbitant privilege," as a former French finance minister complained.[176] It amounts to allowing the United States—and it alone—to issue as means of global payment IOUs that in principle never have to be repaid. As a former top official at the Bank of France complained in the 1960s, "If I had an agreement with my tailor that whatever money I pay him he returns to me the very same day as a loan, I would have no objection at all to ordering more suits from him."[177]

Because of this arrangement, since the mid-1980s the United States has been the world's largest capital *importer*, taking in anywhere from two-thirds to three-quarters of global investment funds. For the United States as a national unit, dollar inflows are really refluxes of dollar *outflows* meant to cover its payment deficits with the world. IOUs thus finance America's deficits with the rest of the world while subsequently returning to sustain its public debt (Treasury bills and bonds). Yet, we should pause before simply characterizing the United States today as an imperialist debtor country that reproduces itself by sucking up enormous inflows of foreign capital. An overriding focus on the "exorbitant privileges" that come from issuing dollars invites the too-hasty conclusion that we live in the age of US "super imperialism."[178]

This sort of analysis seems to gain credence from the fact that among those states recycling dollars into US Treasury securities are many that rely heavily on American military aid and protection—Japan, South Korea, and several Gulf states. Significant as these arrangements are, we lose critical depth if we imagine a *part*, the American state, as greater (i.e., more determinant) than the *whole*, the global capitalist system. Notwithstanding the power of the US state, it remains ultimately determined by the world system of which it is an integral part.[179] In the capitalist world economy that emerged from the downfall of Bretton Woods, the enduring dominance of the dollar, and of US financial markets, is itself a function not just of the needs of the American state, but of the *general needs* of global capital, however much these involve dynamic contradictions. With respect to the operation of the law of value on a world scale—the ultimate regulator of all capitalist production and profitability—the system requires benchmarks that facilitate measures of value, risk, and profitability, and that enforce monetary discipline over labor. The dollar and the US Treasury securities that underpin it have proved crucial in these regards.

And all of this has much to do with two key points we have made: first, that the decline of the Bretton Woods system had its roots in the internationalization of production and investment driven by US multinational corporations (more on this below); and, second, that these processes, combined with heightened capital mobility, led to a geographic expansion of capitalist accumulation and the emergence of a much more global working class. Rather than capitalism having witnessed a *global* slowdown of investment and accumulation—a misapprehension based on a focus on domestic data in the historic capitalist core—there has instead been a geographic restructuring of investment and accumulation, with the highest rates taking place in so-called newly industrializing countries. Moreover, once we introduce foreign direct investment flows and the earnings they generate into the picture, the United States no longer appears simply as an imperialist debtor country.[180] For, as Brett Fieberger and Cédric Durand have shown, the income the US economy earns from its overseas investments more than outweighs the payments it makes on other deficits with the rest of the world—and the same is true for Germany, France, and Japan.[181] It is the flow of surplus value from overseas investment that "rebalances" the finance of the main imperialist powers. In this context, one of the key things the US dollar has done is to provide a highly liquid world money in an age of exceptional globalization of production, investment, and exchange. It is precisely this that has made the dollar significantly "functional" for world capitalism. Nevertheless, its role in providing a world measure of value and a highly liquid means of payment and exchange also involves contradictory dynamics—indeed, ones that might ultimately upset the very global structure it is meant to support.

World Money in the Age of Floating Currencies and Financial Turbulence

The new role of the dollar was prefigured in the growth of Eurodollar markets across the 1960s. These Euromarkets represented dollarized spaces outside the control and regulation of the US state, or any other. Greenbacks deposited overseas, especially in banks in the City of London, were beyond the authority of the American state and also evaded regulation by foreign central banks. At first, these markets were meant as a place where Russian-bloc governments could park dollars. However, it was the financial needs and operations of American-based multinational enterprises that really fueled Eurodollar growth. These transnational firms, driving a boom in foreign direct investment, regularly raised funds outside the United States, just as they often deposited profits in offshore dollar accounts. Across the 1960s, as industrial capital broke out of the largely national forms it had assumed since the Great Depression, US banks followed them into these offshore markets. Indicative of this globalizing trend was the growth of international trade, which expanded 40 percent more rapidly than did world output. Ever-larger shares of commodities were thus being produced for global markets, rather than for local ones. But even more striking, as corporations outgrew national markets, was the growth of foreign direct investment, which expanded twice as fast as gross domestic product.[182] But as much as dollar outflows for foreign investment by US multinationals sparked the new era of capital mobility, it was America's Vietnam War–fueled deficits that caused the offshore dollar market to explode. As US deficits soared, requiring the American economy to ship dollars overseas, total deposits in the Eurodollar market expanded more than fifty times over between 1960 and 1970, rocketing from roughly $1 billion to $57 billion. Following the breakdown of the dollar–gold exchange system, a further explosion pushed Eurodollar holdings over $1 trillion by 1983.[183]

When the Bretton Woods system of dollar–gold convertibility and fixed exchange rates collapsed after 1971, the global monetary regime essentially adapted itself to the deregulated norms of the Eurodollar market. In so doing, it caught up with spatio-structural transformations in productive capital—in particular, the rise of a global manufacturing system and the foreign direct investment that sustained it. This process of adaptation was piecemeal, haphazard, and largely unplanned. Indeed, it seems clear that the managers of the US state did not grasp how the reconfiguration of money and finance might rebuild US financial power.[184] But the legal and institutional adjustments introduced by the US state in the post–Bretton Woods era obeyed a clear logic: the deregulation and internationalization of finance in conformity with the new world of global manufacturing and production.[185] Viewed as an overarching historical process, what the US state did in the decade after 1973 was to redesign American finance in keeping with the *already*-multinational configuration of industrial capital. To be sure, new forms of imperial hegemony were constructed in the process. But, and this is a point downplayed by those who incline to a theory of American super-imperialism, US rulers were able to do this in large measure because the arc of transformation was conducive to *global* capital in general. As economic geographer Neil Smith observed, "However powerful US capital and the American state are . . . globalization is not the same as Americanization. Ruling classes around the world are heavily invested in globalization for their own interests."[186]

If the rise of globalized manufacturing was the dominant economic story of the 1960s, financial globalization was the saga of the 1970s. Fueling this transformation was an explosion in foreign exchange trading. As currencies became unmoored from gold and fixed rates of exchange, new levels of risk and uncertainty entered financial calculations. For instance, currency devaluations could cause profits made by a multinational enterprise in one country to effectively disappear when repatriated to banks in the home country. For this reason, multinational corporations, banks among them, sought to protect their earnings by shifting out of depreciating currencies and into appreciating ones (or by trying to correctly anticipate such movements). Once currencies began to float, monetary volatility produced an eruption in foreign exchange (forex) trading—which jumped ten times over (from $15 billion to $150 billion per day) between 1973 and 1985. By this time, however, currency trading had become a profitable business as an end in itself, and all kinds of institutions developed financial models designed to profit from the smallest of currency fluctuations. For most of these, forex trading became a mode of gambling, the placing of currency bets in the roaring markets of casino capitalism. As table 5.1 indicates, daily forex trading zoomed to $1.2 trillion in 1995, adding another $2 trillion a day by 2007 (when it hit $3.2 trillion), only to surpass $5 trillion a day by 2016. Throughout this rise, speculative activity utterly eclipsed the buying and selling of currencies for the actual needs of business.[187] Whereas 80 percent of forex transactions were tied to regular business activities in 1975, and merely 20 percent to speculation, by the early 1990s speculative trading had come to account for 97 percent of forex transactions—a level it has sustained since then.[188]

Table 5.1: Daily Turnover in Foreign Exchange Markets (selected years 1973–2016)

Year	Amount
1973	$15 billion
1980	$80 billion
1985	$150 billion
1995	$1.2 trillion
2004	$1.9 trillion
2007	$3.2 trillion
2016	$5.1 trillion

Source: Bank for International Settlements, Triennial Central Bank Survey, multiple years

While all this was transpiring, one government after another recognized the writing on the wall and signed on to the so-called "financial revolution" of the 1980s and 1990s. After all, if governments endeavored to regulate the national space, firms could simply enter "stateless" zones like the Eurodollar market, where borrowing was often cheaper and less constrained by regulations. In order to retain financial business, nation-states inclined to the rules of the game simply mimicked these stateless spaces by deregulating finance and eliminating capital controls. As financial deregulation caught wind, gross capital outflows from the fourteen largest industrial economies jumped from an average of about $65 billion a year in the late 1970s to $460 billion per year by 1989.[189] Capital now flowed more readily across borders than at any time since before the Great Depression of the 1930s, as the global investment activities of multinational firms were complemented by globalizing finance. Increasingly, the US domestic economy was a chief beneficiary. During the 1980s, after the American economy had been restructured and stabilized, capital flows *into* the United States, especially for purchases of US bonds and equities, grew twenty times over in real terms.[190] Where capital *outflows* driven by US multinationals had propelled economic globalization in the 1950s and 1960s, capital *inflows* now joined continuing outflows as part of the complex financial architecture of the dollar-based regime of global fiat money.

It wasn't just that capital was flowing more feely around the globe, however. It was also that financial assets were increasing as a share of world gross domestic product. As the McKinsey Global Institute has shown, the global stock of financial assets relative to world GDP began mounting steadily in the 1990s from a level equal to 15 percent of world gross domestic product in 1995 to 103 percent of global GDP by 2007.[191] This is one aspect of the phenomenon often described as *financialization*. Yet, we need to remind ourselves that much of this international movement of finance was for productive investment in the global South, not simply for speculative activity.[192]

Nonetheless, there has been an increase in speculative movements of capital, as well. Too often, however, pundits lose sight of the degree to which this was fueled by tremendous growth in the world money supply once the dollar was delinked from gold. Figure 5.1 illustrates the growth in the base money supply (known as MZM, for "money of zero maturity") in the United States since the late 1950s. Particularly evident is the formidable expansion of the US monetary base after 1980, when the American economy was stabilized following the "dollar crises" of 1968–73, and the inflationary decade of the 1970s.

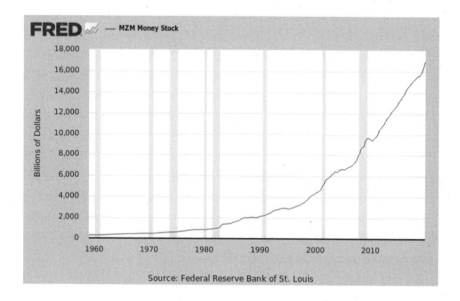

Figure 5.1: MZM Money Stock

Freed from its "metallic barrier," as figure 5.1 demonstrates, the money supply could now grow without the constraining effects of a fixed exchange rate with gold. Monetary growth on this scale also fostered new dynamics of price formation: no longer tied to the market value of gold, prices became much more responsive to the quantity of money and the velocity with which it circulated.[193] This generates a tendency toward permanent price inflation under money's third modal form, at least during periods of expansion—and this is one reason why central banks moved toward "inflation targeting," in hopes of achieving predictable yet modest price increases.[194]

Not only do governments and big business wish to avoid excessive volatility, which can render pricing and investment highly unpredictable. They also seek to avoid explosive strike waves of the sort that occurred between 1965 and 1976 in response to mounting rates of inflation, which were eroding real wages. Under the gold standard, labor could be disciplined when, in the face of currency decline and a rush to gold, the central bank raised interest rates in order to draw gold back to its coffers. Rising interest rates in a moment of financial crisis tended to induce deep slumps that, in pushing hundreds of thousands out of work, acted to reduce wages and worker militancy. In the post–Bretton Woods monetary order, however, central bank policy has substituted for the disciplinary effects of the gold standard. Through control over the interest rate charged to commercial banks (the *discount rate*), central bankers assume the enforcement role previously performed by the treasury in its obligation to convert notes into gold. This took one of its most dramatic forms in the punishing deployment of record-high interest rates by the Federal Reserve under Paul Volcker in the late 1970s and early 1980s. Draconian levels of interest drove down the annual inflation rate in the United States from 14 to 3 percent, and restored global investor confidence in the dollar—all at the price of a bruising world recession.[195]

More recently, the German central bank, the Bundesbank, has attempted to impose a similar sort of financial discipline on the Eurozone, notwithstanding the anti-stimulative effects of such policy in the midst of a global slump.[196] The irony is that since the onset of the 2007 downturn, central banks have struggled to avoid *deflation* of the sort that has ailed Japan since the 1990s, where it has produced chronic stagnation. Generating inflation, rather than curbing it, became the order of the day in a period of slump. The sort of obsession with financial discipline displayed by German governments is not, in these circumstances, geared toward fighting inflation. Instead, it is about the exercise of *class discipline* over labor—the use of austerity as a means to compress wages in the interests of profitability.[197]

Notwithstanding the commitment of central banks to modest inflation and economic discipline, however, the international monetary stock has in fact exploded since gold (as shown in figure 5.1), and this has been one source of continued financial turbulence. At issue here is the inability of central banks to control the production of money. This reality has exposed the monetarist fallacy about controlling the money supply. For the fact is that private banks today create about 95 percent of all money, with central banks issuing merely 5 percent.[198] Contrary to most economic theory, the bulk of money originates as bank credit, in loans to borrowers (for investments, mortgages, credit card payments, student loans, etc.). When my local bank agrees to provide me with a line of credit or mortgage of one hundred thousand dollars, it does not actually go and find already-existing dollars somewhere to lend me. Instead, it *creates* the money ex nihilo. It simply registers that amount digitally in an account bearing my name. I can now proceed to spend that money by promising to make payments from future earnings. This means that my bank has *pre-validated* my debt as full-fledged money.[199] In other words, it has increased the money supply by one hundred thousand dollars—an amount I have merely *promised* to repay—with the stroke of a few keys on a keyboard. Of course, my mortgage or line of credit is small potatoes compared to the billions that are being created every day to satisfy the borrowing needs of corporations (financial and nonfinancial), investors, and governments.

All of this private credit-money creation typically proceeds smoothly until a downturn in the economy or a financial shock induces a credit crisis. At that moment, it becomes clear that much of the bank credit money that had been created (such as my line of credit), alongside much of the stockpile of private nonbank credit instruments (corporate bonds, commercial paper, etc.) is as worthless as the IOUs passed by a penniless person. It then turns out that pre-validation—the treatment of a loan as full-fledged money—has involved a considerable amount of *pseudo-validation*, and much of this debt capital is exposed as largely fictitious, as mortgage-backed securities and other collateralized debt obligations (CDOs) were in 2007–2009. At such moments, there ensues a stampede to "safety," represented by the world's most valued currencies—and gold. And where financial institutions have been buying and selling toxic fictitious capitals to one another, the effects of a credit crunch can be calamitous, as they were in 2007–2009, when a global financial meltdown rocked the international banking system.[200]

When such crises occur outside the imperial centers of the system, local economies are frequently forced to endure the devastations of "structural adjustment," in order to borrow to pay off creditors and thus exit the crisis. Mexico, Brazil, Argentina, Thailand, Malaysia, Iceland, Latvia, Greece, and many others have had such programs inflicted on them by international financial institutions. But when panic shakes the core of the system, the rules abruptly change. Rather than cutting its debt, as most states are compelled to do, the US imperial state massively expanded its borrowing throughout the crisis that commenced in 2008. Operating as the world central bank, the US Federal Reserve intervened to *monetize* trillions of dollars of pre-validated credit money created by private banks, alongside trillions of toxic assets produced by banks, "shadow banks," and other institutions. Figure 5.2 captures the

the dramatic growth of assets owned by the US Federal Reserve banks, which more than quintupled between 2008 and 2014 as the central bank monetized holdings throughout the global credit system.[201]

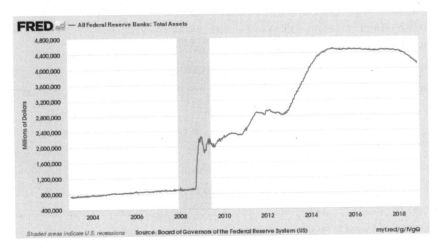

Figure 5.2: Total Assets of US Federal Reserve Banks

To understand the economic processes involved in the monetization of private credit monies like this, let us compare the current modal form of money with its second form. To be sure, money was also produced as private credit notes under the second modal form. The Bank of England, after all, was a private bank at its inception. And outside London, country banks were also empowered to print banknotes. But that second modal form of money was hybrid, as Marx argued. Not only did it obey the dictates of the credit system; it had another master: gold. A credit crunch thus induced a scramble to convert all other forms of money to gold, which was even more valued than Bank of England notes. What had been pre-validated (private bank credit money) had now to be *post-validated*; it had to be subjected to the test of conversion into the most universal form of money, gold. At such moments, fictitious capitals had to find their equivalent in *past* labor—a test that much credit money failed. Given the relative scarcity of gold (the product of past labor), the financial system invariably underwent a forced *deflation*, involving price declines, bankruptcies, wage cuts, and so on, as a range of fictitious capitals (paper claims to future wealth) were repudiated and suffered massive devaluation. The money supply would then contract, as it did during the bank failures of the 1930s, and would be brought into a more appropriate proportion to the existing reserves of gold. Of course, this often took place by way of a devastating slump.

Removed from the gold constraint, however, central banks today can easily *reflate* in the face of a credit crunch. This means pushing down interest rates in order to encourage borrowing (which, as we have seen, is a form of monetary expansion) and to directly expand the money supply. (Often this is accomplished by giving commercial banks "high-powered money"—central bank cash—in exchange for their toxic paper assets.) Put slightly differently, central banks can act to preserve the values pre-validated by private banks (as credit money) since they are under no requirement to convert them to gold. Removed from the metallic barrier, a central bank can offer high-powered money for debased credit money virtually without limit—which is why the money supply just keeps expanding. And this means, of course, that financialization continues in the face of financial crisis. In fact, the panic of 2008–2009 proved just how malleable central bank policy could be in that regard, as trillions upon trillions were pumped into a financial system in the throes of a global meltdown, and "quantitative easing" was used as if there were no limit to the production of money.[202] As early as November 2011, the US Federal Reserve alone had already pumped over $13 trillion into the rescue of the global banking system—even before the Fed introduced its formal quantitative easing programs.[203] And China's massive bailout and stimulus program, along with more modest interventions by the Eurozone, added many trillions more to the global rescue package.

Fault Lines and Histories as yet Unwritten

As we have seen, the Great Depression of 1929–39 was the paradigmatic expression of crisis under the gold standard, where slumps were deep and enduring, involving massive destruction of capital—in the form of widespread business bankruptcies—and mass unemployment. Global capitalism drifted off the gold standard during that crisis, never to fully return (the gold–dollar exchange standard devised in 1944 was already a half step in the direction of a post-gold monetary order). The world financial meltdown that broke out in 2007, triggering a global slump, is symptomatic of the new pattern of capitalist crisis under the third modal form of money.

Unconstrained by a metallic barrier, the third modal form enables central banks to monetize private credit monies, in ways discussed above, in order to avert a 1930s-style slump. However, this tends to block the purge of inefficient capitals on the massive scale necessary to open vistas for new waves of investment and accumulation.[204] As a result, the decade of economic recovery after 2009 was the slowest on record, due, in particular, to sluggish capital investment.[205] While profitability was restored in the United States after 2009 thanks to the squeezing of workers—by way of layoffs, precarious forms of employment, speedups, and wage compression—followed by corporate tax cuts, no sustained investment boom has been generated, nor is one likely in the absence of a deep slump that destroys the least efficient capitals.

A classic capitalist downturn induces widespread industrial restructuring, with plant closures, bankruptcies, and job loss on a tremendous scale. But when central banks drive down interest rates and offer high-powered money for devalued assets, then slumps are arrested—and severe restructuring forestalled. The "cleansing" function of a depression—Joseph Schumpeter's "creative destruction"[206]—is thereby stalled. But without the disappearance of the weakest capitals, the stage is not cleared for new rounds of deep and sustained investment. The result is a sluggish economy awash in cheap money: relative economic stagnation combined with repeated bubbles in financial investments like stocks, collateralized mortgage obligations, emerging market debt, "junk" bonds, and so on. Late capitalism under the third modal form of money thus experiences both ongoing financialization and a recurring pattern of speculative fevers and bursting bubbles. Indeed, that pattern is now well established: the so-called Third World debt crisis of 1982, the Mexican meltdown of 1994–95, the Asian crisis of 1997, Russia's credit crunch and the collapse of Long Term Capital Management in 1998, the bursting of the dot-com bubble in 2000–2001, and the global financial slump of 2007–2009, to name the most significant.

All of this returns us to the role of the dollar as world money. In the midst of these shocks, as financial institutions tumble and billions worth of fictitious capital evaporates, there is a rush to safe assets. One of these is gold. But more than anything else, it is the world's most liquid dollar-based assets—US Treasury securities—that serve as capital's safe haven. For this reason, says economist François Chesnais, "US treasury securities come the nearest to being what Marx called 'hard cash', i.e., they are the closest thing today to what gold was in the past."[207]

But US government securities serve as more than a shelter from the storm. They also function as a critical measure of value and profitability. Having the deepest and most liquid market in the world, along with low credit risk (the US state has never defaulted on its debts and it can always produce more dollars), US Treasury securities provide a benchmark against which all other risks can be measured. This is not to say that the interest rate on Treasuries determines profit rates.[208] Far from it. But once those rates are structurally determined, the degree of assessed risk a financial investment carries can be expressed in the premium that must be paid *above* the interest rate on Treasury assets. So long as US public debt instruments play these essential roles—as safe haven and as benchmark measure of value, risk, and profitability—then a dollar-based international monetary system will have a rudimentary functionality for global capital, notwithstanding the system's inner tensions and contradictions. To be sure, other currencies could operate to fulfill these roles, and the euro, in particular, has demonstrated some traction in this regard, albeit on a more limited (and largely regional) scale. But the Eurozone's financial markets are not at all as deep and liquid as those of the United States, and the European Central Bank is a long way from playing the part of a *world* central bank; that has been unique to the US Federal Reserve.

Yet this should not mislead us into assuming that the dollar-based world monetary order is solid and impervious to change. On the contrary, this regime is characterized by two axes of conflict that might yet undo dollar hegemony in the third modal form. The first of these is *inter-capitalist tensions* that provoke rival blocs to search for alternatives to the dollar as world money. The second, and ultimately the most crucial, is the set of *class tensions* running through the financialized regime of late capitalist dollar hegemony. While these contradictions are inscribed within the very relations of the global fiat money regime, their resolution is not. Their working out will be determined only in the course of real social-historical contestations. With that in mind, let us take each of these axes of conflict in turn.

The "exorbitant privilege" that accrues to the US state as producer of global fiat money frustrated other major capitalist states, even before Treasury Secretary John Connally declared, in 1971, "It's our currency, but it's your problem." The formation of the euro as a global currency was in large measure about escaping that problem. By creating another transnational currency—the euro is now the second-largest reserve currency in the world—and one that dominates trade in Europe, the Eurozone reduced the volume of formally inconvertible American IOUs it is forced to accept in the course of international trade and finance.[209] Notwithstanding all the economic and institutional turmoil of the Eurozone since 2009, the social logic of the euro project is to reduce the bounds of dollar hegemony.

More recently, China has started to move down a similar track, albeit one "with Chinese characteristics." In 2016, the *yuan* was recognized as a world currency by the International Monetary Fund, which incorporated it into the basket of currencies that make up IMF "special drawing rights."[210] Two years later, the Chinese government relaxed restrictions on banking and finance, making it much easier for foreign banks and nonfinancial corporations to buy and sell yuan and invest in China's banking sector. At roughly the same time, China's leaders launched the Shanghai oil futures market, where all prices are denominated in yuan.[211] All of these moves are designed to position the yuan as a more genuinely global currency.[212] And while the dollar will not be dethroned in short order, it is significant that the yuan bloc, as measured by analysts at the International Monetary Fund, is now the world's second-largest currency zone.[213]

There can be little doubt that the global financial crisis of 2007–2009 gave a fillip in this direction. In the throes of the panic, Chinese holdings of US financial assets began to melt down. China's leaders then directly intervened with US officials to ensure that mortgage lenders Fannie Mae and Freddie Mac would be backstopped by the American state. This was the context in which Gao Xiqing—manager of China's enormous sovereign wealth fund (with over $200 billion in foreign assets), alumnus of Duke University Law School, and a former Wall Street lawyer—issued a powerful rebuke to the United States:

> This generation of Americans is so used to your supremacy. . . . It hurts to think, Okay, now we have to be on equal footing to other people. . . . The simple truth today is that your economy is built on the global economy. And it's built on the support, the gratuitous support, of a lot of countries. So why don't you . . . be nice to the countries that lend you money. Talk to the Chinese! Talk to the Middle Easterners! And pull your troops back!

Rhetorically charged as this statement was, it also implied a deliberate program: the redesign of global financial institutions. Discussing foreign ownership of US assets, Gao continued, "If China has $2 trillion, Japan has almost $2 trillion, and Russia has some, then . . . get all the relevant people together and think up what people are calling a second Bretton Woods system."[214] Such statements suggest that China's financial liberalization is part of a campaign to push world capitalism toward a new set of monetary arrangements in which at least three major currencies—the dollar, the euro, and the yuan—would coexist as world monies, effectively sharing the monetary throne in the interests of pluralizing global finance. At the time of writing, China has cut deals with oil companies in Russia, Iran, and Venezuela to accept the yuan in payment for China's foreign purchases of oil.[215] As the world's largest importer, China's move here will incrementally reshape global currency markets. So will its $1 trillion One Belt, One Road initiative, which will link it more powerfully with economies across Europe, Africa, and Asia. The program has also recently been supplemented by the formation of the Shanghai Cooperation Council, which will integrate the Chinese economy ever more closely with those of Russia, India, and Pakistan.

China's track toward monetary diversification is fueled by the enduring dilemma posed for capitalism's most dynamic trading nations by a dollar-based regime of global fiat money: in payment for goods, they are forced to accumulate dollars that have little use other than to purchase American financial assets. What's more, those very assets are inherently unstable under a world monetary regime rife with endemic financial speculation, asset bubbles, and financial crises. Every panic threatens the very dollar-based assets that US trade partners purchase with America's IOUs—and such panics are endemic to a world awash with formally inconvertible greenbacks. This is what China discovered in 2008 when the debt it purchased in government-sponsored enterprises like Fannie Mae and Freddie Mac began to implode.

However, it is one thing for China to want a new Bretton Woods–type agreement to redesign the global monetary system, and quite another for it to get it. As discussed above, American representatives used their global dominance to force through that "agreement." And if there is one lesson of the history we have tracked across this book, it is that wars are often the fearsome engines of "regime change" in the domain of world money. As one analyst rightly notes, "What will resolve the current tension is a power grab by a new stakeholder determined to have its way."[216] It is difficult to foresee a scenario in which the American government would tolerate such a power grab and accept the dethroning of the dollar without extremely bitter conflict, involving at least the *threat* of war. Certainly, that threat might forestall "a new stakeholder determined to have its way." But that simply leaves us with a bloody US empire, intent on belligerent assertion of its state power. Whatever the future holds in this regard, it can only be a repetition of the vicious cycle of blood for money—that is, unless the system of money as second nature is overturned.

To be sure, the prospects for such an upheaval often appear remote. Indeed, late capitalism not only threatens humankind with an intensification of violence and war, but also with catastrophic climate change. Understandably, many are filled with despair in the face of such dangers. But, as Marxist philosopher Ernst Bloch observed, this is in part because capitalist society drapes the future in its own incapacity to promote human development.[217] "On bourgeois ground," he wrote, "change is impossible anyway even if it were desired. In fact, bourgeois interest would like to draw every other interest opposed to it into its own failure; so, in order to drain the new life, it makes its own agony apparently fundamental, apparently ontological. The futility of bourgeois existence is extended to be that of the human situation in general, of existence per se."[218] Invoking the principle of hope, Bloch reminds us that critical-revolutionary thought seeks out forces of world transformation that are struggling to form themselves on the current terrain of violence and domination. This gesture is in tune with Marx's insistence that in capitalist society, radical powers of subversion are always burrowing, often undetected, beneath the surface. In seeking out traces of those forces, he reminds us, "we recognize our old friend, our old mole, who knows so well how to work underground, suddenly to appear: the revolution."[219]

As of this writing, intimations of the old mole's burrowing can be detected on a variety of terrains. One can sense them in the growing restiveness of China's massive industrial working class.[220] They can be discerned in the recent, if short-lived, seizures of city squares—from Occupy Wall Street, to Tahrir Square in Cairo, to Taksim Gezi Park in Istanbul, to the insurgent streets of Sudan, Chile, Ecuador, and Lebanon—in the name of the struggle against austerity and inequality. And it can be seen in community uprisings like those in Ferguson, Missouri, with their insistence that Black Lives Matter, and in the International Women's Strikes and climate justice rebellions in country after country. The mole's subterranean movement can be glimpsed in the new global waves of feminist, anti-racist, queer, environmental, and migrant justice struggles. And it can be detected in the revival of teachers' strikes and the rebirth of socialism in the

United States.[221] It cannot be known if our old friend, the revolution, will triumph in the coming decades. If not, the socialist Left will have to remake itself for new conditions. It may seem at times that this is a thankless task. But in a world entrapped in the rule of war and money, it is helpful to recall the words of a central character in Tony Kushner's play *A Bright Room Called Day*:

> *Pick any era in history, Agnes.*
> *What is really beautiful about that era?*
> *The way the rich lived?*
> *No.*
> *The way the poor lived?*
> *No.*
> *The dreams of the Left*
> *are always beautiful.*
> *The imagining of a better world*
> *the damnation of the present one*
> *This faith,*
> *this luminescent anger,*
> *these alone*
> *are worthy of being called human.*[222]

Conclusion

If to be human is to suffer we are not human to suffer only
this is why I think so often, these days, of the great river
of this meaning that goes forward between banks of herbs and weeds
and animals that graze and slake their thirst and people that sow and reap
and even of great tombs and small dwellings of the dead.
This flowing that follows its course and is not so different from human blood
from the eyes of men when they look straight ahead without fear in their hearts
    —George Seferis, "An Old Man on the River Bank" (1942)

The poor have suffered. The blood has flowed. Everywhere, the bleeding has occurred in the service of war, empire, slavery, and money. Yet, as George Seferis notes in the passage above, "we are not human to suffer only." Beyond suffering, there is joy, love, community, festivity, defiance, celebration. All of this nourishes what Walter Benjamin called a "tradition of the oppressed"—of solidarity and insurgence—that sustains stories and practices at odds with those of the conquerors.[1] And in that space reside resources of hope and intimations of utopia.

As much as recorded history has resembled Hegel's "slaughter-bench," it has also been something more, something that overspills the bounds of oppression.[2] There are currents of human life that move outside the circuits of money and violence. This is a flow that "follows its course and is not so different from human blood." If the common meal was the first money, a communal ceremony

241

bound to sustenance of life, it has long lost that hallowed character. Like blood, communal wealth was meant to flow, circulate, and nourish. The original material and semiotic link between blood and money may be located at this juncture.

But for too long, human blood has been bound to the circuits of money and power. And all the while, this bondage has fueled the depredations of class domination. "They seize possessions by force, and order has been destroyed. There is no longer an equitable distribution," wrote Theognis. Money had become an instrument of dispossession and a means of war. When Cicero exulted over the "120,000 sesterces on the platform" in front of him, he expressed this perverse power of money over persons.[3] Capitalism elevated these reifying forces to unprecedented heights. So much so that, in the words of the young Marx, money turned "real human and natural powers into purely abstract representations"— coin, paper notes, and financial derivatives.[4] And these abstract representations, derived from the "sacred hunger for gold," continue to consume blood and life.[5]

Ancient democracy was meant to break this power. It was intended to instate the sovereignty of the people over that of wealth, and to undo slavery and oppression. This was the spirit in which Solon declared:

> I brought back to their god-given homeland Athens
> many who had been sold, one unjustly,
> another justly, others fleeing
> from dire necessity . . .
> Others here held in shameful slavery
> Trembling at their masters whims
> I freed.[6]

But ancient democracy could not overturn the domination of life by property. The ties of the Greek polis to slavery, patriarchy, and empire simply allowed too much license for the dominion of money over blood. And so, the cycle of violence and oppression continued, reconfiguring itself some centuries ago into the form of modern capitalism. With it came cyclonic storms and destruction. "On a ship at sea: a tempestuous noise of thunder and lightning heard," wrote Shakespeare.[7] While the tempest raged, the oceans filled with blood—and the bones of the enslaved.

But many arrived on the other side, their blood mixing with tobacco, indigo, coffee, sugar, cotton . . . and money—always the money. Their owners sought to render them socially dead, to remake them as zombie laborers. But their songs, their stories, their freedom dreams preserved the zombie's hidden power: awakening.[8]

"Are we not your *Money?*" asked the enslaved person in Tryon's *Friendly Advice to the Gentelmen* [*sic*] *Planters of the East and West Indies* (1684).[9] Indeed, they were. As one Saint-Domingue planter remarked in the face of slave uprisings, "It is in these slaves that our fortunes exist."[10] This was both their suffering—and their power. For in those whose labor generates the wealth of this world resides an immense capacity to remake it. And on the sugar plantations of Saint-Domingue, enslaved people lived and worked in communities of hundreds, making them, as C. L. R. James noted, "closer to a modern proletariat than any group of workers in existence at the time."[11] Their potential for collective insurgence, for turning the world upside down, haunted their masters' dreams—as would the name Toussaint Louverture.[12] Deny it as they might, the oppressors sensed the capacity of the enslaved for that dialectical reversal which brings liberation.[13]

Today, the memories of those freedom struggles constitute resources for the struggles of the oppressed. They are signposts on the road to a life "without fear in their hearts," to again cite George Seferis.[14] They are Benjamin's reserves of the "courage, humor, cunning and fortitude" that keep alive the tradition of the oppressed.[15] They nourish the "faith" and "the luminescent anger" that Kushner describes as "worthy of being called human." They are the reason why the image of liberation will not die, notwithstanding a world of violence, hunger, bondage, and catastrophic climate change.

$

"I hear a drum beating on the far bank of the river. A breeze stirs and catches it. The resonant pounding is borne on the wind."[16] In his 1802 sonnet to Toussaint Louverture, William Wordsworth called that breeze "the common wind."[17] It speaks of hope and resistance. Of a world without war and cruelty. Of an end to the chains of oppression.

It whispers, *No more blood for money.*

Notes

Introduction

1. Ann Pettifor, *The Production of Money: How to Break the Power of Bankers* (London and New York: Verso, 2017), 4.

2. For important critiques of barter theories of the origins of money and markets, see Caroline Humphrey, "Barter and Economic Disintegration," *Man* 20, no.1 (1985), 48–72; and David Graeber, *Debt: The First 5,000 Years* (New York: Melville House, 2011), ch. 2.

3. All systems of societal reproduction are contradictory, however, and money may simultaneously be involved in reproducing *and* undermining a given social system.

4. By "critical theory," I refer in the first instance to that developed by Karl Marx, from his early critique of the state to his later critique of political economy. Key aspects of this approach are described by Max Horkheimer, "Traditional and Critical Theory," in *Critical Theory: Selected Essays*, Matthew J. O'Connell, trans. (New York: Herder & Herder, 1972), 188–243. Critical-dialectical theory, deriving from Hegel and Marx, also insists that the history of objects includes the history of ways of interacting with and knowing them. This is why, for critical philosophy, "the process of knowledge becomes the process of history." Herbert Marcuse, *Reason and Revolution: Hegel and the Rise of Social Theory* (Boston: Beacon, 1960), 95.

5. Seth Rockman, "What Makes the History of Capitalism Newsworthy?," *Journal of the Early Republic* 34 (Fall 2014), 462. Important exceptions to this trend are Ed Baptist, *The Half Has Never Been Told: Slavery and the Making of American Capitalism* (New York: Basic Books, 2014); and Sven Beckert, *Empire of Cotton: A Global History* (New York: Vintage, 2014). While I have some differences with both Baptist and Beckert, each restores to capitalism its bloody dimensions.

6. For important works that do not forget these relations, see François Chesnais, *Finance Capital Today: Corporations and Banks in the Lasting Global Slump* (Chicago: Haymarket, 2017); and Cédric Durand, *Fictitious Capital: How Finance Is Appropriating Our Future*, David Broder, trans. (London and New York: Verso, 2017).

7. Karl Marx, "Excerpts from James Mill's *Elements of Political Economy*," in *Early Writings*, Quintin Hoare, ed. (Harmondsworth: Penguin, 1975), 264.

8. See my *Monsters of the Market: Zombies, Vampires, and Global Capitalism* (Chicago: Haymarket, 2012).

9. See my *Bodies of Meaning: Studies on Language, Labor, and Liberation* (Albany: State University of New York Press, 2001).

10. There is an important and growing literature on Marxist monetary theory. Some key texts include Suzanne de Brunhoff, *Marx on Money*, Maurice Goldboom, trans. (New York: Urizen Books, 1976); Fred Moseley, *Money and Totality* (Chicago: Haymarket, 2017); Costas Lapavitsas, *Marxist Monetary Theory: Collected Papers* (Chicago: Haymarket, 2017). See also the essays collected in Fred Moseley, ed., *Marx's Theory of Money: Modern Appraisals* (New York: Palgrave Macmillan, 2005). On modern money and finance, see Chesnais, *Finance Capital Today*.

11. In fact, Marx specifically includes the public debt, national finance, and colonialism as conditions of original capitalist accumulation in his illuminating discussion in part 8 of *Capital*, volume 1, "The Secret of Primitive Accumulation."

12. Karl Marx, *Capital*, vol. 1, Ben Fowkes, trans. (Harmondsworth: Penguin, 1976), 221–22.

13. See the opening sentence to the preface of Marx's *Contribution to the Critique of Political Economy* (1859): "I examine the system of bourgeois economy in the following order: *capital, landed property, wage-labour; the State, foreign trade, the world market*" (available at https://www.marxists.org/archive/marx/works/download/Marx_Contribution_to_the_Critique_of_Political_Economy.pdf). There is an important debate as to whether Marx eventually abandoned this plan. I seriously doubt it, though I cannot enter into a sustained discussion of this here. Marx was an incredibly ambitious and comprehensive thinker. That he failed to complete his overarching plan does not indicate that he abandoned it. Certainly, a powerful case can be made that his examination of the "system of bourgeois economy" logically required a theory of the state, international trade, and the world market.

14. J. Lawrence Broz, "The Origins of Central Banking: Solutions to the Free Rider Problem," *International Organization* 52, no. 2 (1998), 239.

15. Marx, *Capital*, vol. 1, 926.

16. It should go without saying that general historical accounts can (and must) attend to societal specificities and differentiations, as I hope I have done here. At the same time, all systems of social and economic domination have shared features—such as relations of exploitation—that enable the historian to locate continuities amid discontinuities. This is certainly true where money, slavery, and colonization are concerned.

17. Of course, how long the third epoch will be is yet to be determined.

18. These developments were related to a prolonged crisis of European feudalism, which is explored in chapter 3.

19. Peter Frankopan, *The Silk Roads: A New History of the World* (New York: Vintage, 2015), 181–82. Throughout this work I use the acronyms CE for the dates of the Christian era (often denoted as AD) and BCE for dates before the Christian era.

20. Janice E. Thompson, *Mercenaries, Pirates, and Sovereigns* (Princeton: Princeton University Press, 1996), 3.

21. This is why I dissent from those theorists, such as David Harvey in *The New Imperialism* (Oxford: Oxford University Press, 2003), who consider that capital and the state pursue two distinct logics that coexist and intertwine. I advance in chapter 4 a unitary account of this social-historical process.

22. In *Empire of Cotton*, Sven Beckert coins the term "war capitalism" to describe a specific phase in the emergence of modern capitalism as a system. Notwithstanding the considerable insights of Beckert's analysis, I theorize war as integral to capitalism in *all* its iterations.

23. Frankopan, *Silk Roads*, 154.

24. John Kenneth Galbraith, *Money: Whence It Came, Where It Went* (New York: Bantam, 1975), 5.

25. Vincent Harding, *There Is a River: The Black Struggle for Freedom in America* (San Diego: Harcourt Brace, 1981), xi.

Chapter 1: *"Droves I Took Alive and Auctioned Off as Slaves"*

1. Cicero, *Letters to Atticus*, 5.20.5, as cited by Sandra R. Joshel, *Slavery in the Roman World* (Cambridge, UK: Cambridge University Press, 2010), 84.

2. Ann Pettifor, *The Production of Finance: How to Break the Power of Bankers* (London and New York: Verso, 2017), 5.

3. In speaking of money here, I have coinage specifically in mind.

4. Ronald S. Stroud, "An Athenian Decree on Silver," *Hesperia* 43, no. 2 (1974), 159, 166. This decree was enacted in 375–374 BCE.

5. There is a debate among historians as to whether the basanos was largely a ritualized legal threat during a trial or an actually deployed practice of judicial torture. Michael Gagarin, for example, argues that it was rarely if ever practiced: "The Torture of Slaves in Athenian Law," *Classical Philology* 91 (1986), 1–18. But this claim, for which we have little evidence one way or the other, misses the essential points: (a) that this was a procedure encoded in Athenian law and thus tells us something significant about the slave body as a touchstone of truth; and (b) that it was entirely consistent with all the codes of a society in which, as Virginia Hunter aptly puts it, "slaves answered for all their offences with their bodies." See Hunter, "Constructing the Body of the Citizen: Corporal Punishment in Classical Athens," *Échos du Monde Classique/Classical Views* 36 (1992), 278. Consistent with this, David Mirhady makes a compelling case for the centrality of slave torture to Athenian law. See his "The Athenian Rationale for Torture," in *Demosthenes: Statesman and Orator*, Ian Worthington, ed. (London: Routledge, 2001), 53–74.

6. Page duBois, *Torture and Truth* (London: Routledge, 1991), 21, original emphasis. My discussion of basanos is deeply indebted to duBois's text.

7. *Sylloge*, no. 984, lines 8ff, as cited by Glenn R. Morrow, *Plato's Law of Slavery in its Relation to Greek Law* (Urbana: University of Illinois Press, 1939), 68.

8. Aristotle, *The Politics*, rev. ed., T. A. Sinclair, trans. (Harmondsworth: Penguin, 1981), 1253b23–1254a1.

9. See Orlando Patterson, *Slavery and Social Death* (Cambridge, MA: Harvard University Press, 1985). I treat social death as a fundamental existential *tendency* of enslaved life—one that is countered by the multiple ways in which the enslaved sought to reclaim identity and personhood and to forge social and communal relations.

10. As Aristotle implies, those who held that slavery was purely conventional opened the door to the idea that it might be entirely unjust, and based fundamentally on force and conquest.

See *Politics*, 1253b14. Indeed, the Sophist Alcadimas is reported to have said that "the deity gave liberty to all men and nature created no one a slave." Cited in Yvon Garland, *Slavery in Ancient Greece*, rev. ed., Janet Lloyd, trans. (Ithaca: Cornell University Press, 1988), 125.

11. See G. W. F. Hegel, *The Phenomenology of Spirit*, A. V. Miller, trans. (Oxford: Oxford University Press, 1969), part B, ch. IV(A). Hegel's account of this master–slave dialectic is replete with ambiguities. On one reading, Christianity represents the spiritual revolution in which the enslaved come to a new consciousness, even though slavery itself persisted for centuries after Christianity's appearance. On another reading, masters and slaves come through conflict to a mutual recognition as equals. For a sampling of interpretations, see John O'Neill, ed., *Hegel's Dialectic of Desire and Recognition* (Albany: State University of New York Press, 1996). More recently, Susan Buck-Morss has argued that one hears in Hegel's account echoes of the great slave revolution in Haiti (1791–1804), even if Hegel refuses to register their theoretical significance. See her *Hegel, Haiti, and Universal History* (Pittsburgh: University of Pittsburgh Press, 2009).

12. This tradition encounters one of its greatest challenges in Hegel. After Hegel, this challenge reappears in a variety of—quite distinct—forms of social theory, from Marxism to psychoanalysis to poststructuralism.

13. There is no doubt that hostility to the rise of the laboring citizen—the touchstone of democracy—played a crucial role here, as will become more evident below. In complicated ways, the statuses of slave and laboring citizen were linked, as Plato himself intimated in trying to bar both groups from politics.

14. Plato's argument itself is fraught with internal tensions. The slave boy is shown to be capable of solving mathematical problems—suggesting a universal aptitude for knowledge. But Socrates later proceeds to question the conclusion that seems to follow from this: that if virtue is wisdom, then virtue must be teachable. See Plato, *Meno*, in Plato, *Protagoras and Meno*, W. K. C. Guthrie, trans. (Harmondsworth: Penguin, 1956), 89C: 143–44. In-text citations of book and line numbers refer to this edition. These sorts of tensions run through Plato's texts, embodying, on one hand, the contradictions between the philosopher's aristocratic social and political commitments, and, on the other, his attempt to rebuild elitist politics (in opposition to democracy) by way of universal claims for the "good life" that are free from utilitarian calculus and monetary quantification.

15. While Socrates seeks to reveal the difference between having the correct opinion about something and knowing why that opinion is right (knowledge), a close reading of the *Meno* suggests that in fact Socrates struggles to demonstrate the practical significance of this distinction.

16. Avery Gordon, *Ghostly Matters: Haunting and the Sociological Imagination* (Minneapolis: University of Minnesota Press, 1997), 25.

17. Friedrich Nietzsche, *Beyond Good and Evil*, Walter Kaufmann, trans. (New York: Vintage, 1989), 169, 201. I have discussed Nietzsche's aristocratic radicalism in *Bodies of Meaning: Studies on Language, Labor, and Liberation* (Albany: State University of New York Press, 2011), ch. 1.

18. Walter Benjamin, "Theses on the Philosophy of History," in *Illuminations*, Hannah Arendt, ed. (New York: Schocken, 1968), 256.

19. Catherine Eagleton and Jonathan Williams, *Money: A History*, 2nd ed. (London: British Museum Press, 2007), 19–20, 17–18.

20. The concept of special-purpose money was developed by Karl Polanyi. See, for instance, "The Semantics of Money-Uses," in *Primitive, Archaic and Modern Economies: Essays of Karl Polanyi*, George Dalton, ed. (Boston: Beacon, 1971), 178–79.

21. Colin M. Kraay, "Small Change and the Origins of Coinage," *Journal of Hellenic Studies* 84 (1964), 76–91.

22. Richard Seaford, "Monetisation and the Generation of the Western Subject," *Historical Materialism* 20, no. 1 (2012), 81–82, original emphasis.

23. David M. Schaps, *The Invention of Coinage and the Monetization of Ancient Greece* (Ann Arbor: University of Michigan Press, 2004), 16.

24. Aristotle, *Ethics*, rev. ed., J. A. K. Thompson, trans. (Harmondsworth: Penguin, 1976), 1133a21–1133b19.

25. I deliberately refer to an economy of gift exchange here, rather than a mode of production. After all, what was exchanged had first to be produced, largely by peasant and slave labor. I shall return below to questions relevant to the mode of production in the ancient Greek world. The crucial thing here is that where market regulation does not dominate, we find various forms of reciprocity—including aristocratic gift exchange—as distributive principles, alongside others, in noncapitalist economies.

26. See M. I. Finley, "Marriage, Sale, and Gift in the Homeric World," *Seminar* 12 (1954), 61–68; and Anthony Snodgrass, *Archaic Greece* (Berkeley: University of California Press, 1980), 132. The term "competitive generosity" is from Oswyn Murray, *Early Greece* (London: William Collins, 1980), 50–51. *Xenia* is frequently translated as "guest-friendship" or "hospitality."

27. For terrible confusion on this score, see Jacques Derrida, *Given Time*, vol. 1, *Counterfeit Money*, Peggy Kamuf, trans. (Chicago: University of Chicago Press, 1992); and my critique in McNally, *Bodies of Meaning*, 60–66. Recent research has rightly emphasized that one-way gift giving, without any obligation for a counter-gift, was much more widespread than some anthropologists and historians believed. On this point see, for example, Frederic L. Pryor, *The Origins of the Economy* (New York: Academic Press, 1977). For a brief summary of recent debates in this area, see Schaps, *Invention of Coinage*, 72–73.

28. Caroline Mytinger, *Headhunting in the Solomon Islands* (New York: Macmillan, 1942), 148.

29. Finley, "Marriage, Sale, and Gift," 65.

30. John Gould, *Give and Take in Herodotus* (Oxford: Leopard's Head Press, 1991), 12.

31. See, for instance, Karl Polanyi, "Societies and Economic Systems" in *Primitive, Archaic, and Modern Economies*, 3–25.

32. Marshall Sahlins, *Stone Age Economics* (Chicago: Aldine Publishing, 1972), 191–99.

33. Paul Bohannan, "The Impact of Money on an African Subsistence Economy," *Journal of Economic History* 19, no. 4 (1959), 492.

34. Walter Beringer, "'Servile Status' in the Sources for Early Greek History," *Historia* 31, no. 1 (1982), 28. Orlando Patterson makes a similar point: "This condition of belonging, of participating, of being protected by the community, constitutes the ideal non-slave condition . . . in nearly all traditional societies." Patterson, *Freedom*, vol. 1 (New York: Basic Books, 1991), 23.

35. Annette B. Weiner, *Inalienable Possessions: The Paradox of Keeping-While-Giving* (Berkeley: University of California Press, 1992), 33. See also Marcel Mauss, *The Gift: Forms and Functions of Exchange in Archaic Societies* (Glencoe, IL: Free Press, 1954), 42–43.

36. See, for instance, Paul Einzig, *Primitive Money: In Its Ethnological, Historical, and Economic*

Aspects, 2nd ed. (Oxford: Pergamon, 1966), 29–30.

37. In-text citations of book and line numbers refer to Martin Hammond's translation of the *Iliad* (Harmondsworth: Penguin, 1987). It is true that there appears in Homer a concept—*ʒoagria*—that can be translated as "the price of a life." But in the *Iliad* this is a term used by Trojans to indicate what they will offer as ransom in order to save themselves.

38. Sitta von Reden, *Exchange in Ancient Greece* (London: Duckworth, 1995), 45.

39. Schaps, *Invention of Coinage*, 79.

40. Gould, *Give and Take*, 14.

41. Finley, "Marriage, Sale, and Gift," 66.

42. I follow convention in referring to the *Iliad* and the *Odyssey* as Homer's texts, even though they were almost certainly written down by a scribe who did not invent these epics. "Homer" is the name we give to the greatest poetic innovator and conveyor of these oral epics. See Andrew Dalby, *Rediscovering Homer: Inside the Origins of the Epic* (New York: W. W. Norton, 2006), chs. 6–7. For the argument that "Homer" may well have been a female poet, see Gregory Nagy, "An Evolutionary Model for the Making of Homeric Poetry: Comparative Perspectives," in *The Ages of Homer*, Jane B. Morris and Sarah P. Morris, eds. (Austin: University of Texas Press, 1994), 163–79; and Dalby, 139–53.

43. In-text citations of book and line numbers refer to Robert Fagles's translation of the *Odyssey* (Harmondsworth: Penguin, 1996).

44. Richard Seaford, *Money and the Early Greek Mind* (Cambridge, UK: Cambridge University Press, 2004), 44.

45. Kurt A. Raaflaub, "Homer to Solon: The Rise of the Polis," in *The Ancient Greek City-State*, Mogens Herman Hansen, ed. (Copenhagen: Royal Danish Academy of Sciences and Letters, 1993), 51.

46. For a thorough documentation, see David W. Tandy, *Warriors into Traders: The Power of the Market in Early Greece* (Berkeley: University of California Press, 1997), 19–58.

47. Murray, *Early Greece*, 105. On enslavement of women in Homeric Greece see Gerda Lerner, *The Creation of Patriarchy* (Oxford: Oxford University Press, 1986), 83–87.

48. Murray, *Early Greece*, 73–74.

49. S. C. Humphreys, *Anthropology and the Greeks* (London: Henley and Boston, 1978), 167.

50. Mogens Herman Hansen, *Polis: An Introduction to the Ancient Greek City-State* (Oxford: Oxford University Press, 2006), 44.

51. Murray, *Early Greece*, 119.

52. Walter Burkert, *The Orientalizing Revolution: Near Eastern Influence on Greek Culture in the Early Archaic Age* (Cambridge, MA: Harvard University Press, 1992).

53. W. G. Forrest, *The Emergence of Greek Democracy, 800–400 BC* (New York: McGraw-Hill, 1966), 77.

54. As Tandy points out, the fact that some colonies introduced laws prohibiting the alienation of land is highly suggestive that they hoped to combat an actually existing trend toward alienability (*Warriors into Traders*, 131–33). Forrest (*Greek Democracy*, 148) holds that land in Attica (the area of the Attic Peninsula that includes Athens) had long been alienable, but proof for this is sketchy.

55. James M. Redfield, "The Development of the Market in Archaic Greece," in *The Market in History*, B. L. Anderson and A. J. H. Latham, eds. (London: Croom Helm, 1986), 50–51.

56. Forrest, *Greek Democracy*, 150.

57. Murray, *Early Greece*, 184–85.

58. In-text citations of line numbers refer to M. L. West's translation of Hesiod's text in *Theogony, and Works and Days* (Oxford: Oxford University Press, 1988), though in one case (citation for line 341), I have preferred to deploy the Greek term *kleros*, indicating its possible translations.

59. As quoted in *Theognis of Megara: Poetry and the Polis*, ed. Thomas Figueria and Gregory Nagy (Baltimore: Johns Hopkins University Press, 1985): 23.

60. See G. E. M. de Ste. Croix, *The Class Struggle in the Ancient Greek World* (London: Duckworth, 1981), 162–70; and Garlan, *Slavery in Ancient Greece*, 88–91. Tandy suggests that Perses, having lost his own land, may have brought legal action against Hesiod in an attempt to claim some from his brother (*Warriors into Traders*, 212).

61. Ian Morris, "The Strong Principle of Equality and the Archaic Origins of Greek Democracy," in *Demokratia: A Consideration on Democracies, Ancient and Modern*, Josiah Ober and Charles Hedrick, eds. (Princeton: Princeton University Press, 1996), 218; Raaflaub, "Homer to Solon," 59.

62. Beringer, "'Servile Status,'" 29.

63. *Constitution of Athens*, ch. 2, available at http://oll.libertyfund.org/titles/580.

64. On the periodization of Homer's written epics, see Dalby, *Rediscovering Homer*, 4. On the social values expressed in these epics, see Ian Morris, "The Use and Abuse of Homer," *Classical Antiquity* 5, 81–138. See also Tandy, *Warriors into Traders*, 9–11; and Murray, *Early Greece*, 38.

65. Redfield, "Development of the Market," 31.

66. Paul Millett, "Hesiod and His World," *Proceedings of the Cambridge Philological Society* 210 (1984), 84–115. See also Tandy, *Warriors into Traders*, ch. 8. Note that an increased role for markets does not at all imply the presence of capitalist social relations.

67. See Murray, *Early Greece*, 179. It should be noted that Hesiod's social justice outlook has distinct limits: neither women nor slaves are viewed as deserving of fair treatment.

68. In-text citations of fragment and line numbers refer to M. L. West's translation of Solon's verse in *Greek Lyric Poetry* (Oxford: Oxford University Press, 1999).

69. Ellen Meiksins Wood, *Peasant-Citizen and Slave: The Foundations of Athenian Democracy* (London: Verso, 1988), 95.

70. Murray, *Early Greece*, 183.

71. M. I. Finley, "Between Slavery and Freedom," *Comparative Studies in Society and History* 6, no. 3 (1964), 235.

72. In fragment 5, Solon implies that he balanced the interests of the contending social classes.

73. Wood, *Peasant-Citizen and Slave*, chs. 3–4.

74. Plutarch, "Solon," in *Plutarch's Lives*, John Dryden, trans. (New York: Modern Library, 2001), 114.

75. Garlan, *Slavery in Ancient Greece*, 20–21.

76. Murray, *Early Greece*, 169.

77. This reality has produced a divergence in major Marxist interpretations of ancient Greece. Emphasizing the role of slaves in producing a growing share of social surplus, G. E. M. de Ste. Croix (*Class Struggle*) characterized ancient Greek society as one based upon a slave mode of production. Underlining the fact that the majority of citizens (and producers) were

peasants reproducing their households largely through their own labors and those of their kin, Ellen Meiksins Wood disputed this position in *Peasant-Citizen and Slave*. In my view, these two positions can be reconciled, but to do so will require a more complex notion of an ancient mode of production—one that combines self-reproducing peasant households with widespread exploitation of slave labor.

78. Garlan, *Slavery in Ancient Greece*, 53. Of course, enslaved people were sometimes first captured by Athenians, although this may have been a minority of cases.

79. Karl Marx, *Capital*, vol. 1, Ben Fowkes, trans. (Harmondsworth: Penguin), 182. See also Karl Polanyi, "The Economy as Instituted Process," in *Primitive, Archaic, and Modern Economies*, 159; M. I. Finley, "Marriage, Sale, and Gift," 235; Sahlins, *Stone Age Economics*, 302–3.

80. M. I. Finley, *Economy and Society in Ancient Greece* (London: Chatto and Windus, 1981), 235.

81. If we were to follow Redfield ("Development of the Market") here, we might conclude that this, too, was a strategic omission. However, as I argue below, it is in fact one particular kind of trade—that in slaves—that is depicted in the epics. Crucially, however, markets in slaves involved trade *of* foreigners *with* foreigners.

82. Emile Benveniste, *Indo-European Language and Society*, Elizabeth Palmer, trans. (Coral Gables: University of Miami Press, 1973), 129–37. This connection is insightfully discussed by Sitta von Reden, *Exchange in Ancient Greece* (London: Duckworth, 1995), 67.

83. This seems to have been the case in much of West Africa during the era of the Atlantic slave trade. See Hugh Thomas, *The Slave Trade* (New York: Simon & Schuster, 1997), 47. On the general principle that people might be made property where land could not be, see John Thornton, *Africa and Africans in the Making of the Atlantic World*, 2nd ed. (New York: Cambridge University Press, 1998), 84–95.

84. See Isaac Mendelsohn, *Slavery in the Ancient Near East* (Oxford: Oxford University Press, 1949); Bernard J. Siegel, "Slavery during the Third Dynasty of Ur," part 2, *American Anthropologist* 49, no. 1 (January 1947).

85. Patterson, *Slavery and Social Death*, 149.

86. Peter Frankopan, *The Silk Roads: A New History of the World* (New York: Vintage, 2015), 116. See also Fuad Matthew Caswell, *The Slave Girls of Baghdad* (London: I. B. Tauris & Co., 2011).

87. Jean Andreau and Raymond Descat, *The Slave in Ancient Greece and Rome*, Mario Leopold, trans. (Madison: University of Wisconsin Press, 2011), 21.

88. N. R. E. Fischer, *Slavery in Classical Greece* (London: Bristol Classical Press, 1993), 37.

89. Heraclitus, fragment B53, as translated by Jonathan Barnes in *Early Greek Philosophy* (Harmondsworth: Penguin, 1987), 102.

90. Finley, "Between Slavery and Freedom," 233–49. See also Orlando Patterson, *Freedom*, vol. 1 (New York: Basic Books, 1991), parts 2 and 3.

91. Murray, *Early Greece*, 227.

92. Redfield, "Development of the Market," 30, 38.

93. Redfield, "Development of the Market," 43.

94. Claude Nicolet, *The World of the Citizen in Republican Rome* (Berkeley: University of California Press, 1980), 122.

95. For powerful critiques of barter theories of the origins of trade and markets, see Caroline Humphrey, "Barter and Economic Disintegration," *Man* 20, no. 1 (1985), 48–72; and David

Notes | 253

Graeber, *Debt: The First 5,000 Years* (New York: Melville House, 2011), ch. 2.

96. Patterson, *Slavery and Social Death*, 148.

97. Giuseppe Salvioli, *Le Capitalisme dans le Monde Antique* (Paris: Girard and Briere, 1906).

98. Max Weber, *The Agrarian Sociology of Ancient Civilizations*, R. I. Frank, trans. (London: Verso, 1976), 393.

99. Joseph C. Miller, *The Problem of Slavery as History: A Global Approach* (New Haven: Yale University Press, 2012), 49. See also Joseph C. Miller, "Introduction: Women as Slaves and Owners of Slaves," in *Women and Slavery: Africa, the Indian Ocean World, and the Medieval North Atlantic*, Gwyn Campbell, Suzanne Miers, and Joseph C. Miller, eds. (Athens: Ohio University Press, 2007), 1–40. Of course, there must have been nonbinary persons among captive populations, but slavers would have tended to impose gender identity in the same way they did clothing, habits, and even names.

100. On Delos, see Junius P. Rodriguez, *Chronology of World Slavery* (Santa Barbara: ABC-CLIO, 1999), 31. For Athens, see Garlan, *Slavery in Ancient Greece*, 53–55.

101. This is the view, for instance, of Keith Hopkins, *Conquerors and Slaves* (Cambridge, UK: Cambridge University Press, 1978), 8n14, 25–26, 102.

102. Sandra R. Joshel, *Slavery in the Roman World* (Cambridge, UK: Cambridge University Press, 2010), 84.

103. Joshel, *Slavery in the Roman World*, 66–68.

104. Polybius, *The Histories* (Bloomington: Indiana University Press, 1962), 4.38.

105. Of course, this was true of other societies, such as that of the ancient Hebrews. The Old Testament informs us, for instance, that Jacob's wealth included "much cattle, and maidservants, and menservants, and camels, and asses" (Genesis 30:43).

106. Garlan, *Slavery in Ancient Greece*, 20.

107. Finley, *Ancient Slavery and Modern Ideology* (Harmondsworth: Penguin Books, 1983), 76.

108. Patterson, *Slavery and Social Death*, 13. There is, of course, great variation in the forms of slavery across human societies and historical time. Chattel slavery, for instance, is far from its only form. Patterson's definition of slavery as "the permanent, violent domination of natally alienated and generally dishonored persons" remains most useful.

109. Patterson, *Slavery and Social Death*, 42, 377n32.

110. 'Abd al-Muhsin Bakir, *Slavery in Pharaonic Egypt* (Cairo: l'Institut francais d'archéologie orientale, 1952), ch. 2.

111. Claude Meillassoux, *The Anthropology of Slavery*, Alide Dasnois, trans. (Chicago: University of Chicago Press, 1991), 35.

112. "Ancient Egypt," *Macmillan Encyclopedia of World Slavery*, Paul Finkelman and Joseph C. Miller, eds. (New York: Macmillan, 1998), 282.

113. See Einzig, *Primitive Money*, 80, 111, 131–80, 238–41.

114. Page duBois, *Slaves and Other Objects* (Chicago: University of Chicago Press, 2003), 107.

115. Patterson, *Slavery and Social Death*, 32.

116. Hopkins, *Conquerors and Slaves*, 142–43.

117. Aristotle, *Politics*, 1254b16.

118. Pliny the Elder, *Natural History*, book 29, ch. 8, available at http://www.perseus.tufts.edu/hopper/text?doc=Perseus%3Atext%3A1999.02.0137%3Abook%3D29%3Achapter%3D8.

119. Andreau and Descat, *Slave*, 64.

120. Andreau and Descat, *Slave*, 64; Alan Watson, ed., *The Digest of Justinian* (Philadelphia: University of Pennsylvania Press, 1985), 9.2.2.2.

121. Marx, *Capital*, vol. 1, 377.

122. Patterson, *Slavery and Social Death*, 5.

123. Lucius Annaeus Seneca, *Moral Epistles*, vol. 2, Richard M. Gunnemore, trans. (Cambridge, MA: Harvard University Press, 1917–25), available at http://www.stoics.com/seneca _epistles_book_2.html#%E2%80%98LXXX1.

124. Joshel, *Slavery in the Roman World*, 105.

125. Aristophanes, *The Frogs* (Cambridge, MA: Harvard Classics, 1909–14), line 1532, available at http://www.bartleby.com/8/9/3.html. In this instance, I prefer this older translation, although I will turn to a more modern one below.

126. Hunter, "Body of the Citizen," 278, 273, 280, 284.

127. Joshel, *Slavery in the Roman World*, 116, 119–21; Hunter, "Body of the Citizen," 281–82.

128. Xenophon, *Memorabilia*, Amy L. Bonnette, trans. (Ithaca: Cornell University Press, 1994), 1.16.

129. Hunter, "Body of the Citizen," 285.

130. Aristophanes, "The Frogs," in *The Wasps, the Poet, and the Women*, David Barrett, trans. (Harmondsworth: Penguin, 1964), 644–51.

131. Aristophanes, "The Frogs" (1964 ed.), 734–49.

132. Aristophanes, "Wealth," in *Birds and Other Plays*, Stephen Halliwell, trans. (Oxford: Oxford University Press, 1998), 146.

133. Xenophon, *Memorabilia*, 2.5.2.

134. This point is powerfully argued by Seaford, *Money*.

Chapter 2: The Law of the Body

1. See my *Political Economy and the Rise of Capitalism: A Reinterpretation* (Berkeley: University of California Press, 1988), ch. 3.

2. William H. Desmonde, *Magic, Myth, and Money* (New York: Free Press of Glencoe, 1962), 23. While the analysis in this book is sometimes reductively psychoanalytic, it contains important insights into the historical relations between food and money in the ancient world.

3. Within critical Marxist thought, the concept of "second nature" refers to the naturalization and reification of social processes that present them as emanating from natural laws that evade human control. See Georg Lukács, *History and Class Consciousness: Studies in Marxist Dialectics*, Rodney Livingstone, trans. (London: Merlin Press, 1971), 86; and Alfred Sohn-Rethel, "The Curse of the Second-Nature," in *Intellectual and Manual Labour: A Critique of Epistemology* (London: Macmillan, 1978), ch. 34.

4. Ellen Meiksins Wood, *The Origin of Capitalism: A Longer View* (London and New York: Verso, 2002). I would add to Wood's analysis that market dependence also involves the subjection of work to the capitalist value form, and, with it, new forms of alienated labor.

5. Lukács, *History and Class Consciousness*, 111.

6. While this subsumption of labor to capital is contractually a "temporary" condition regularly renewed through the wage form, in fact the working class as a whole is in bondage

to capital's "golden chain." See Karl Marx, *Capital*, vol. 1, Ben Fowkes, trans. (Harmondsworth: Penguin), 769.

7. Alfred Sohn-Rethel, *Intellectual and Manual Labour: A Critique of Epistemology* (London: Macmillan, 1978), 118.

8. Walter Donlan, "Reciprocities in Homer," *Classical World* 75, no. 3 (1982), 155–56, 163.

9. Desmonde, *Magic, Myth, and Money*, 97.

10. Jane Ellen Harrison, *Ancient Art and Ritual* (Bradford-on-Avon: Moonraker Press, 1978), 41–47; Robert Parker, *Athenian Religion: A History* (Oxford: Clarendon, 1996), 92.

11. Richard Seaford, "Money and Tragedy," in *The Monetary System of the Greeks and the Romans*, W. V. Harris, ed. (Oxford: Oxford University Press, 2008), 53; Harrison, *Ancient Art and Ritual*, 2–3; Parker, *Athenian Religion*, ch. 1.

12. Harrison, *Ancient Art and Ritual*, 45.

13. Bernhard Laum, *Heiliges Geld: Eine historische Untersuchung uber den sakralen Ursprung des Geldes* (Tubingen: Mohr, 1924). Remarkably, this book remains untranslated into English. For useful summaries of some of Laum's arguments, see Desmonde, *Magic, Myth, and Money*, 110–19; Alla Semenova, "Would You Barter with God? Why Holy Debt and Not Profane Markets Created Money," *American Journal of Economics and Sociology* 70, no. 2 (2011), 376–400; Mark Peacock, "The Political Economy of Homeric Society," *Contributions to Political Economy* 30 (2011), 47–65; and Louis Gernet, "'Value' in Greek Myth," in *Myth, Religion, and Society*, R. L. Gordon, ed. (Cambridge, UK: Cambridge University Press, 1981), 112–14.

14. Paul Einzig, *Primitive Money: In Its Ethnological, Historical, and Economic Aspects*, 2nd ed. (Oxford: Pergamon, 1966), 382; Richard Seaford, *Money and the Early Greek Mind: Money, Tragedy, Philosophy* (Cambridge, UK: Cambridge University Press, 2004), 61.

15. Ian Morris, "The Strong Principle of Equality and the Archaic Origins of Greek Democracy," in *Demokratia: A Consideration on Democracies, Ancient and Modern*, Josiah Ober and Charles Hedrick, eds. (Princeton: Princeton University Press, 1996).

16. Seaford, *Money*, 24; Desmonde, *Magic, Myth, and Money*, 116; Semenova, "Would You Barter with God?," 387–88.

17. Martin Ostwald, *Nomos and the Beginnings of the Athenian Democracy* (Oxford: Clarendon, 1969), 20–27.

18. Parker, *Athenian Religion*, ch. 6.

19. To paraphrase Semenova, one does not barter with the gods.

20. James Q. Whitman, "At the Origins of Law and the State: Supervision of Violence, Mutilation of Bodies, or Setting of Prices?" *Chicago-Kent Law Review* 71, no. 1 (1995), 41–84.

21. James Lindgren, "Measuring the Values of Slaves and Persons in Ancient Law," *Chicago-Kent Law Review* 71, no. 1 (1995), 162–64. While Lindgren's article suffers from the mania for quantification characteristic of a "new empiricism" in legal studies, it nevertheless sheds interesting light on the issues we are exploring here.

22. As we shall see, this monetization of law did not derive from market processes.

23. Lindgren, "Values of Slaves," 166–172.

24. As erroneously does Lindgren: "Values of Slaves," 205, 210.

25. Whitman, "Law and the State," 49–52.

26. Philip Grierson, "The Origins of Money," *Research in Economic Anthropology* 1 (1978), 10.

27. Jairus Banaji has made a powerful argument, albeit a highly controversial one, about the existence of "merchant capitalism" across long swathes of human history prior to the emergence of agrarian and industrial capitalism. See, for instance, Banaji, "Guide de lecture: Pour une historiographie du capitalisme marchand," *Période*, available at http://revueperiode.net/breve-bibliographie-annotee-sur-le-capitalisme-marchand/.

28. Sitta von Reden, "Money, Law, and Exchange: Coinage in the Greek Polis," *Journal of Hellenic Studies* 117 (1997), 157–58, 167.

29. Julie Vélissarapoulos-Karakostas, "Merchants, Prostitutes, and the 'New Poor': Forms of Contract and Social Status," in *Money, Labour, and Land: Approaches to the Economies of Ancient Greece*, Paul Cartledge, Edward E. Cohen, and Lin Foxhall, eds. (London: Routledge, 2002), 134.

30. Ronald S. Stroud, "An Athenian Decree on Silver," *Hesperia* 43, no. 2 (1974), 159.

31. Norman Biggs, *Quite Right: The Story of Mathematics, Measurement, and Money* (Oxford: Oxford University Press, 2016), 18–19, 24.

32. Witold Kula, *Measures and Men*, R. Szeter, trans. (Princeton: Princeton University Press, 1986).

33. Kula, *Measures and Men*, 15–16, 25.

34. Sohn-Rethel, *Intellectual and Manual Labour*, 47. Sohn-Rethel's brilliantly original work suffers from a tendency to conflate the exchange abstraction with the capitalist mode of production as a whole. But this shortcoming does not greatly affect his illuminating analysis of Greek mathematics and philosophy.

35. Marx, *Capital*, vol. 1, 128.

36. Marc Shell, *The Economy of Literature* (Baltimore: Johns Hopkins University Press, 1978), 24.

37. In what follows, in-text citations refer to the 1894 English translation of *The Republic* by Benjamin Jowett (Mineola, NY: Dover Publications, 2000).

38. Edith Ayres Copeland, "The Institutional Setting of Plato's *Republic*," *International Journal of Ethics* 34, no. 3 (1924), 228–42. An excellent discussion of book 1 of *The Republic* is provided by Thomas Noutsopoulos, "The Role of Money in Plato's *Republic*, Book I," *Historical Materialism* 23, no. 2 (2015), 131–56.

39. Aristotle, *The Politics*, 1257b30–31, 1257b42.

40. Seaford, *Money*, 175, 231–58.

41. Karl Marx, *Economic and Philosophic Manuscripts*, in *Early Writings*, Rodney Livingstone and Gregor Benton, trans. (Harmondsworth: Penguin, 1973), 383.

42. Karl Marx and Friedrich Engels, *The German Ideology* (Moscow: Progress Publishers, 1976), 50.

43. Plato, *The Laws*, Trevor J. Saunders, trans. (Harmondsworth: Penguin, 1970), 806, 296.

44. Plato, *The Laws*, 777, 258–9. On use of the whip, see Morrow, *Plato's Law of Slavery*, 47, 66–68.

45. Anthony Snodgrass, *Archaic Greece* (Berkeley: University of California Press, 1980), 52–54; Murray, *Early Greece*, 65.

46. Ian Morris, "Gift and Commodity in Archaic Greece," *Man*, n.s. 21 (1986), 12.

47. Beate Dignas, *Economy of the Sacred in Hellenistic and Roman Asia Minor* (Oxford: Oxford University Press, 2002), 14–15.

48. David M. Schaps, *The Invention of Coinage and the Monetization of Ancient Greece* (Ann Arbor: University of Michigan Press, 2004), 82–83.

49. As cited by William Ridgeway, *The Origin of Metallic Currency and Weight Standards*

(Cambridge, UK: Cambridge University Press, 1892), 214.

50. Paul Courbin, "Dans la Grèce archaique: Valeur compare du fer et de làrgent lors de l'introduction du monnayage," *Annales, Économies-Sociétés-Civilisations* 14 (1959), 211–33. See also Alison Hingston Quiggin, *A Survey of Primitive Money* (London: Methuen, 1963), 282, who gives a different figure for the number of spits discovered.

51. Herodotus, *The Histories*, rev. ed., trans Aubrey de Sèlencourt (Harmondsworth: Penguin Books, 2003), II.135.

52. See, for instance, Ingrid Strom, "Obeloi of Pre- or Proto-Monetary Value in the Greek Sanctuaries," in *Economics of Cult in the Ancient Greek World*, Tullia Linders and Brita Alroth, eds. (Upsula: Proceedings of the Upsula Symposium, 1992).

53. David W. Tandy, *Warriors into Traders: The Power of the Market in Early Greece* (Berkeley: University of California Press, 1997), 160. John H. Kroll affirms Tandy's interpretation in his "Observations on Monetary Instruments in Pre-Coinage Greece," in *Hacksilber to Coinage: New Insights into the Monetary History of the Near East and Greece*, Miriam S. Balmuth, ed. (New York: American Numismatic Society, 2001), 87. Seaford (*Money*) and Schaps (*Invention of Coinage*) come to the same conclusion concerning the proto-monetary role of spits, as does R. M. Cook, "Speculations on the Origins of Coinage," *Historia* 7, no. 3 (1958), 257–62.

54. See Courbin, "Dans la Grèce archaique"; and Cook, "Origins of Coinage."

55. Seaford, *Money*, 79–80.

56. See Ian Morris, "The Strong Principle of Equality and the Archaic Origins of Greek Democracy," in Ober and Hedrick, *Demokratia*, 19–48. The example of Hesiod alone makes the case for Morris's claim for an anti-aristocratic or "middling" tradition in archaic Greek cultural life.

57. Ian Morris, *Death-Ritual and Social Structure in Classical Antiquity* (Cambridge, UK: Cambridge University Press, 1992), 118–29, 151–53. My claim for the ascendance of the polis at this time is not a claim for its origins, which are surely much earlier. I am more concerned with its broadening and encroachment upon aristocratic privilege and prerogative.

58. Herodotus, *Histories*, 1.94.3–5.

59. Catherine Eagleton and Jonathan Williams, *Money: A History*, 2nd ed. (London: British Museum Press, 2007), 23–26.

60. Herodotus, *Histories*, 1.93–94.

61. Leslie Kurke, *Coins, Bodies, Games, and Gold: The Politics of Meaning in Archaic Greece* (Princeton: Princeton University Press, 1999). Kurke rightly points out that Herodotus's text is a "profoundly dialogic" one (29). As much as aristocratic themes and values run through it, as in his description of Lydia, so are there countercurrents that owe more to "the middling tradition" identified by Morris.

62. Kurke, *Coins, Bodies, Games*, 47.

63. I have modified Barker's translation here to substitute "people" for "populace."

64. W. G. Forrest, *The Emergence of Greek Democracy, 800–400 BC* (New York: McGraw-Hill, 1966), 94. On the new form of warfare, see also Snodgrass, *Archaic Greece*, 111–13; and Murray, *Early Greece*, 120–31. Building on more recent historical argument, Kurt A. Raaflaub offers a somewhat more gradualist account, less committed to the idea of a "military revolution." See his "Equalities and Inequalities in Athenian Democracy," in Ober and Hedrick,

Demokratia, 151–52.

65. Victor D. Hanson, "Hoplites into Democrats: The Changing Ideology of Athenian Infantry," in Ober and Hedrick, *Demokratia*, 289–312.

66. Forrest, *Greek Democracy*, 112–15.

67. Parker, *Athenian Religion*, 88–89.

68. Kurt A. Raaflaub, "Homer to Solon: The Rise of the Polis," in *The Ancient Greek City-State*, Mogens Herman Hansen, ed. (Copenhagen: Royal Danish Academy of Sciences and Letters, 1993), 52.

69. Parker, *Athenian Religion*, 71, 75.

70. Seaford, "Money and Tragedy," 55; and, with some qualifications, Harrison, *Ancient Art and Ritual*, 82–84.

71. Parker, *Athenian Religion*, 91.

72. Parker, *Athenian Religion*, 103.

73. Harrison, *Ancient Art and Ritual*, 68–77.

74. Seaford, "Money and Tragedy," 56, 61.

75. Christopher Howgego, *Ancient History from Coins* (London: Routledge, 1995), 97; Colin M. Kraay, *Archaic and Classical Greek Coins* (Berkeley: University of California Press, 1976), 55, 60, 63, 72–73. To be sure, this was a regional world money. Full-fledged world money emerges only with the capitalist mode of production and its accompanying world market.

76. Ellen Meiksins Wood, *Peasant-Citizen and Slave: The Foundations of Athenian Democracy* (London: Verso, 1988), 43, 189n3.

77. R. M. Cook, "Speculations on the Origins of Coinage," *Historia* 7 (1958), 257–62; John Melville-Jones, "Why Did the Ancient Greeks Strike Coins?," *Journal of the Numismatic Association of Australia* 17 (2006), 21–30.

78. Karl Marx, *Grundrisse*, Martin Nicolaus, trans. (Harmondsworth: Penguin, 1973), 105.

79. Herodotus, *Histories*, I.64.4–5.

80. H. W. Parke, *Greek Mercenary Soldiers* (Chicago: Ares Publishers, 1933), 15–17, 19, 23–33, 4–6.

81. N. G. L. Hammond, *Alexander the Great*, 2nd ed. (Bristol: Bristol Classical Press, 1994).

82. Glyn Davies, *A History of Money* (Cardiff: University of Wales Press, 2002), 89.

83. Jairus Banaji, *Agrarian Change in Late Antiquity: Gold, Labour, and Aristocratic Dominance* (Oxford: Oxford University Press, 2002), 43.

84. The exception here involves citizen-soldiers under the Roman Empire, who might be awarded slaves that served them in the army. But this is a very different case from that of hired mercenaries. See Sara Elise Phang, "Soldiers' Slaves, 'Dirty Work,' and the Social Status of Roman Soldiers," in *A Tall Order: Writing the Social History of the Ancient World*, Jean-Jacques Aubert and Zsuzsanna Varhelyi, eds. (Leipzig: K. G. Saur Munchen, 2005), 203–25.

85. David B. Hollander, "Veterans, Agriculture, and Monetization in the Late Roman Republic," in Aubert and Varhelyi, *A Tall Order*, 229.

86. Sitta von Reden, *Money in Ptolemaic Egypt* (Cambridge, UK: Cambridge University Press, 2007), 52.

87. Yvon Garlan, *Slavery in Ancient Greece*, rev. ed., trans. Janet Lloyd (Ithaca: Cornell University Press, 1988), 93. I have explored the dubious liberal separation of labor from the body in "The Commodity Status of Labor," in *Not for Sale: Decommodifying Public Life*, Dennis Soron and Gordon Laxer, eds. (Toronto: Broadview Press, 2006), 38–54.

88. Xenophon, *Memorabilia*, Amy L. Bonnette, trans. (Ithaca: Cornell University Press, 1994), 2.8. 1–4.

89. M. I. Finley, "Between Slavery and Freedom," *Comparative Studies in Society and History* 6, no. 3 (1964), 234.

90. Edward E. Cohen, "An Unprofitable Masculinity," in Cartledge, Cohen, and Foxhall, *Money, Labour and Land*, 101.

91. For discussions of this issue, which also touch on the Roman case of slaves and wage labor, see Jean Andreau and Raymond Descat, *The Slave in Ancient Greece and Rome*, Mario Leopold, trans. (Madison: University of Wisconsin Press, 2011), 72–74, 81–89; Cohen, "An Unprofitable Masculinity," 102–3; Hopkins, *Conquerors and Slaves* (Cambridge, UK: Cambridge University Press, 1978), 124–28; and Garlan, *Slavery in Ancient Greece*, 70–72.

92. Hopkins, *Conquerors and Slaves*, 126–28.

93. Sandra R. Joshel, *Slavery in the Roman World* (Cambridge, UK: Cambridge University Press, 2010), 167.

94. Hugo Grotius, *The Rights of War and Peace*, 3 vols., Richard Tuck, ed. (Indianapolis: Liberty Fund, 2005), vol. 2, 556–7, and vol. 3, 1483.

95. David McNally, *Monsters of the Market: Zombies, Vampires, and Global Capitalism* (Chicago: Haymarket, 2012).

96. Emile Benveniste, *Indo-European Language and Society*, Elizabeth Palmer, trans. (Coral Gables: University of Miami Press, 1973), 137.

97. Karl Marx to Friedrich Engels, September 25, 1857, in *Marx-Engels Selected Correspondence*, 2nd ed., I. Lasker, trans. (Moscow: Progress Publishers, 1965), 96. The text is available in a different translation at http://marxists.anu.edu.au/archive/marx/works/1857/letters/57_09_25.htm.

98. Marx, *Grundrisse*, 529n. Marx also makes clear here that this form of wage labor is not capitalist, as the production of surplus value is not its imperative. Nevertheless, he insists that this is where the wage relation first developed on an extensive scale.

99. As quoted by Hollander, "Veterans, Agriculture, and Monetization," 233.

100. von Reden, *Money in Ptolemaic Egypt*, 39.

101. Eagleton and Williams, *Money*, 51.

102. Daphne Nash, "Coinage and State Development in Central Gaul," in *Coinage and Society in Britain and Gaul*, Barry Cunliffe, ed. (London: Council for British Archaeology, 1981), 14–16, 11; von Reden, *Money in Ptolemaic Egypt*, 60–61.

103. The reigns of the Ptolemaic kings were as follows: Ptolemy I (323–282/3 BCE); Ptolemy II (282/3–246); Ptolemy III (246–222); Ptolemy IV (222–204).

104. von Reden, *Money in Ptolemaic Egypt*, 21, 32, 56. Later, a bronze coinage was developed for smaller payments in currency, and it was commonly used for paying wages.

105. Payment in money could originate with those directly taxed, or it could derive from tax farmers, who were contracted to collect and submit predetermined tax revenues, while taking a cut for themselves—and who might collect payments at least partially in kind, but then convert them into cash for submission to government officials. See von Reden, *Money in Ptolemaic Egypt*, 94–99.

106. von Reden, *Money in Ptolemaic Egypt*, 84, 103, 60.

107. von Reden, *Money in Ptolemaic Egypt*, 63, 104.

108. J. G. Manning, "Coinage as 'Code' in Ptolemaic Egypt," in *The Monetary System of the Greeks and Romans*, W. V. Harris, ed. (Oxford: Oxford University Press, 2008), 109.

109. von Reden, *Money in Ptolemaic Egypt*, 36, 39.

110. See, for instance, Peter Spufford, *Money and Its Use in Medieval Europe* (Cambridge, UK: Cambridge University Press, 1988), 14–17.

111. For an overview, see Hugh Kennedy, *The Great Arab Conquests* (Philadelphia: Da Capo, 2007). The background story is laid out in Maxine Rodinson, *Muhammad*, 2nd English ed., Ann Carter, trans. (Harmondsworth: Penguin, 1971).

112. Peter Frankopan, *The Silk Roads: A New History of the* World (New York: Vintage, 2015), 86–93.

113. Orlando Patterson, *Slavery and Social Death* (Cambridge, MA: Harvard University Press, 1982), 152–57.

114. Ralph A. Austen, "The Trans-Saharan Slave Trade: A Tentative Census," in *The Uncommon Market: Essays in the Economic History of the Atlantic Slave Trade*, Henry A. Gemery and Jan S. Hogendorn, eds. (New York: Academic Press, 1979), 23–76; Thomas M. Ricks, "Islamic World," in *Macmillan Encyclopedia of World Slavery*, vol. 2, Paul Finkelman and Joseph C. Miller, eds. (New York: Macmillan, 1988), 833–34; Patterson, *Slavery and Social Death*, 159.

115. Frankopan, *Silk Roads*, 104, 111–17; Dimitrij Mishan, "The Saqaliba Slaves in the Aghlabid State," in *Annual of Medieval Studies at CEU, 1996–97* (Budapest: Central European University, 1998), 236–44.

116. Thomas S. Noonan, "Early Abbasid Mint Output," *Journal of Economic and Social History* 29 (1986), 113–75.

117. J. M. Dent, ed., *The Travels of Marco Polo* (London: J. M. Dent and Sons, 1908), 202–5.

118. I have drawn here on the accounts in Lien-sheng Yang, *Money and Credit in China: A Short History* (Cambridge, MA: Harvard University Press, 1952), chs. 1, 6, and 7; and Eagleton and Williams, *Money*, ch. 6.

119. Yang, *Money and Credit*, 61, 53–55.

120. Frankopan, *Silk Roads*, 191–93; Yang, *Money and Credit*, 66–67.

121. Notwithstanding a number of difficulties with his arguments, Kenneth Pomeranz is right on China's relative development into the fifteenth century CE. See Pomeranz, *The Great Divergence: China, Europe, and the Making of the Modern World Economy* (Princeton: Princeton University Press, 2000). His attempt to extend the claim through the eighteenth century is seriously flawed.

122. Frankopan, *Silk Roads*, 137, 139.

123. Bernard of Clairvaux, *The Letters of St. Bernard of Clairvaux*, Bruno Scott James and Beverley Mayne Kienzle, eds. and trans. (Sutton: Stroud, 1998), 391.

124. David Abulafia, *The Great Sea: A Human History of the Mediterranean* (Oxford: Oxford University Press, 2011), 298.

125. See, among other texts, Henri Pirenne, *Economic and Social History of Medieval Europe*, I. E. Clegg, trans. (New York: Harcourt Brace, 1937), part 1. Pirenne's analysis famously influenced the market-centered position taken by Paul Sweezy in the Marxist "transition debate" of the early 1950s, which was prompted by Maurice Dobb's *Studies in the Development of Capitalism* (New York: International Publishers, 1947; rev. ed. 1963). See Paul Sweezy, "A Critique," in *The Tran-*

sition from Feudalism to Capitalism, Rodney Hilton, ed. (London: New Left Books, 1976), 33–56.

126. Charles Verlinden, *The Beginnings of Modern Colonization*, Yvonne Freccero, trans. (Ithaca: Cornell University Press, 1970), 11–17. Knight service was less typical of the later Portuguese colonies.

127. Again, I want to stress that this has to do with logics of retro-determination. It is not that the earlier form *must* develop in a singular direction. Instead, once a new stage is reached it becomes possible to reconstruct the historical logic by which it emerged from earlier forms.

128. Janet Abu-Lughod, *Before European Hegemony: The World System, A.D. 1250–1350* (New York: Oxford University Press, 1989); Roxann Prazniak, "Sienna on the Silk Roads: Ambrogio Lorenzetti and the Mongol Global Century, 1250–1350," *Journal of World History* 21, no. 2 (2010), 177–217.

129. Spufford, *Money in Medieval Europe*, 152–60; Frankopan, *Silk Roads*, 190–93, 181.

130. Spufford, *Money in Medieval Europe*, ch. 12.

131. Abu-Lughod, *Before European Hegemony*, 85.

132. John Day, "The Great Bullion Famine of the Fifteenth Century," *Past and Present* 79 (1979), 3–54.

133. William S. Atwell, "Time, Money, and the Weather: Ming China and the 'Great Depression' of the Mid-fifteenth Century," *Journal of Asian Studies* 61, no. 1 (2002), 84.

134. H. Cross, "South American Bullion Production and Export, 1550–1750," in *Precious Metals in the Later Medieval and Early Modern Worlds*, John F. Richards, ed. (Durham: Carolina Academic Press, 1983), 402–4; Pierre Vilar, *A History of Gold and Money, 1450–1920*, Judith White, trans. (London: New Left Books, 1976), 103–4, 138.

135. Verlinden, *Modern Colonization*, 18–24. See also Eric Wolf, *Europe and the People without History* (Berkeley: University of California Press, 1997), 149–51.

136. Frankopan, *Silk Roads*, 250.

Chapter 3: From the Bones of Princes to the Blood of the Commonwealth

1. Barnardo Davanzati, *A Discourse upon Coins*, John Toland, trans. (London: Awnsham and John Churchil, 1969[1588]), available at https://avalon.law.yale.edu/16th_Century/coins.asp.

2. See Nicholas Oresme, *De Moneta*, Charles Johnson, ed., Latin text with English translation (New York: Thomas Nelson, 1956), 43–44. On the use of the metaphor into the eighteenth century, see Jerah Johnson, "The Money=Blood Metaphor," *Journal of Finance* 21, no. 1 (March 1966), 119–22.

3. Edmund Plowden, *Commentaries or Reports* (London, 1816), as cited by Ernst H. Kantorowicz, *The King's Two Bodies: A Study in Medieval Political Theology* (Princeton: Princeton University Press, 1957), 177.

4. Baldus de Ubaldis, *Consilia* (Venice, 1575), as cited by Kantorowicz, *King's Two Bodies*, 185.

5. Kantorowicz, *King's Two Bodies*, 179–80, 209.

6. Christine Desan, *Making Money: Coin, Currency, and the Coming of Capitalism* (Oxford: Oxford University Press, 2014), 268–70.

7. *The Case of Mixed Money* (1605), in *Cobbett's Complete Collection of State Trials and Pro-*

ceedings for High Treason and Other Crimes and Misdemeanours, T. B. Howell, ed., vol. 2 (London: R. Bagshaw, 1809), 114–18.

8. The Case of Mixed Money, 225–27.

9. For an excellent overview of Hobbes's political thought, see Ellen Meiksins Wood and Neal Wood, A Trumpet of Sedition: Political Theory and the Rise of Capitalism, 1509–1688 (London: Pluto, 1997), ch. 5.

10. Thomas Hobbes, Leviathan (Harmondsworth: Penguin, 1968), ch. 15, 208. C. B. Macpherson's treatment of Hobbes's "market model" of society builds on passages such as this and remains compelling—see his The Political Theory of Possessive Individualism: Hobbes to Locke (Oxford: Oxford University Press, 1962)—though his attempt to make him a part of the liberal tradition clearly founders on the overwhelming evidence of Hobbes's absolutism.

11. For an overview of bourgeois economic thought and its social-historical context, see my Political Economy and the Rise of Capitalism: A Reinterpretation (Berkeley: University of California Press, 1988).

12. Hobbes, Leviathan, 296.

13. Hobbes, Leviathan, 300–1.

14. Rodney Hilton, "Feudalism in Europe: Problems for Historical Materialists," Class Conflict and the Crisis of Feudalism, 2nd ed. (London: Verso, 1990), 2.

15. Georges Duby, The Early Growth of the European Economy: Warriors and Peasants from the Seventh to the Twelfth Century, Howard B. Clarke, trans. (London: Weidenfeld and Nicolson, 1974), 157.

16. Guy Bois, The Revolution of the Year One Thousand, Jean Birrell, trans. (Manchester: Manchester University Press, 1983), 50.

17. John Hatcher, "English Serfdom and Villeinage: Towards a Reassessment," Past and Present 90 (1981), 3–39.

18. As does Jane Whittle in her important study, The Development of Agrarian Capitalism: Land and Labour in Norfolk 1440–1580 (Oxford: Clarendon, 2000), 11–15. As will become clear below, I differ with Whittle on significant points of historical analysis and judgement.

19. Rodney Hilton, "A Crisis of Feudalism," in The Brenner Debate: Agrarian Class Structure and Economic Development in Pre-industrial Europe, T. H. Aston and C. H. E. Philpin, eds. (Cambridge, UK: Cambridge University Press, 1985), 124.

20. See Whittle, Agrarian Capitalism, 46–63, who does acknowledge that these courts endured a partial decline in the fifteenth century (83).

21. Perry Anderson, Passages from Antiquity to Feudalism (London: New Left Books, 1974), 148. It is certainly true that the medieval English state was considerably less decentralized than its continental counterparts, and the crown more powerful, but this represented a comparatively stronger monarchy on a continuum that was still recognizably feudal.

22. Sidney Painter, Studies in the History of the English Feudal Barony (Baltimore: Johns Hopkins University Press, 1943), 170–78.

23. Marc Bloch, Feudal Society, vol. 1, L. A. Manyon, trans. (Chicago: University of Chicago Press, 1961), ch. 11.

24. Jack Goody, The Development of the Family and Marriage in Europe (Cambridge, UK: Cambridge University Press, 1983), 125–27.

25. Michael Mann, The Sources of Social Power, vol. 1 (Cambridge, UK: Cambridge University

Press, 1986), 418, 428.

26. Christopher Dyer, *An Age of Transition? Economy and Society in England in the Later Middle Ages* (Oxford: Clarendon, 2005), 18–20. On the general processes throughout Western Europe, see Georges Duby, *Rural Economy and Country Life in the Medieval West*, Cynthia Postan, trans. (Columbia: University of South Carolina Press, 1968), 67–80.

27. On agricultural productivity trailing the rate of population increase, see Hilton, "Crisis of Feudalism," 122. The notion of a *weak* tendency toward technological improvement refers to the idea that humans are cultural creatures with the capacity to retain and innovate upon forms of social knowledge (including technologies). I touch on this point in my *Bodies of Meaning: Studies in Labor, Language, and Liberation* (Albany: State University of New York Press, 2002), ch. 3. However, what is retained and transmitted depends overwhelmingly on the social relations of production and the degree to which these foster or discourage technological change. The capitalist mode of production is unique in its intrinsic requirement for continuous and systematic technological innovation; the tendency to project this capitalist dynamic as a transhistorical law has done considerable damage to historical materialism. For a critique of this tendency, see Ellen Meiksins Wood, "History or Technological Determinism," in *Democracy against Capitalism: Renewing Historical Materialism* (Cambridge, UK: Cambridge University Press, 1995), ch. 4.

28. See Lynn White Jr., *Medieval Technology and Social Change* (London: Oxford University Press, 1962); Robert S. Lopez, *The Commercial Revolution of the Middle Ages, 950–1350* (Cambridge, UK: Cambridge University Press, 1976).

29. For evidence of a systemic contraction beginning around 1280 in England, see H. E. Hallam, "Population Density in the Medieval Fenland," *Economic History Review*, 2nd series, no. 14 (1961–62), 78–79. On the general question of system crisis in medieval England at this time, see Ian Kershaw, "The Great Famine and Agrarian Crisis in England 1315–22," in *Peasants, Knights and Heretics: Studies in Medieval English Social History*, Rodney Hilton, ed. (Cambridge, UK: Cambridge University Press, 1976), 85–132.

30. Hilton, *Class Conflict*, 170.

31. For the suggestion of a slow rise in agricultural productivity until the twelfth century, see Georges Duby, "Medieval Agriculture, 900–1500," in *The Fontana Economic History of Europe*, vol. 1, Carlo M. Cipolla, ed. (London: Collins/Fontana, 1972), 195–96. For a more skeptical view, see Hilton, "Was There a General Crisis?" in *Class Conflict*, 169, who argues that "there is no indication of a general and permanent increase in yields."

32. Hilton, "Was There a General Crisis?," 170–71.

33. Duby, *Rural Economy*, 124, 298–301.

34. Hilton, *Class Conflict*, 74.

35. Guy Bois, *La Grande Dépression medievale* (Paris: Actuel Marx, 2000). This book extends Bois's earlier attempt at constructing a historical materialist account of the systemic laws of motion of feudalism that led to breakdown and decline. For the earlier study, see Bois, *Crise du féodalisme* (Paris: Presses de la foundations nationale des sciences politiques, 1976). I consider Bois's analysis to be highly insightful, notwithstanding my reservations about delineating purely economic laws of motion for modes of production in which the "economic" and the "political" have not been formally separated.

36. Robert Brenner, "The Agrarian Roots of European Capitalism," in Aston and Philpin, *The*

Brenner Debate, 238.

37. Duby, *Rural Economy*, 206.

38. Brenner, "Agrarian Roots," 239.

39. Geoffrey Parker, *The Military Revolution: Military Innovation and the Rise of the West, 1500–1800* (Cambridge, UK: Cambridge University Press, 1988); Michael Duffy, ed., *The Military Revolution and the State* (Exeter: Exeter University Press, 1980). While the social-historical analyses in these books are lacking, they are descriptively insightful.

40. As quoted by Michael Mann, *The Sources of Social Power*, vol. 1 (Cambridge, UK: Cambridge University Press, 1986), 454.

41. Richard Bean, "War and the Birth of the Nation State," *Journal of Economic History* 33, no. 1 (1973), 216–17.

42. Mann, *Social Power*, table 13.2, 425; P. K. O'Brien and P. A. Hunt, "The Rise of a Fiscal State in England, 1485–1815," *Historical Research* 66 (1993), 151.

43. Michael Mann (*Social Power*, 432) correctly points out, in response to the sometimes-excessive claims of Charles Tilly, that the increase in the capacity of medieval and early modern states to extract resources was "hardly impressive." For Tilly's view, see "Reflections on the History of European State-Making," in *The Formation of National States in Western Europe*, Charles Tilly, ed. (Princeton: Princeton University Press, 1975), 73–74.

44. J. H. Elliott, *Imperial Spain, 1469-1716* (New York: Mentor, 1966), 203, 282–83.

45. The concept of impersonal power is developed by way of comparative historical analysis by Heide Gerstenberger, *Impersonal Power: History and Theory of the Bourgeois State* (Leiden: Brill, 2007).

46. Karl Marx and Friedrich Engels, *The German Ideology*, 3rd ed. (Moscow: Progress Publishers, 1976), 98.

47. As quoted by G. R. Elton, *England under the Tudors*, 2nd ed. (London: Methuen & Co., 1974), 107.

48. As quoted by Elton, *England under the Tudors*, 160–61. On Thomas Cromwell's political career, see chs. 6 and 7.

49. Lawrence Stone, *The Crisis of the Aristocracy, 1558–1641* (New York: Oxford University Press, 1967), 97.

50. Elton, *England under the Tudors*, 160.

51. Christopher Hill, "A Bourgeois Revolution?," in *Three British Revolutions: 1641, 1688, 1776*, J. G. A. Pocock, ed. (Princeton: Princeton University Press, 1980), 117.

52. Kenneth R. Andrews, *Elizabethan Privateering: English Privateering during the Spanish War, 1585–1603* (Cambridge, UK: Cambridge University Press, 1964), 7–10.

53. Andrews, *Elizabethan Privateering*, 5, 94, 21.

54. Andrews, *Elizabethan Privateering*, ch. 7.

55. Theodore K. Rabb, *Enterprise and Empire: Merchant and Gentry Investment in the Expansion of England, 1575–1630* (Cambridge, MA: Harvard University Press, 1967), 13, 13n16, 27, 31, 38–39.

56. As is made clear by Nicholas Canny, *The Elizabethan Conquest of Ireland: A Pattern Established 1565–76* (Brighton: Harvester, 1976).

57. Andrews, *Elizabethan Privateering*, 15.

58. Rabb, *Enterprise and Empire*, 13.

59. On Bohemia, see Arnošt Klima, "Agrarian Class Structure and Economic Development in Pre-industrial Bohemia," in *The Brenner Debate*, 192–212. On Prussia, see Terence Byers, *Capitalism from Above and Capitalism from Below: An Essay in Comparative Political Economy* (Houndmills: Palgrave Macmillan, 1996).

60. It is impossible to do justice to the debate over the economic development of the Nether-lands here. My view that it represented a highly developed commercial republic dominated by merchant capital is briefly sketched in *Monsters of the Market: Zombies, Vampires, and Global Capitalism* (Chicago: Haymarket, 2012), 35–36. An excellent discussion of the role of war in the making of the Dutch republic can be found in Pepijn Brandon, *War, Capital, and the Dutch State* (Chicago: Haymarket, 2016), who points out, "From the early eighteenth century onwards, if not earlier . . . the economy of the Dutch republic had lost most of its erstwhile dynamism" (66). The two key representatives of "Political Marxism," Robert Brenner and Ellen Meiksins Wood, disagreed as to whether the Netherlands had transi-tioned into agrarian capitalism, with Brenner in the affirmative. See Robert Brenner, "The Low Countries in the Transition to Capitalism," *Journal of Agrarian Change* 1, no. 2 (April 2001), 169–241, and Ellen Meiksins Wood, "The Question of Market Dependence," *Journal of Agrarian Change* 2, no.1 (January 2002), 50–87.

61. The overarching comparative analysis here is indebted to the seminal work of Robert Brenner (see his essays in *The Brenner Debate*). However, I depart from Brenner with respect to chronology and social agency. The largest difference revolves around my view that social differentiation of the peasantry was a crucial precondition of agrarian capitalist transforma-tion in England. Building on the work of Rodney Hilton, among others, I suggest that rich peasants drove the earliest movements toward enclosure and agricultural improvement in the period 1380 to 1520, creating conditions that would prove to be conducive to new waves of enclosure and capital investment on the lands by landowners themselves. For Hilton's work, see especially *The English Peasantry in the Later Middle Ages* (Oxford: Clarendon, 1975); *The Decline of Serfdom in Medieval England* (London: Macmillan, 1969); *Bond Men Made Free: Medieval Peasant Movements and the English Rising of 1381* (London: Methuen, 1973); and *Class Conflict and the Crisis of Feudalism*; as well as Hilton, ed., *Peasants, Knights and Heretics: Studies in Medieval English Social History* (Cambridge, UK: Cambridge University Press, 1976). The importance of the point about social differentiation of the peasantry has been persuasively made by Terence J. Byers, "Differentiation of the Peasantry under Feudalism and the Transition to Capitalism: In Defence of Rodney Hilton," *Journal of Agrarian* Change 6, no. 1 (2006), 17–68. Similar amendments to Brenner's argument are found in Colin Mooers, *The Making of Bourgeois Europe* (London: Verso, 1991). My analysis in *Political Economy and the Rise of Capitalism* (ch. 1) is also much influenced by the work of Hilton. An interesting attempt to defend Brenner on these grounds—or, perhaps better, one which takes on board aspects of these critical amendments and integrates them into a more nuanced version of the Brenner thesis—can be found in Spencer Dimmock, *The Origin of Capitalism in England, 1400–1600* (Chicago: Haymarket Books, 2015). Some of the classic historical scholarship in tune with the basic argument I make here includes R. A. Tawney, *The Agrarian Problem in the Sixteenth Cen-tury* (London, 1912; reprint, New York: Harper & Row, 1967); W. G. Hoskins, *The Midland Peasant* (London: Macmillan, 1957); Margaret Campbell, *The English Yeoman under Elizabeth and the Early Stuarts* (New Haven: Yale University Press, 1942); Joan Thirsk, *Agrarian Regions*

and Agrarian History in England (London: Macmillan, 1987). Recent works of considerable significance to these issues include Dyer, *An Age of Transition?*; Keith Wrightson, *Earthly Necessities: Economic Lives in Early Modern Britain* (New Haven: Yale University Press, 2000); and Whittle, *Agrarian Capitalism.*

62. Dyer, *An Age of Transition?*, 1.

63. David Underdown, *Revel, Riot and Rebellion: Popular Politics and Culture in England, 1603–1660* (Oxford: Oxford University Press, 1985), 26.

64. Whittle, *Agrarian Capitalism*, 37.

65. Duby, *Rural Economy*, 158

66. Dimmock, *Capitalism in England*, 146.

67. On the cooperative ethos of unenclosed communities, see J. M. Neeson, *Commoners: Common Right, Enclosure, and Social Change in England, 1700–1820* (Cambridge, UK: Cambridge University Press, 1993).

68. Joan Thirsk, *Tudor Enclosures* (London: Routledge & Kegan Paul, 1959), 4.

69. Whittle, *Agrarian Capitalism*, 196–203; W. G. Hoskins, *The Age of Plunder: The England of Henry VIII 1500–1547* (London: Longman, 1976), 57.

70. Campbell, *English Yeoman*, 87.

71. J. R. Wordie, "The Chronology of English Enclosure, 1500–1914," *Economic History Review* 36 (1983), 484–505.

72. Campbell, *English Yeoman*, 102.

73. Wrightson, *Earthly Necessities*, 101.

74. Hoskins, *Age of Plunder*, 30–32.

75. A point I first made in *Political Economy and the Rise of Capitalism*, 5–6.

76. What follows here is based on the account by Whittle, *Agrarian Capitalism*, 59–62.

77. Interestingly, Bisshop did suffer the penalty of having his lease for the "great enclosure" withdrawn. But this seems not to have seriously deterred him or to have cost him a significant loss of status in the village community.

78. Whittle, *Agrarian Capitalism*, 70–71.

79. See R. B. Outhwaite, *Inflation in Tudor and Stuart England* (London: Macmillan, 1969). On the effects of these price rises, see Wrightson, *Earthly Necessities*, ch. 5.

80. John E. Martin, *Feudalism to Capitalism: Peasant and Landlord in English Agrarian Development* (London: Macmillan, 1983), 129.

81. For examples, see Dyer, *An Age of Transition?*, 81–85.

82. Wrightson, *Earthly Necessities*, 135, 139.

83. Rodney Hilton, "A Study in the Pre-history of English Enclosure in the Fifteenth Century," in *The English Peasantry*, 168.

84. A. L. Beier, "Social Problems in Elizabethan London," *Journal of Interdisciplinary History* 9 (1978), 204–5. See also Paul Slack, *Poverty and Policy in Tudor and Stuart England* (London: Longman, 1988).

85. In what follows concerning the crown and the church, I draw on Elton, *England under the Tudors*, 143–49, and Hoskins, *Age of Plunder*, 121–36.

86. Wrightson, *Earthly Necessities*, 142–43; Hoskins, *Age of Plunder*, 136–38.

87. Wrightson, *Earthly Necessities*, 144.

88. Wordie, "Chronology of English Enclosure," 502, 495.

89. F. M. L. Thompson, "The Social Distribution of Landed Property in England since the Sixteenth Century," *Economic History Review*, 2nd series, vol. 19, no. 3 (1966), 515. ·

90. Richard Lachman, *From Manor to Market: Structural Change in England, 1536–1640* (Madison: University of Wisconsin Press, 1987), 129.

91. Lachman, *Manor to Market*, 17.

92. Dimmock (e.g., 155) tends to locate the "origin" of capitalism in the fifteenth century. There is something to this, given the scale of social change in that era. But I find it more prudent to suggest that capitalist transformations had become overwhelming by 1640, though they required a reconstitution of state power (the revolutions of the 1640s and 1688–89) to make them effectively irreversible.

93. Ann Kussmaul, *Servants in Husbandry in Early Modern England* (Cambridge, UK: Cambridge University Press, 1981), 3, 4, 11.

94. There is now a massive literature on early industrialization, some of which I reviewed in my *Against the Market: Political Economy, Market Socialism, and the Marxist Critique* (London: Verso, 1983), 24–42. For a comprehensive and considerably more up-to-date overview and analysis, see Michael A. Zmolek, *Rethinking the Industrial Revolution: Five Centuries of Transition from Agrarian to Industrial Capitalism in England* (Leiden: Brill, 2013).

95. On Baconianism in seventeenth-century England, see McNally, *Political Economy*, 36–40 (on number, weight and measure, see 38). On abstract space, see Henri Lefebvre, *The Production of Space*, Donald Nicholson-Smith, trans. (London: Blackwell, 1991). For an interesting discussion of the changing landscapes of rural capitalism, see Matthew Johnson, *An Archaeology of Capitalism* (London: Blackwell, 1996).

96. Derek Gregory, *Geographical Imaginations* (Oxford: Blackwell, 1994), 392.

97. On Petty and the Down Survey, see McNally, *Political Economy*, 47–49.

98. Anon., *A ruful complaynt of the publyke weale to England* (London, 1550). See also John U. Nef's comment that the during the period 1540–1640, the economic interests of English gentry and merchants "tended to become identical": *Industry and Government in France and England, 1540–1640* (Ithaca: Cornell University Press, 1964), 9.

99. John Guy, *Tudor England* (Oxford: Oxford University Press, 1988), 208.

100. See the fine study by Andy Wood, *The 1549 Rebellions and the Making of Early Modern England* (Cambridge, UK: Cambridge University 2007), 56, 60.

101. S. T. Bindhoff, *Ket's Rebellion* (London: Historical Association, 1949), 9.

102. Nicholas Canny, *Kingdom and Colony: Ireland in the Atlantic World 1560–1800* (Baltimore: Johns Hopkins University Press, 1988), 13.

103. As quoted by Nicholas Canny, *The Elizabethan Conquest of Ireland: A Pattern Established 1565–76* (London: Harvester, 1976), 122. This paragraph draws on Canny, *Elizabethan Conquest*, 65–74, 154.

104. Canny, *Elizabethan Conquest*, 92; D. B. Quinn, *Raleigh and the British Empire* (New York: Collier, 1962); Quinn, *The Roanoke Voyages, 1584–90*, 2 vols. (Cambridge, UK: Cambridge University Press, 1955); Canny, *Kingdom and Colony*, 29, 100–1, 105.

105. John Davies, *Historical Tracts* (London: John Stockdale, 1786), 288.

106. Canny, *Kingdom and Colony*, 79–80, discusses this emphasis on colonialism as agricultural improvement.

107. Ellen Meiksins Wood, *Empire of Capital* (London and New York: Verso, 2003), 38. For a

general history, see Elliott, *Imperial Spain*.

108. Andrews, *Elizabethan Privateering*, 2–4.

109. As Andrews notes, the "distinction between privateering and piracy" comes down to the purely legal one between plundering activity with a document of commission or without (*Elizabethan Privateering*, 5).

110. As Robert Brenner demonstrates in *Merchants and Revolution* (London and New York: Verso, 2003).

111. Robert Brenner, "The Social Basis of English Commercial Expansion, 1550–1650," *Journal of Economic History* 32, no. 1 (1972), 374. See also Brenner, *Merchants and Revolution*, 89, 113–16.

112. Richard Pares, *Merchants and Planters* (London: Cambridge University Press, 1960), 7. In this respect, the new merchants had moved beyond the classical behavior of commercial capitalists who invest "in inventory, not directly in production," in the words of John R. Gillis, "Islands in the Making of an Atlantic Oceana," in *Seascapes: Maritime Histories, Littoral Cultures, and Transoceanic Exchanges*, Jerry H. Bentley, Renate Bridenthal, and Karen Wigen, eds. (Honolulu: University of Hawai'i Press, 2007), 28.

113. Rabb, *Enterprise and Empire*, 27, 38–39n27.

114. "From the beginning they were the main champions of plantation": Kenneth R. Andrews, *Trade, Plunder and Settlement* (Cambridge, UK: Cambridge University Press, 1984), 18.

115. Andrews, *Elizabethan Privateering*, 17, 189–90.

116. Rabb, *Enterprise and Empire*, 41–42n33.

117. "Surplus population" refers, of course, not to some simple demographic relation, but to the impoverished small tenants and some pauperized landless "vagrants" who were rendered *socially* surplus to capitalist agriculture. It should also be noted that enslavement of indigenous peoples was much more widely practiced than generally believed, though the leading colonial power in this regard was Spain, and the settlers who came via its colonial activity.

118. See Kussmaul, *Servants in Husbandry*.

119. I am drawing upon and extrapolating the figures provided by Henry A. Gemery, "Markets for Migrants: English Indentured Servants and Emigration in the Seventeenth and Eighteenth Centuries," in *Colonialism and Migration: Indentured Labour before and after Slavery*, P. C. Emmer, ed. (Leiden: Martinus Nijhoff, 1986), 38.

120. Not only were the numbers of indentured workers exported from the Netherlands dramatically lower than the numbers from England, but a much larger percentage seem to have entered nonagricultural jobs. See Ernst van den Boogaart, "The Servant Migration to New Netherland, 1624–1664," in Emmer, *Colonialism and Migration*.

121. Nuala Zahedieh, *The Capital and the Colonies: London and the Atlantic Economy, 1660–1700* (Cambridge, UK: Cambridge University Press, 2010), 32–33.

122. David Eltis, *The Rise of African Slavery in the Americas* (Cambridge, UK: Cambridge University Press, 2000), 14, 36, 53.

123. For a few of the best sources, see Christopher Hill, *The World Turned Upside Down* (Harmondsworth: Penguin, 1968); *A Century of Revolution* (London: Sphere, 1969); *Intellectual Origins of the English Revolution Revisited* (Oxford: Oxford University Press, 1997); Brian Manning, *The English People and the English Revolution* (London: Heineman, 1976); Michael Walzer, *The Revolution of the Saints: A Study in the Origins of Radical Politics*

(Cambridge, MA: Harvard University Press, 1982); H. N. Brailsford, *The Levellers and the English Revolution* (Stanford: Stanford University Press, 1961); and Ian Gentles, *The New Model Army in England, Ireland, and Scotland, 1645–1653* (Oxford: Blackwell Publishers, 1992).

124. Hill, "A Bourgeois Revolution?," 116.

125. A most useful source on this is Christopher Hill, *God's Englishman: Oliver Cromwell and the English Revolution* (New York: Harper & Row, 1970), chs. 5–6.

126. Hill, *God's Englishman*, 117.

127. See Susan Dwyer Amussen, *Caribbean Exchanges: Slavery and the Transformation of English Society, 1640*–1700 (Chapel Hill: University of North Carolina Press, 2007), 154–73; Richard S. Dunn, *Sugar and Slaves: The Rise of the Planter Class in the English West Indies, 1624–1713* (New York: W. W. Norton, 1972), 72–73; Daniel P. Mannix, *Black Cargoes: A History of the Atlantic Slave Trade* (Harmondsworth: Penguin, 1976), 60–66. Key theoretical and political extrapolations include Theodor Allen, *The Invention of the White Race*, 2 vols. (London and New York: Verso, 1994); and David Roediger, *The Wages of Whiteness: Race and the Making of the American Working Class* (London and New York: Verso, 1991).

128. Eltis, *African Slavery*, 38–39, 49.

129. Brenner, *Merchants and Revolution*, 115.

130. My account of Thomson draws on J. E. Farnell, "The Navigation Act of 1651, the First Dutch War, and the London Merchant Community," *Economic History Review* 16, no. 3 (1964), 443–44; Brenner, *Merchants and Revolution*, 115, 118, 135, 158, 127, 134; and Gerald Horne, *The Apocalypse of Settler Colonialism: The Roots of Slavery, White Supremacy, and Capitalism in Seventeenth-Century North America and the Caribbean* (New York: Monthly Review, 2018), 15, 48.

131. Hill, *God's Englishman*, 160. Following the lead of Farnell, "Navigation Act," Hill (131) suggests Thomson as the author of the 1651 act.

132. See Brenner, "Social Basis," 382.

Chapter 4: Blood in the Water

1. Barry Unsworth, *Sacred Hunger* (Harmondsworth: Penguin, 1992), 352.

2. Karl Marx, *Capital*, vol. 1, Ben Fowkes, trans. (Harmondsworth: Penguin, 1976), 922.

3. Thomas Hobbes, *Leviathan*, C. B. Macpherson, ed. (Harmondsworth: Penguin, 1968), ch. 24, 300.

4. As cited by Hans Koning, *Columbus: His Enterprise* (New York: Monthly Review, 1991), 107–8. For more on Columbus's obsession with gold, see Kirkpatrick Sale, *The Conquest of Paradise: Christopher Columbus and the Columbian Legacy* (New York: Penguin, 1991), 106–7.

5. Andrés Reséndez, *The Other Slavery: The Uncovered Story of Indian Enslavement in America* (Boston: Mariner, 2016), 19–39.

6. Charles Davenant, *Discourses on the Public Revenues and the Trade of England in Two Parts*, in *The Political and Commercial Works of the Celebrated Writer Charles Davenant*, Charles Whitworth, ed., 5 vols. (London: R. Horsfield et. al., 1771), vol. 1, 381–83. On the distinction between Spanish colonialism and the English and French variants, see also Sidney Mintz, *Sweet-*

ness and Power: The Place of Sugar in Modern History (Harmondsworth: Penguin, 1985), 35–36.

7.   For background, see Pierre Vilar, *Spain: A Brief History*, 2nd. ed., Brian Tate, trans. (Oxford: Pergamon, 1967). See also Vilar, *A History of Gold and Money, 1450–1920*, Judith White, trans. (London: Verso, 1976), ch. 17.

8.   John Taylor, *Multum in Parvo*, as cited by Susan Dwyer Amussen, *Caribbean Exchanges: Slavery and the Transformation of English Society, 1640–1770* (Chapel Hill: University of North Carolina Press, 2007), 59.

9.   David Eltis, *The Rise of African Slavery in the Americas* (Cambridge, UK: Cambridge University Press, 2000), 150–51.

10.   Christopher Hill, *God's Englishman: Oliver Cromwell and the English Revolution* (New York: Harper Collins, 1972), 132.

11.   My account of the Stop of the Exchequer and its aftermath is indebted to Bruce G. Carruthers, *City of Capital: Politics and Markets in the English Financial Revolution* (Princeton: Princeton University Press, 1996), 122–26; and Christine Desan, *Making Money: Coins, Currency, and the Coming of Capitalism* (Oxford: Oxford University Press, 2014), 281–87. See also Henry Roseveare, *The Financial Revolution, 1660–1760* (London: Longman, 1991), 21–22.

12.   See Desan, *Making Money*, 246–48; Roseveare, *Financial Revolution*, 34.

13.   *The Case of the Bankers* (1699–1700), in *Cobbett's Complete Collection of State Trials and Proceedings for High Treason and Other Crimes and Misdemeanours*, T. B. Howell, ed., vol. 14 (London: R. Bagshaw, 1809), 55.

14.   *The Case of the Bankers*, 37.

15.   See Nuala Zahedieh, *The Capital and the Colonies: London and the Atlantic Economy, 1660–1700* (Cambridge, UK: Cambridge University Press, 2010), ch. 6.

16.   Christopher Hill, *The Century of Revolution* (London: Sphere, 1969), 187, 189.

17.   Carruthers, *City of Capital*, 125.

18.   Carruthers, *City of Capital*, 193. As we have seen, not all of this sum was in fact repaid, though the courts defended the creditors' rights to it.

19.   *Debates of the House of Commons: From the Year 1667 to the Year 1694*, vol. 10 (London: D. Henry and R. Cave, 1763), 18.

20.   D. W. Jones, *War and Economy in the Age of William III and Marlborough* (London: Blackwell, 1988), 7–11.

21.   John Brewer, *The Sinews of Power: War, Money, and the English State, 1688–1783* (Cambridge, MA: Harvard University Press, 1990), 34.

22.   Pepijn Brandon, *War, Capital, and the Dutch State, 1588–1795* (Leiden: Brill, 2015), 57.

23.   John Clapham, *The Bank of England: A History*, vol. 1, *1694–1797* (Cambridge, UK: Cambridge University Press, 1966), 26. A careful account of the early history of the bank can be found in Richard Kleer, "'Fictitious Cash': English Public Finance and Paper Money," in *Money, Power, and Print: Interdisciplinary Studies on the Financial Revolution in the British Isles*, Charles Ivar McGrath and Chris Fauske, eds. (Newark: University of Delaware Press, 2008), 70–103.

24.   On the origins of the tally, see Hilary Jenkinson, "Medieval Tallies, Public and Private," *Archaeologia* 74 (1925). See also Glyn Davies, *A History of Money: From Ancient Times to the Present Day*, 3rd ed. (Cardiff: University of Wales Press, 2002), 146–52.

25. Carl Wennerlind, *Casualties of Credit: The English Financial Revolution, 1620–1720* (Cambridge, MA: Harvard University Press, 2011), 169.

26. How precisely such debts were to be honored is a tricky question—and one of the reasons that world currencies remained tied to gold until 1971, a point I shall explore below and in the next chapter.

27. Desan, *Making Money*, 319.

28. Patrick Hyde Kelly, "General Introduction," in *Locke on Money*, vol. 1, Patrick Hyde Kelly, ed. (Oxford: Clarendon, 1991), 49.

29. J. G. A. Pocock, *Virtue, Commerce, and History* (Cambridge, UK: Cambridge University Press, 1985), 112.

30. Patrick Brantlinger, *Fictions of State: Culture and Credit in Britain, 1694–1994* (Ithaca: Cornell University Press, 1996), 21.

31. Clapham, 17, 24.

32. See Brewer, *Sinews of Power*, figure 4.8, 118.

33. P. K. O'Brien and P. A. Hunt, "The Rise of a Fiscal State in England, 1485–1815," *Historical Research* 66, no. 160 (1993), 151.

34. Brewer, *Sinews of Power*, 89.

35. O'Brien and Hunt, "Fiscal State," 163, 168.

36. Brewer, *Sinews of Power*, 40.

37. This term has been widely used by historians working on the British state, such as John Brewer, Patrick K. O'Brien, and M. S. Anderson, *War and Society in Europe of the Old Regime 1618–1780* (Leicester: University of Leicester Press, 1988).

38. Craig Muldrew, "'Hard Food for Midas': Cash and Its Social Value in Early-Modern England," *Past and Present* 170 (2001), 170–228.

39. See my discussion of these writers in *Political Economy and the Rise of Capitalism* (Berkeley: University of California Press, 1988), 29–35.

40. Eric Kerridge, *Trade and Banking in Early Modern England* (Manchester: Manchester University Press, 1988), 99.

41. J. Keith Horsefield, "The Beginnings of Paper Money in England," *Journal of European Economic History* 6 (1977), 117–32.

42. Deborah Valenze, *The Social Life of Money in the English Past* (Cambridge, UK: Cambridge University Press, 2006), 37.

43. Ming-Hsun Li, *The Great Recoinage of 1696 to 1699* (London: Weidenfeld and Nicolson, 1963), 53.

44. Li, *Great Recoinage*, 51; J. Keith Horsefield, *British Monetary Experiments, 1650–1710* (Cambridge, MA: Harvard University Press, 1960), 26.

45. The next few pages draw upon arguments I originally made in "The Blood of the Commonwealth: War, the State, and the Making of World Money," *Historical Materialism* 22, no. 2 (2014), esp. 17–22.

46. John Craig, "Isaac Newton and the Counterfeiters," *Notes and Records of the Royal Society of London* 18, no. 2 (1963), 129. See also James Gleick, *Isaac Newton* (New York: Vintage, 2004, 160–1); and Thomas Levenson, *Newton and the Counterfeiter: The Unknown Detective Career of the World's Greatest Scientist* (Boston: Houghton Mifflin Harcourt, 2009).

47. Wennerlind, *Casualties of Credit*, 147. So zealous was Newton in the cause of the death pen-

alty as monetary policy that he had himself made a justice of the peace in order to oversee prosecutions personally.

48. Peter Linebaugh, *The London Hanged: Crime and Civil Society in the Eighteenth Century*, 2nd ed. (London and New York: Verso, 2003), 50.

49. John Locke, *The Works of John Locke*, vol. 4 (London: F. C. & J. Rivington, 1824 [1696]), 198, available at http://oll.libertyfund.org/people/john-locke.

50. Neal Wood, *John Locke and Agrarian Capitalism* (Berkeley: University of California Press, 1984), 106–7.

51. See John Locke, "Draft of a Representation Containing a Scheme of Methods for the Employment of the Poor," in *Political Writings of John Locke*, David Wootton, ed. (New York: Mentor, 1993), 449, 453, 450, 448.

52. Modern economists have been decidedly hostile to Locke's arguments, particularly his notion that the nominal value of coin should correspond with its "intrinsic value." Instead, dogmatically ensconced in the subjective utility notions that underpin neoclassical economics, they have championed the position of real estate developer and financial speculator Nicholas Barbon, who *proclaimed*, "Things have no Value in themselves, it is opinion and fashion gives them a value": *Discourse Concerning Coining the New Money Lighter* (London: Richard Chiswell, 1696), available at http://quod.lib.mich.edu/e/eebo/A33802.0001.001?view=toc. For economists' endorsements of Barbon's views, see, for example, Joyce Appleby, *Economic Thought and Ideology in Seventeenth-Century England* (Princeton: Princeton University Press, 1978), 222–39; and Li, *Great Recoinage*, 1963, 106–7.

53. John Locke, "Some Considerations of the Consequences of the Lowering of Interest and Raising the Value of Money" (1691), in Kelly, *Locke on Money*, vol. 1, 307. Also available in Locke, *Works*, 84. Note that Locke wrote this even before the recoinage debate of 1694–96.

54. John Locke, "Further Considerations Concerning Raising the Value of Money" (1696), in Kelly, *Locke on Money*, vol. 2, 465–66, 430, 415.

55. Locke, "Some Considerations," 223, 213.

56. Locke, "Further Considerations," in *Locke on Money*, vol. 2, 469.

57. Locke, "Further Considerations," 442.

58. Locke, "Some Considerations," 265, 267.

59. See Vilar, *Gold and Money*, 205.

60. Constantine George Caffentzis, *Clipped Coins, Abused Words, and Civil Government* (New York: Autonomedia, 1989), 119—a book that deserves a much wider readership in the literature on Locke, classical political economy, and the rise of capitalism.

61. Gleick, *Isaac Newton*, 142–45.

62. Hugh Thomas, *The Slave Trade: The Story of the Atlantic Slave Trade, 1440–1870* (New York: Touchstone, 1997), 199–200; Maurice Cranston, *John Locke: A Biography* (London: Macmillan, 1957), 115n3.

63. The full title of the body was "His Majesty's Commissioners for Promoting the Trade of this Kingdom, and for Inspecting and Improving His Plantations in America and Elsewhere."

64. See Peter Laslett, "John Locke, the Great Recoinage, and the Origins of the Board of Trade: 1695–1698," *William and Mary Quarterly*, 3rd series, vol. 14, no. 3 (1957), 371. Laslett describes Locke's colonialism as "a striking paradox."

65. On the Whiggism of the Bank of England, and its associations with "republicanism," see Clapham, *Bank of England*, 10; P. G. M. Dickson, *The Financial Revolution in England* (London: Macmillan, 1967), 55–56; Brewer, *Sinews of Power*, 153, 207; and David Stasavage, "Partisan Politics and Public Debt: The Importance of the 'Whig Supremacy' for Britain's Financial Revolution," *European Review of Economic History* 2 (2007), 123–53. On Locke's investment in the Bank of England, see Laslett, "John Locke," 395n64.

66. Robert Weir, *Colonial South Carolina: A History* (Columbia: University of South Carolina Press, 1983), 26.

67. Brad Hinshelwood, "The Carolinian Context of John Locke's Theory of Slavery," *Political Theory* 41, no. 4 (2013), 570.

68. John Locke, "The Fundamental Constitution of Carolina," in *Political Writings*, 230. For Locke's role in writing this document, see Cranston, *Biography* (Oxford: Oxford University Press, 1957), 119; and K. H. D. Haley, *The First Earl of Shaftesbury* (Oxford: Oxford University Press, 1968), 242.

69. Robert Filmer, *Patriarcha, or the Natural Power of Kings* (London: Richard Chiswell, 1680), available at https://oll.libertyfund.org/titles/filmer-patriarcha-or-the-natural-power-of-kings.

70. As I show in "Locke, Levellers, and Liberty: Property and Democracy in the Thought of the First Whigs," *History of Political Thought* 10, no. 1 (1989), 17–40.

71. In-text citations of Locke's *Two Treatises* refer to Peter Laslett's scholarly edition: John Locke, *Two Treatises of Government*, rev. ed. (Cambridge, UK: Cambridge University Press, 1963).

72. James Farr, "Locke, Natural Law, and New World Slavery," *Political Theory* 36, no. 4 (2008), 495, 516.

73. A term coined by Valenze, *Social Life of Money*, 27, 202.

74. I have explored money's demonic powers in *Monsters of the Market: Zombies, Vampires, and Global Capitalism* (Chicago: Haymarket, 2012).

75. John Bunyan, *The Pilgrim's Progress* (Ware: Wordsworth Editions, 1996), 72.

76. Malachy Postlethwayte, *The African Trade, the Great Pillar, and Support of the British Plantation Trade in America*, in *English Historical Documents*, vol. 10, *1714–1783*, D. B. Horn and Mary Ransome, eds. (New York: Oxford University Press, 1969), 825.

77. Postlethwayte, *African Trade*, 824.

78. As quoted by Eltis, *Rise of African Slavery*, 141.

79. Humphrey Morice to Captain Weedon, March 25, 1725, as cited by James A. Rawley, *London, Metropolis of the Slave Trade* (Columbia: University of Missouri Press, 2003), 50.

80. Andrés Reséndez, *The Other Slavery: The Uncovered Story of Indian Enslavement in America* (Boston: Mariner, 2016).

81. Abbot E. Smith, *Colonists in Bondage: White Servitude and Convict Labor in America, 1607–1776* (Chapel Hill: University of North Carolina Press, 1947); Hilary M. Beckles, *White Servitude and Black Slavery in Barbados, 1627–1715* (Knoxville: University of Tennessee Press, 1989); Daniel P. Mannix, *Black Cargoes: A History of the Atlantic Slave Trade* (Harmondsworth: Penguin, 1976), 56–59; Eric Williams, *Capitalism and Slavery* (London: Andre Deutsch, 1964), 10; Eltis, *Rise of African Slavery*, 49.

82. Williams, *Capitalism and Slavery*, 7. As Reséndez demonstrates, Williams ought to have

added "red," i.e., indigenous.

83. See Russell R. Menard, "The Africanization of the Workforce in English America," in *Debt and Slavery in the Mediterranean and Atlantic Worlds*, Gwyn Campbell and Alessandro Stanziani, eds. (London: Pickering & Chato, 2013), 93–103.

84. Edmund S. Morgan, *American Slavery, American Freedom: The Ordeal of Colonial Virginia* (New York: W. W. Norton, 1975), 297–99.

85. Richard S. Dunn, *Sugar and Slaves: The Rise of the Planter Class in the English West Indies, 1624–1713* (New York: W. W. Norton, 1972), 70–3; Amussen, *Caribbean Exchanges*, 129–38.

86. I date the origins of the Atlantic slave trade from the Portuguese importation of bound Africans into Madeira in 1443–44. See Barbara L. Solow, "Capitalism and Slavery in the Exceedingly Long Run," in *British Capitalism and Caribbean Slavery: The Legacy of Eric Williams*, Barbara L. Solow and Stanley L. Engerman, eds. (Cambridge, UK: Cambridge University Press, 1987), 58; Thomas, *Slave Trade*, 48–60.

87. Eltis, *Rise of African Slavery*, 231, 121–23.

88. Thomas, *Slave Trade*, 318.

89. Colin Palmer, *Human Cargoes: The British Slave Trade to Spanish America, 1700–1739* (Urbana: University of Illinois Press, 1981), 101–2.

90. Dieudonné Rinchon, *La traité et l'esclavage Congolais par le Européens: Histoire de la deportations des 13 millions 250.00 noirs en Amérique* (Brussels: J. de Meester Wetteren, 1929), 32; Thomas, *Slave Trade*, 110, 318, 395; Vincent Brown, *The Reaper's Garden: Death and Power in the World of Atlantic Slavery* (Cambridge, MA: Harvard University Press, 2008), 28.

91. Walter Johnson, *Soul by Soul: Life inside the Antebellum Slave Market* (Cambridge, MA: Harvard University Press, 1999), 118.

92. The basic narrative is laid out in Robert Weisbord, "The Case of the Slave-Ship 'Zong', 1783," *History Today* (August 1, 1969), 561–67. An excellent in-depth treatment is provided by James Walvin, *The Zong: A Massacre, the Law, and the End of Slavery* (New Haven: Yale University Press, 2011).

93. Lee and Mansfield, as cited by Brown, *Reaper's Garden*, 172, my emphasis.

94. Thomas, *Slave Trade*, 206.

95. As cited by William A. Pettigrew, *Freedom's Debt: The Royal African Company and the Politics of the Atlantic Slave Trade, 1672–1752* (Chapel Hill: University of North Carolina Press, 2013), 104–5.

96. Philip D. Curtin, *The Atlantic Slave Trade: A Census* (Madison: University of Wisconsin Press, 1969), table 41, 142. A number of scholars have proposed modifications to Curtin's figures. For a synthesis of various estimates, see Paul E. Lovejoy, "The Volume of the Atlantic Slave Trade: A Synthesis," *Journal of African History* 23, no. 4 (1982), 473–501. Lovejoy arrives at figures quite close to Curtin's estimates. His calculation of exported slaves for Britain alone in the eighteenth century is just over 2.5 million (table 4, 483). Detailed figures across temporal periods are available at http://www.slavevoyages.org/.

97. Jacob Price, "Heathcote, Sir Gilbert, first baronet (1652–1833)," *Oxford Dictionary of National Biography*, September 2004, http://www.oxforddnb.com.ezproxy.library.yorku .ca/view/10.1093/ref:odnb/9780198614128.001.0001/odnb-9780198614128-e-12847 ?rskey=ceQF3D&result=1; Pettigrew, *Freedom's Debt*, 139, 158.

98. Rawley, *London*, 40–44; Marcus Rediker, *The Slave Ship: A Human History* (New York:

Viking, 2007), 33–35.

99. Ian Baucom, *Specters of the Atlantic: Finance Capital, Slavery, and the Philosophy of History* (Durham: Duke University Press, 2005), 96, 67, 94.

100. For the term *collateralized labor*, see Joseph Miller, *The Problem of Slavery as History: A Global Approach* (New Haven: Yale University Press, 2012), 142.

101. Richard Sheridan, *Sugar and Slavery: An Economic History of the British West Indies, 1623–1775* (Kingston: University of the West Indies, 1974), 219; Roger Lloyd-Jones and A. A. Le Roux, "The Size of Firms in the Cotton Industry: Manchester 1815–41, *Economic History Review* 33 (1980), 72–81; Robin Blackburn, *The Making of New World Slavery: From the Baroque to the Modern* (London and New York: Verso, 1997), 410, 415; Maxine Berg, *The Age of Manufactures, 1700–1820* (London: Fontana, 1985), 230–31; Dunn, *Sugar and Slaves*, 189–96.

102. C. L. R. James, *The Black Jacobins: Toussaint L'Ouverture and the San Domingo Revolution*, 2nd ed. (New York: Vintage, 1963), 392. James is documenting the case of a French slave colony, not an English one. As much as France lagged behind England in terms of capitalist development, the colonies were a site in which forms of planter capitalism could be more readily imposed, as there were not entrenched feudal relations to overcome.

103. Peter Kolchin, *American Slavery*, rev. ed. (New York: Hill & Wang, 2003), 172. Blackburn, *New World Slavery*, 374–76, takes a similar position. A classic statement of this approach is Eugene Genovese, *The Political Economy of Slavery: Studies in the Economy and Society of the Slave South* (New York: Vintage, 1967). A more theoretically sophisticated version of this position (although to my mind still an erroneous one) is advanced in Elizabeth Fox-Genovese and Eugene Genovese, *Fruits of Merchant Capital: Slavery and Bourgeois Property in the Rise and Expansion of Capitalism* (New York: Oxford University Press, 1983), ch. 2.

104. In a forthcoming book, I will have occasion to show that the New World relationship between masters and plantation slaves was indeed market mediated, notwithstanding the different form in which markets allocated the labor power of slaves as in opposition to that of wage laborers.

105. Jairus Banaji, "Modes of Production in a Materialist Conception of History," *Capital and Class* 3 (1977), 1–44, now reprinted as chapter 2 of Banaji, *Theory as History: Essays on Modes of Production and Exploitation* (Leiden: Brill, 2010); Karl Marx, *Capital*, vol. 1, Ben Fowkes, trans. (Harmondsworth: Penguin, 1976), 345; Rosa Luxemburg, *The Accumulation of Capital: An Anti-Critique* published along with Niklolai Bukharin, *Imperialism and the Accumulation of Capital* (New York: Monthly Review Press, 1972), 56. Note as well Marx's remark that "we now not only call the plantation owners in America capitalists, but . . . they are capitalists": *Grundrisse*, Martin Nicolaus, trans. (Harmondsworth: Penguin, 1973), 513.

106. This approach is associated with the historical work of Robert Brenner, which I have discussed above. The clearest summary statement of this position is Ellen Meiksins Wood, *The Origin of Capitalism* (London and New York: Verso, 2002).

107. John Clegg, "Capitalism and Slavery," *Critical Historical Studies* 2, no. 2 (Fall 2015), 299. Intriguingly, in *Merchants and Revolution* (London: Verso, 2003), 159, Brenner refers to "West Indian Sugar Capitalism" in the 1640s.

108. Trevor Burnard, *Planters, Merchants, and Slaves: Plantation Societies in British North America, 1650–1820* (Chicago: University of Chicago Press, 2015), 27, 33, 38, 54, 78–89.

Edward E. Baptist has also identified the importance of terror as an organizing principle of plantation slavery in the US South. More precisely, he has described "torture" as a "factor of production" (I prefer *force* of production). See *The Half Has Never Been Told: Slavery and the Making of American Capitalism* (New York: Basic Books, 2014), 141. This is a valuable insight, but it does not require the conclusion, to which Baptist inclines, that *all* increases in productivity represented intensifications of torture. Despotic, even terroristic, labor discipline is meant, in part, to enable other kinds of productive innovations to be imposed on workers, no matter how unfriendly they are to the pace and quality of work. There is no need to reduce all such increases to terror (or torture) itself.

109. Lorena S. Walsh, "Slave Life, Slave Society, and Tobacco Production in the Tidewater Chesapeake, 1620–1820," in *Cultivation and Culture: Labor and the Shaping of Slave Life in the Americas*, Ira Berlin and Philip D. Morgan, eds. (Charlottesville: University of Virginia Press, 1993), 170–99.

110. Marx, *Capital*, vol. 1, ch. 16.

111. Bill Cooke, "The Denial of Slavery in Management Studies," *Journal of Management Studies* 40 (2003), 1895–918; R. Keith Aufhauser, "Slavery and Scientific Management," *Journal of Economic History* 33 (1973), 811–24; Amussen, *Caribbean Exchanges*, 229; Burnard, *Planters, Merchants, and Slaves*, 114; David Roediger and Elizabeth Esch, "'One Symptom of Originality': Race and the Management of Labor in US History," in Roediger, *Race, Class and Marxism* (London and New York: Verso, 2017), 115–56. See also James Oakes, *The Ruling Race: A History of American Slaveholders* (New York: Alfred A. Knopf, 1982), ch. 6. The most systematic study of these trends is Caitlin Rosenthal, *Accounting for Slavery: Masters and Management* (Cambridge, MA: Harvard University Press, 2018).

112. On the legal differentiation of European servants from African slaves in seventeenth-century Barbados, see Amussen, *Caribbean Exchanges*, 90, 121–35; and Burnard, *Planters, Merchants, and Slaves*, 139–41.

113. See Stephen Marglin, "What Do Bosses Do? The Origins and Function of Hierarchy in Capitalist Production," *Review of Radical Political Economics* 6 (1974), 60–112. Also of interest in this regard are Sidney Pollard, "Factory Discipline in the Industrial Revolution," *Economic History Review* 16 (1963–64), 254–71; E. P. Thompson, "Time, Work-Discipline, and Industrial Capitalism," *Past and Present* 38 (1967), 56–97; and Neil McKendrick, "Josiah Wedgwood and Factory Discipline," *Historical Journal* 4, no. 1 (1961), 30–55.

114. Gavin Wright, *Slavery and American Economic Development* (Baton Rouge: Louisiana State University Press, 2006), 95.

115. David Eltis, Frank D. Lewis, and David Richardson, "Slave Prices, the Africa Slave Trade, and Productivity in the Caribbean, 1674–1807," *Economic History Review* 58, no. 4 (2005), 693, 698. As Gavin Wright points out, there is some confusion in these accounts between a growth of labor inputs and growth of labor productivity—or between what Marx would call absolute and relative surplus value. See Wright, *Slavery*, 24–26.

116. Alan L. Olmstead and Paul W. Rhode, "Biological Innovation and Productivity Growth in the Antebellum Cotton Economy," *Journal of Economic History*, 68, no. 4 (2008), 1123–71. As indicated above, I believe these increases involved an interrelated set of "improvements" in technology, including use of new seed strains, and labor management.

117. Dale W. Tomich, *Through the Prism of Slavery: Labor, Capital, and World Economy* (Lanham:

Rowman & Littlefield, 2004), ch. 3.

118. J. R. Ward, "The Profitability of Sugar Planting in the British West Indies, 1650–1834," *Economic History Review* 31, no. 2 (1978), 197–213.

119. Eltis, *Rise of African Slavery*, 220.

120. See Wright, *Slavery*, 36–40.

121. Williams, *Capitalism and Slavery*.

122. Solow, "Capitalism and Slavery," 72. As Wright puts it, "The evidence suggests there are more than a few grains of truth in the Williams thesis" (*Slavery*, 17).

123. During the heyday of neoliberalism's influence on historical research (sometimes joined to idealist obsessions with "discursivity"), it was fashionable to question whether anything like an Industrial Revolution had occurred. But serious historical scholarship has consistently recognized that a widespread social transformation to mechanized and steam-powered production did indeed revolutionize the forces of production in late-eighteenth- and early-nineteenth-century Britain. For general accounts, see T. S. Ashton, *The Industrial Revolution, 1760–1830* (London: Oxford University Press, 1948); Paul Mantoux, *The Industrial Revolution in the Eighteenth Century*, rev. ed. (New York: Harper & Row, 1962); Peter Mathias, *The First Industrial Nation: An Economic History of Britain 1700–1914* (New York: Scribner, 1969); Phyllis Deane, *The First Industrial Revolution*, 2nd ed. (Cambridge, UK: Cambridge University Press, 1979); Berg, *Age of Manufactures*, and Michael A. Zmolek; *Rethinking the Industrial Revolution: Five Centuries of Transition from Agrarian to Industrial Capitalism in England* (Leiden: Brill, 2013).

124. Nicholas F. R. Crafts, "British Economic Growth," *Economic History Review* 36 (1983), 177–99.

125. David Richardson, "The Slave Trade, Sugar, and British Economic Growth, 1748–1776," in Solow and Engerman, *British Capitalism and Caribbean Slavery*, 124–25. See also Joseph E. Inikori, "Slavery and the Development of Industrial Capitalism in England," in *British Capitalism and Caribbean Slavery*, 79–101.

126. Ralph Davis, "English Foreign Trade, 1700–1774," *Economic History Review* 15 (1962), 302–3.

127. Paul Bairoch, "Commerce international et genèse de la revolution industrielle anglaise," *Annales* 27 (1973), 561.

128. Blackburn, *New World Slavery*, 541–42, deploying data from C. H. Feinstein, "Capital Expenditure in Great Britain," in *Cambridge Economic History of Europe* (Cambridge, UK: Cambridge University Press, 1978), 74.

129. Triangular trade credit had deep roots in Africa, of course, where slaves were often used to pay off debts to European traders. This is a link in the structure of transatlantic debt relations that I am unable to adequately explore here. See Joseph C. Miller, *Way of Death: Merchant Capitalism and the Angolan Slave Trade, 1730–1830* (Madison: University of Wisconsin Press, 1988), 98–99, 105–39.

130. Thomas, *Slave Trade*, 441; Eltis, *Rise of African Slavery*, 217; Baucom, *Specters of the Atlantic*, 61.

131. Larry Neal, *The Rise of Financial Capitalism: International Markets in the Age of Reason* (Cambridge, UK: Cambridge University Press, 1990), 12.

132. Williams, *Capitalism and Slavery*, 43, 101.

133. Calvin Schermerhorn, *The Business of Slavery and the Rise of American Capitalism, 1815–*

1860 (New Haven: Yale University Press, 2015), 105.

134. John Briscoe, *A Discourse on the Late Funds of the Million-Act, and Bank of England* (London: J. B. Briscoe, 1694), available at https://quod.lib.umich.edu/e/eebo /A29540.0001.001?view=toc. On Briscoe, about whom little is known, see Kleer, "'Fictitious Cash,'" 85–92.

135. For one example, see Marieke de Goede, *Virtue, Fortune, and Faith: A Genealogy of Finance* (Minneapolis: University of Minnesota Press, 2005), who argues that "processes of knowledge and interpretation . . . are precisely *the way in which 'finance' materializes*" (7, emphasis in original). To be sure, knowledge and interpretation are part of the practical ensemble through which social-material financial relations are lived. But they are not "the way" in which financial relations—from the sale of a slave to the purchase of a share—are materialized. For a critique of some of the theoretical confusions here, see my *Bodies of Meaning: Studies on Language, Labor, and Liberation* (Albany: State University of New York Press, 2001).

136. Neal, *Financial Capitalism*, 4.

137. P. K. O'Brien, "Mercantilist Institutions for the Pursuit of Power with Profit: The Management of Britain's National Debt, 1756–1815," working paper no. 95/06, Department of Economic History, London School of Economics (October 2006), 3, available at http://eprints.lse.ac.uk/22322/1/wp95.pdf.

138. Dickson, *Financial Revolution*, 254, 260, 273.

139. See Wennerlind, *Casualties of Credit*, 175–77.

140. See Marx, *Capital*, vol. 1, ch. 28. For the eighteenth century, see the superb essays by Douglas Hay and others in *Albion's Fatal Tree: Crime and Society in Eighteenth-Century England* (New York: Pantheon, 1975).

141. Linebaugh, *The London Hanged*, 82.

142. Valenze, *Social Life of Money*, 198.

143. E. P. Thompson, "The Sale of Wives," in *Customs in Common: Studies in Traditional Popular Culture* (New York: New Press, 1991), 442. See also Valenze, *Social Life of Money*, 246–52.

144. Peter Wilson Coldham, *Emigrants in Chains: A Social History of Forced Emigration to the Americas, 1607–1776* (Baltimore: Genealogical Publishing, 1992), 61.

145. McNally, *Monsters of the Market*, ch. 1.

146. Valenze, *Social Life of Money*, 7.

147. Karl Marx, *Wage Labour and Capital* (Moscow: Progress Publishers, 1952), 21, 20.

148. Marx, *Capital*, vol. 1, 176.

149. Richard K. Meeker, "Bank Note, Corkscrew, Flea, and Sedan: A Checklist of Eighteenth-Century Fiction," *Library Chronicle* 35 (1969), 52–57.

150. Christopher Flint, "Speaking Objects: The Circulation of Stories in Eighteenth-Century Prose Fiction," *Publications of the Modern Languages Association* 113, no. 2 (March 1998), 215, 219.

151. Joseph Addison, *The Tatler*, no. 249 (November 11, 1710), available at https://quod.lib .umich.edu/e/ecco/004786805.0001.000/1:64?rgn=div1;view=fulltext.

152. Charles Johnstone, *Chrysal: Or the Adventures of a Guinea* (London: George Routledge & Sons, 1769), vols. 1, 4, 6, 7.

153. John Richetti, "Introduction," Daniel Defoe, *Robinson Crusoe* (Harmondsworth: Penguin Classics, 2001 [1719]), xviii.

154. Defoe, *Robinson Crusoe*, 47.

155. Daniel Defoe, *Review of the State of the English Nation* 3, no. 5 (January 10, 1706), available at https://babel.hathitrust.org/cgi/pt?id=mdp.39015019363376;view=1up;seq=37.

156. A number of commentators have detected genuine sympathy toward women in Defoe's *Moll Flanders* (Amersham: Transatlantic Press, 2012 [1722]). A useful point of departure for these debates is Lois A. Chaber, "Matriarchal Mirror: Women and Capital in *Moll Flanders*," in *Critical Essays on Daniel Defoe*, Roger D. Lund, ed. (New York: G. K. Hall & Co., 1997), 181–201.

157. Defoe, *Moll Flanders*, 142.

158. Defoe, *Robinson Crusoe*, 17, 28–33, 157–61, 154.

159. Daniel Defoe, *Colonel Jack*, in *Defoe's Works*, vol. 1, *Captain Singleton and Colonel Jack* (London: George Bell & Sons, 1882), 401, 377.

160. For an insightful overview, see Patrick J. Keane, "Slavery and the Slave Trade: Crusoe as Defoe's Representative," in *Critical Essays*, 97–120.

161. Wennerlind, *Casualties of Credit*, 221–23.

162. Daniel Defoe, *A True Account of the Design, and Advantages of the South-Sea Trade* (London: J. Morphew, 1711), 20, available at https://quod.lib.umich.edu/e/ecco/004834143.0001.000?view=toc.

163. Neal, who radically understates the company's slaving activities (*Financial Capitalism*, 52–53), is a prime example. He describes the company as "primarily an organization for the conversion of government debt" (94). While this was indeed its origins, what boosted it into the top rank of English joint-stock companies was its shipment of thousands of slaves to the New World. In *Financial Revolution*, Dickson, too, downplays the company's slaving activities. On the very considerable extent of the South Sea Company's engagement in the slave trade, see Palmer, *Human Cargoes*.

164. Wennerlind, *Casualties of Credit*, 199.

165. Dickson, *Financial Revolution*, 145.

166. See Neal, *Financial Capitalism*, ch. 4–5.

167. Dickson, *Financial Revolution*, 143.

168. Thomas, *Slave Trade*, 241.

169. Wennerlind, *Casualties of Credit*, 237.

170. Dickson, *Financial Revolution*, 179; Neal, *Financial Capitalism*, 112–17.

171. Dickson, *Financial Revolution*, 216–28.

172. *Miller v. Race*, Court of King's Bench, 1 Burrows 457, 97 Eng. Rep. 398 (King's Bench 1758). For a discussion of this ruling, see Benjamin Geva, *The Payment Order of Antiquity and the Middle Ages: A Legal History* (Oxford: Hart Publishing, 2011), 518.

173. Davies, *History of Money*, 282.

174. Desan, *Making Money*, 374.

175. Rondo Cameron, "England 1750–844," in Rondo Cameron et. al., *Banking in the Early Stages of Industrialization* (Oxford: Oxford University Press, 1967), 42.

176. Desan, *Making Money*, 318.

177. Since the recoinage of 1696, the government had tried to maintain the primary connection between silver and the pound. In fact, gold guineas had become increasingly central to the British monetary system. But the reality was only recognized in official policy long after it

prevailed in practice. See Davies, *History of Money*, 284–304.

178. *Report*, Select Committee on the High Price of Gold Bullion, House of Commons (London: Richard Taylor & Company, 1810), 73.

179. Barry Eichengreen, *Globalizing Capital: A History of the International Monetary System* (Princeton: Princeton University Press, 1996), 33–35. On the "managed gold standard," see Michael D. Bordo, "The Gold Standard: The Traditional Approach," in *A Retrospective on the Classical Gold Standard, 1821–1931*, Michael D. Bordo and Anna J. Schwartz, eds. (Chicago: University of Chicago Press, 1984), 45.

180. Karl Marx, *Capital*, vol. 3, Ben Fowkes, trans. (Harmondsworth: Penguin, 1981), 708.

181. An insightful discussion of this can be found in Matt Hampton, "Hegemony, Class Struggle, and the Radical Historiography of Global Monetary Standards," *Capital and Class* 89 (2006), 145–47. It is a limitation of this important article that it does not tease out the complex mediations between the interconnected dynamics of disciplining wage labor *and* organizing world money to express capital's law of value on a global level. On the historical experience, see Barry Eichengreen, *Golden Fetters: The Gold Standard and the Great Depression, 1919–1939* (New York: Oxford University Press, 1995).

182. W. M. Scammell, "The Working of the Gold Standard," in *The Gold Standard in Theory and History*, Barry Eichengreen, ed. (New York: Methuen, 1985), 103–19.

Chapter 5: Imperial War, Imperial Money

1. Robert E. Wright, *Origins of Commercial Banking in America, 1750–1800* (Lanham: Rowman & Littlefield, 2001), 195.

2. As quoted in Gary Clayton Anderson, *Ethnic Cleansing and the Indian: The Crime That Should Haunt America* (Norman: University of Oklahoma Press, 2014), 315.

3. Patrick Wolfe, "Settler Colonialism and the Elimination of the Native," *Journal of Genocide Research* 8, no. 4 (2006), 388.

4. Benjamin Franklin, *A Modest Enquiry into the Nature and Necessity of a Paper-Currency* (Philadelphia, 1729), available at https://founders.archives.gov/documents/Franklin/01–01–02–0041.

5. John Grenier, *The First Way of War: American War Making on the Frontier, 1607–1814* (New York: Cambridge University Press, 2005), 5. On "extirpative war," see 21–23.

6. Karl Marx, *Capital*, vol. 1, Ben Fowkes, trans. (Harmondsworth: Penguin, 1976), part 8. As many commentators have pointed out, the term Marx uses—"ursprünglich"—might more accurately be translated as "primary" or "original."

7. On the timing of fully capitalist development in the US Northeast, see Charles Post, *The American Road to Capitalism* (Leiden and Boston: Brill, 2011), ch. 2, pt. iii.

8. Fred Anderson and Andrew Cayton, *The Dominion of War: Empire and Liberty in North America, 1500–2000* (New York: Penguin, 2005), 169–71.

9. "Instructions to Major General John Sullivan," May 31, 1779, in *The Writings of George Washington*, vol. 15, John C. Fitzpatrick, ed. (Washington, DC: US Government Printing Office, 1936), 189.

10. Anderson, *Ethnic Cleansing*, 102, 104, 109, 113, 125–26.

11. See Roxanne Dunbar-Ortiz, *An Indigenous Peoples' History of the United States* (Boston: Beacon, 2014); and André Reséndez, *The Other Slavery: The Uncovered Story of Indian Enslavement in America* (New York: Mariner, 2017). For the view that these processes amount to a system of ethnic cleansing, see Anderson, *Ethnic Cleansing*; and Anderson and Cayton, *Dominion*, 170.

12. Anderson, *Ethnic Cleansing*, 335.

13. Grenier, *First Way of War*, 39–47; Henry J. Young, "A Note on Scalp Bounties in Pennsylvania," *Pennsylvania History* 24, no. 3 (July 1957), 207–218.

14. On an "Old World" corpse economy, see my *Monsters of the Market: Zombies, Vampires, and Global Capitalism* (Chicago: Haymarket, 2012), ch. 1. On "grim commerce," see Margaret Haig Roosevelt Sewall Ball, "Grim Commerce: Scalps, Bounties, and the Transformation of Trophy-Taking in the Early American Northwest, 1450–1770," PhD diss., University of Colorado, Boulder, Spring 2013.

15. Scott Reynolds Nelson, *A Nation of Deadbeats: An Uncommon History of America's Financial Disasters* (New York: Vintage, 2012), 7.

16. Anderson, *Ethnic Cleansing*, 102–4; Nelson, *Nation of Deadbeats*, 27–30.

17. Robert E. Wright, "Thomas Willing (1731–1821): Philadelphia Financier and Forgotten Founding Father," *Pennsylvania History* 63 (1996), 527–29, 533.

18. Wright, "Thomas Willing," 526, 543.

19. Anderson and Cayton, *Dominion*, 107–8, 111, 113, 134, 145, 148; Edmund Morgan, *American Slavery, American Freedom* (New York: W. W. Norton, 1975), 4. For socioeconomic context, see the essays in Warren Hofstra, ed., *George Washington and the Virginia Backcountry* (Madison: Madison House, 1998).

20. Anderson and Cayton, *Dominion*, 174–75.

21. Nelson, *Nation of Deadbeats*, 41.

22. Fisher Ames as quoted in Nelson, *Nation of Deadbeats*, 42.

23. Robert E. Wright, *Origins of Commercial Banking in America, 1750–1800* (Lanham: Rowman & Littlefield, 2001), 62.

24. Nelson, *Nation of Deadbeats*, 7.

25. Wright, *Origins*, 64.

26. John Adams to James Warren (Philadelphia), July 23, 1775, in *Letters of Delegates to Congress, 1774–1789*, 26 volumes, Paul H. Smith, ed. (Washington, DC: Library of Congress, 1976–2000), vol. 1, 650.

27. Bray Hammond, *Banks and Politics in America from the Revolution to the Civil War* (Princeton: Princeton University Press, 1957), 25–27.

28. Wright, *Origins*, 62–63; Hammond, *Banks and Politics*, 6; Robert E. Wright, *Hamilton Unbound: Finance and the Creation of the American Republic* (Westport, CT: Greenwood Press, 2002), 119, 117.

29. On "pawnshops for promises," a fecund metaphor originating with Thomas Paine, see Nelson, *Nation of Deadbeats*, 13.

30. To redeem paper notes for gold or silver, the holder had to appear in person at a branch of the bank that had issued the currency.

31. Jane Kamensky, *The Exchange Artist* (New York: Viking, 2008), 158–60.

32. Kamensky, *Exchange Artist*, 114–31.

33. Nelson, *Nation of Deadbeats*, 55–56; Hammond, *Banks and Politics*, 188.

34. See Richard H. Timberlake Jr., *The Origins of Central Banking in the United States* (Cambridge, MA: Harvard University Press, 1978), 13–17, 22.

35. See, for instance, the extreme individualist conception of "the link between finance and growth" articulated by Wright in *Hamilton Unbound*, 123–24, and elaborated into a full "finance-focused explanation" of growth in his *The Wealth of Nations Rediscovered: Integration and Expansion in American Financial Markets, 1750–1850* (Cambridge, UK: Cambridge University Press, 2002), 4. As I have argued in *Global Slump: The Economics and Politics of Crisis and Resistance* (Oakland: PM Press, 2012), ch. 3, world capitalism *has* become more financialized since the 1970s, but this is not about a sort of coup or usurpation led by bankers, as has too often been argued, but instead expresses structural transformations associated with the legal severing of the US dollar from gold.

36. A counter-position promoted by Charles Sellers in his otherwise important and insightful work, *The Market Revolution: Jacksonian America, 1815–1846* (New York: Oxford University Press, 1991), 4–6.

37. Hammond, *Banks and Politics*, 279–80.

38. Jonathan Levy, "The Mortgage Worked the Hardest: The Fate of Landed Independence in Nineteenth-Century America," in *Capitalism Takes Command: The Social Transformation of Nineteenth-Century America*, Michael Zakim and Gary J. Kornblith, eds. (Chicago: University of Chicago Press, 2012), 58. On the earlier transition in the Northeast, and the capitalist dynamics of petty commodity production, see Post, *American Road*, ch. 2.

39. See, for instance, Stephen Hahn and Jonathan Prude, *The Countryside in the Age of Capitalist Transformation* (Chapel Hill: University of North Carolina Press, 1985); Christopher Clark, *The Roots of Rural Capitalism: Western Massachusetts, 1780–1860* (Ithaca: Cornell University Press, 1990); Allan Kulikoff, *The Agrarian Origins of American Capitalism* (Charlottesville: University of Virginia Press, 1992); Post, *American Road*; and Christopher Clark, "The Agrarian Context of American Capitalist Development," in Zakim and Kornblith, *Capitalism Takes Command*, 13–38. Post's book is especially important in developing the view that it is *market dependence* that is foundational to agrarian capitalism. I dissent from Post, however, in seeing the slave-based plantation system of the US South as a form of agrarian capitalism.

40. Alan Dawley, *Class and Community: The Industrial Revolution in Lynn* (Cambridge, MA: Harvard University Press, 1976); Mary H. Blewett, *Men, Women, and Work: Class, Gender, and Protest in the New England Shoe Industry, 1989–1910* (Urbana: University of Illinois Press, 1988); Jonathan Prude, *The Coming of Industrial Order: Town and Factory Life in Rural Massachusetts, 1810–1860* (New York: Cambridge University Press, 1983).

41. Nelson, *Nation of Deadbeats*, 38, 35.

42. Robert E. Wright, "Capitalism and the Rise of the Corporation Nation," in Zakim and Kornblith, *Capitalism Takes Command*, 148–49.

43. Hammond, *Banks and Politics*, 148–49, 145.

44. Walter Johnson, *Soul by Soul: Life Inside the Antebellum Slave Market* (Cambridge, MA: Harvard University Press, 1999), 26. On slave traders as rationalizing businessmen utilizing "modern accounting practices," see Steven Deyle, "Rethinking the Slave Trade: Slave Traders and the Market Revolution in the South," in *The Old South's Modern Worlds: Slavery, Region, and Nation in the Age of Progress*, L. Diane Barnes, Brian Schoen, and Frank Towers, eds. (New York: Oxford University Press, 2011), 104–19.

45. Michael Tadman, *Speculators and Slaves: Masters, Traders, and Slaves in the Old South* (Madison: University of Wisconsin Press, 1989), 54.

46. Calvin Schermerhorn, *The Business of Slavery and the Rise of American Capitalism* (New Haven: Yale University Press, 2015), 120.

47. I dissent strongly here from Marc Egnal's view, which is couched in the categories of a static Weberianism, in "Counterpoint: What If Genovese Is Right? The Premodern Outlook of Southern Planters," in Barnes et al., *The Old South's Modern Worlds*.

48. Schermerhorn, *Business of Slavery*, 43.

49. This unfailing commitment to cotton contributed to the downfall of the Second BUS after 1836. See Hammond, *Banks and Politics*, chs. 15 and 16.

50. Edward E. Baptist, "Toxic Debt, Liar Loans, Collateralized and Securitized Human Beings, and the Panic of 1837," in Zakim and Kornblith, *Capitalism Takes Command*, 80–82.

51. Schermerhorn, *Business of Slavery*, 53.

52. These social tensions are perceptively treated by Sellers, *Market Revolution*, though I prefer to speak of this period as one of "capitalist transformation" rather than "market revolution."

53. Anderson and Cayton, *Dominion*, 222–33. On Jackson's background, see Sellers, *Market Revolution*, 174–78.

54. Sellers, *Market Revolution*, 91–100.

55. Sellers, *Market Revolution*, 108.

56. Hammond, *Banks and Politics*, 329.

57. Stephen Mihm, *A Nation of Counterfeiters: Capitalists, Con-Men, and the Making of the United States* (Cambridge, MA: Harvard University Press, 2007), 180.

58. A. Barton Hepburn, *A History of Currency in the United States* (New York: Macmillan, 1915), 180. Hepburn's figure for counterfeits may have been high, as it represented a cumulative total over several decades. But, of course, a counterfeit might stay in circulation for some time, even after its issuer was defunct.

59. Timberlake, *Origins of Central Banking*, 64–65, 72–73, 77–79.

60. See Jessica M. Lepler, *The Many Panics of 1837: People, Politics, and the Creation of a Trans-Atlantic Financial Crisis* (Cambridge, UK: Cambridge University Press, 2013).

61. To be sure, *individual* capitals will often take advantage of fragmentation and regionalization of powers in order to expand markets and profits. I have discussed examples of this in *Monsters of the Market*, 221–22. But localized power conflicts, often resulting in civil wars, are far from optimal for the general interests of capital.

62. John Sherman, *New York Times*, January 16, 1863.

63. I use *nationalize* here to indicate the bringing of institutional powers under the sovereign authority of the national state.

64. Abraham Lincoln, "Message to Congress in Special Session," July 4, 1861, in *Lincoln: Political Writings and Speeches*, Terrence Ball, ed. (Cambridge, UK: Cambridge University Press, 2013), 131.

65. See Joseph T. Glatthaar, *Forged in Battle: The Civil War Alliance of Black Soldiers and White Officers* (New York: Free Press, 1990).

66. John Kenneth Galbraith, *Money: Whence It Came, Where It Went* (New York: Bantam, 1975), 112–13.

67. Bray Hammond, *Sovereignty and an Empty Purse: Banks and Politics in the Civil War* (Prince-

ton: Princeton University Press, 1970), 227.

68. Fiat money classically consists of a token, like paper, carrying little intrinsic value, but representing a value decreed by the state. It differs from *fiduciary* money in that the latter, while also consisting of a close-to-worthless material, carries a guaranteed rate of conversion into precious metal.

69. As quoted by Hammond, *Sovereignty*, 179, 181.

70. Thaddeus Stevens, *The Selected Papers of Thaddeus Stevens*, vol. 1, *April 1865–August 1868* (Pittsburgh: University of Pittsburgh Press, 1997), 247.

71. *New York Times*, April 14 and May 12, 1862, as cited by Hammond, *Sovereignty*, 245–46.

72. Karl Marx to Friedrich Engels, May 27, 1862, as cited in Robin Blackburn, *Marx and Lincoln: An Unfinished Revolution* (London and New York: Verso, 2011), 192–93.

73. Paul Kennedy, *The Rise and Fall of the Great Powers: Economic Change and Military Conflict from 1500 to 2000* (London: Fontana Press, 1989), 252–53. The quote refers, of course, to *previous* history.

74. Mihm, *Nation of Counterfeiters*, 321, 329–30.

75. Hammond, *Sovereignty*, 257.

76. On the multifaceted forms of black insurgency during the Civil War, see David Williams, *I Freed Myself: African American Self-Emancipation in the Civil War Era* (New York: Cambridge University Press, 2014). See also Vincent Harding, *There Is a River: The Black Struggle for Freedom in America* (New York: Harcourt Brace & Co., 1981), ch. 11. On the general strike of the slaves, see W. E. B. Du Bois, *Black Reconstruction in America, 1860–1880* (New York: Free Press, 1992 [1935]).

77. Abraham Lincoln, *Speeches and Writings, 1859–1865*, vol. 1, Don E. Fehrenbacher, ed. (Boone, IA: Library of America, 1989), 431.

78. In a February 10, 1863, speech, as cited by Hammond, *Sovereignty*, 326.

79. *Appendix to the Congressional Globe*, 37th Congress, 3rd session, January 8, 1863, 50.

80. National banknotes had been created under the National Bank Act of 1863, which was extended in June 1864 under an act of the same name authorizing commercial banks to create notes backed by deposits of US government bonds with the Treasury.

81. Hammond, *Banks and Politics*, 731–34.

82. Timberlake, *Origins of Central Banking*, 90.

83. Thomas Hobbes, *Leviathan*, C. B. Macpherson, ed. (Harmondsworth: Penguin, 1968 [1651]), ch. 24, 300.

84. Levy, "Mortgage Worked the Hardest," 45.

85. Kennedy, *Great Powers*, 312.

86. William Cronon, *Nature's Metropolis: Chicago and the Great West* (New York: W. W. Norton, 1991), 68.

87. Cronon, *Nature's Metropolis*, 26–28, 70, 124–25, 210.

88. James Livingston, *Origins of the Federal Reserve: Money, Class, and Corporate Capitalism, 1890–1913* (Ithaca: Cornell University Press, 1986), 138.

89. William Greenleaf, "Introduction," in *American Economic Development Since 1860*, William Greenleaf, ed. (New York: Harper & Row, 1968), 27, 10.

90. Greenleaf, "Introduction," 56.

91. Ian M. Drummond, *The Gold Standard and the International Monetary System* (London:

Macmillan, 1987), 12.

92. The British pound sterling was often interchangeable with gold. But it too was regularly redeemed for gold due to the latter's greater universality.

93. US Congress, 41st Congress, 2nd session, *The Gold Panic Investigation: House Report No. 31*, 19, available at: https://archive.org/details/cu31924032442679.

94. Some commentators consider the US to have gone onto the gold standard in 1873, when it stopped minting silver coins. But it did not return to convertibility at this point, which makes any "gold standard" purely nominal.

95. Cited by Steven Bryan, *The Gold Standard at the Turn of the Twentieth Century: Rising Powers, Global Money, and the Age of Empire* (New York: Columbia University Press, 2010), 57.

96. On this concept, see Joseph-Achille Mbembe, "Necropolitics," *Public Culture* 15, no. 1 (Winter 2003), 11–40.

97. *Congressional Record*, 53rd Congress, 1st session, 205.

98. *Congressional Record*, 53rd Congress, 1st session, 310.

99. *Annual Report of the Secretary of the Treasury, 1897*, lxxiv, available at https://fraser.stlouisfed.org/title/194/item/5543.

100. George C. Herring, *From Colony to Superpower: US Foreign Relations since 1777* (New York: Oxford University Press, 2008), ch. 8.

101. The official title was the Currency Standard Act (1900).

102. Bryan, *Gold Standard*, 20. Commentators like Bryan attribute the downward price trend primarily to a slowdown in world gold production. Among other things, this tends to ignore the possibilities of increasing the money supply via credit and paper currency issues, or of accelerating the velocity of monetary circulation. Put simply, price movements are complex phenomena. Moreover, a period of technological transformations and resultant declines in socially necessary labor time will have a powerful tendency to reduce prices.

103. James Livingston provides far and away the best account of this corporate campaign. See his *Origins of the Federal Reserve System: Money, Class, and Corporate Capitalism, 1890–1913* (Ithaca: Cornell University Press, 1986). Timberlake (ch. 13) provides details on the legislative creation of the Federal Reserve Bank, but with effectively no social-historical analysis.

104. J. Lawrence Broz, "Origins of the Federal Reserve System: International Incentives and the Domestic Free Rider Problem," *International Organization* 53, no. 1 (1999), 44.

105. The legislation was known as the Aldrich-Vreeland Act of 1908.

106. *Washington Post*, August 1, 1914, as quoted by Silber, *Wall Street*, 24.

107. William L. Silber, *When Washington Shut Down Wall Street: The Great Financial Crisis of 1914 and the Origins of America's Financial Supremacy* (Princeton: Princeton University Press, 2007), 151–52, 153–54.

108. Eric Hobsbawm, *The Age of Extremes: A History of the World, 1914–1991* (New York: Vintage, 1996), 44–45.

109. Silber, *Wall Street*, 15, 41, 10.

110. As quoted by Lester V. Chandler, *Benjamin Strong, Central Banker* (Washington, DC: Brookings Institution, 1958), 84. Broz ("Federal Reserve System," 45–55) is entirely clear about the international dimension of the US government's commitment to gold, notwithstanding his use of political science models whose value I deeply question.

111. Barry Eichengreen, *Exorbitant Privilege: The Rise and Fall of the Dollar and the Future of the*

International Monetary System (Oxford: Oxford University Press, 2011), 26–27.

112. In fact, a small amount of trading did continue, but it was conducted out of the public eye.

113. Silber, *Wall Street*, 2.

114. Fernand Braudel, "Historie et Sciences sociale: La longue durée," *Annales: Histoire, Sciences Sociales*, 13e Année, no. 4 (October–December 1958), 725–753. For an appreciative yet critical assessment of Braudel in this regard, see Ulysses Santamaria and Anne M. Bailey, "A Note on Braudel's Structure as Duration," *History and Theory* 23, no. 1 (1984), 78–83. Important criticism of Braudel's tendency to discount human agency is made by David Abulafia in his introduction to *The Great Sea: A Human History of the Mediterranean* (Oxford: Oxford University Press, 2011), xxvi.

115. An indispensable source for understanding this thirty-year conjuncture is Enzo Traverso, *Fire and Blood: The European Civil War, 1914–1945* (London and New York: Verso, 2017).

116. Traverso, *Fire and Blood*, 163.

117. Rosa Luxemburg, "The Crisis of German Social Democracy," in Luxemburg, *Selected Political Writings*, Dick Howard, ed. (New York: Monthly Review, 1971), 324.

118. Walter Benjamin, "One Way Street," in *Selected Writings*, vol. 1, *1913–1926* (Cambridge, MA: Harvard University Press, 1996), 487

119. Winston Churchill, *The World Crisis, 1911–1918* (New York: Macmillan, 1942), 19–20, as cited by George Lichtheim, *Europe in the Twentieth Century* (New York: Praeger, 1972), 105–6.

120. Hannah Arendt, *The Origins of Totalitarianism* (New York: Harcourt, 1986 [1951]).

121. Hobsbawm, *Age of Extremes*, 45.

122. A first-rate account can be found in John Kenneth Galbraith, *The Great Crash, 1929*, 2nd ed. (Boston: Houghton Mifflin, 1961).

123. Charles P. Kindelberger, *The World in Depression, 1929–1939* (London: Allen Lane, 1973), 117.

124. This was the beginning of the transition away from commodity money and toward global fiat money. However, so long as the dollar was officially anchored by gold and convertible for it at a set rate—an arrangement whose durability was determined by its reserves of gold on the one hand and its balance of payments on the other—then it did not yet function as mere fiat money. That transition would come after 1973.

125. Anwar Shaikh, *Capitalism: Competition, Conflict, Crises* (London: Oxford, 2016), ch. 12.

126. John Kenneth Galbraith, *American Capitalism: The Concept of Countervailing Power* (Boston: Houghton Mifflin, 1952), 65.

127. Alan S. Milward, *War, Economy, and Society, 1939–1945* (Berkeley: University of California Press, 1977), 63, 64–5, 67.

128. A. D. H. Kaplan, *The Liquidation of War Production* (New York: McGraw-Hill, 1944), 3.

129. Philip Armstrong, Andrew Glyn, and John Harrison, *Capitalism Since World War II: The Making and Breakup of the Great Boom* (London: Fontana, 1984), 26.

130. Hobsbawm, *Age of Extremes*, 259, 258; Armstrong, Glynn, and Harrison, *Capitalism Since World War II*, 168; Angus Maddison, "Growth and Slowdown in Advanced Capitalist Economies," *Journal of Economic Literature* 25 (June 1987), 650.

131. John Kenneth Galbraith, *The Affluent Society* (New York: Houghton Mifflin, 1958).

132. On the shift of people in Japan and Western Europe from farm to city, see Jeffry A. Frieden, *Global Capitalism: Its Fall and Rise in the Twentieth Century* (New York: W. W. Norton, 2006), 282.

133. The background to and terms of the Bretton Woods Agreement are laid out concisely by Barry Eichengreen, *Globalizing Capital: A History of the International Monetary System* (Princeton: Princeton University Press, 1996), ch. 4.

134. Fred L. Block, *The Origins of International Economic Disorder* (Berkeley: University of California Press, 1977), 103–8.

135. *Survey of Current Business*, June 1972 (Washington, DC: US Department of Commerce, 1972).

136. Joyce Kolko, *America and the Crisis of World Capitalism* (Boston: Beacon, 1974), 73; Paul M. Sweezy and Harry Magdoff, "Gold, Dollars, and Empire," *Monthly Review*, February 1968, reprinted in Sweezy and Magdoff, *The Dynamics of US Capitalism* (New York: Monthly Review, 1972), 160.

137. For a first-rate assessment of the war and its effects on US society, see Robert Buzzanco, *Vietnam and the Transformation of American Life* (Oxford: Blackwell, 1999). Also highly recommended is Frances Fitzgerald, *Fire in the Lake: The Vietnamese and the Americans in Vietnam* (New York: Vintage, 1989), originally published in 1972, while the war was still raging.

138. US Congress, Joint Economic Committee, Subcommittee on Economic Policy, *Hearings: A Foreign Economic Policy for the 1970s* 91, no. 2, September–October 1970, part 5, 1067.

139. Kolko, *Crisis of World Capitalism*, 60.

140. I discuss this in *Global Slump*, ch. 2. For further evidence, see Armstrong, Glynn, and Harrison, *Capitalism Since World War II*, 255–59. Using US government data, Robert Guttman dates the profit decline in that country from 1966. See his *How Credit-Money Shapes the Economy: The United States in a Global System* (Armonk: M. E. Sharpe, 1994), 120–21.

141. Armstrong, Glynn, and Harrison, *Capitalism Since World War II*, 219, 232; Lukin Robinson, "The Downfall of the Dollar," *Socialist Register 1973* (London: Merlin Press, 1973), 407.

142. Robinson, "Downfall of the Dollar," 426.

143. As quoted by Frieden, *Global Capitalism*, 345.

144. In fact, gold does not actually leave the US but moves to the vaults or into the accounts of foreign holders at the Federal Reserve Bank of New York. Today, 98 percent of all the gold held by the Federal Reserve Bank of New York belongs to thirty-six foreign central banks.

145. Frieden, *Global Capitalism*, 345.

146. William Safire, *Before the Fall: A View of the Pre-Watergate White House* (Garden City: Doubleday Books, 1975), 510.

147. Quoted in Safire, *Before the Fall*, 514.

148. Stephen Schulmeister, "Globalization without Global Money: The Double Role of the Dollar as National Currency and World Currency," *Journal of Post Keynesian Economics* 22, no. 3 (Spring 2002), 369. At the same time, the dollar's relative decline made foreign investments by US corporations more expensive, as their dollars were worth relatively less in foreign markets.

149. For the data, see McNally, *Global Slump*, table 4.1, 93.

150. German Chancellor Helmut Schmidt, as quoted by Joel Kurtzman, *The Death of Money* (Boston: Little, Brown & Co., 1993), 51.

151. Kurtzman, *Death of Money*, ch. 4.

152. Quoted in Eichengreen, *Globalizing Capital*, 136.

153. For two examples, originating in quite distinct Marxist traditions, see Paul M. Sweezy and Harry Magdoff, "The End of US Hegemony," *Monthly Review*, October 1971, reprinted in

Sweezy and Magdoff, *Dynamics of US Capitalism*, 197–212; and Ernest Mandel, *Decline of the Dollar: A Marxist View of the Monetary Crisis* (New York: Monad Press, 1972).

154. Anwar Shaikh (193) also deploys this term in his monumental theorization of modern capitalism.

155. John Niehans, *The Theory of Money* (Baltimore: Johns Hopkins University Press, 1980), 140.

156. Patrick Brantlinger, *Fictions of State: Culture and Credit in Britain, 1694–1994* (Ithaca: Cornell University Press, 1996), 21; Marieke de Goede, *Virtue, Fortune, and Faith: A Genealogy of Finance* (Minneapolis: University of Minnesota Press, 2005), 5, emphasis in original.

157. Philip Goodchild, *Theology of Money* (Durham: Duke University Press, 2009), 165.

158. Jacques Derrida, *Given Time: I. Counterfeit Money*, Peggy Kamuf, trans. (Chicago: University of Chicago Press, 1992), 124, 161.

159. Jean Baudrillard, *The Transparency of Evil: Essays on Extreme Phenomena*, James Benedict, trans. (London and New York: Verso, 1993), 34; Baudrillard, *Symbolic Exchange and Death*, Iain Hamilton and Mike Gane, trans. (London: Sage Publications, 1993), 20; Baudrillard, *Transparency*, 33. I have explored the fetishistic theory that runs through these analyses by Derrida and Baudrillard in my *Bodies of Meaning: Studies on Language, Labor, and Liberation* (Albany: State University of New York Press, 2001), 60–66.

160. The theory of immaterial labor proposed by Michael Hardt and Antonio Negri—in both *Empire* (Cambridge, MA: Harvard University Press, 2000) and *Multitude* (New York: Penguin, 2004)—is decidedly unhelpful in these areas. For a clear critique, see David Camfield, "The Multitude and the Kangaroo: A Critique of Hardt and Negri's Theory of Immaterial Labour," *Historical Materialism* 15, no. 2 (2007), 21–52.

161. Ole Berg, *Making Money: The Philosophy of Crisis Capitalism* (London and New York: Verso, 2014), 242. This position is consistent with the Lacanian analysis of "the real," but also sits at odds with the more interesting parts of Berg's text, which are devoted to analyzing "post-credit money" and "monetary exploitation." While I have differences with those analyses, they at least move into a more historical idiom. Remarkably, as I indicate below (see next note), Berg also recycles arguments by right-wing libertarians about "funny money" (106–7).

162. Stephan Kinsella, "The Bank of England and Me," March 21, 2010, available at: http://www.stephankinsella.com/2010/03/the-bank-of-england-and-me/. Kinsella's blog bears the subtitle, "Austro-Anarchist Libertarian Legal Theory," making it a curious source for Berg's Lacanian interpretation of money.

163. Josh Ryan-Collins et. al., *Where Does Money Come From?*, 2nd. ed. (London: New Economics Foundation, 2011), 7.

164. The same naive position runs through those analyses that treat the Marxian concept of "value" as metaphysical. A case in point is Joan Robinson, who asks about value, "Where can we find it?" See Robinson, *Economic Philosophy* (Harmondsworth: Pelican, 1964), 29. A similarly empiricist approach is taken by Jonathan Nitzan and Shimshon Bichler in *Capital as Power: A Study of Order and Creorder* (London: Routledge, 2009).

165. See McNally, *Bodies of Meaning*.

166. On a particularly egregious form of such irresponsibility—Baudrillard's claim that the First Gulf War did not happen—see Christopher Norris, *Uncritical Theory: Postmodernism, Intellectuals, and the Gulf War* (London: Lawrence & Wishart, 1992). A powerful critique of similar lines of irresponsible social theory, from the standpoint of the ecological crisis,

can be found in Andreas Malm, *The Progress of This Storm: Nature and Society in a Warming World* (London and New York: Verso, 2018).

167. Richard Freeman, "The Great Doubling: The Challenge of the New Global Labor Market," August 2006, available at: https://eml.berkeley.edu/~webfac/eichengreen/e183_sp07/great_doub.pdf.

168. See McNally, *Global Slump*, ch. 4.

169. See, for instance, Peter Kennedy, "A Marxist Account of the Relationship between Commodity Money and Symbolic Money in the Context of Contemporary Capitalist Development," in John Smithin, ed., *What Is Money?* (London: Routledge, 2000), 201. In the same volume, Steve Fleetwood approximates the same position in his "A Marxist Theory of Commodity Money Revisited" (189). Approaches of this sort are also adopted by some adherents of the Uno School of Marxian political economy.

170. G. W. F. Hegel, *The Phenomenology of Spirit*, A. V. Miller, trans. (Oxford: Oxford University Press, 1977), 20.

171. To be sure, capitalism could in principle so mutate as to become something radically other. But in that case, we would reasonably expect that its central properties—commodification, regulation by markets and money, the production of surplus value, ongoing primitive accumulation—would no longer be systemic features of our society.

172. David Harvey, *The Limits to Capital* (Chicago: University of Chicago Press, 1982), 244.

173. Duncan Foley, "Marx's Theory of Money in Historical Perspective," in *Marx's Theory of Money*, Fred Moseley, ed. (Houndmills: Palgrave Macmillan, 2005), 46.

174. Robert Stein, "Issues Regarding Dollarization," staff report, Subcommittee on Economic Policy, US Senate Committee on Banking, Housing, and Urban Affairs, July 1999, 7.

175. Note two things here, however. First, the US is not, in practice, a single "national economic unit," as it is US capital and its state that principally benefits from this arrangement. Second, foreign dollar-holders (ultimately foreign central banks) may elect to purchase other dollar-denominated assets, as China did in 2007 when it bought nearly 10 percent of American-based real estate firm Blackstone. But for the most part, foreign governments have stuck with Treasury securities.

176. Quoted in Eichengreen, *Globalizing Capital*, 4.

177. Jacques Rueff and Fred Hirsch, *The Role and the Rule of Gold: An Argument*, Essays in International Finance, no. 47 (Princeton: Princeton University Press, 1965), 3.

178. This is the position of Michael Hudson, *Super Imperialism: The Origins and Fundamentals of US World Dominance*, 2nd ed. (London: Pluto, 2002). A variant of this position, albeit with much greater emphasis on the American state, is also advanced by Leo Panitch and Sam Gindin, *The Making of Global Capitalism: The Political Economy of American Empire* (London and New York: Verso, 2012), esp. ch. 11.

179. To be sure, there is a reciprocal determination in effect here: one in which parts shape the whole that, in turn, determines them. But it remains the case that "the true is the whole" (Hegel), albeit a whole that is constituted in and through its parts, not over and against them.

180. Ramaa Vasudevan, "From the Gold Standard to the Floating Dollar Standard: An Appraisal in the Light of Marx's Theory of Money," *Review of Radical Political Economics* 41, no. 4 (2009), 473.

181. Brett Fieberger, "Rethinking the Financialisation of Non-financial Corporations: A Reap-

praisal of US Empirical Data, *Review of Political Economy* 28, no. 3 (2016), 354–79; Cédric Durand, *Fictitious Capital: How Finance Is Appropriating Our Future*, David Broder, trans. (London and New York: Verso, 2017), 148–50. These are both exceptionally important studies deserving of sustained attention.

182. Peter Dicken, *Global Shift: Reshaping the Global Economic Map in the 21st Century* (New York: Guilford, 2003), 52. With these developments there emerged a much more genuinely global working class as well.

183. Gary Burn, *The Reemergence of Global Finance* (Basingstoke: Palgrave Macmillan, 2006), 17; Eric Helleiner, *States and the Reemergence of Global Finance: From Bretton Woods to the 1990s* (Ithaca: Cornell University Press, 1994), 135.

184. See Eric Newstadt, "Neoliberalism and the Federal Reserve," in *American Empire and the Political Economy of Global Finance*, Leo Panitch and Martijn Konings, eds. (Houndmills: Palgrave Macmillan, 2008), 99.

185. One of the many strengths of François Chesnais's work has been to underline how globalized manufacturing drove the development of globalized finance. See, for instance, Chesnais, *Finance Capital Today: Corporations and Banks in the Lasting Global Slump* (Chicago: Haymarket, 2017), ch. 2.

186. Neil Smith, *The End Game of Globalization* (New York: Routledge, 2005), 126. While Panitch and Gindin (*Making of Global Capitalism*) rightly emphasize the internationalization of the state, their narrative tends too much toward seeing the American state as a largely autonomous actor. Hudson (*Super Imperialism*) offers an even more extreme version of the super-imperialism analysis.

187. Data on foreign exchange trading comes from the Bank for International Settlements, *Triennial Central Bank Survey*, multiple years.

188. Bernard Lietaer, "Global Currency Speculation and Its Implications," *International Forum on Globalization News* 2 (1997), reproduced by *Third World Network* available at https://www.twn.my/title/nar-cn.htm.

189. Philip Turner, "Capital Flows in the 1980s: A Survey of Major Trends," *BIS Economic Papers*, no. 30 (Basel: Bank for International Settlements, April 1991), 12.

190. Robert Solomon, *Money on the Move: The Revolution in International Finance since 1980* (Princeton: Princeton University Press, 1999), 110.

191. McKinsey Global Institute, *The New Dynamics of Financial Globalization* (August 2017), exhibit E4, 7.

192. Durand, *Fictitious Capital*, 145.

193. Shaikh, *Capitalism*, ch. 15; Costas Lapavitsas, "Money and the Analysis of Capitalism: The Significance of Commodity Money," in *Marxist Monetary Theory: Collected Papers*, Costas Lapavitsas, ed. (Chicago: Haymarket, 2017), 112. While exponents of the quantity theory of money utterly misunderstand price formation in capitalist society (particularly with commodity money), the dynamics of the latter within a regime of fiat money do follow some of the patterns described by the QTM.

194. It should be emphasized here that central banks lack the capacity to control capitalism's macro-dynamics (hence crises like that of 2007–2009).

195. See my discussion in *Global Slump*, 33–36.

196. As is persuasively shown by Adam Tooze, *Crashed: How a Decade of Financial Crises*

Changed the World (New York: Viking, 2018), part 3.

197. See C. Omney, I. Greer, and O. Onaran, "The State and Class Discipline: European Labour Market Policy after the Financial Crisis," *Capital and Class* 42, no. 2 (2018), 333–51.

198. Sir Mervyn King, "Lunch with the *FT*," *Financial Times*, June 14, 2013, available at https://www.ft.com/content/350a10a2-d284–11e2–88ed-00144feab7de. King is a former governor of the Bank of England.

199. On "pre-validation," see Alain Lipietz, *The Enchanted World: Inflation, Credit, and the World Crisis* (London: Verso, 1985), 60, 72–76.

200. McNally, *Global Slump*, ch. 4.

201. "Monetization" here refers to turning dubious forms of credit money issued by private institutions into full-fledged central bank money through the mechanism of the central bank buying up devalued financial assets.

202. However, while central banks can boost the supply of money, they have much less control over its *velocity*, i.e., the number of transactions it moves through in a given period of time. There are major indications that as the money supply increased from 2009, the velocity of money slowed down, partially countering central bank policy.

203. See Bob Ivry, Bradley Keoun, and Phil Kuntz, "Secret Fed Loans Gave Banks $13 Billion Undisclosed to Congress," *Bloomberg News*, November 27, 2011, available at https://www.bloomberg.com/news/articles/2011–11–28/secret-fed-loans-undisclosed-to-congress-gave-banks-13-billion-in-income.

204. A notable exception was the recession of 1981–82, when the Federal Reserve under Paul Volcker induced a deep slump by means of record-high interest rates—all in order to break working-class bargaining power and reduce inflation. See Panitch and Gindin, *Making of Global Capitalism*, 167–70.

205. L. H. Summers, "US Economic Prospects: Secular Stagnation, Hysteresis, and the Zero Lower Bound," *Business Economics* 49, no. 2 (2014), 65–74. Summers lacks any serious theoretical account of this phenomenon, but his observations are on point.

206. Joseph Schumpeter, *Capitalism, Socialism, and Democracy*, 3rd ed. (New York: Harper & Row, 1950).

207. Chesnais, *Finance Capital Today*, 61–62.

208. On profit rates as structurally determined, see Shaikh, *Capitalism*, ch. 10, who also acknowledges the "benchmark" role of interest rates (443).

209. Guglielmo Carchedi, *For Another Europe: A Class Analysis of European Economic Integration* (London and New York: Verso, 2001), 149.

210. SDRs are a special currency created by the IMF for a variety of financing reasons. They are a synthetic currency, composed of a mix of national monies. China's yuan is the first "emerging market" currency incorporated into the SDR.

211. Henning Gloystein, "Shanghai Crude Futures Eat into Western Benchmarks as China Pushes Yuan," *Reuters*, August 30, 2018, available at https://www.reuters.com/article/us-china-crude-oil-futures-analysis/shanghai-crude-futures-eat-into-western-benchmarks-as-china-pushes-yuan-idUSKCN1LF2RE.

212. See Betty Huang and Le Xia, "What Do China's Renewed Opening Efforts Mean for Foreign Banks?" *BBVA Research*, June 2018, available at https://www.bbvaresearch.com/wp-content/uploads/2018/06/201806_China-Financial-Liberalization_HK-Chamber

_EDI.pdf.

213. Camilo E. Tavor and Tania Mohd Nor, "Reserve Currency Blocs: A Changing International Monetary System?," International Monetary Fund Working Paper, January 2018.

214. James Fallows, "'Be Nice to the Countries that Lend You Money!'," *Atlantic*, December 2008, available at https://www.theatlantic.com/magazine/archive/2008/12/be-nice-to-the-countries-that-lend-you-money/307148/.

215. Steve Johnson, "Rise of the renminbi is 'story of the next cycle'," *Financial Times*, April 25, 2019.

216. Adam Tooze, "Everything You Know about Global Order Is Wrong," *Foreign Policy*, January 30, 2019.

217. Note that I underline "*human* development" here, which is by no means identical with progress in technique.

218. Ernst Bloch, *The Principle of Hope*, vol. 1, Neville Plaice, Stephen Plaice, and Paul Knight, trans. (Cambridge, MA: MIT Press, 1986), 4.

219. This passage comes from Marx's 1856 speech at the anniversary of the *People's Paper*. An intriguing discussion of the use of this metaphor in Shakespeare, Hegel, and Marx can be found in Margreta de Grazia, "Teleology, Delay and the 'Old Mole'," *Shakespeare Quarterly* 50, no. 3 (1999), 251–67.

220. Ching Kwan Lee, *Against the Law: Labor Protests in China's Rustbelt and Sunbelt* (Berkeley: University of California Press, 2007); Hsiao-Hung Pai, *Scattered Sand: The Story of China's Rural Migrants* (London and New York: Verso, 2013); Tim Pringle, *Trade Unions in China: The Challenge of Labour Unrest* (London: Routledge, 2011); Chris King-Chi Chan, *The Challenge of Labour in China: Strikes and the Changing Labour Regime in Global Labour Factories* (Ithaca: ILR Press, 2010).

221. See Tithi Bhattacharya, Eric Blanc, Kate Doyle Griffiths, and Lois Weiner, "Return of the Strike: A Forum on the Teachers' Rebellion in the United States," *Historical Materialism*, 2018, available at http://www.historicalmaterialism.org/articles/return-strike; Tithi Bhattacharya, "Women Are Leading the Wave of Strikes in America. Here's Why," *Guardian*, April 10, 2018; Kate Doyle Griffiths, "When Women Organize We Win: Lessons from the West Virginia Teachers' Strike," *Truthout*, March 7, 2018; Eric Blanc, "Betting on the Working Class," *Jacobin*, May 29, 2018.

222. Tony Kushner, *A Bright Room Called Day* (New York: Broadway Play Publishing, 1992), 65.

Conclusion

1. Walter Benjamin, "On the Concept of History," in *Selected Writings*, vol. 4, Howard Eidland and Michael Jennings, eds. (Cambridge, MA: Harvard University Press, 2003), 392.

2. G. W. F. Hegel, *The Philosophy of History*, J. Sibree, trans. (Buffalo: Prometheus, 1991), 21. Where Hegel rationalizes this human suffering as part of the advance of human freedom, the Marxist insistence on the imperative "to brush history against the grain" refuses this move. See Benjamin, "On the Concept of History," 392.

3. Cicero, *Letters to Atticus*, 5.20.5, as cited by Sandra R. Joshel, *Slavery in the Roman World* (Cambridge, UK: Cambridge University Press, 2010), 84.

4.   Karl Marx, *Economic and Philosophic Manuscripts*, in Marx, *Early Writings*, Rodney Livingstone and Gregor Benton, trans. (Harmondsworth: Penguin, 1975), 378.

5.   On sacred hunger, see John Taylor, *Multum in Parvo*, as cited by Susan Dwyer Amussen, *Caribbean Exchanges: Slavery and the Transformation of English Society, 1640–1770* (Chapel Hill: University of North Carolina Press, 2007), 58.

6.   As reproduced in M. L. West, *Greek Lyric Poetry* (Oxford: Oxford University Press, 1999), fragment 36, lines 8–14.

7.   William Shakespeare, *The Tempest*, Barbara A. Mowat and Paul Werstine, eds. (New York: Washington Square Press, 1994), setting for scene 1, 7.

8.   David McNally, *Monsters of the Market: Zombies, Vampires, and Global Capitalism* (Chicago: Haymarket, 2012), conclusion.

9.   Thomas Tryon, *Friendly Advice to the Gentelmen* [sic] *Planters of the East and West Indies* (London: Printed by Andrew Soyle, 1684), 214, available at https://quod.lib.umich.edu/e/eebo/A63791.0001.001?view=toc. As Deborah Valenze notes, "Tryon presented an enslaved African in possession of a complex subjectivity." See Valenze, *The Social Life of Money in the English Past* (Cambridge, UK: Cambridge University Press, 2006), 227.

10. As cited by Laurent Dubois, *Avengers of the New World: The Story of the Haitian Revolution* (Cambridge, MA: Belknap Press of Harvard University Press, 2004), 141–42.

11. C. L. R. James, *The Black Jacobins: Toussaint L'Ouverture and the San Domingo Revolution* (New York: Vintage, 1963), 86.

12. Matthew Clavin, *Toussaint Louverture and the American Civil War: The Promise and Peril of a Second Haitian Revolution* (Philadelphia: University of Pennsylvania Press, 2010).

13. "Now, however, he destroys this alien negative moment." G. W. F. Hegel, *The Phenomenology of Spirit*, A. V. Miller, trans. (New York: Oxford University Press, 1977), 118.

14. The quote from Seferis comes from "An Old Man on the River Banks," as cited at the outset of this conclusion. Seferis's reference to a life "without fear in their hearts" resonates with jazz great Nina Simone's declaration, "Freedom is a feeling! Freedom is no fear!" (Nina Simone in *What Happened Miss Simone?* documentary directed by Liz Garbus (2015).

15. Benjamin, "On the Concept of History," 390.

16. Caryl Phillips, *Crossing the River* (Toronto: Alfred A. Knopf Canada, 1993), 235.

17. See William Wordsworth, "To Toussaint L'Ouverture," *Morning Post* (London), February 2, 1803, available at https://en.wikisource.org/wiki/Poems_(Wordsworth,_1815)/Volume_2/To_Toussaint_L%27Ouverture. Wordsworth's term has been insightfully deployed by Julius S. Scott, *The Common Wind: Afro-American Currents in the Age of the Haitian Revolution* (London and New York: Verso, 2018).

Index

ABOUT HAYMARKET BOOKS

Haymarket Books is a radical, independent, nonprofit book publisher based in Chicago. Our mission is to publish books that contribute to struggles for social and economic justice. We strive to make our books a vibrant and organic part of social movements and the education and development of a critical, engaged, international left.

We take inspiration and courage from our namesakes, the Haymarket martyrs, who gave their lives fighting for a better world. Their 1886 struggle for the eight-hour day—which gave us May Day, the international workers' holiday—reminds workers around the world that ordinary people can organize and struggle for their own liberation. These struggles continue today across the globe—struggles against oppression, exploitation, poverty, and war.

Since our founding in 2001, Haymarket Books has published more than five hundred titles. Radically independent, we seek to drive a wedge into the risk-averse world of corporate book publishing. Our authors include Noam Chomsky, Arundhati Roy, Rebecca Solnit, Angela Y. Davis, Howard Zinn, Amy Goodman, Wallace Shawn, Mike Davis, Winona LaDuke, Ilan Pappé, Richard Wolff, Dave Zirin, Keeanga-Yamahtta Taylor, Nick Turse, Dahr Jamail, David Barsamian, Elizabeth Laird, Amira Hass, Mark Steel, Avi Lewis, Naomi Klein, and Neil Davidson. We are also the trade publishers of the acclaimed Historical Materialism Book Series and of Dispatch Books.

ALSO AVAILABLE FROM
HAYMARKET BOOKS

Marxism and the Oppression of Women: Toward a Unitary Theory
Lise Vogel, introduction by Susan Ferguson and David McNally

Marxist Monetary Theory: Collected Papers
Costas Lapavitsas

Marx's Theory of the Genesis of Money
How, Why, and Through What is a Commodity Money?
Samezō Kuruma, edited and translated by Michael Schauerte

Monsters of the Market: Zombies, Vampires and Global Capitalism
David McNally

The Political Economy of Racism
Melvin Leiman

Repair: Redeeming the Promise of Abolition
Katherine Franke

ABOUT THE AUTHOR

David McNally is the Cullen Distinguished Professor of History and Business at the University of Houston and director of the Center for the Study of Capitalism. McNally is the author of seven books and has won a number of awards, including the Paul Sweezy Award from the American Sociological Association for his book *Global Slump* and the Deutscher Memorial Award for *Monsters of the Market*.